VASE-PAINTING IN ITALY

Red-Figure and Related Works

VASE-PAINTING IN ITALY

*Red-Figure and Related Works in the
Museum of Fine Arts, Boston*

*J. Michael Padgett, Mary B. Comstock,
John J. Herrmann, and Cornelius C. Vermeule*

*with contributions by Amy E. Raymond,
Emily T. Vermeule, and Florence Z. Wolsky*

MUSEUM OF FINE ARTS, BOSTON

Library of Congress Catalogue Card Number: 93-080374
ISBN 0-87846-406-9

Typeset by DEKR Corporation, Woburn, Massachusetts
Printed and bound by The Stinehour Press, Lunenburg,
Vermont

Designed by Cynthia Rockwell Randall

This catalogue was published with the assistance of the
Getty Grant Program and a grant from the National
Endowment for the Arts, a Federal agency.

Cover illustrations:
Details of cat. no. 38

Frontispiece:
Detail of cat. no. 42

To

Sir John D. Beazley
In Memory

Arthur Dale Trendall
With Gratitude

CONTENTS

Places Mentioned in the Text

Adriatic Sea

Tyrrhenian Sea

Ionian Sea

ETRURIA

CAMPANIA

APULIA

LUCANIA

SICILY

Lipari Islands

Siena

Rome

Naples

Taranto

Syracuse

1
2
3
4
5
6
7
8
9
10
11
12
13
14
15
16
17
18
19
20
21
22
23
24
25
26
27
28
29
30
31

Avella	12	Cumae	10	Pisticci	21
Bari	18	Falerii	5	Reggio	28
Brindisi	24	Gela	30	Ruvo	17
Caere	6	Gnathia	20	Suessula	11
Canosa	15	Heraclea (Policoro)	23	Tarquinia	4
Capri	13	Himera	31	Teano	8
Capua	9	Lecce	25	Thurii	26
Ceglie del Campo	19	Locri	27	Volterra	1
Centuripe	29	Metapontum	22	Vulci	3
Chiusi	2	Paestum	14		
Corato	16	Palestrina	7		

PREFACE

This catalogue is the first comprehensive publication in recent years of the South Italian and Etruscan red-figure, Gnathian, and mold-made vases in the Museum of Fine Arts, Boston. Because virtually every major South Italian vase in Boston is listed and often illustrated in one or more of the books, monographs, and articles by Arthur Dale Trendall, the task of placing these vases in their proper historical, mythological, and aesthetic contexts has been made much easier. In the case of attributed works, it is taken as understood that the best place to look for comparable examples of shape, style, and subject is among the other vases attributed to the painter in question in Trendall's *The Red-figured Vases of Lucania, Campania and Sicily* and *The Red-Figured Vases of Paestum;* in A. D. Trendall and A. Cambitoglou, *The Red-figured Vases of Apulia;* and in the latest supplements to these works. No effort is made here to index or cross-reference these magisterial volumes but, where possible, reference is made to articles, monographs, and catalogues that supplement, clarify, or update the information they provide. Professor Trendall read a draft of this catalogue and provided important observations and corrections; any remaining errors are the responsibility of the authors.

With the exception of plastic vases, no unpainted or black-glazed wares, including gutti with relief medallions, are catalogued in this volume. Among the wares excluded are Calenian, Daunian, Messapian, Peucetian, Etruscan bucchero, and black-figure of all types. Many of these were catalogued with full descriptions by Arthur Fairbanks in *Catalogue of Greek and Etruscan Vases,* I: *Early Vases, Preceding Athenian Black-Figured Ware,* published for the Museum of Fine Arts by Harvard University Press in 1928. It is hoped that a future publication will re-study those pieces and include the more recently acquired examples of these wares.

Most of the vases in the present catalogue were made in the fourth century B.C., although several are of the fifth century, and the vases from Centuripe and some of the Gnathian pieces date from the third century. With the exception of two Etruscan examples, vases decorated in the Gnathian technique are grouped together; although most are Apulian, it is sometimes difficult to determine in what region a particular work was created, despite the considerable progress in this area made by Professor J. R. Green. Etruscan vases in the Gnathian technique along with those decorated with added, or superposed, color are included with the red-figure wares. As is customary, Faliscan vases are included with Etruscan.

Unless otherwise indicated, all the attributions to specific South Italian painters or groups are by Professor Trendall. Most attributions to Gnathian vase-painters are by T. B. L. Webster or J. R. Green. Sir John D. Beazley knew nearly every Etruscan vase in Boston and incorporated almost all of them in *Etruscan Vase-Painting,* his famous monograph of 1947; unless otherwise indicated, all attributions to Etruscan painters and groups are his. Thus our debt to his landmark work is also acknowledged.

The catalogue descriptions and commentaries are mainly the work of Michael Padgett, who expanded my summary listing. John Herrmann and Michael Padgett wrote the Etruscan entries jointly. John Herrmann examined the objects for the entire catalogue, verifying the added colors and the physical condition of the vases. He is also responsible for the entries for nos. 3, 22–23, 144a and 145. Michael Padgett wrote the introductory essays for the various Italiote schools of painting, while John Herrmann wrote those for the Etruscan section and for the use of color in South Italian vase-painting. Mary Comstock has maintained the records on each vase since the mid-1970s. For this catalogue she traced the circumstances of acquisition where possible, compiled the bibliography, prepared the indexes and concordances, and coordinated the writing of the other authors; to a significant extent she is responsible for the consistency and accuracy of this publication.

Amy Raymond produced the map and supervised most of the new photography carried out for the catalogue from 1990 to 1993. Emily Vermeule lent her expertise in unraveling the complex mythology of several pieces, particularly those by the Darius Painter. Florence Wolsky gave valuable aid in proofreading and collaborated with Michael Padgett in compiling the glossary. Arthur Fleischman and Rebecca Reed assisted John Herrmann in making additional measurements of the vases for the catalogue. Elaine Banks, Herbert Hoffmann, Mary Ellen Carr (Soles), Carolyn Graham Townsend, Marion True, and Penelope von Kersburg Truitt made contributions in various ways during the years when they were members of the Department of Classical Art.

The Museum's Research Laboratory cleaned, strengthened, reassembled, and restored these vases, and many are now significantly more legible than in the past. Members of the Research staff who have been involved since the 1950s include Pamela Hatchfield, Jean-Louis Lachevre, Margaret Leveque, Maureen Russell, Peter Williams, William J. Young, and the late Joseph Harrington and Merville E. Nichols. In the Department of Ancient Egyptian, Nubian, and Near Eastern Art, Peter Der Manuelian gave technical advice on the preparation of the original text. Rima Boulos, Steven Harvey, and Karen Kennedy, former members of that department, also offered help.

Former members of the Museum's Department of Development, Janet Spitz, Lisa Harris, and Martha Reynolds, found the funds to make this catalogue possible: in particular, generous grants from the National Endowment for the Arts and from the Getty Grant Program. In this respect, Professor Trendall kindly wrote letters of support for the project. Three directors — Perry T. Rathbone, Jan Fontein, and, currently, Alan Shestack — have nourished the collection by encouraging donations and purchases. Most recently, Alan Shestack provided the initiative that brought this publication into being.

The design and copy editing of the catalogue were the work of Cynthia R. Randall and Margaret Jupe. The photographs were taken by the Museum's photographers who have worked with the Department of Classical Art over the past century. They include the late Baldwin Coolidge, Edward J. Moore, and John McQuade; more recently, Joseph E. Logue, Herbert C. Hamilton, Wayne O. Lemmon, and William R. Buckley; and the present members of the Depart-

ment of Photographic Services, under the overall guidance of Janice Sorkow: Thomas P. Lang, John C. Lutsch, and John D. Woolf. The new photographs and transparencies made especially for this catalogue were produced by John Woolf.

Dietrich von Bothmer of the Metropolitan Museum of Art, New York, has offered advice during his many visits to the Department of Classical Art over a period of half a century. Joan R. Mertens, also of the Metropolitan Museum of Art, gave key assistance with genealogy. Arielle P. Kozloff and Sharon Herene of the Cleveland Museum of Art provided photographs of and information on the volute-krater by the Darius Painter with the scene of the Departure of Amphiaraos that helps to explain a large fragment in Boston (cat. no. 44). Gerry D. Scott, III, of the San Antonio Museum of Art supplied a new photograph of the plastic mouse (cat. no. 95) lent to that institution in 1990. Pamela J. Russell of the Tampa Museum of Art measured the three vases from Boston currently on extended loan to that museum. Susan B. Matheson, at the Yale University Art Gallery, proffered counsel based on her own experiences as a cataloguer and exhibitor of Greek vases. Robert E. Hecht, Jr., contributed to the scholarly content of the catalogue through discussions of many of the vases with members of the Department of Classical Art.

Finally, the Museum would like to express profound thanks and appreciation to the many generous donors who have made possible the acquisition of the vases described and illustrated in this volume. Although the Museum has managed to acquire several South Italian vases with its own funds in recent years, the major purchases that have added so many splendid later Apulian vases to the collection were realized only through this magnanimous external support.

C. C. V.

HISTORY OF THE COLLECTION

The first South Italian vases were given to the Museum of Fine Arts by Thomas Gold Appleton, a Bostonian, in the year of the United States centennial. His vases were mostly purchased from the noble jeweler-collector-scholar Alessandro Castellani in Rome and came with provenances. They include one Lucanian (cat. no. 2), eight Apulian (cat. nos. 19, 25, 35, 53, 56–57, 62, 73), and four Gnathian (cat. nos. 117, 119, 129, 132) vases. Alessandro Castellani was to become a great benefactor of the municipal collections of Rome and is remembered, *inter alia*, for his part in the development of the Sala Castellani in the Palazzo dei Conservatori. In the same year, John James Dixwell, also a Bostonian, presented a collection of Etruscan vases, several of which belong to the fourth-century Sokra Group (cat. nos. 155–158). He had purchased his vases in Florence in 1875 at an auction of material deaccessioned from a public collection in Chiusi. In 1880 four Gnathian vases (cat. nos. 116, 124, 136, 140) were purchased by Charles C. Perkins, the Museum's honorary director. The last major donor before the era of Edward Perry Warren was Henry P. Kidder, who, in 1880, gave a Campanian plastic mouse (cat. no. 95), a Faliscan phiale (cat. no. 174), and two Apulian rhyta (cat. nos. 31–32).

Random donations were received in the decade of the 1890s, some of them vases of importance. Edward Perry Warren, soon to be Boston's chief collector, gave an Apulian pelike in 1890 (cat. no. 24). A large Apulian column-krater was the gift of Nathan Appleton in 1892 (cat. no. 36). Mrs. Samuel D. Warren, mother of E. P. Warren, donated an Apulian boar's-head rhyton in 1897 (cat. no. 67), and the famous orientalist Dr. William Sturgis Bigelow was responsible for a series of gifts of South Italian vases in every category.

During the years 1900 to 1910 the South Italian collection grew rapidly both in numbers and importance, thanks to funds provided by a variety of donors. Acquisitions were made throughout Europe by Edward Perry Warren and John Marshall, and the provenances they supplied for the vases that passed through their hands are recorded verbatim in the appropriate entries of this catalogue. After this burst of growth, there were further gifts from Warren, from

the philhellenes Mr. and Mrs. William de Forest Thomson, and from the Misses Norton, who donated vases from the collections of Richard and Charles Eliot Norton.

In the 1950s Horace L. Mayer donated a number of vases he had acquired from old collections in Switzerland in the 1920s and 1930s. A group of three monumental Apulian vases was presented to the Museum by Robert E. Hecht, Jr., in 1970 (cat. nos. 9–10, 21), and there were selected gifts and purchases in the 1970s and 1980s, all designed to add important myths and interesting shapes to the collection.

The huge Faliscan calyx-krater by the Nazzano Painter (cat. no. 166), purchased in 1970, with a vivid representation of the myth of Telephos holding the infant Orestes hostage at the altar in the palace of Mycenae, quickly gathered a substantial bibliography in the literature of visual mythology after its hegira from exhibition in New York to its permanent home in Boston.

The Apulian calyx-krater by an artist close to the Darius Painter (cat. no. 39), the gift of Edythe K. Shulman, had a long history in private hands in Germany before entering the collection of the late William Randolph Hearst. Its last public appearance in the United States before coming to the Museum of Fine Arts was at a Parke-Bernet sale in the spring of 1963. Two considerably larger calyx-kraters, major mythological vases by the Darius Painter, were acquired by gift and purchase in 1987 and 1989. On the first of the pair (cat. no. 41) is the story of the exposure of the baby Aigisthos, in the presence of Thyestes and Pelopeia, his incestuous parents. On the second calyx-krater (cat. no. 43) is the abortive attempt of Amphitryon to kill his wife, Alkmene, by burning her to death, a tragedy prevented by her lover Zeus. In 1991 the Museum was presented by the Jerome Levy Foundation with a half-interest in the large amphora of Panathenaic shape showing the death of Atreus (cat. no. 42), another important mythological vase by the Darius Painter. Aigisthos and his father, Thyestes, appear here as the murderers of Atreus, in a sequel to the scene on the calyx-krater acquired in 1987.

From 1988 to 1991 Dr. and Mrs. Jerome M. Eisenberg donated vases of types not previously represented in the collection: a Paestan fish-plate (cat. no. 101), an Apulian red-figure situla (cat. no. 40), and a rare Apulian head-vase, or guttus (cat. no. 34). The latest acquisition to be included in this catalogue, a purchase of June 1992, is a situla (cat. no. 37) attributed to the Varrese Painter, showing Dionysos with maenads. The Varrese Painter's refined drawing was the source for the style of the Darius Painter, and the situla thus fittingly caps the Museum's recent purchases of major late Apulian vases.

C. C. V.

SHORT TITLES

Aellen, Cambitoglou, and Chamay, *Peintre de Darius*
C. Aellen, A. Cambitoglou, and J. Chamay. *Le Peintre de Darius et son Milieu: Vases grecs d'italie méridionale.* Geneva, 1986.

Ann Arbor, *Greek Vases*
S. Herbert. *Greek Vases from Boston, c. 600–300 B.C.* September 30 - December 10, 1976. The Kelsey Museum of Archaeology, University of Michigan. Ann Arbor, 1976.

Balensiefen, *Spiegelbildes*
L. Balensiefen. *Die Bedeutung des Spiegelbildes als ikonographisches Motiv in der antiken Kunst.* Tübingen, 1990.

Barr-Sharrar and Borza, *Macedonia and Greece*
B. Barr-Sharrar and E. N. Borza, eds. *Macedonia and Greece in Late Classical and Early Hellenistic Times.* Washington, D.C., 1982.

Beazley, *ARV²*
J. D. Beazley. *Attic Red-figure Vase-painters.* 2nd ed. Oxford, 1963.

Beazley, *EVP*
J. D. Beazley. *Etruscan Vase-Painting.* Oxford, 1947.

Bernardini, *Vasi*
M. Bernardini. *Vasi dello stile di Gnathia, vasi a vernice nera.* Museo Provinciale "S. Castromediano" Lecce. Bari, 1961.

Bieber, *Theater*
M. Bieber. *The History of the Greek and Roman Theater.* Princeton, 1939.

Bieber, *Theater,* **1961**
M. Bieber. *The History of the Greek and Roman Theater.* 2nd ed., revised and enlarged. Princeton, 1961.

Brijder, *Enthousiasmos*
H. A. G. Brijder, A. A. Drukker, and C. W. Neeft, eds. *Enthousiasmos: Essays on Greek and Related Pottery Presented to J. M. Hemelrijk.* Amsterdam, 1986.

Brockton Art Center, *The Ancient Mediterranean*
S. K. Morgan. *The Ancient Mediterranean.* September 4, 1975 - July 1977. The Brockton Art Center-Fuller Memorial. Brockton, Mass., 1975.

Brommer, *Denkmälerlisten,* **II**
F. Brommer, with A. Peschlow-Bindokat and D. Lindemann. *Denkmälerlisten zur griechischen Heldensage,* II: *Theseus-Bellerophon-Achill.* Marburg, 1974.

Brommer, *Denkmälerlisten,* **III**
F. Brommer, with D. Kemp-Lindemann. *Denkmälerlisten zur griechischen Heldensage,* III: *Übrige Helden.* Marburg, 1976.

Brommer, *Göttersagen*
F. Brommer. *Göttersagen in Vasenlisten.* Marburg, 1980.

Brommer, *Vasenlisten*
F. Brommer. *Vasenlisten zur griechischen Heldensage.* 1st ed., Marburg/Lahn, 1956; 2nd ed., Marburg/Lahn, 1960; 3rd ed., Marburg, 1973.

Cambitoglou, *Studies Trendall*
A. Cambitoglou, ed. *Studies in Honour of Arthur Dale Trendall.* Sydney, 1979.

Cambitoglou and Trendall, *Plain Style*
A. Cambitoglou and A. D. Trendall. *Apulian Red-figured Vase-painters of the Plain Style.* Rutland and Tokyo, 1961.

Cambitoglou and Trendall, *Plain Style, Addenda*
A. Cambitoglou and A. D. Trendall. "Addenda to *Apulian Red-figure Vase-painters of the Plain Style,*" AJA 73 (1969), pp. 423–433.

Carpenter, *Art and Myth*
T. H. Carpenter. *Art and Myth in Ancient Greece: A Handbook.* London, 1991.

Caskey and Beazley
L. D. Caskey and J. D. Beazley. *Attic Vase Paintings in the Museum of Fine Arts, Boston.* I-III. Boston, 1931–1963.

Catteruccia, *Pitture*
L. M. Catteruccia. *Pitture Vascolari Italiote di Soggetto Teatrale Comico.* Rome, 1951.

Cavagnaro Vanoni and Serra Ridgway, *Vasi etruschi*
L. Cavagnaro Vanoni and F. R. Serra Ridgway. *Vasi etruschi a figure rosse: Dagli scavi della fondazione Lerici nella necropoli dei Monterozzi a Tarquinia.* Rome, 1989.

Chase, *Antiquities*
G. H. Chase. *Greek and Roman Antiquities: A Guide to the Classical Collection.* Boston, 1950.

Chase and Vermeule, *Greek, Etruscan and Roman Art*
G. H. Chase and C. C. Vermeule III. *Greek, Etruscan and Roman Art: The Classical Collections of the Museum of Fine Arts, Boston.* Boston, 1963. 2nd rev. ed., 1972.

Corpus Christi, *Greek Vases*
Greek Vases from the Boston Museum of Fine Arts. March 12 to May 2, 1976. Art Museum of South Texas, Corpus Christi, Texas.

Del Chiaro, *Caere*
M. A. Del Chiaro. *Etruscan Red-Figured Vase-Painting at Caere.* Berkeley, Los Angeles, and London, 1974.

Del Chiaro, *Funnel Group*
M. A. Del Chiaro. *The Etruscan Funnel Group: A Tarquinian Red-Figured Fabric.* Florence, 1974.

Descoeudres, *Greek Colonists*
J.-P. Descoeudres, ed. *Greek Colonists and Native Popula-tions: Proceedings of the First Australian Congress of Classical Archaeology held in honour of Emeritus Profes-sor A. D. Trendall.* Oxford, 1990.

Eisenberg, *Ancient World,* **IV**
J. M. Eisenberg. *Art of the Ancient World: A Guide for the Collector and Investor,* IV. Royal Athena Galleries, New York and Beverly Hills, 1985.

Fairbanks, *Philostratus*
A. Fairbanks, trans. *Philostratus The Elder, The Younger, Imagines; Callistratus, Descriptions.* Cambridge, Mass. (Loeb Classical Library), 1969.

Festschrift Arias
ΑΠΑΡΧΑΙ: Nuove ricerche e studi sulla Magna Grecia e la Sicilia antica in onore di Paolo Enrico Arias. Pisa, 1982.

Festschrift von Blanckenhagen
G. Kopcke and M. B. Moore, eds. *Studies in Classical Art and Archaeology: A Tribute to Peter Heinrich von Blanck-enhagen.* Locust Valley, N.Y., 1979.

Festschrift Cambitoglou
J.-P. Descoeudres, ed. *ΕΥΜΟΥΣΙΑ: Ceramic and Icono-graphic Studies in Honour of Alexander Cambitoglou.* Sydney, 1990.

Festschrift Hanfmann
D. G. Mitten, J. G. Pedley, and J. A. Scott, eds. *Studies Presented to George M. A. Hanfmann.* Cambridge, Mass., 1971.

Festschrift Hausmann
B. von Freytag gen. Löringhoff, D. Mannsperger, F. Pra-yon, et al., eds. *Praestant Interna: Festschrift für Ulrich Hausmann.* Tübingen, 1982.

Forman Sale Catalogue
C. H. Smith, in *The Forman Collection: Catalogue of the Egyptian, Greek & Roman Antiquities and Objects of Art of the Renaissance, &.* Sotheby, Wilkinson & Hodge. June 19, 1899. London, 1899.

Forti, *Gnathia*
L. Forti. *La Ceramica di Gnathia.* Naples, 1965.

Freytag gen. Löringhoff, *Giebelrelief*
B. von Freytag gen. Löringhoff. *Das Giebelrelief von Tela-mon und seine Stellung innerhalb der Ikonographie der 'Sieben gegen Theben.'* (*RM,* Ergänzungsheft 27). Mainz, 1986.

Furtwängler and Reichhold
A. Furtwängler and K. Reichhold, et al. *Griechische Va-senmalerei: Auswahl hervorragender Vasenbilder.* I-III. Munich, 1904–1932.

Ghali-Kahil, *Hélène*
L. B. Ghali-Kahil. *Les Enlèvements et le Retour d'Hélène dans les Textes et les Documents figurés.* Paris, 1955.

Giambersio, *Pisticci*
A. M. Giambersio. *Il pittore di Pisticci: Il mondo e l'opera di un ceramografo della seconda metà del V secolo a.c.* Galatina, 1989.

Ginouvès, *Balaneutikè*
R. Ginouvès. *Balaneutikè: Recherches sur le bain dans l'antiquité grecque.* Paris, 1962.

Green, *Gnathia*
J. R. Green. *Gnathia Pottery in the Akademisches Kunst-museum Bonn.* Mainz, 1976.

Hamdorf, *Kultpersonifikationen*
F. W. Hamdorf. *Griechische Kultpersonifikationen der vorhellenistischen Zeit.* Mainz, 1964.

Harari, *Gruppo Clusium*
M. Harari. *Il "Gruppo Clusium" nella ceramografia etrusca.* Rome, 1980.

Hayes, *Black-Gloss*
J. W. Hayes. *Greek and Italian Black-Gloss Wares and Related Wares in the Royal Ontario Museum.* Toronto, 1984.

Heldring, *Sicilian*
B. Heldring. *Sicilian Plastic Vases.* Utrecht, 1981.

Herbig and Simon, *Götter*
R. Herbig and E. Simon. *Götter und Dämonen der Etrus-ker.* Mainz, 1965.

Hoffmann, *Tarentine*
H. Hoffmann. *Tarentine Rhyta.* Mainz, 1966.

Hoorn, *Choes*
G. van Hoorn. *Choes and Anthesteria.* Leiden, 1951.

Hornbostel, *Schätze*
W. Hornbostel, et al. *Kunst der Antike: Schätze aus nord-deutschem Privatbesitz.* Mainz, 1977.

Jentoft-Nilsen, *CVA Getty 4*
M. R. Jentoft-Nilsen and A. D. Trendall. *CVA,* The J. Paul Getty Museum 4. Malibu, 1991.

Jircik, *Pisticci*
N. R. Jircik. *The Pisticci and Amykos Painters: The Begin-nings of Red-Figured Vase Painting in Ancient Lucania.* Ann Arbor, 1990. Ph.D. diss., University of Texas. Micro-fiche.

Jolivet, *Recherches*
V. Jolivet. *Recherches sur la céramique étrusque à figures rouges tardive du musée du Louvre: Département des an-tiquités grecques et romaines* (*Notes et Documents des musées de France 6*). Paris, 1982.

Kossatz-Deissmann, *Dramen*
A. Kossatz-Deissmann. *Dramen des Aischylos auf westgriechischen Vasen.* Mainz, 1978.

Krauskopf, *Thebanische Sagenkreis*
I. Krauskopf. *Die Thebanische Sagenkreis und andere Sagen in der etruskischen Kunst.* Mainz, 1974.

Lohmann, *Grabmäler*
H. Lohmann. *Grabmäler auf unteritalischen Vasen (Archäologische Forschungen,* vol. 7). Berlin, 1979.

Maas and Snyder, *Stringed Instruments*
M. Maas and J. M. Snyder. *Stringed Instruments of Ancient Greece.* New Haven, 1989.

Martelli, *Ceramica*
M. Martelli, ed. *La Ceramica degli Etruschi: La pittura vascolare.* Novara, 1987.

Mayo, *Magna Graecia*
M. E. Mayo, ed. *The Art of South Italy: Vases from Magna Graecia.* Virginia Museum of Fine Arts, Richmond, 1982.

McPhee and Trendall, *Fish-plates*
I. McPhee and A. D. Trendall. *Greek Red-figured Fish-plates (AntK,* Beiheft 14). Basel, 1987.

MFA, *Gods and Heroes*
G. H. Chase and H. Palmer. *Greek Gods & Heroes.* Museum of Fine Arts. 5th ed., fully revised. Boston, 1962.

MFA, *Illustrated Handbook,* **1976**
Illustrated Handbook, Museum of Fine Arts Boston 1976. Boston, 1975. Reprinted, Boston, 1988.

MFA, *Trojan War*
M. Comstock, A. Graves, E. Vermeule, and C. Vermeule. *The Trojan War in Greek Art: A Picture Book.* Museum of Fine Arts, Boston [1965].

Oliver, *Reconstruction*
A. Oliver, Jr. *The Reconstruction of Two Apulian Tomb Groups (AntK,* Beiheft 5). Bern, 1968.

Pianu, *Figure rosse*
G. Pianu. *Ceramiche etrusche a figure rosse (Materiali del Museo Archeologico Nazionale di Tarquinia,* I). Rome, 1980.

Pianu, *Sovradipinte*
G. Pianu. *Ceramiche etrusche sovradipinte (Materiali del Museo Archeologico Nazionale di Tarquinia,* III). Rome, 1982.

Piotrovsky, Galanina, and Grach, *Scythian*
B. Piotrovsky, L. Galanina, and N. Grach. *Scythian Art.* Translated by V. Sobolev. Leningrad and Oxford, 1987.

Prag, *Oresteia*
A. J. N. W. Prag. *The Oresteia: Iconographic and Narrative Tradition.* Warminster, Wiltshire, 1985.

Rasmussen and Spivey, *Greek Vases*
T. Rasmussen and N. Spivey, eds. *Looking at Greek Vases.* Cambridge, 1991.

Rawson, *Marsyas*
P. B. Rawson. *The Myth of Marsyas in the Roman Visual Arts: An Iconographic Study* (BAR International Series 347). Oxford, 1987.

Robertson, *History*
M. Robertson. *A History of Greek Art.* Cambridge, 1975.

Robinson, *Catalogue*
E. Robinson. *Catalogue of Greek, Etruscan, and Roman Vases* (Museum of Fine Arts, Boston). Boston and New York, 1893.

Robinson, Harcum, and Iliffe, *Greek Vases*
D. M. Robinson, C. G. Harcum, and J. H. Iliffe. *A Catalogue of the Greek Vases in the Royal Ontario Museum of Archaeology, Toronto.* Toronto, 1930.

RVAp
A. D. Trendall and A. Cambitoglou. *The Red-figured Vases of Apulia,* I: *Early and Middle Apulian.* Oxford, 1978; II: *Late Apulian.* Oxford, 1982; Suppl. I (*BICS,* Suppl. 42), London, 1983; Suppl. II, Parts 1–3 (*BICS,* Suppl. 60), London, 1991–1992.

Schefold and Jung, *Argonauten*
K. Schefold and F. Jung. *Die Sagen von den Argonauten, von Theben und Troia in der klassischen und hellenistischen Kunst.* Munich, 1989.

Schefold and Jung, *Göttersage*
K. Schefold and F. Jung. *Die Göttersage in der klassischen und hellenistischen Kunst.* Munich, 1981.

Schefold and Jung, *Urkönige*
K. Schefold and F. Jung. *Die Urkönige: Perseus, Bellerophon, Herakles und Theseus in der klassischen und hellenistischen Kunst.* Munich, 1988.

Schmidt, Trendall, and Cambitoglou, *Grabvasen*
M. Schmidt, A. D. Trendall, and A. Cambitoglou. *Eine Gruppe apulischer Grabvasen in Basel: Studien zu Gehalt und Form der unteritalischen Sepulkralkunst.* Mainz, 1976.

Schneider-Herrmann, *Paterae*
G. Schneider-Herrmann. *Apulian Red-figured Paterae with Flat or Knobbed Handles (BICS,* Suppl. 34). London, 1977.

Shepard, *Monster*
K. Shepard. *The Fish-tailed Monster in Greek and Etruscan Art.* New York, 1940.

Smith, *Funerary Symbolism*
H. R. W. Smith. *Funerary Symbolism in Apulian Vase-Painting.* Edited by J. K. Anderson (University of California Publications: Classical Studies, vol. 12). Berkeley, 1976.

Söldner, *Bonn 3*
M. Söldner. *CVA,* Bonn Akademisches Kunstmuseum 3. Munich, 1990.

Sommella, *Enea nel Lazio*
P. Sommella. In *Enea nel Lazio: Archeologia e mito.* Rome, 1981.

St. Paul's School, *The Classical Shape*
M. G. Braverman (catalogue) and T. R. Barrett (introduction). *The Classical Shape: Decorated Pottery of the Ancient World.* The Art Center at Hargate, St. Paul's School, Concord, N.H., 1984.

Studies Mildenberg
A. Houghton, S. Hurter, P. E. Mottahedeh, and J. A. Scott, eds. *Studies in Honor of Leo Mildenberg: Numismatics, Art History, Archaeology.* Wetteren, Belgium, 1984.

Studies Webster, II
J. H. Betts, J. T. Hooker, and J. R. Green, eds. *Studies in Honour of T.B.L. Webster.* Vol. II. Bedminster, Somerset, 1988.

Taplin, *Comic Angels*
O. Taplin. *Comic Angels and Other Approaches to Greek Drama through Vase-Paintings.* Oxford, 1993.

Taranto, *Letteratura*
Letteratura e arte figurata nella Magna Grecia. Taranto, Museo Nazionale, ottobre 1966.

Theater in Ancient Art
F. F. Jones. *The Theater in Ancient Art: An Exhibition.* The Art Museum, Princeton University. December 10, 1951–January 6, 1952.

Trendall, *Early*
A. D. Trendall. *Early South Italian Vase-painting.* Revised ed., 1973. Mainz, 1974.

Trendall, *Frühitaliotische*
A. D. Trendall. *Frühitaliotische Vasen.* Leipzig, 1938.

Trendall, *Handbook*
A. D. Trendall. *Red Figure Vases of South Italy and Sicily: A Handbook.* London, 1989.

Trendall, *LCS*
A. D. Trendall. *The Red-figured Vases of Lucania, Campania and Sicily.* 2 vols. Oxford, 1967. *LCS,* Suppl. I (*BICS,* Suppl. 26), London, 1970. *LCS,* Suppl. II (*BICS,* Suppl. 31), London, 1973. *LCS,* Suppl. III (*BICS,* Suppl. 41), London, 1983.

Trendall, *Phlyax,* **1959**
A. D. Trendall. *Phlyax Vases* (*BICS,* Suppl. 8). London, 1959.

Trendall, *Phlyax,* **1967**
A. D. Trendall. *Phlyax Vases.* 2nd ed., revised and enlarged (*BICS,* Suppl. 19). London, 1967.

Trendall, *PP*
A. D. Trendall. *Paestan Pottery: A Study of the Red-figured Vases of Paestum.* British School at Rome, 1936.

Trendall, *RVP*
A. D. Trendall. *The Red-Figured Vases of Paestum.* British School at Rome, 1987.

Trendall, *Vasi antichi,* **II**
A. D. Trendall. *Vasi antichi dipinti del Vaticano,* II: *Vasi italioti ed etruschi a figure rosse.* Vatican City, 1955.

Trendall and Webster, *Illustrations*
A. D. Trendall and T. B. L. Webster. *Illustrations of Greek Drama.* London, 1971.

Venedikov and Gerassimov, *Thracian*
I. Venedikov and T. Gerassimov. *Thracian Art Treasures.* Translated by M. Alexieva and P. Drenkov, assisted by M. Holman and R. Healey. Sofia, 1975.

Webster, *Gnathia*
T. B. L. Webster. "Towards a Classification of Apulian Gnathia," *BICS* 15 (1968), pp. 1–33.

Webster, *Old and Middle Comedy*
T. B. L. Webster. *Monuments Illustrating Old and Middle Comedy.* 2nd ed. (*BICS,* Suppl. 23). London, 1969.

Webster, *Tragedy and Satyr-Play*
T. B. L. Webster. *Monuments Illustrating Tragedy and Satyr-Play.* 2nd ed. with Appendix (*BICS,* Suppl. 20). London, 1967.

Webster and Green, *Old and Middle Comedy*
T. B. L. Webster and J. R. Green. *Monuments Illustrating Old and Middle Comedy.* 3rd ed., revised and enlarged by J. R. Green (*BICS,* Suppl. 39). London, 1978.

ABBREVIATIONS

AA	Archäologischer Anzeiger	JHS	Journal of Hellenic Studies
AJA	American Journal of Archaeology	JOAI	Jahreshefte des Österreichischen Archäologischen Instituts
AntK	Antike Kunst		
ArchCl	Archeologia Classica	LIMC	Lexicon Iconographicum Mythologiae Classicae
AuA	Antike und Abendland		
BABesch	Bulletin van de Vereeniging tot Bevordering der Kennis van de Antieke Beschaving	MarbWPr	Marburger Winckelmann-Programm
		Meded	Mededelingen van het Nederlands Instituut te Rome
BCH	Bulletin de correspondance hellénique		
BClevMus	The Bulletin of the Cleveland Museum of Art	MeditArch	Mediterranean Archaeology
		MEFRA	Mélanges de l'École française de Rome, Antiquité
BdA	Bollettino d'arte		
BdArch	Bollettino di Archeologia	MFA AnnRep	Museum of Fine Arts, Boston, Annual Report
BICS	Bulletin of the Institute of Classical Studies of the University of London		
		MonAnt	Monumenti antichi
		NSc	Notizie degli Scavi
BMFA	Bulletin of the Museum of Fine Arts, Boston	NumAntCl	Numismatica e antichità classiche. Quaderni ticinesi
BMMA	Bulletin of the Metropolitan Museum of Art		
		OpRom	Opuscula Romana
BSR	Papers of the British School of Archaeology at Rome	OudMed	Oudheidkundige Mededelingen
		PAPS	Proceedings of the American Philosophical Society
BullCom	Bullettino della Commissione archeologica comunale di Roma		
		PCPS	Proceedings of the Cambridge Philological Society
BurlMag	Burlington Magazine		
CJ	The Classical Journal	RA	Revue archéologique
CVA	Corpus Vasorum Antiquorum	RdA	Rivista di Archeologia
DialArch	Dialoghi di Archeologia	RM	Mitteilungen des Deutschen Archäologischen Instituts, Römische Abteilung
EAA	Enciclopedia dell'arte antica, classica e orientale		
		TAPA	Transactions of the American Philological Association
FastiA	Fasti Archeologici		
GettyMusJ	The J. Paul Getty Museum Journal	TAPS	Transactions of the American Philosophical Society
JdI	Jahrbuch des Deutschen Archäologischen Instituts		

COLOR IN SOUTH ITALIAN
VASE-PAINTING

The techniques employed by potters and vase-painters to create the painted vases of South Italy and Sicily have been admirably described by Joseph V. Noble. He has recreated the processes of preparation of clay, throwing of vases, molding of ornaments, preparation of black glaze from highly refined clay, and the complex and precarious processes of firing. The role of color, which took on increasing importance throughout the history of vase-painting in South Italy, deserves a further mention here, however, if only to clarify the descriptions in the text of this catalogue.

In the earliest South Italian red-figure vases in Boston — the late fifth-century works of the Lucanian school — the technique is the one traditionally employed in the red-figure workshops of Attica; figures are reserved on the reddish orange clay of the body of the vase and silhouetted by the surrounding black glaze. Black glaze is also applied within the figures as wiry linear detail. Dilute glaze is used for anatomical details, and occasionally it is applied in a looser and more painterly way to render the transparency of sideburns or the edges of flowing hair. In late fifth-century Athens, however, a richer use of color effects had been developed. White was used extensively for details of costume like wreaths and especially for the flesh of female figures and Erotes. Details within these large white fields were added in a golden brown tone created with dilute glaze. The wings of Erotes were frequently gilded. Inlays in metal vessels were suggested by beads or lines of clay that were painted white to evoke silver or tinted yellow with dilute glaze or gilded to represent gold inlays. Contemporary Attic white-ground vases, on the other hand, may have imitated wall-paintings; figures were outlined in thin black glaze, and yellows and browns were created with diluted glaze. Reds, yellows, blues, and greens were also produced with added earth and vegetable colors.

The vase-painters of South Italy tended to build on the Attic red-figure tradition of adding white and yellow, but they were evidently more interested in painterly illusionistic effects than in suggesting gold and silver overlays on metal vessels. A white color (produced with a slip of iron-poor clay) and dilute glaze were both taken up in fourth-century red-fig-

ure vase-painting in South Italy, and the range of application of these colors was enormously expanded. Primarily, such color was used to articulate differences in the materials of the subjects represented. Metal was most often so distinguished, but other materials were so articulated as well. White was added very extensively for every kind of jewelry, ribbon, or strap embellishing the figures and for all kinds of weaponry, furniture, musical instruments, or other gear employed in the scenes. Bracelets, anklets, earrings, hair ribbons, necklace pendants, and similar ornaments were almost invariably rendered entirely with added white — usually painted on the black-glazed background — while shoes were usually overpainted in white on the reserved red ground. Landscape props might be touched with white. White was often used for the pelts of animals like dogs and horses, which might be so colored naturally.

In most schools of South Italian Greek vase-painting, however, added white was no longer used to color the skin of women and Erotes, as it had been in Attic red-figure. This convention, on the other hand, was frequently employed farther to the north and west in the Campanian and Etruscan schools, and these varying practices show how the different regions in Italy could have different relationships to the Attic motherland of red-figure vase-painting. In Apulia, added white was used for the skin of women and Erotes in Gnathian vases — that is, in vases painted entirely in added color without the reserved red-brown color of red-figure painting. This is, however, a special situation; normally, added white was employed only for radically different contrasts of material rather than for the distinction between suntanned male and tender, protected female skin. In Apulian red-figure, human figures were colored white almost exclusively when they were not living beings; these exceptional cases include statues and, especially, figures in funerary naiskoi, where they are distinguished from the living mortals around them. The white figures in naiskoi can be thought of as statues of the deceased in their tombs or else as the deceased transferred to the realm of the blessed dead. An even more ambiguous use of added white for female skin occurs in the female heads in vine scrolls, which normally appear on the necks and shoulders of vases. These disembodied heads, which are surely not sculptures, must have been colored white to indicate their superhuman, otherworldly character.

In all schools of South Italian red-figure, dilute glaze was used to create brown linear detail on white objects, and even more frequently it was used as a thin wash over white objects to tint them a honey-yellow color. This yellow was often used to create the effects of metalwork — whether bronze, gold, or gilding — but it can also suggest other yellowish colors, like the reddish blond hair of the frontal heads on the handles of volute kraters or the flowery vegetation of a landscape. As the occasion required, dilute glaze was applied more densely on a white substratum to create the brown mottling of a serpent's back, or it was applied in broad, brownish areas to the reserved surface of a fish's back to modulate its red-brown color. In figures of actors, costumes were toned a uniform brown with dilute glaze to give the effect of skins and leather. Uneven groundlines were frequently indicated by lines of white and yellow dots. Yellow dilute glaze was also used for an artistically more ambitious purpose: to create the effects of painterly illusionism. Not only were objectively different materials given different colors, but, in addition, purely optical effects like reflections, highlights, shadows, and transparencies (as of hair), were suggested by the application of yellowish or brownish dilute glaze. These effects are seen most often when yellow dilute glaze was modulated over a white substratum to give the illusion of highlighting and shadowing on a fully rounded metal object. Highlights were created with added white on the reserved red surface of a flower and could be supplemented by shadows of dilute glaze, also placed on the reserved red surface.

A few other colors were used on rarer occasions. Iron-rich slip produced a red-brown hue that approaches the color of the body clay of the vase, and this fluent red was used to paint vine decoration or the colors of flesh, especially in Gnathian pottery. A more intense, dark red color (like the added red familiar from Archaic vase-painting) was also employed for colored drapery and at times even for blood stains. Rainbows were suggested by rings of this red enclosed by rings of white and yellow. In the red-figure vases of the Lipari Islands (not represented in the Boston collection) blue and blue-greens were also applied in tempera after the vase had been fired.

The desire for color and for illusionistic effects led eventually to the abandonment of the sharply outlined red-figure technique. This tendency manifested itself precociously in Gnathian pottery, in which the colors mentioned above (minus the blues and blue-greens) were painted on the uniformly black-glazed surface of the vase. Painting in tempera colors in the workshops of Canosa and Centuripe during the third century was the culmination of this process. Black glaze, the basic medium of the traditional Greek decorator of vases, was completely given up, as the effects of wall- or panel-painting were imitated on a three-dimensional ceramic support.

Bibliography: J. V. Noble in Mayo, *Magna Graecia*, pp. 37–47. For the background of Greek color theory, see V. J. Bruno, *Form and Color in Greek Painting* (New York, 1977).

PLATE I. 8A. Stamnos. Attributed to the Ariadne Painter.
Apulian, ca. 400–390 B.C. Theseus abandoning Ariadne

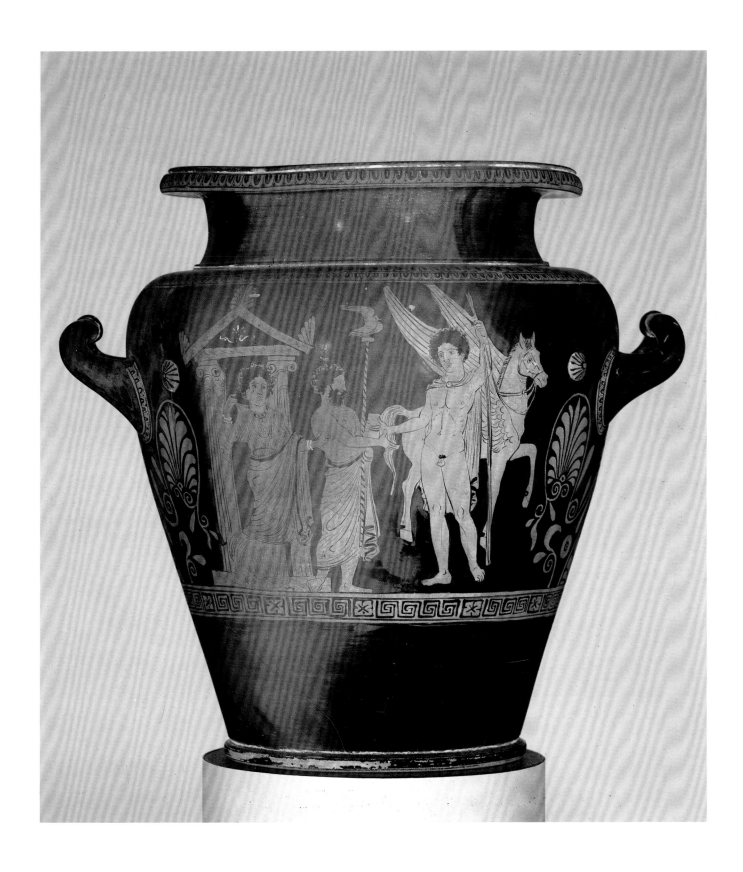

PLATE II. 8B. Stamnos. Attributed to the Ariadne Painter.
Apulian, ca. 400–390 B.C. The departure of Bellerophon

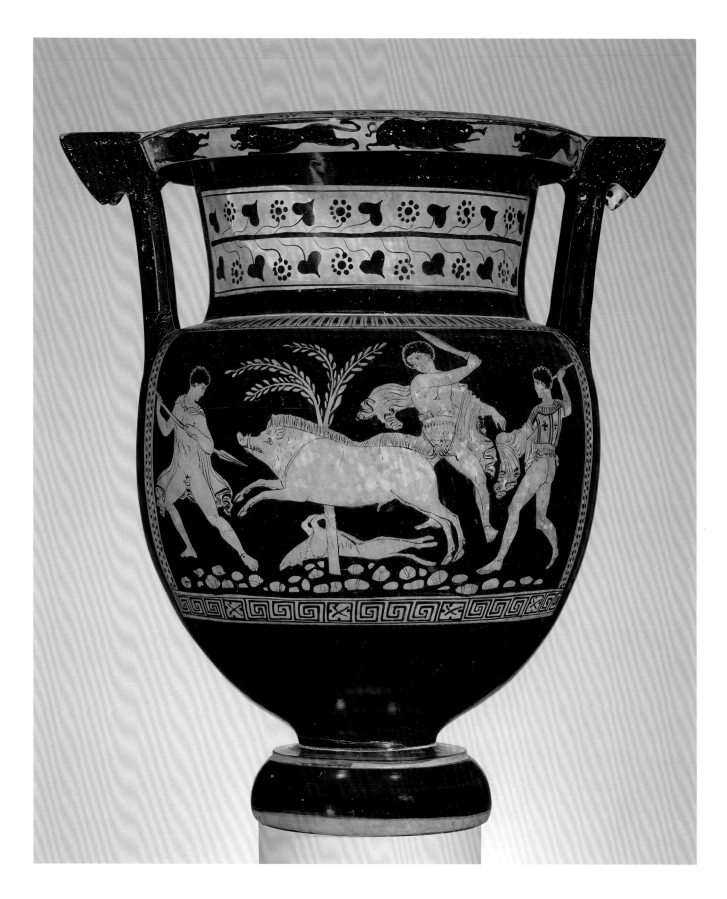

PLATE III. 9. Column-krater. Attributed to the Sisyphus
Group. Apulian, ca. 400–390 B.C. A boar hunt

PLATE IV. 10. Bell-krater. Attributed to the Tarporley
Painter. Apulian, ca. 400–385 B.C. Athena with the head
of Medusa

PLATE V. 13. Bell-krater. Apulian, ca. 380–370 B.C.
Two phlyax actors

PLATE VI. 17. Bell-krater. Closely associated with the
Judgement Painter. Apulian, ca. 370–360 B.C. Orestes at
Delphi

PLATE VII. 18. Bell-krater. The name-vase of the Painter of
Boston 00.348. Apulian, ca. 370–360 B.C. Athena playing
the auloi

PLATE VIII. 21. Volute-krater. Attributed to the Iliupersis
Painter. Apulian, ca. 365–355 B.C. Perhaps Polyneikes
bribing Eriphyle

PLATE IX. 28. Alabastron. Related to the V. and A. Group.
Apulian, ca. 350–340 B.C. Menelaos and Helen

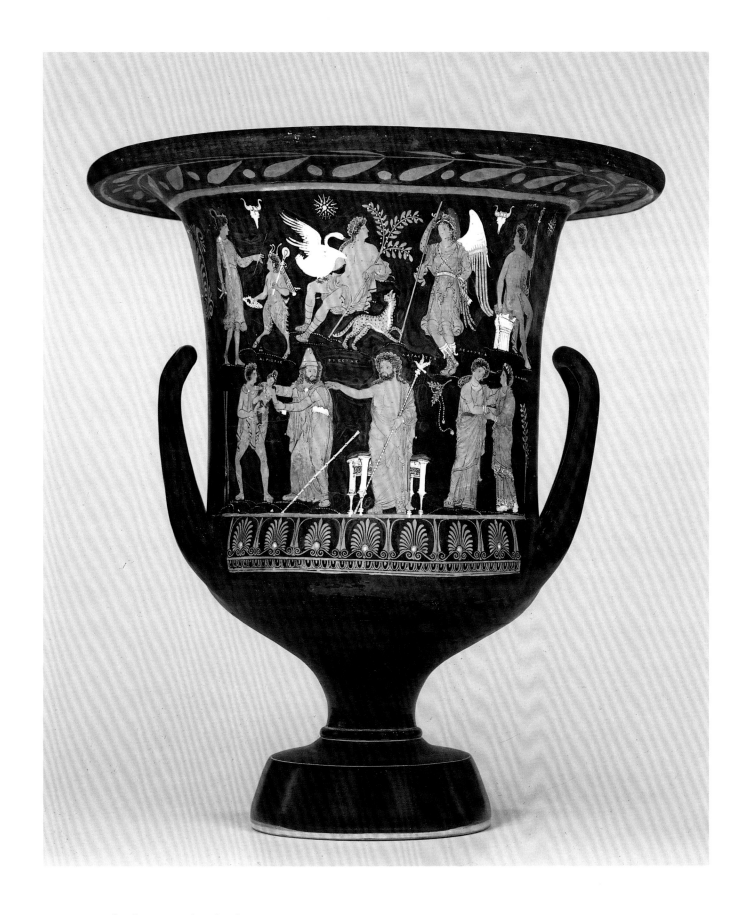

PLATE X. 41. Calyx-krater. Attributed to the Darius Painter.
Apulian, ca. 340–330 B.C. The exposure of the baby Aigisthos

PLATE XI. 42. Amphora. Attributed to the Darius Painter.
Apulian, ca. 340–330 B.C. The death of Atreus

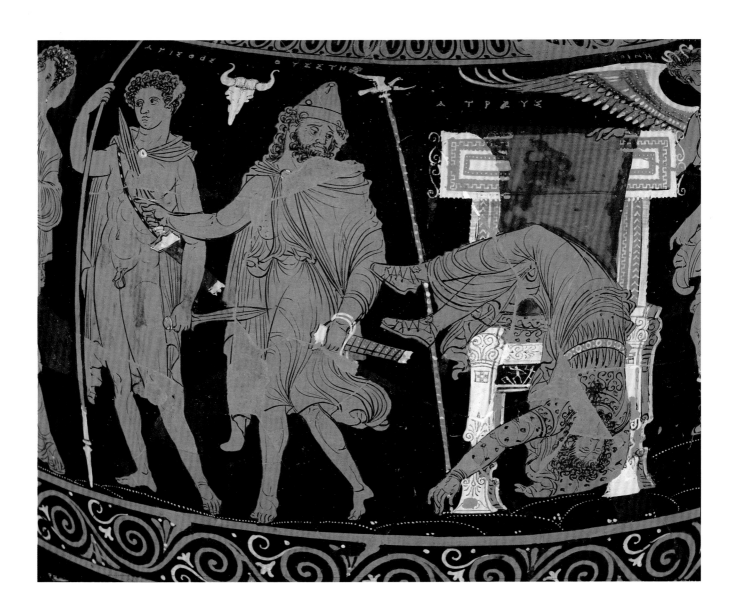

PLATE XI. 42. Amphora. Detail

PLATE XII. 47. Knob-handled patera. Attributed to the
Perrone-Phrixos Group. Apulian, 340–330 B.C.

PLATE XIII. 52. Skyphos. Attributed to the Alabastra Group.
Apulian, ca. 330–320 B.C.

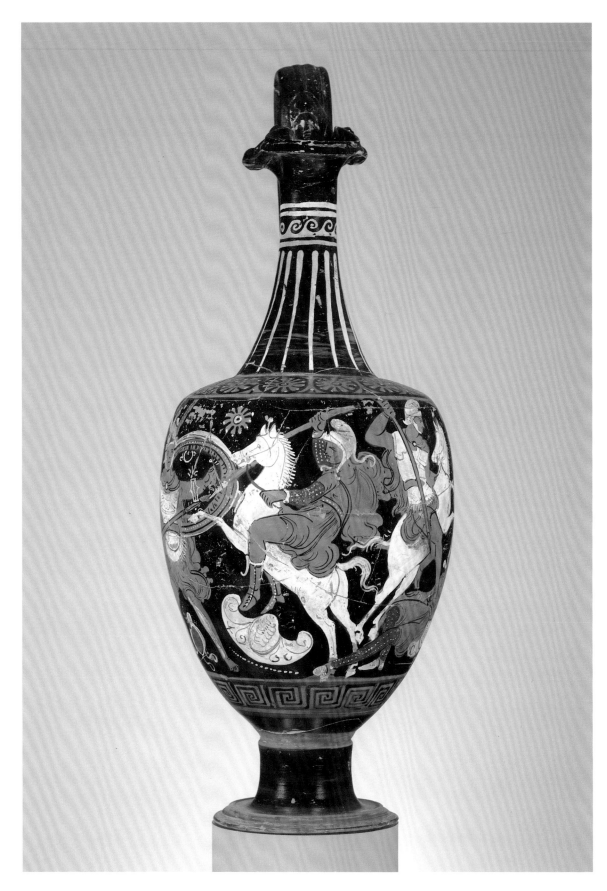

PLATE XIV. 66. Oinochoe. Attributed to the Helios Group.
Apulian, 320–310 B.C. A battle of Greeks and Amazons

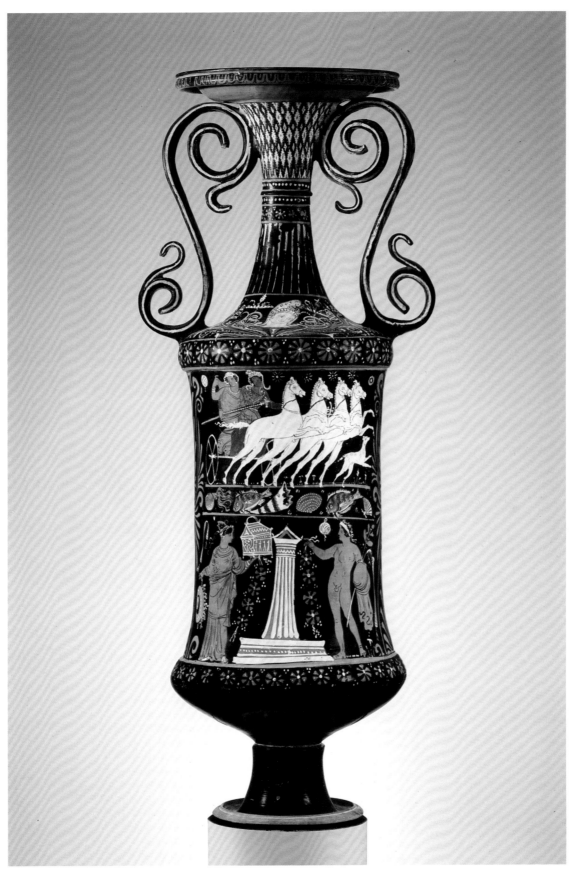

PLATE XV. 69. Loutrophoros. Attributed to the White Sakkos
Painter. Apulian, 320–310 B.C. Pelops and Hippodameia
in a quadriga

PLATE XVI. 85. Hydria. Attributed to the Whiteface-
Frignano Painter. Campanian, ca. 345–335 B.C. Kadmos
and the serpent

PLATE XVII. 88. Fish-plate. Related to the D'Agostino
Painter. Campanian, 3rd quarter of 4th century B.C.

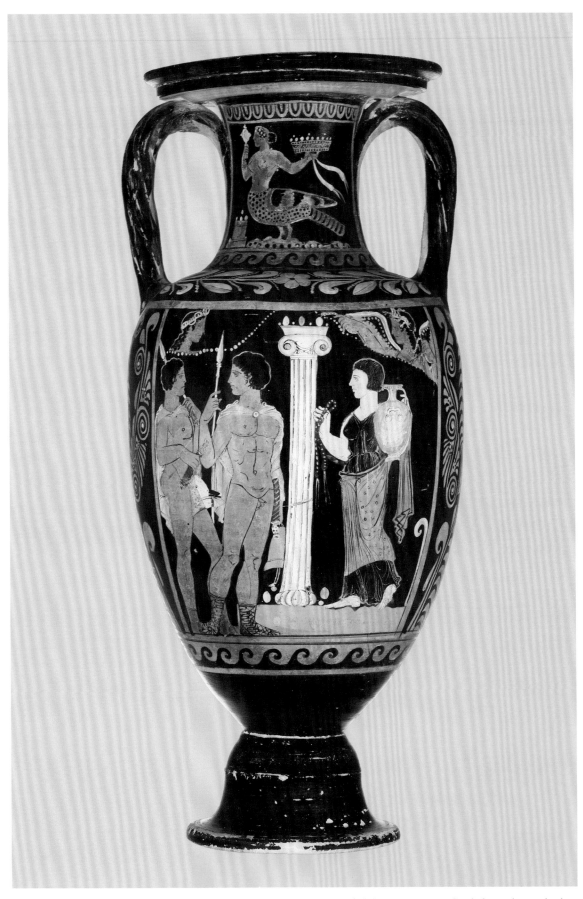

PLATE XVIII. 105. Neck-amphora. The name-vase of the
Boston Orestes Painter. Paestan, 335–320 B.C. The
meeting of Elektra, Orestes, and Pylades at the tomb of
Agamemnon

PLATE XIX. 108. Calyx-krater. Attributed to the Konnakis
Painter. Gnathian Ware, Apulian, ca. 350 B.C. A phlyax actor

PLATE XX. 111. Squat lekythos. Gnathian Ware, Apulian,
ca. 350 B.C. Eros

PLATE XXI. 130. Bell-krater. Gnathian Ware, Apulian, end
of 4th century B.C. Eros driving a biga drawn by hounds

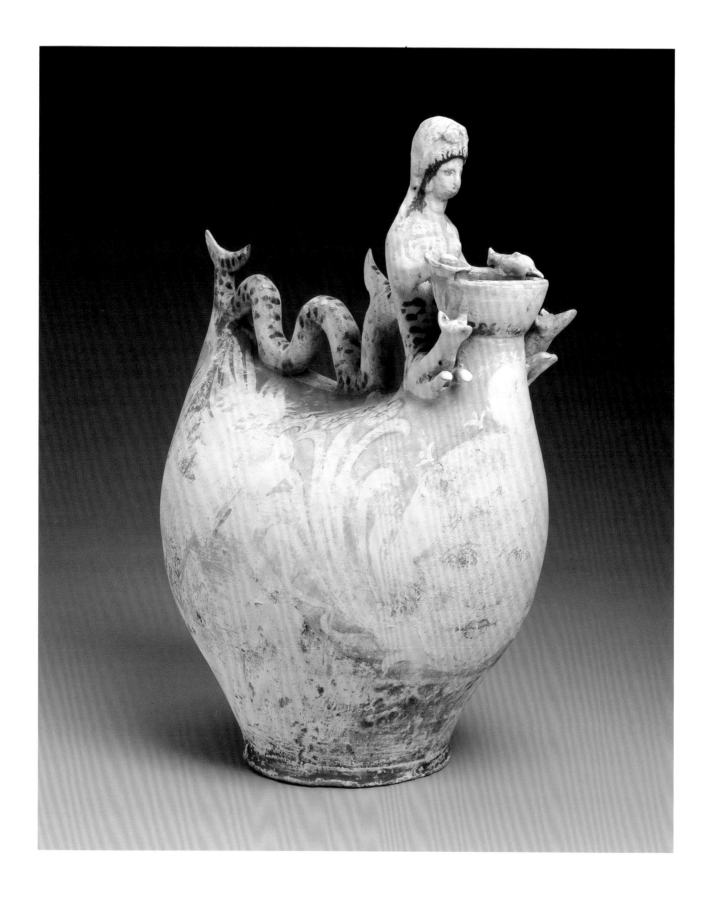

PLATE XXII. 149. Askos. Attributed to the Group of the
Skylla Askoi. Canosan, ca. 300 B.C.

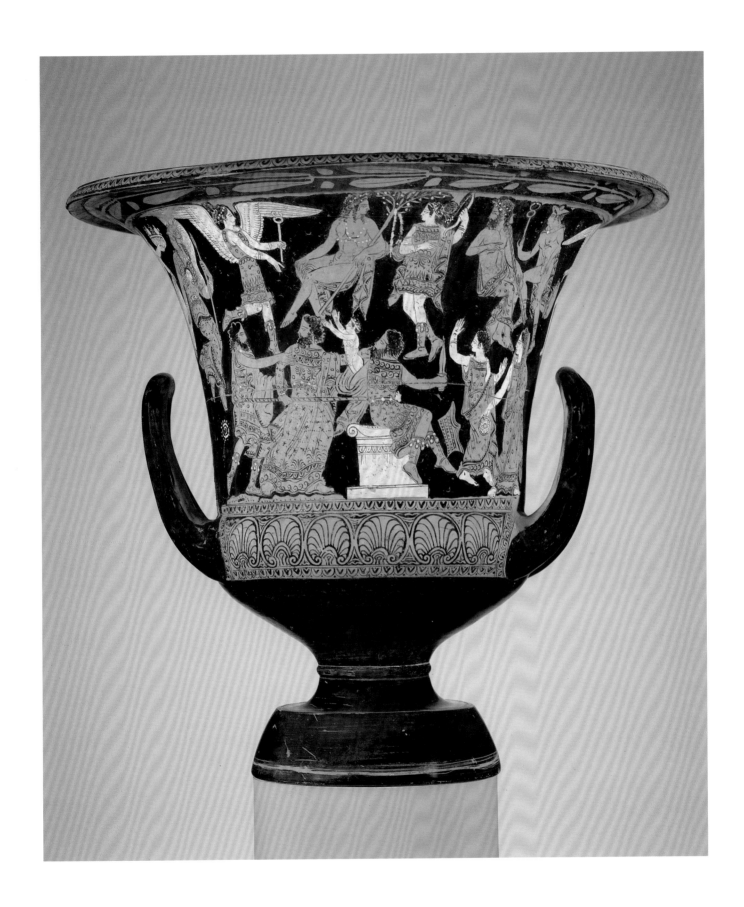

PLATE XXIII. 166. Calyx-krater. Attributed to the Nazzano
Painter. Faliscan, ca. 380–360 B.C. Telephos and the infant
Orestes

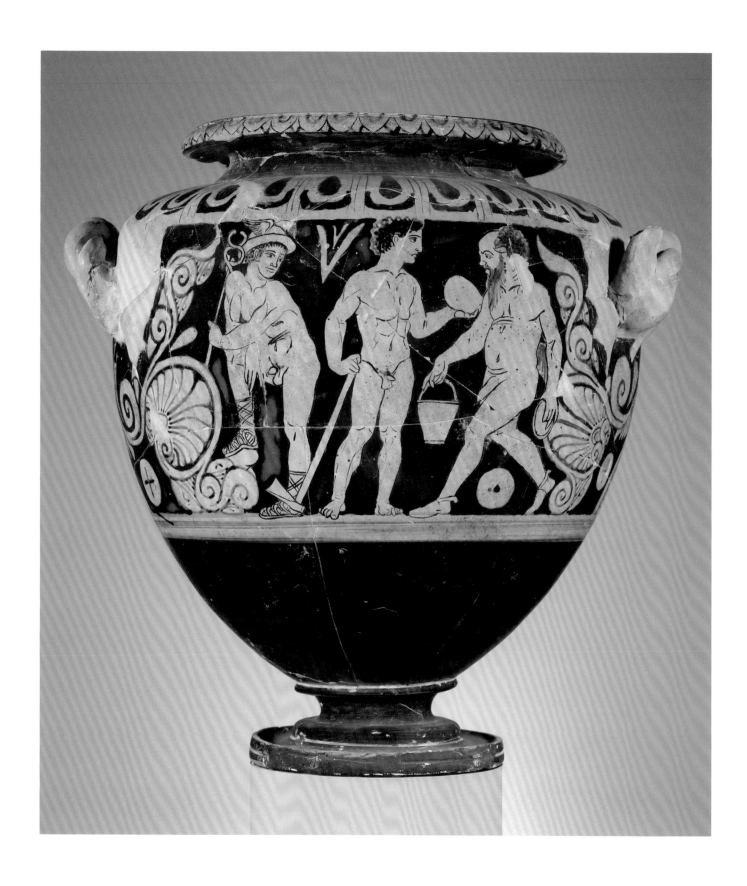

PLATE XXIV. 167. Stamnos. Attributed to the Painter of the
Oxford Ganymede. Etruscan or Faliscan, 1st half of 4th
century B.C. Polydeukes holding the egg containing Helen

PLATE XXV. 174. Phiale mesomphalos. Attributed to the
Fluid Group. Faliscan, 330–310 B.C. A row of geese

USE OF THE CATALOGUE

The catalogue has been divided into the basically Greek schools of South Italy and Sicily and the Italic schools of central Italy. Within these two divisions, the catalogue has been arranged according to technique: red-figure; the Gnathian technique; its close relation, superposed color; and tempera painting. Plastic vases have been included in the red-figure sections, although some have no painted decoration. In the South Italian section, each technical division is subdivided according to regional schools, and these subsections have a roughly chronological arrangement. In the central Italian section, the Etruscan and Faliscan schools have been treated together since they are so closely interrelated on many levels.

The names of mythological figures are usually given in Greek. Latin equivalents are used when they are more familiar than the Greek versions. In the central Italian section, Faliscan and Etruscan designations are given only when the mythological figures represented appear to differ significantly in some respect from their closest Greek counterparts.

In the listing of dimensions, the diameters of the rim and the body are the maximum dimension unless otherwise specified. The diameters of the neck and stem are the minimum dimension unless otherwise indicated. The diameter of the foot is at the lowest point, which is not necessarily the widest.

The provenance is given in reverse chronological order, beginning with the most recent previous owner and proceeding to the earliest known.

Entries in the indexes refer only to the vases in the Museum of Fine Arts.

CATALOGUE OF THE COLLECTION

South Italian

LUCANIAN
Red-Figure

The discovery in 1973 of kilns containing fragments of vases by the Amykos Painter and his followers the Creusa and Dolon Painters proves beyond a doubt that the center of Lucanian vase-painting in the late fifth and early fourth century was at Metapontum. Vases by the Pisticci Painter found nearby are not in his early style, of around 450 B.C. and somewhat thereafter, but their presence nevertheless suggests that this earliest of Lucanian vase-painters also worked at or near Metapontum, perhaps at the site of Pisticci itself in Metapontum's hinterland, where many of his vases have been found. Both the early works of the Pisticci Painter, such as the chous in Boston (cat. no. 1), and his developed works, like the kalpis and bell-krater in Boston (cat. nos. 3, 2), show a strong Attic influence; not only his style but also the shapes of his bell-kraters and hydriai are Attic in derivation. The Pisticci Painter was probably an immigrant from Athens, and it has recently been maintained by Nancy Jircik that the artist began his career in the circle of the Niobid Painter as early as 460 B.C. and had moved to South Italy before the middle of the century (Jircik, *Pisticci*, pp. 54–61, 186–187). If she is right, then the artist's style, subjects, and general mood underwent a sea change during the voyage to Magna Graecia.

The Pisticci Painter tended to repeat figures and a limited number of compositional schemes. His kalpis in Boston (cat. no. 3) is unusual in taking up innovative motifs like a figure seated on a rock that is shaded with dilute glaze. Such progressive ideas stemming ultimately from the wall-paintings of Polygnotos of Thasos could well have been transmitted via imported Attic vases rather than remembered from direct experience. The Pisticci Painter's followers were active borrowers of such novelties on Athenian vases. The Pisticci Painter's subject matter tends to be as limited as his compositions, generally being restricted to Dionysiac, domestic, athletic, and abduction scenes. Jircik speculates that the infrequency of literary or mythological themes may have reflected the not-fully-Hellenized tastes of his public; the known find spots of his vases are chiefly in the native areas of inland Lucania. When the subject matter is seen in the funerary context for which the vases were probably intended, its generalized images assume eschatological connotations. Motifs of abduction signify apotheosis in death. Revelry or scenes of domestic tranquillity allude to a joyful ex-

istence in another life (Jircik, *Pisticci*, pp. 141–150, 189–193). Similar arguments can and have been made for many South Italian vase-paintings, so many of which seem to have been manufactured exclusively for funerary use.

The Cyclops and Amykos Painters, followers of the Pisticci Painter, made the bell-krater their favorite shape, but the Amykos Painter also decorated a few nestorides, a variant of the native Italic trozzella; one of his best is the nestoris in Boston (cat. no. 4), with an Oscan warrior arming and a satyr pursuing a maenad. Both the warrior and the shape of the vessel may have been in response to the tastes prevalent in the Amykos Painter's markets, which, like those of the Pisticci Painter, lay to a great extent in inland, Italic areas (Jircik, *Pisticci*, pp. 148, 192–193). More literary themes began, however, to make headway as well. The name-vase of the Cyclops Painter, a calyx-krater in the British Museum with Odysseus blinding Polyphemos in the presence of two capering satyrs, was probably inspired by Euripides' satyr-play *Cyclops*, of about 406 B.C., one of the earliest in a long series of South Italian vase-paintings inspired by the works of the great Athenian tragedians of the fifth century.

The Amykos Painter was the most prolific and influential of the Pisticci Painter's followers, strongly influencing a group of painters whose workshop seems to have been located at Policoro, the ancient Heraclea. Among these are the Palermo, Karneia, and Policoro Painters, whose large vases, including several volute-kraters, reflect the contemporary Apulian taste for mythological compositions on the grand scale and continue the taste for scenes derived from Euripidean tragedy.

Slightly later than these is the workshop of the Creusa (cat. no. 5) and Dolon Painters, active until about 370 B.C. Vases by the Amykos and Creusa Painters were found together in the same tomb at Policoro. Like the Amykos Painter, the Dolon Painter decorated several nestorides and, like the earlier painters at Policoro, was strongly influenced by artists of the Apulian Plain style, being especially close to the Tarporley Painter.

Around 370 B.C., the workshops at Metapontum and Policoro seem to have shut down, as far fewer Lucanian vases of a later date have been found at Apulian sites. Production shifted to the Lucanian hinterland, where artists were more removed from new inspiration and stylistic influences. The quality of Lucanian vases rapidly declined, the best work exhibiting a strong Apulian influence. The Choephoroi Painter, active around midcentury, is notable for the scenes of Aeschylean tragedy that give him his name, but later artists, such as the Primato (cat. no. 6) and Roccanova Painters, brought the Lucanian style to a relatively inglorious termination at the end of the third quarter of the fourth century.

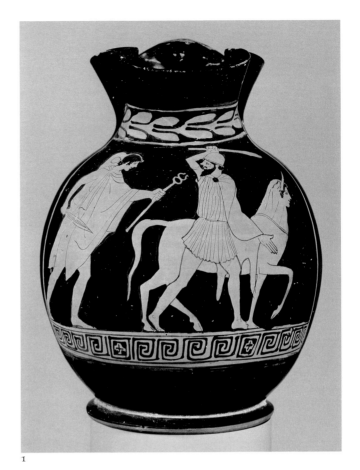

1

1

OINOCHOE (shape 3)
Attributed to the Pisticci Painter
Early style. Ca. 450 B.C.
Henry Lillie Pierce Residuary Fund. 00.366

PROVENANCE: E. P. Warren collection

DIMENSIONS AND CONDITION: Height: 22.7 cm; diameter neck: 8.2 cm; diameter body: 17.7 cm; diameter foot: 11.8 cm
Unbroken

SHAPE: A so-called chous, both in shape and probably in capacity (i.e., 12 kotylai), although this has not been measured. The body is nearly spherical; wide disk foot; trefoil mouth; low handle.

Io, in the form of a cow, is being driven along by Argos, who stands in the foreground. Hermes follows from the left, his herald's staff in his extended left hand, his sword drawn back in his right. Argos looks back at Hermes and with his right hand raises his staff over his head to defend himself. Argos wears a chitoniskos, a cap of wool or skin, and a cloak of skin pinned at the throat. Hermes wears a chlamys and petasos. The drawing is in the Attic style, but unlike most Athenian renderings of the myth, Io is given a human face, and Argos is not *panoptes*.

The picture has lateral frames of narrow reserved lines. The upper frame is a large laurel wreath. The broad groundline consists of groups of four linked maeanders to right alternating with cross-squares. On top of the handle, where it meets the rim, is an enclosed, upright palmette.

Trendall and Webster (*Illustrations*, p. 32) thought it possible this picture was inspired by the lost Sophoclean satyr-play, *Inachos*, but the subject and basic composition precede Sophocles' work; see Brommer, *Göttersagen*, pp. 31–32; and E. Simon, *AA* 1985, pp. 265–280.

1

PUBLISHED: E. Robinson, *MFA AnnRep* 1900, pp. 62–63, no. 21; *AA* 1901, p. 167, no. 21; R. Engelmann, *JdI* 18 (1903), pp. 38–42 (fig. 1), 54; *AJA* 7 (1903), p. 476; Trendall, *Frühitaliotische*, pp. 9 (note 8, no. 60, as 00.346), 33 (no. 60); A. B. Cook, *Zeus: A Study in Ancient Religion*, III: *Zeus God of the Dark Sky* (Cambridge, 1940), p. 635, fig. 432; van Hoorn, *Choes*, p. 112, no. 374 (as 00.346); E. Paribeni, *EAA*, IV,

p. 170; Webster, *Tragedy and Satyr-Play*, p. 149; Trendall, *LCS*, p. 16, no. 9; Trendall and Webster, *Illustrations*, p. 32, pl. 2, 6; J. Henle, *Greek Myths: A Vase Painter's Notebook* (Bloomington, 1973), p. 174, note 2, ch. 3; Trendall, *Early*, pp. 4, 30, no. 99; N. R. Oakeshott, *JHS* 95 (1975), p. 297; K. Schauenburg, *AA* 1977, p. 296, note 49; A. H. Sommerstein, *BICS* 24 (1977), p. 74; D. A. Amyx, *Archaeological News* (Tallahassee) 8 (1979), pp. 107, 115, note 58; I. McPhee, *AntK* 22 (1979), p. 38; Brommer, *Göttersagen*, p. 32, no. D 2; Schefold and Jung, *Göttersage*, pp. 136, 351, note 268; C. Weiss, *Griechische Flussgottheiten in vorhellenistischer Zeit (Beiträge zur Archäologie*, no. 17, Würzburg, 1984), pp. 107–108, 215, note 691, pl. 11, 1; N. Yalouris, in *Iconographie classique et identités régionales* (*BCH*, Suppl. 14, Paris, 1986), pp. 10–12, no. 13, fig. 7; Giambersio, *Pisticci*, pp. 64, 72, 90–93 (fig. 22), 170, no. 9; J.-M. Moret, *RA* 1990, p. 5; G. Siebert, *LIMC*, V, 1, pp. 356–357 (no. 839, as 1901.562); N. Yalouris, ibid., V, 1, pp. 667 (no. 33, as 1901.562), 674–675; V, 2, pl. 444.

2

2

BELL-KRATER
Attributed to the Pisticci Painter
Developed style. Ca. 445–425 B.C.
Gift of Thomas G. Appleton. 76.50

PROVENANCE: Alessandro Castellani collection; from Ruvo

DIMENSIONS AND CONDITION: Height: 29.4 cm; diameter rim: 32.0 cm; diameter body below handles: 26.6 cm; diameter stem: 10.2 cm; diameter foot: 14.6 cm
A piece of the foot has been reattached; otherwise intact.

SHAPE: Canonical shape for both Attic and Lucanian bell-kraters of this period, with disk foot (reserved on the side), tapering lower body, upturned handles, and flaring rim in two degrees.

A: Three figures are walking in procession to the right. At the left is a bearded man wearing a himation and laurel wreath and carrying a staff in his right hand. Ahead of him is a woman wearing a chiton, himation, and sakkos and playing the double flutes. At the right is a youth wearing a himation and laurel wreath and carrying a staff in his right hand; he looks back at the woman as he walks.

B: A boy stands between two youths with staffs in their right hands. All three wear himatia, the boy's covering both arms and the lower face.

A laurel wreath circles the vase below the lip. The groundline consists of groups of three stopt maeanders to right alternating with cross-squares.

2

PUBLISHED: Robinson, *Catalogue*, p. 161, no. 439; E. M. W. Tillyard, *The Hope Vases: A Catalogue and A Discussion of the Hope Collection of Greek Vases with An Introduction on the History of the Collection and on Late Attic and South Italian Vases* (Cambridge, 1923), p. 10, no. 8; Trendall, *Frühitaliotische*, p. 9, pl. 1 b; L. Budde, *AJA* 53 (1949), p. 33, note 12; Trendall, *LCS*, p. 19, no. 32; idem, *Early*, pp. 3–6, 27, no. 20, pl. I; Giambersio, *Pisticci*, p. 173, no. 32.

3

Kalpis

Attributed to the Pisticci Painter (Herrmann)
Developed style. Ca. 445–430 B.C.
Gift of Edward Jackson Holmes. Res. 41.56

DIMENSIONS AND CONDITION: Height: 44.5 cm; diameter rim: 17.5 cm; diameter neck: 10.1 cm; diameter body below handles: 33.5 cm; diameter stem: 9.4 cm; diameter foot: 15.6 cm Reassembled from fragments. There are gaps and abraded cracks through the figured zone, particularly at the left and in the center; areas are missing in the head and bottom left of the left figure, the face and shoulders of the next woman, across the body of the seated woman, and in the lower left leg of the woman facing her. Breaks in the palmette and tendrils behind the left woman have been retouched, as have gaps and abraded cracks in the ornamental bands below the figures.

Prior to acquisition in 1941, all missing areas had been repainted. The repainting extended over the original parts of the figures, and the deceptive treatment had been concealed with a cosmetic coating. In 1991 and 1992, the coating and repainting were removed in the Museum's Research Laboratory, and the ornament was newly retouched.

SHAPE: Of standard kalpis type, it bears comparison with hydriai by the Policoro, Amykos, and Creusa Painters from the Policoro tomb, which likewise have "domestic" scenes on the shoulder (N. Degrassi, *BdA* ser. 5, 50 [1965], pp. 10–12, nos. 4–6, figs. 4, 13–14, 18, 21–24, 29–32). The foot is in two degrees, with a torus base and sloping riser.

The figures on the shoulder are organized in three facing pairs. At the left, a woman reaches out to receive a casket being offered by another woman approaching from the right. Between the two is a kalathos. The woman at the left wears a peplos with belted overfold and a chlaina. She is barefoot, like all the figures on the vase. The top of her head is missing, but its rear contour is preserved; the compact silhouette suggests that her hair was covered with a sakkos. The woman facing her is clad only in a chiton. A ribbon wound repeatedly around her head supports her chignon. The central group is formed by a woman seated on a rocky outcropping, who is offered an exaleiptron by a standing woman. The seated woman wears a chiton and himation, and her hair, which hangs down her back, is bound on her head by a ribbon, into which three olive or laurel leaves are inserted. The rocky outcropping is darkened with a wash of dilute glaze. The standing woman with the exaleiptron wears a peplos with belted overfold and a chlaina, which is draped over her left shoulder and held with her outstretched left hand. A ribbon, into which four small leaves are inserted, is wrapped around her head and supports her chignon. Between the central and the right pair of figures, a piece of dotted fabric with borders at either end is hung, apparently over two pegs. In the right hand group, a woman spinning wool faces Eros

3

3

3

across a wool basket. The woman again wears a peplos and a headband, which this time is embellished with a continuous row of nine leaves. She holds the distaff in her raised left hand, and a line of yarn is guided by her lowered right hand to the hanging spindle, which appears to be completely wrapped in yarn. There is some ambiguity in the representation since the "distaff" is crosshatched as if it were wrapped with yarn rather than rougher, unfinished wool or flax. The "spindle," moreover, is an amorphous shape like a roving of wool. A break passing through the lower part of the spindle may have destroyed the spindle-whorl, which would have identified the object with certainty. Eros holds a small pyxis-like basket in his left hand. Details of his anatomy are sketched in with dilute glaze.

At either end of the figured zone on the shoulder is a palmette springing from and encircled by a long, vine-like tendril. Two small tendrils spring from the groundline below the palmette. An inverted palmette, enclosed in a heart-shaped band, decorates the base of the vertical handle.

The lip is decorated with a dotted egg-pattern. The neck is embellished with a network of black lotus buds on a reserved ground. Below the figures is a

band of dotted egg-pattern, and below this a broader band of lotus and palmette. The handle roots are surrounded by tongue-pattern on the outer two-thirds of their circumference. The zones under the side handles are reserved. A reserved band circles the base of each step of the foot.

The vase was long considered a forgery of an Attic vase and published as such in an exhibition in Minneapolis on fakes, with a comment on the hydria's "unbelievably perfect" condition. In 1990, Arthur Beale, director of conservation research at the Museum of Fine Arts, questioned the condemnation. On examination by the Research Laboratory, it was revealed that a heavy surface coating concealed breaks and gaps and gave the surface its disturbingly slick appearance. There had been an effort to deceive, but it was directed toward concealing the true condition of an ancient object rather than creating an entirely modern imposture. Even after cleaning, however, the body clay still has a dark, dull surface, undoubtedly resulting from the penetration of the resins used in the original deceptive treatment. The vase was then recognized as Lucanian by Michael Padgett.

The figures, moreover, are clearly the work of the

Pisticci Painter. Many can be connected with his early phase. The Eros can be perfectly paralleled in nude males on the squat lekythos in Palermo (999) and the oinochoe in Adolphseck (170) (Trendall, *LCS*, p. 15, nos. 5, 8, pl. 2). The wool baskets are virtually identical with one on the Palermo lekythos. The women, however, find their best parallels in the painter's developed style. Not only the heads but also the chitons with belted overfold and a multitude of fine pleats are repeated on the bell-krater in Denver (AN 108) and a Panathenaic amphora in Taranto (I.G. 8001: *LCS*, pp. 17 [no. 14], 22 [no. 57], pls. 3, 5; Giambersio, *Pisticci*, pp. 16 [fig. 2], 61). Long, straight lines of dilute glaze continue to be used to sketch the leg muscles of nude youths, as on a developed-style fragment with athletes in Taranto (12562: *LCS*, p. 21, no. 45; Giambersio, *Pisticci*, pp. 121, 122 [fig. 32], 123–125, color pl. 9).

The hydria is something of an anomaly in the work of the Pisticci Painter, who rarely presented compositions with more than four figures. Rocky outcroppings and specific vignettes from daily life like the spinner are also rare or unique. His women normally wear a simply detailed himation over their chiton. The hydria with figured shoulder is apparently otherwise unknown in his work. This lotus-and-palmette is more elaborate than that on his hydria in Taranto (I.G. 6997: *LCS*, p. 18, no. 25; Giambersio, *Pisticci*, pp. 22 [fig. 3], 102 [fig. 25], 103, color pl. 5) and much richer than his usual simple and stereotyped ornament. The black lotus-bud chain is rare in South Italian vases in general. The lines of drapery folds are denser than usual in his work, and their movement is more natural. In general, this hydria must be accounted one of his most ambitious works.

Hydriai with a band of lotus-and-palmette at the level of the handles and women in domestic or musical scenes on the shoulder are fairly popular in mid-fifth-century Attic workshops. Several such hydriai were produced in the circle of Polygnotos (A. Greifenhagen, *CVA* Braunschweig, pp. 30–34, pls. 23–27; *CVA* British Museum 6, III, 1, c, pl. 83; Beazley, *ARV*[2], p. 1060, nos. 138–140). An unattributed Attic hydria of about 450 B.C. in Berlin even has a woman (a Muse?) seated on a rock, as on this vase (Berlin F. 2388: P. Jacobsthal, *Ornamente griechischer Vasen* [Berlin, 1927], pp. 86, 88, 90, 152, 183, pl. 64 b).

EXHIBITED: Minneapolis Institute of Arts, *Fakes and Forgeries*, July 11–September 29, 1973 (Minneapolis, 1973), no. 5, illus.; Museum of Fine Arts, Boston, "Unlocking the Hidden Museum," July 3–September 9, 1990.

3

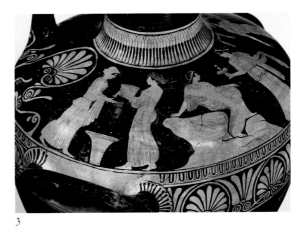

3

4

4

NESTORIS (type 1)
Attributed to the Amykos Painter
Ca. 420–410 B.C.
Frederick Brown Fund. 1971.49

DIMENSIONS AND CONDITION: Height to rim: 23.0 cm; height
with handles: 28.5 cm; diameter rim: 13.0 cm; diameter
neck: 8.7 cm; diameter body: 19.4 cm; diameter stem below
molding: 5.2 cm; diameter foot: 9.5 cm
Unbroken

SHAPE: This nestoris may be the earliest known red-figure example (A. D. Trendall, in Descoeudres, *Greek Colonists*,
p. 223). It is of type 1, with a biconical body and flaring
mouth. There are crossbars and spurs on the vertical handles
and horizontal handles resembling those on hydriai. A thick
fillet separates the foot and lower body. Below the stem, the
foot is a narrow disk, reserved on the side, with a groove
around the upper edge.

A: An Oscan warrior is seated on a rock at left with
a pair of spears held upright in his left hand and a
shield resting against his left knee. He is wearing a
striped tunic, a himation, and a tall, pointed cap of
spotted skin, with long flaps by the ears. With his
right hand, the warrior reaches for his sword, which
is proffered by a woman wearing a chiton, himation,
and sphendone. The shield has a star device. Growing at the far right is a spindly tree.

B: A maenad wearing a belted chiton and sphendone
runs to the left, her cloak in the raised right hand and
a thyrsos in the lowered left. She looks back toward

an entreating, ithyphallic satyr, who prances after
her, his arms outstretched and his right leg raised.

There are laurel wreaths around the inner and
outer rim. On the outer face of each vertical handle
are four superimposed rows of chevrons above a single band of egg-pattern. The pictures have lateral
frames of narrow reserved lines and upper frames of
tongues. A single groundline of linked maeanders to
right circles the lower body.

For red-figure nestorides, see K. Schauenburg, *JdI*
89 (1974), pp. 137–186; and G. Schneider-Herrmann (see reference below). For the rapid evolution of
the shape, compare two later nestorides by the Amykos Painter: Richmond 81.71 (Trendall, *LCS*, Suppl.
III, p. 15, no. 188a, pl. 2, 2–4) and Geddes Collection, Melbourne (*LCS*, Suppl. III, p. 390, no. 188b).

PUBLISHED: C. C. Vermeule, *MFA AnnRep* 1970–71, p. 36;
Trendall, *LCS*, Suppl. II, pp. 145, 156, no. 137b, pl. 30, no. 1;
idem, *Early*, pp. 6, 34, no. 236 (ref. to Trendall, *Gli Indigeni*,
figs. 1–2); K. Schauenburg, *JdI* 89 (1974), pp. 155–156, 159,
figs. 28–30; Schmidt, Trendall, and Cambitoglou, *Grabvasen*,
p. 110, note 409; C. C. Vermeule, *BMFA* 78 (1980), pp. 22,
36–37, no. 15, 3 illus.; G. Schneider-Herrmann, *Red-figured
Lucanian and Apulian Nestorides and their Ancestors* (Amsterdam, 1980), pp. 31–33 (text fig. 1, 1), 46, 49, 59, 69, figs.
43, 43 a-b; M. E. Mayo, in Mayo, *Magna Graecia*, p. 59, under no. 4; K. Schauenburg, *Gnomon* 55 (1983), p. 57; Trendall, *LCS*, Suppl. III, p. 14, no. 137b; idem, *Handbook*,
pp. 20–21, 35 (fig. 11), 277; Jircik, *Pisticci*, pp. 37, 126, figs.
110–111; A. D. Trendall, in Descoeudres, *Greek Colonists*,
p. 223; K. Schauenburg, *JdI* 106 (1991), p. 188, note 48.

4

4

5

5

FRAGMENT OF A SKYPHOS
Attributed to the Creusa Painter
Ca. 380–370 B.C
Lent by Mr. and Mrs. Cornelius C. Vermeule III.
172.1970

DIMENSIONS AND CONDITION: Height: 6.5 cm; width: 8.5 cm

Hermes stands to the left, his chlamys and petasos
hanging behind him, the latter tied with a red cord.
A fillet binds his hair, which hangs in ringlets on his
cheeks. A round pin fastens his chlamys. His left
hand is on his hip, and he holds his caduceus in the
extended right hand. His lower body, most of the
right forearm, and all but the left "horn" and tip of
the right "horn" of the caduceus are missing.

There is no clue as to the subject; the presence of
Hermes does not necessarily denote a mythological
theme. Compare the Hermes on Policoro 35298
(Trendall, *LCS*, p. 87, no. 425, pl. 40, 6; idem,
Handbook, fig. 69) and Naples 2181 (Trendall, *LCS*,
p. 90, no. 445, pl. 42, 3).

6

SQUAT LEKYTHOS
Attributed to the Primato Painter
Ca. 350–340 B.C.
Gift of Edward Austin. 76.455

DIMENSIONS AND CONDITION: Height: 36.0 cm; diameter rim:
8.7 cm; diameter neck: 2.5 cm; diameter body: 16.7 cm; diameter foot: 11.3 cm
The mouth has been reassembled from fragments. The vase is
otherwise intact.

SHAPE: Standard, with ovoid body, broad grooved foot in three
degrees, tall neck, and tall chimney-pot mouth

A woman is seated, with her lower body partly to the
left and her upper body turned to the right. She is
gazing at a mirror in her left hand. The mirror has its
center, handle, axial attachments, and a ring of beads
on its frame rendered in added white. A touch of yellow glaze suggests that the center was gilded. In her
right hand the woman holds two small palm
branches, whose fronds and stems are touched with
white. She wears a chiton, himation, shoes, kekryphalos, necklace, and bracelets. Her earrings, the
pendants of her necklace, the ribbon tying her chignon, details of her shoes, and four tall, feather-like
projections from her kekryphalos are rendered in
white. Two large flowers grow in the area below her
left elbow. Eros flies toward the woman from the
right, holding a long garland in both hands. His
wings have white highlights overlaid with glaze. He
wears shoes, a wreath, and a spiraling anklet. In the
field above are flowers and a hanging fillet. The flowers on the vase are shaded with dilute glaze and highlighted with white.

On the front of the neck is a band of rays above a
narrower band of tongues; in back is a dotted band.
There are enclosed, upright palmettes on the shoulder. Three white dots ornament the base of each palmette, and two more dots flank the tip of its central
petal. The band above the palmette is covered with
white. The upper frame of the figure zone consists
of egg-pattern and dots; the groundline of linked
maeanders to right, with a single, dotted saltire-
square below the woman's feet. Below the handle is
an elaborate palmette complex.

PUBLISHED: Robinson, *Catalogue*, p. 192, no. 528; Trendall,
LCS, p. 174, no. 1014, pl. 76, no. 4; *LIMC*, III, p. 898, no.
560c.

6

APULIAN
Red-Figure and Plastic Vases

Apulian red-figure began a little later than Lucanian, around 430–425 B.C., and for a while the two schools were very close in style. To judge by the Lucanian pottery found in Apulia, it may have been the dominant fabric there until the beginning of the fourth century. Early Apulian vase-painters were also strongly influenced by Attic red-figure and in particular seem to have been more impressed than their Lucanian counterparts by large volute-kraters with mythological subjects and complex, multi-figured compositions, like those by the Kadmos, Pronomos, and Talos Painters found at Ruvo. The influence of such works was manifested in a preference for larger shapes, including every type of krater, and for mythological subjects in the grand manner. Attic influence is also discernible in more modest works, such as owl-skyphoi and choes with scenes of children (cat. no. 7).

When Attic exports to Italy fell off sharply after the Peloponnesian War and production of Attic volute-kraters ceased, the latter shape continued in Apulia, where vase-painting developed along lines increasingly divorced from Attic models. Painted South Italian vases, of which by far the most numerous are Apulian, are distinguishable from their Attic counterparts not only by differences in shape, which may be subtle or glaring, but also by style. Attic and Apulian vases were the products of different worlds, one Ionian Greek, with a long tradition of painted ceramics, the other colonial, mostly Dorian Greek, with a strong native element—Daunian, Messapian, Peucetian—and with a history of importing Attic pottery and drawing inspiration from it for local manufactures. It would make little sense to compare them in qualitative terms, for although the prolific Apulian workshops produced thousands of minor pieces that are little more than hackwork, many of them made specifically as grave goods, these are no worse than the poorest Athenian products, and the best works of artists such as the Black Fury Painter and the Darius Painter are superior to most contemporary Attic works, with varied and occasionally elevated subjects rendered with consummate skill and a flair for dramatic narrative.

In very general terms, Attic drawing of the fourth century is less labored and self-conscious than Apulian. In the better works, figures have a sketchy, impressionistic quality, an easy naturalism that perhaps reflects the influence of contemporary wall-paintings. Apulian vase-paintings, with notable exceptions, seem more self-contained, more reliant on internalized ceramic traditions: the interplay of relief lines and dilute glaze and the bold use of added color for highlighting and visual variety. Although Attic vase-painting is also dependent on older figural types and compositions, it is nevertheless less formulaic than Apulian, in which the very number of works, particularly from the second half of the fourth century, contributes to a misleading impression of numbing homogeneity. Many Apulian vases, particularly the big, showpiece volute-kraters and loutrophoroi, are decorated with a wealth of added color and elaborate floral ornament that is jarring to modern taste, which may find them gaudy and superficial. Although there is some validity to this judgment, it too is superficial and takes no account of the undoubted excellence of many individual artists and pieces, some of which stand among the greatest achievements of Greek art in Italy. The unevenness in quality may be attributed in part to funerary practices that seem to have called for a large variety of cheap, painted ceramics as grave goods. Although many vessels bound for the grave were decorated with mythological subjects that can be plausibly related to funerary cult or expectations for the afterlife, far more numerous are minor works with languid offering bearers, androgynous Erotes, and oversize female heads, all of which undoubtedly had greater significance for their creators and purchasers than we are now able to discern.

The very terms "South Italian" and "Apulian" reveal a traditional uneasiness in accepting the painted pottery of this region as fully Greek, even though the shapes, subjects, and techniques of manufacture are wholly in the Greek tradition. In contrast, works in other media, such as gold jewelry or sculpture in stone or terracotta are commonly referred to as "Tarentine" but almost never as "Apulian." The Greek city of Taras (Taranto) was undoubtedly the most important producer of painted pottery in the region until late in the fourth century, and it would not be inaccurate to call a work such as the stamnos by the Ariadne Painter (cat. no. 8) "Tarentine." However, the appearance of characters in native dress, such as the boar hunters on cat. no. 9, demonstrates that vase-painters were at the very least aware of the native peoples, and there is some evidence that they may have been adjusting their designs with an eye to Italian markets. Vases of the early Ornate style are often found in and around Taranto itself, while early Plain-style works are frequently found at inland sites, possibly indicating that they were directed toward markets in Peucetia and Messapia. The boar hunt mentioned above is on a column-krater, a shape that remained popular in Peucetia long after its extinction in Attica; on the other hand, Apulian painters avoided decorating the native nestoris shape until the second quarter of the fourth century, long after their Lucanian counterparts. It is likely that native Italians, Hellenized in various degrees, actively participated in the production of painted pottery, particularly after the establishment of workshops at inland centers such as Canosa.

The earliest recognizable personality among Apulian vase-painters is the Painter of the Berlin Dancing Girl, an artist of considerable skill and an active imitator of the Attic style. It was, however, his younger colleague and follower, the Sisyphus Painter, who had the greater impact. A prolific artist who was active until the end of the fifth century, the Sisyphus Painter produced both large mythological works and numerous more modest pieces, particularly small bell-kraters. Although he too was aware of Attic models, Italic influence is apparent in the Oscan costume of some of his youths, perhaps indicating a conscious attempt at catering to the native market. One of the most talented of his late followers was the Ariadne Painter, whose name-vase, a particularly elegant stamnos, is in Boston (cat. no. 8). Another follower, also active in the early years of the fourth century, was the Painter of the Birth of Dionysos, who stands at the head of one of the major branches of Apulian vase-painting, the so-called Ornate style. His volute-kraters in particular, with openwork handles, complex compositions, mythological subjects, and increased polychromy, set the tone for subsequent developments. Careful analysis of drawing styles permits the tracing of these various influences and workshop traditions throughout the rest of the century, as younger painters adapted and varied the styles of their masters, sometimes moving to establish workshops in different regions, where new ideas were absorbed and old ones transmitted.

Another follower of the Sisyphus Painter, the Tarporley Painter, was the most influential of the early painters in the so-called Plain style. His bell- and calyx-kraters eschew the florid ornament that proliferated on vases of the Ornate style. He favored Dionysiac and genre subjects instead of mythology, although on at least three occasions he represented Perseus and Athena with the head of Medusa (e.g., cat. no. 10). The Tarporley Painter's phlyax vases were the first in Apulia and began a tradition continued by the McDaniel Painter (cat. no. 13) and others (cat. no. 20), including the Adolphseck Painter, who also tried his hand at Ornate works (cat. no. 14). To the extent that they represent actual stage performances, the phlyax vases may be said to belong to the category of genre scenes, a class less numerous than in Attica, unless one counts the innumerable depictions of offering bearers holding the baskets, phialai, fillets, and tympana associated with funerary cults. Here one must also mention the many scenes of two or more youths standing in conversation on the reverse of two-sided vases, where, in the Attic manner, they do little more than fill the available space. As Trendall has noted, the very sameness of the figures can be an aid in attributing a vase to a specific painter, as each artist developed particular habits of drawing his "back men."

The Tarporley Painter influenced a generation of painters who continued working in the Plain style, including the Hoppin Painter, one of the most talented of Apulian draftsmen (cat. no. 15). Among other practitioners of the Plain style were the Lecce Painter (cat. no. 19), the Judgement Painter (cat. no. 17), the Bendis Painter (cat. no. 16), and the Painter of Boston 00.348 (cat. no. 18), the last a master of austere but complex mythological compositions. It was in this Middle Apulian period, roughly corresponding to the second quarter of the fourth century, that the first rhyta appeared, with mold-made animal heads and painted rims, a type looking back to Attic models and continuing throughout the century (cat. nos. 31–32, 64, 67). The relationship between the potters and the coroplasts must have been a close one, particularly at Taranto, where the sculptor Lysippos lived for a while in the last quarter of the century.

The Ornate and Plain styles ran parallel in the first third of the century, and most artists worked in either one or the other. The Early Apulian painters of the Black Fury Group brought the Ornate style to a high level of excellence, combining grand mythological themes with masterly drawing and sumptuous ornament. It is one of the tragedies of South Italian vase-painting that this group survives primarily in fragments, but these are themselves sometimes sufficient to suggest the grandeur of the original works (e.g., cat. no. 12).

The principal canons followed by later painters in the Ornate style were established by the Iliupersis Painter, who was active about 370–355 B.C., when Taranto, under the guidance of the philosopher Archytas, was at the height of its power and prosperity. The volute-kraters of the Iliupersis Painter, with plastic masks or other relief decoration on the handles, were particularly influential. On his later kraters he introduced a further innovation, painting on the neck a female head emerging from a colorful bouquet of flowers and scrolling tendrils, possibly a reflection of the flower paintings of Pausias, a noted Greek muralist. The painter's volute-krater in Boston (cat. no. 21) may be the earliest example of this type of neck decoration, which became progressively more elaborate as the century advanced and was adapted for use on other shapes, such as amphorae and loutrophoroi (e.g., cat. nos. 42 and 69). These volute-kraters set the standard for the second half of the century, when they became increasingly larger and even more elaborately decorated, with the female heads in some cases now grown to fill both sides of the body. The Iliupersis Painter also introduced what was to become the standard funerary scheme on Apulian vases: on one side, a naiskos with an image of the deceased, on the other, a grave stele, both flanked by offering bearers. Both types—naiskos and stele—continued to the end of the century and might be used alone or in combination with each other or a mythological or Dionysiac subject (cat. no. 69).

The Late Apulian period commenced early in the third quarter of the fourth century, but there is no hard boundary between it and Middle Apulian. Its early development occurred against a backdrop of increasing strife between the South Italian Greeks, supported by Sparta and Epiros, and the native Messapians and Lucanians. After the Iliupersis Painter, there was a noticeable increase in vase production;

over twice as many vases were produced in Late Apulian as in the Early and Middle periods combined. The number of smaller vases increased dramatically, and large vases are even larger, perhaps partly because of the growing popularity of chamber tombs; a volute-krater in Boston is one of the largest (cat. no. 38), being well over a meter in height. A greater uniformity of style in this period makes it more difficult to trace stylistic influences and workshop relationships. The Plain style continued on bell- and column-kraters, as well as pelikai and smaller vases, with increased use of added color blurring the distinction from the Ornate style. The major Plain-style workshop just before midcentury was that of the Dijon Painter, whose prolific following included the Snub-Nose Painter and his close associate, the Laterza Painter (cat. no. 35). Among painters of the Ornate style, the Lycurgus Painter had his own substantial following, including the Painter of Boston 76.65 (cat. no. 25) and the Varrese Painter (cat. no. 36).

The Varrese Painter, active around midcentury but overlapping in his later career with the early Darius Painter, was a prolific painter who had a major impact on artists of both the Plain and Ornate styles. His mythological scenes feature many of the same stock figures as on his minor works, and the subsidiary ornament on his larger vases is often inventive and brightly colored. The artists in his following led on to the Ornate-style predecessors of the Darius Painter in the 340s, although the precise nature of their workshop relationships is obscure. Among these proto-Darian followers of the Varrese Painter were the Hippolyte Painter (cat. no. 39), the Painter of Copenhagen 4223 (cat. no. 40), and the painter of the great Thersites volute-krater in Boston (cat. no. 38), with its dramatic panorama of hubris and murder.

The large mythological vases of the Darius Painter represent the apogee of the Apulian achievement in vase-painting, combining the grand themes of the classic playwrights with the artist's own elegant hand and distinctive compositions. These vases are a window on a world of obscure myths and lost tragedies, with ranks of haughty deities looking down on the violent actions of deluded, pathetic, and occasionally heroic mortals. Often the protagonists are identified by inscriptions thoughtfully added by the artist, who was among the most literate of South Italian vase-painters. The three mythological works in Boston are among the painter's finest, two of them treating the violent youth of Aigisthos and the woes besetting the house of Pelops (cat. nos. 41–42), the third the rescue of Alkmene by the divine grace of Zeus (cat. no. 43). In these scenes inspired by Sophocles and Euripides, one senses something of the emotion and tragic catharsis experienced by audiences in the ancient theater. The fragment with Amphiaraos (cat. no. 44), on the other hand, is similar to several other versions and may be based on a wall-painting rather than a drama. Numerous more minor works can be attributed to the painter's workshop (cat. nos. 45–48, 53), including a fish-plate (cat. no. 49), a type of vessel that was invented in Athens but that South Italian vase-painters made distinctly their own.

The Darius Painter's decorative schemes were continued in somewhat more elaborate forms by his follower the Underworld Painter, who also continued his penchant for mythological and theatrical subjects. The Darius-Underworld workshop, as it has been called, seems to have been located at Taranto, but by this time red-figure was also produced at other towns in Apulia. Inland centers such as Canosa, Arpi, and Altamura grew prosperous in the last quarter of the century, probably from agricultural exports. The Patera Painter (cat. no. 58) moved from Ruvo to Canosa, where he produced numerous large pots with funerary compositions. His follower in Canosa, the Baltimore Painter, was a prolific producer of mythological and funerary scenes on both large and small vases (cat. nos. 61–62). His volute-kraters, covered with polychrome ornament from handles to feet, brought the Ornate style to new and gaudy heights. Hundreds of minor works are attributed to his workshop (cat. nos. 63–64) and to groups and painters associated with it (cat. nos. 66–68). His principal follower was the White Sakkos Painter, whose barrel-shaped loutrophoros in Boston (cat. no. 69) is a mannered confection of sinuous handles, intricate ornament, and brightly colored depictions of fish, offering bearers, and mythical rape; his two oinochoai (cat. nos. 71–72), for all their rich bravado, seem tame by comparison.

The White Sakkos Painter also had a considerable following (cat. nos. 73–76), which kept the Canosan workshop active to the end of the century, when the red-figure style seems to have exhausted itself. Red-figure production came to an end throughout Apulia, with only scattered continuation into the third century, the final termination roughly coinciding with the conquest of Taranto by Rome in 272 B.C. At Canosa, there was a shift to painting vases with bright tempera colors (see "Canosan," below), but elsewhere the Apulian fabric came to a sputtering and inglorious end.

7

7

Oinochoe (shape 3)
End of 5th century B.C.
Gift of H. P. Arnold. 97.605

DIMENSIONS AND CONDITION: Height: 8.9 cm; width of neck:
2.9 cm; depth of neck: 3.3 cm; diameter body: 6.6 cm; diameter foot: 4.7 cm
Unbroken

SHAPE: A miniature chous, not unlike the earlier and full-size
Lucanian example, cat. no. 1. This example is less spherical,
and later ones are slenderer yet.

A nude boy, a toddler, walks to the left while looking
back to the right at the *streptos* (twisted roll) in his
left hand. In his right hand he holds a miniature
chous, like this very vessel. A string of charms hangs
from his right shoulder. On the right is the left half
of a small table.

The lateral frames are simple reserved lines; the
upper frame a band of dotted egg-pattern.

The shape, style, and subject reflect strong Attic
influence. Attic choes of this type, with scenes of
children, have long been thought to have been connected with the Anthesteria festival, perhaps as
grave goods for tots who died before being able to
participate in the festival, which featured a drinking
contest on the day called "Choes"; see Hoorn, *Choes
and Anthesteria*, and H. W. Parke, *Festivals of the
Athenians* (London, 1977), pp. 107–116. In *Choes*

and Anthesteria: Athenian Iconography and Ritual
(Ann Arbor, 1992), Richard Hamilton, noting the
variety of subjects on miniature choes and the pau-
city of festival-related subjects on full-size choes, the
kind actually used in the drinking contest, has suggested that the relationship between the miniature
choes and the Anthesteria is not clear-cut, or at least
is more complex than previously supposed. How the
Apulian versions can be accounted for is not clear,
but the Anthesteria was apparently celebrated in
some other Ionian towns, to judge by the frequent
occurrence of Anthesterion as the name of a month.

PUBLISHED: E. Robinson, *MFA AnnRep* 1897, p. 29, no. 17;
Hoorn, *Choes*, p. 111, no. 370.

8

Stamnos
Attributed to the Ariadne Painter
Ca. 400–390 B.C.
Henry Lillie Pierce Residuary Fund. 00.349a

PROVENANCE: E. P. Warren collection; from Gela

DIMENSIONS AND CONDITION: Height: 30.0 cm; width including handles: 29.0 cm; diameter upper molding of rim: 21.3
cm; diameter body just above handles: 25.6 cm; diameter base
of body: 15.2 cm; diameter foot: 15.7 cm
Unbroken. A large portion of side B misfired red.

SHAPE: The straight-sided body is almost a truncated cone, not
truly tapering; disk foot; concave neck; overhanging rim in
two degrees; handles tilted upward and rolled back. Stamnoi
are uncommon in Apulia but no longer as rare as when Trendall and Cambitoglou could list only three other Apulian examples (*RVAp*, I, p. 23). Several new stamnoi are now known,
most of them later than this example and none as perfectly
proportioned (e.g., Eisenberg, *Ancient World*, IV, p. 36, nos.
111–112; *RVAp*, Suppl. II, p. 132, nos. 17/64–1 and 17/64–2).
The striped cones standing in relief on either side of each handle are descended from the flanges and knobs on earlier stamnoi, themselves imitating the handle attachments of metal
vessels. For the shape, see A. D. Trendall and A. Cambitoglou, in *Etudes et Travaux* 13 (1983), pp. 405–413.

A: Theseus is abandoning Ariadne, who sleeps on a
low couch decorated with battlements and zigzags
and having a striped pillow at one end. There is no
indication of landscape. She wears white bracelets
and a himation, which has fallen around her waist to
leave her torso nude. Athena is seated above, her
spear in her right hand. She wears a chiton, himation, scaly aegis with gorgoneion and snakes, bracelets, earrings, a necklace, and a sphendone. The
winged boy with a white fillet standing at the right is
Hypnos, who drops poppies (?) on Ariadne's head
from a phiale held in his left hand. Theseus moves
rapidly to the left, his nude body turned frontally

and his face in three-quarter view. His hair is blown back in a leonine mane of wavy locks. A cloak hangs over his shoulders. He is moving toward the stern of his ship, which is decorated with battlements, zig-zags, and fluttering fillets.

B: The departure of Bellerophon. He stands at the right, beside Pegasus, wearing a chlamys pinned at the throat and holding a pair of spears in his left hand. Pegasus stamps the ground in anticipation of departure; white dots fleck his bridle. Proitos, hi-mation about his waist, stands to the right, holding a scepter with a finial in the form of a bird in his left hand. He has just handed to Bellerophon the letter for King Iobates of Lycia asking him to kill the young hero. At the left, Stheneboea (or Anteia) stands in the door of the palace, the porch supported by Ionic columns, the pediment containing a white and yel-low palmette and supporting three palmette akro-teria. She wears a chiton, himation, necklace, and white bracelets and earrings. With her right hand she plucks up her chiton, and with her left touches her husband, encouraging him to rid her of the youth who spurned her advances.

There are enclosed palmettes linked by tendrils around and under the handles. Bands of dotted egg-pattern circle the lower molding of the mouth, the base of the handles, and (in a double band) the shoul-der below the neck. The groundline consists of groups of linked maeanders to left alternating with saltire-squares.

When purchased, the vase had as a "lid" an Attic black-glazed fish-plate (00.349b), which may have been found with it.

For Ariadne abandoned by Theseus, see W. A. Daszewski, *LIMC*, III, 1, pp. 1057–1060; and F. Brommer, *Theseus: Die Täten des griechischen Hel-den in der antiken Kunst und Literatur* (Darmstadt, 1982), pp. 86–92. Earlier Attic representations also show Hypnos by Ariadne's head (Beazley, *ARV²*, p. 405, 1 and p. 560, 5; *LIMC*, III, 1, p. 1057, nos. 52–53; III, 2, pl. 730). The motif of the ship's stern is repeated on a calyx-krater connected with the Painter of the Birth of Dionysos, another follower of the Sisyphus Painter (Taranto 52230: *RVAp*, I, p. 39, no. 2/25, pl. 12, 2). The ship was also depicted in a wall-painting of the subject seen by Pausanias in the sanctuary of Dionysos Eleutherios in Athens (Paus. 1.20.3), but only the Taranto krater follows the mu-ral in having Dionysos already present before The-seus has fully departed. Trendall and Webster, speculating that the Boston and Taranto scenes may have been inspired by Euripides' *Theseus*, suggest that the Theseus on the Boston stamnos may be starting back at the sight of the approaching Diony-

8 (Color Plate I)

8 (Color Plate II)

sos, whose arrival is imminent though undepicted; see Trendall and Webster, *Illustrations*, p. 105; and *RVAp*, I, p. 41.

For Bellerophon, see F. Brommer, *MarbWPr* 1952/1954, pp. 3–16; K. Schauenburg, *JdI* 71 (1956), pp. 59–96; and *AA* 1958, cols. 21–37; compare also cat. no. 27. Very similar representations of Bellerophon delivering the letter to Iobates are distinguished from scenes with Proitos by the Oriental garb of the Lycian monarch; for example, a calyx-krater by the Darius Painter in the Zewadski collection, on loan to the Tampa Museum of Art (W. K. Zewadski, *Ancient Greek Vases from South Italy in Tampa Bay Collections* [Tampa, 1985], no. 8, illus.; *RVAp*, Suppl. II, p. 151, no. 18/65d). In Homer, the wife of Proitos is Anteia (*Il*.6.155ff.), in later accounts, Stheneboea. The scene on the Boston stamnos could have been inspired by Euripides' lost play *Stheneboia*; see Trendall and Webster, *Illustrations*, pp. 102–103.

A follower of the Sisyphus Painter, the Ariadne Painter was active in the first decade or so of the fourth century. He returned to the myth of Bellerophon on a column-krater in Ruvo (inv. 1091: *RVAp*, I, pp. 24–25, no. 1/107; Trendall, *Handbook*, fig. 46), with the hero and Pegasus attacking the Chimaera.

PUBLISHED: E. Robinson, *MFA AnnRep* 1900, pp. 67–69, no. 25; E. Pfuhl, *Malerei und Zeichnungen der Griechen*, III (Munich, 1923), pl. 258, fig. 632 (side A); F. Hauser, in Furtwängler and Reichhold, III, pp. 104–105, fig. 51 (side A); Trendall, *Frühitaliotische*, pp. 24, 40, no. 52, pl. 23; Brommer, *Vasenlisten*, 1956, pp. 130 (no. D 1), 172 (no. D 5); G. Cressedi, *EAA*, I, p. 632, fig. 817; K. Schauenburg, *AA* 1958, col. 27, note 11; W. Hahland, *JOAI* 44 (1959), p. 44; Brommer, *Vasenlisten*, 1960, pp. 167 (no. D 1), 225 (no. D 5); Cambitoglou and Trendall, *Plain Style*, p. 17, no. 1 (ref. to *Atene e Roma* 35 [1932], p. 126, pl. 2, fig. 10); MFA, *Gods and Heroes*, 1962, pp. 81, 83, fig. 70; Hamdorf, *Kultpersonifikationen*, p. 102, no. 345; T. B. L. Webster, *Greece and Rome* XIII, 1 (April 1966), p. 28, pl. III (side A); idem, *Tragedy and Satyr-Play*, pp. 127 (TV 41), 163, 165; G. Hafner, *Art of Rome, Etruria, and Magna Graecia* (New York, 1969), pp. 102–103, illus.; F. Brommer, *Die Wahl des Augenblicks in der griechischen Kunst* (Munich [1969]), pp. 25–26, fig. 34; Fairbanks, *Philostratus*, fig. 6, facing p. 63; Cambitoglou and Trendall, *Plain Style, Addenda*, p. 425; Trendall and Webster, *Illustrations*, p. 105, III.3, 51 (the *Theseus* of Euripides); J. Charbonneaux, R. Martin, and F. Villard, *Classical Greek Art (480–330 B.C.)* (New York, 1972), pp. 302–303 (fig. 349), 394; K. Schauenburg, *RM* 79 (1972), p. 6, note 36; J.-M. Moret, *AntK* 15 (1972), pp. 97 (note 14), 102, pl. 28, 2; Brommer, *Vasenlisten*, 1973, pp. 218 (no. D 1), 297 (no. D 5); idem, *Denkmälerlisten*, II, p. 6 (ref. to Lippold, *Antike Gemäldekopien*, 1951, fig. 32); Trendall, *Early*, pp. 18, 50, no. B 84, pl. 23; Robertson, *History*, pp. 441, 698, note 213; M. Bieber, *Ancient Copies: Contributions to the History of Greek and Ro-*

man Art (New York, 1977), p. 238, note 243; W. A. Daszewski, *La Mosaïque de Thésée* (Nea Paphos, II, Warsaw, 1977), p. 82; *RVAp*, I, pp. 23–24, no. 1/104 (with additional bibliography); E. Richardson, in *Festschrift von Blanckenhagen*, pp. 190–191; Cambitoglou, *Studies Trendall*, p. 49; M. Anderson, in C. Houser, *Dionysos and His Circle: Ancient through Modern* (Cambridge, Mass.: Fogg Art Museum, Harvard University, 1979), p. 104, MFA 13, illus.; F. Brommer, *Konkordanzlisten zu alter Vasenliteratur* (Marburg, 1979), p. 24, no. 105; Schefold and Jung, *Göttersage*, pp. 270, 359, note 588; M. Robertson, *A Shorter History of Greek Art* (Cambridge, 1981), pp. 153, 237; V. M. Strocka, in B. Andreae, ed., *Symposium über die antiken Sarkophage* (*MarbWPr* 1984), pp. 216, 240, note 104 (ref. to G. E. Rizzo, *La Pittura ellenistico-romana* [1929], pl. 38, 1); P. Demargne, *LIMC*, II, 1, p. 1001, no. 492; S. McNally, *Classical Antiquity* 4 (1985), pp. 161–163, fig. 5; Aellen, Cambitoglou, and Chamay, *Peintre de Darius*, p. 107, note 1; W. A. Daszewski, *LIMC*, III, 1, p. 1057, no. 54 (with additional bibliography); III, 2, pl. 730; N. Yalouris, *Pegasus: Ein Mythos in der Kunst* (Mainz, 1987), pp. 19, 61, fig. 44; Schefold and Jung, *Urkönige*, pp. 260, 347 (note 289), 358 (note 679); Trendall, *Handbook*, pp. 26, 48 (fig. 45), 259, 277; Söldner, *Bonn 3*, p. 14, under inv. no. 80; Carpenter, *Art and Myth*, p. 116, fig. 166; Jentoft-Nilsen, *CVA Getty 4*, pp. 8 (under inv. no. 86.AE.680), 33 (under inv. no. 71.AE.445); *RVAp*, Suppl. II, pp. 4, no. 1/104 (with additional bibliography), 485.

EXHIBITED: Dayton Art Institute (*Flight: Fantasy, Faith, Fact: A Loan Exhibition Commemorating the Fiftieth Anniversary of Powered Flight 1903–1953* [Dayton, 1953], December 17, 1953–February 21, 1954, p. 8, no. 46).

9

COLUMN-KRATER
Attributed to the Sisyphus Group; associated with the Ariadne Painter
Ca. 400–390 B.C.
Gift of Robert E. Hecht, Jr. 1970.236

DIMENSIONS AND CONDITION: Height: 53.0 cm; diameter rim: 36.2 cm; width at handles: 48.0 cm; diameter neck: 26.0 cm; diameter body: 37.2 cm; diameter stem: 11.2 cm; diameter foot: 19.1 cm
Unbroken

SHAPE: Column-kraters were out of fashion in Athens when this vase was potted, but both the shape and much of the ornament derive from late mannerist Attic models. The vine on the neck and the silhouettes on the rim are also of Attic inspiration; Alexander Cambitoglou lists several column-kraters connected with the Sisyphus and Ariadne Painters on which such black animals appear on the rim (in *Studies Webster*, II, p. 1). Attic column-kraters were already being imitated in Apulia in the first half of the fifth century, when a single workshop produced a number in the black-figure technique; for example, Boston 99.530 (A. Fairbanks, *Catalogue of Greek and Etruscan Vases*, I: *Early Vases, preceding Athenian Black-figured Ware* [Cambridge, Mass., 1928], pp. 199–200, no. 572, pl. 74). The attenuated lower body, the ivy on the mouth, and the decoration of *both* sides of the neck are distinctly Apulian features.

A: Boar hunt. The central hunter raises his sword in his right hand to slash the hindquarters of the boar, which charges to the left. His hunting companions stand on either side with spears, and there is a dead dog lying below. The hunter at the left braces his spear under his arm to take the charge of the boar. A tree and striped rocks denote the countryside. The hunter at the left wears a Greek chlamys, pinned at the throat, but the other two are in native Italic garb: the middle one with an embroidered loincloth secured by a broad belt, the one on the right in a striped tunic with two swastikas, also held by a belt. Both have cloaks on their left arm. Although the dead dog recalls the dog Ormenos in the depiction of the Calydonian Boar Hunt on the François Krater (J. D. Beazley, *Attic Black-figure Vase-painters* [Oxford, 1956], p. 76, no. 1), there is nothing else to suggest that this is the legendary hunt, and indeed the native costume of the two hunters makes it unlikely.

B: Two pairs of youths in long himatia stand in conversation. The leftmost youth holds a staff in his right hand; the second has a strigil in his raised right hand. Between the two at the right, whose arms are covered, hangs a pair of jumping weights; these act as a space-filler but also combine with the strigil to place the setting in the palaestra. The three youths at the right wear shoes.

Two pairs of confronted boars and lions are drawn in black silhouette on the edge of the obverse rim; on the reverse edge is a degenerate ivy vine. Panels with ivy vines and berries decorate both necks, and a similar vine circles the top of the mouth. There are black palmettes on top of the handle-plates. The pictures have lateral frames of degenerate ivy and upper frames of tongues. The lower frames consist of triple linked maeanders to left alternating with saltire-squares.

Trendall and Cambitoglou note the nearly identical black animals on the rim of a column-krater in Milan ("H.A." collection 345: *RVAp*, I, p. 26, no. 1/117), which also has four similar youths on the reverse and an Amazonomachy with a rocky landscape of this same type. In style, the Boston krater is closely linked with the Sisyphus Painter and the Gravina Painter but is listed by Trendall and Cambitoglou among works associated with another member of the Sisyphus Group, the Ariadne Painter.

PUBLISHED: C. C. Vermeule, *MFA AnnRep* 1969–70, p. 42; K. Schauenburg, *AA* 1973, p. 230, note 17; C. C. Vermeule, *BurlMag* 115 (1973), pp. 117–118, fig. 69; *RVAp*, I, pp. 26 (no. 1/118, with ref. to *Gli Indigeni*, fig. 35), 30, 435–436; A. Cambitoglou, *Studies Webster*, II, p. 1 (as 1970.276); Söldner, *Bonn* 3, p. 23, under inv. no. 96.

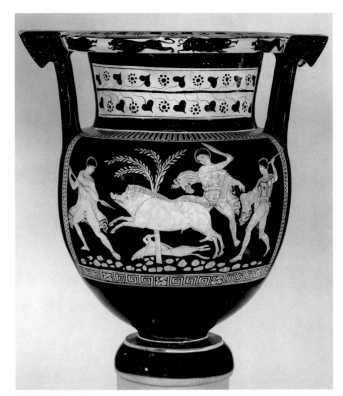

9 (Color Plate III)

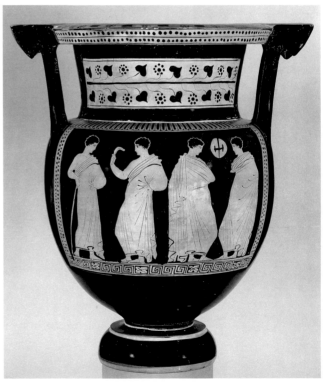

9

10 (Color Plate IV)

10

10

10

BELL-KRATER
Attributed to the Tarporley Painter
Ca. 400–385 B.C.
Gift of Robert E. Hecht, Jr. 1970.237

DIMENSIONS AND CONDITION: Height: 30.5 cm; diameter rim: 35.0 cm; diameter just below handles: 25.5 cm; diameter stem: 9.3 cm; lower diameter foot: 15.3 cm
Unbroken

SHAPE: Standard Early Apulian type, quite close to the Attic prototypes, with overhanging torus rim, rolled-back handles, lower body tapering to a stem, and a reserved groove at the top of a disk foot.

A: Athena holds up the head of Medusa, which is reflected in her shield (quite correctly, upside down). Her left hand rests on the vertical shaft of her long spear, the bronze butt of which is at bottom, the point out of sight at top. The goddess wears a belted chiton embroidered with palmettes, a necklace, earrings, and a sphendone. Her aegis is not in evidence. Perseus, in winged boots, chlamys, and elaborate Phrygian helmet, stands before her, leaning on the spear in his left hand; the helmet is presumably the one that magically confers invisibility. Hermes, a chlamys around his shoulders, leans on a barren tree at the right, his legs crossed, his right hand resting on his caduceus. Perseus will soon return the god's winged boots. All three figures look down to avoid gazing at Medusa's head, and Perseus takes the opportunity to study the reflection of his victim's visage. The reflection presages Athena's attachment of the head to the shield (Apollodorus 2.4.3).

B: A nude youth, with a strigil in the right hand and a staff in the left, stands between two companions wearing shoes and draped in himatia that cover their arms. The strigil suggests an assignation in the palaestra.

A laurel wreath circles the vase under the rim. Rays partly surround the roots of the handles. The groundlines on either side consist of groups of linked maeanders to left alternating with saltire-squares.

Like the Ariadne Painter, the Tarporley Painter was a close follower of the Sisyphus Painter, active in the first quarter of the fourth century. He was an influential practitioner of the Plain style and had several followers and pupils including the Adolphseck, Hoppin, Truro, Lecce, and Dijon Painters, and the Painter of the Long Overfalls. The Tarporley Painter painted mostly bell-kraters, favoring Dionysiac and genre scenes over mythology.

For Trendall's most recent comments on the Tarporley Painter, see *Festschrift Cambitoglou*, pp. 211–215. The closest parallel to the main scene is the painter's pelike in a Taranto private collection, with Perseus, Hermes, and the seated Athena reflecting the head of Medusa in her shield (*RVAp*, I, p. 51, no. 3/44); compare also the version on the calyx-krater Gotha 72, on which Athena reflects the head in a pool, although the shield is still present (*RVAp*, I, p. 51, no. 3/39).

PUBLISHED: Cambitoglou and Trendall, *Plain Style Addenda*, p. 426, no. 3 bis; C. C. Vermeule, *MFA AnnRep* 1969–70, pp. 38–39 (illus.), 42; E. Phinney, Jr., *TAPA* 102 (1971), pp. 461–462, pl. 2; C. C. Vermeule, *BurlMag* 115 (1973), p. 117, figs. 70, 74; Trendall, *Early*, p. 51, no. B 110; Robertson, *History*, pp. 443, 698, note 217; *RVAp*, I, p. 48, no. 3/16; A. D. Trendall, in *Festschrift Cambitoglou*, pp. 211–212; Balensiefen, *Spiegelbildes*, pp. 223–224, no. K 14, pl. 15, 2; *RVAp*, Suppl. II, p. 12, no. 3/16.

11

TWO FRAGMENTS OF AN OINOCHOE (shape 3)
Ca. 400–380 B.C.
Francis Bartlett Donation of 1900. 03.839a-b

PROVENANCE: E. P. Warren collection; bought in Taranto, where it is said to have been found

DIMENSIONS AND CONDITION: Frag. A: Length: 14.6 cm; Frag. B: Length: 6.1 cm

SHAPE: Compare the Lucanian chous, cat. no. 1, and the miniature Apulian chous, cat. no. 7.

Death of Aktaion. On the larger fragment (A), Aktaion, wearing a baldric and a cloak around his shoulders, falls to the right, attacked by three of his hounds. Red blood flows from his thighs. His head, right arm and shoulder, and left hand are missing. A female figure is at the left, moving away from Aktaion, her legs and part of her patterned chiton-skirt remaining, the latter having a fringe and a design of red and black chevrons. Part of her wrist may be preserved to the left of Aktaion's cloak. The smaller fragment (B), from the right side of the scene, preserves the head of Pan, facing left and holding up one or both hands.

Part of the right lateral frame of chevrons is preserved to the right of Pan's head. The groundline consists of groups of maeanders to right alternating with saltire-squares.

Beazley suggested that the female may be Lyssa, the personification of madness, who appears in several representations of this subject (Caskey and Beazley, II, p. 86). Trendall and Webster (*Illustrations*) note that Aeschylus puts Lyssa on the stage to drive the maenads mad in the *Xantriai*. In the playwright's *Toxotides* the Death of Aktaion is described in a messenger's speech; if Lyssa was shown on stage and was the inspiration for the vase-painters to include her in scenes of the hero's death, she was probably shown in a dialogue with Artemis, who urged her to turn the dogs on their master; see Trendall and Webster, *Illustrations*, p. 62; and Kossatz-Deissmann, *Dramen*, pp. 142–165, pls. 27.2–32. Pan appears in several paintings of the Death of Aktaion, as do satyrs, perhaps as symbols of the wild, uncivilized setting and of Aktaion's transformation from man to beast. For an example with Lyssa, Pan, and a satyr, compare a volute-krater in Taranto by the Gravina Painter (*RVAp*, I, p. 32, no. 2/1, pl. 8, 1–2); for Lyssa

11

and Pan, but no satyr, compare Gothenburg R. K. 13–71 (*RVAp*, II, p. 476, no. 18/7, pl. 169, 3–4); for Pan and a satyr, without Lyssa, compare a chous by the Felton Painter in Taranto (*RVAp*, I, p. 175, no. 7/63, pl. 57, 2) and the volute-krater Naples Stg. 31 (*RVAp*, I, p. 203, no. 8/100). Several versions of Aktaion's death include Pan but neither Lyssa nor a satyr; for example, the situla Bloomington 70.97.1 (*RVAp*, II, p. 478, no. 18/11). For the subject, see P. Jacobsthal, *Marburger Jahrbuch für Kunstwissenschaft* 5 (1929), pp. 1–23; K. Schauenburg, *JdI* 84 (1969), pp. 29–46; L. Guimond, *LIMC*, I, 1, pp. 454–469; I, 2, pls. 346–363. For Lyssa, see A. Kossatz-Deissmann, *LIMC*, VI, 1, pp. 322–329; VI, 2, pls. 166–168.

12

PUBLISHED: E. Robinson, *MFA AnnRep* 1903, p. 73, no. 69 (partial); Caskey and Beazley, II, p. 86, no. 3; Brommer, *Vasenlisten*, 1960, p. 337, no. D 6; K. Schauenburg, *RM* 69 (1962), p. 32, no. 80, pl. 16, 2; Webster, *Tragedy and Satyr-Play*, p. 146; K. Schauenburg, *JdI* 84 (1969), p. 29, note 5; Brommer, *Vasenlisten*, 1973, p. 474, no. D 10; Kossatz-Deissmann, *Dramen*, pp. 150 (no. K 48), 153, pl. 28, 1; L. Guimond, *LIMC*, I, 1, pp. 459 (no. 48 b), 467; L. Kahil and N. Icard, *LIMC*, II, 1, p. 733, no. 1417 (with ref. to Moret, *Ilioupersis*, pl. 57, 1); II, 2, pl. 562; C. C. Schlam, *Classical Antiquity* 3 (1984), p. 94, note 54; Freytag gen. Löringhoff, *Giebelrelief*, pp. 138, 153, 288, no. E 10: dated 400/390–370/60; E. Mugione, *DialArch* ser. 3, 6 (1988), p. 132, no. 38; A. Kossatz-Deissmann, *LIMC*, VI, 1, pp. 325 (no. 3), 328.

12

FRAGMENT OF A KRATER
Attributed to the Black Fury Painter
390–380 B.C.
Francis Bartlett Donation of 1912. 13.206

PROVENANCE: E. P. Warren collection; from Taranto

DIMENSIONS AND CONDITION: Length: 12 cm
Unbroken

Callisto being turned into a bear. Her head, with ursine ears, and one clawed hand are visible to the right of a pollarded laurel tree. She is skillfully drawn in three-quarter view, with attention to such details as pupils, irises, eyelashes, and the hairs on the nape. Her long locks are rendered with a multitude of relief lines. The spotted cloak of another figure (Artemis?) appears at the left, possibly a shoulder and forearm.

This piece well illustrates the early stages of the Ornate style, and the quality of the drawing supports Trendall's comment that "Fragments . . . from vases in the Black Fury Group must rank among the finest examples of early Apulian vase-painting" (*Handbook*, p. 78).

An oinochoe in the Getty Museum (72.AE.128) presents the subject in fuller form: see A. D. Trendall, *AntK* 20 (1977), pp. 99–101; *RVAp*, I, pp. 165–167, no. 7/12. For Callisto, see I. McPhee, *LIMC*, V, 1, pp. 940–944; V, 2, pls. 604–605.

PUBLISHED: F. Hauser, in Furtwängler and Reichhold, II, p. 265, fig. 94 b; L. D. Caskey, *MFA AnnRep* 1913, p. 93; M. H. Swindler, *Ancient Painting: From the Earliest Times to the Period of Christian Art* (New Haven, 1929), p. 231, fig. 381; G. Pesce, *BullCom* 58 (1930), p. 59, fig. 1; Fairbanks, *Philostratus*, fig. 18, facing p. 139; A. D. Trendall, *AntK* 20 (1977), p. 100, pl. 22, 5; *RVAp*, I, pp. 165–166 (no. 7/10), 263, under no. 27a, pl. 54, 2; E. Vermeule, *Aspects of Death in Early Greek Art and Poetry* (Berkeley, 1979), p. 129, fig. 2; J.-M. Moret, *RA* 1980, p. 363, note 5; Brommer, *Göttersagen*, p. 35, no. D 3; Schefold and Jung, *Göttersage*, pp. 231–232 (fig. 322), 372; M. E. Mayo, in Mayo, *Magna Graecia*, p. 89, under no. 19; *RVAp*, Suppl. I, p. 21, no. 7/10; A. D. Trendall, *LIMC*, II, 1, pp. 609–610, under no. 3a; L. Kahil and N. Icard, ibid., p. 730, no. 1388; Schefold and Jung, *Urkönige*, p. 315; I. McPhee, *LIMC*, V, 1, pp. 941 (no. 5), 944; V, 2, pl. 604; *RVAp*, Suppl. II, p. 484, no. 7/10.

13

BELL-KRATER
Compared to the McDaniel Painter
Ca. 380–370 B.C.
Otis Norcross Fund. 69.951

PROVENANCE: From Pisticci

DIMENSIONS AND CONDITION: Height: 28.6 cm; diameter rim: 32.9 cm; diameter just below handles: 23.1 cm; diameter stem: 7.9 cm; diameter foot: 14.4 cm
Unbroken; flaking of black glaze; incrustation on rim and handles

SHAPE: Standard. Compared with cat. no. 10, this example is somewhat more tapering, with a higher stem and proportionately larger foot.

A: Two phlyax actors wearing masks and padded tights stand on a low stage. The taller, at the left, is a youth, who points accusingly at the old man at the right, whose white hair is rendered with a reddish cream slip. The youth's staff is held vertical by the extended finger of his left hand. Behind him, at the left, is a herm, on which the youth has placed his clothes and an aryballos. The herm has a black beard and erect phallus and wears a pilos. The old man pours oil from an aryballos into his left hand. Behind him, at the right, is a carrying-stick with a basket at each end and a goose tied by the neck. In each basket is a small animal, probably a goat's kid.

B: Two youths are running to the right, the one at the left carrying a chous and staff, the one at the right nude and gesturing back at his friend (or pursuer?). Both wear cream-colored fillets. The one at the left wears a himation; the one at the right has a cloak over his left arm.

A wreath of laurel circles the vase under the lip. The groundline consists of groups of stopt maeanders to left alternating with cross-squares. Tongues surround the roots of the handles, which have palmettes and spiraling tendrils beneath them.

C. Vermeule (*BurlMag* 112; see reference below) identified the subject of the obverse as a scene from the same phlyax play illustrated on an earlier bell-krater by the Tarporley Painter, New York 24.97.104 (J. D. Beazley, *AJA* 56 [1952], pp. 193–195, pl. 32; Trendall, *Phlyax*, 1967, p. 53, no. 84; *RVAp*, I, p. 46, no. 3/7). On the New York krater, a youth with a stick accosts an old man, who holds his hands up as though he were suspended from a post and about to be whipped. At the right, on a tall platform representing a stage, is an old woman next to a dead goose and a basket containing a live kid. Watching the scene at left is a fourth figure, labeled *Tragoidos*. Further inscriptions provide what may be actual dialogue from the play, with the old man saying "He has bound my hands up high," and the old woman crying "I shall supply," perhaps meaning that she will give testimony to the old man's thievery. Beazley interpreted the nonsense syllables uttered by the youth as indicating that he is a foreign-born policeman, about to use his stick on the miscreant. The goose and the basket with the kid are clear links with the Boston krater, as are the youth with the stick and the old man. Dearden notes that both protagonists wear the same types of masks as their counterparts in New York: type ZA for the youth ("clean shaven, longish hair") and type E for the old man ("scanty white hair, short beard, short nose"). Clearly, the same play, "The Punishment of

13 (Color Plate v)

13

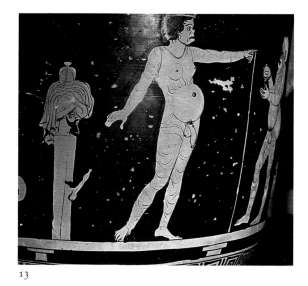

13

13

13

the Thief," inspired both vase-painters. On the Boston krater, the God of Thievery himself is present in the form of the herm. Taplin suggests that because the goose is alive on the Boston krater and dead on the New York vase, the former represents an earlier scene in the play, and "the demise of the goose may have been a significant event in the plot" (*Comic Angels*, p. 32).

The use of Attic rather than Doric letter forms in the inscriptions on the New York krater suggests that the play was an Attic comedy produced or revived in Taranto (A. D. Trendall, in Rasmussen and Spivey, *Greek Vases*, p. 164). For Dearden, this is further proof that the phlyax vases reflect performances of "sophisticated" Attic comedy in permanent theaters, many of which had wooden stages, rather than the informal and impromptu farces they are often said to be. He is answered by Trendall, who believes the vases "reflect in some measure contemporary Middle Comedy in Athens, but also, no doubt, local productions," by itinerant actors with their own stages and properties, "without the need for a formal presentation in a theatre" (in Rasmussen and Spivey, *Greek Vases*, pp. 168–169). Taplin (*Comic Angels*) believes that the importance of imported Attic comedies has been underrated and that many of the vase scenes are misidentified as phlyax plays.

For phlyax vases, see A. D. Trendall and J. R. Green, *Phlyax Vases*, 3rd ed. (forthcoming). See also Trendall, *Phlyax*, 1967; idem, in Rasmussen and Spivey, *Greek Vases*, pp. 151–182; idem, *BClevMus* 79 (Jan. 1992), pp. 2–15; C. W. Dearden, in *Studies Webster*, II, pp. 151–182; O. Taplin, *PCPS* 213 (1987), pp. 92–104; idem, *Comic Angels*; J. R. Green, *NumAntCl* 20 (1991), pp. 49–56. For the carrying-stick and baskets, see J. Chamay, *AntK* 20

(1977), pp. 57–60, who compares the stick with one carried by a phlyax on an oinochoe in a Geneva private collection (pl. 14, 1), where it is used to support a bundle, a basket, a situla, and a haunch of venison. A similar stick and bundle appear on stage on a phlyax krater in London (F 151: *RVAp*, I, p. 100, no. 4/252) which Trendall associates with the style of the Boston krater (Trendall, *Phlyax*, 1967, p. 35, no. 37). For types of comic masks on phlyax vases, see Trendall, *Phlyax*, 1967, pp. 12–13; and Webster and Green, *Old and Middle Comedy*, pp. 13–26.

PUBLISHED: C. C. Vermeule, *MFA AnnRep* 1969–70, p. 40; W. M. Whitehill, *Museum of Fine Arts Boston: A Centennial History*, II (Cambridge, Mass., 1970), p. 664; C. C. Vermeule, *BurlMag* 112 (1970), pp. 628–629, figs. 103–104; J. R. Green, *BICS* 19 (1972), p. 14, note 48; MFA, *Illustrated Handbook*, 1976, pp. 116–117, illus.; J. Chamay, *AntK* 20 (1977), p. 58, pl. 14, 2; *RVAp*, I, p. 100, no. 4/251; C. W. Dearden, *Studies Webster*, II, pp. 35, 37, pl. 3, 2–3 (as 69.695); G. Siebert, *LIMC*, V, 1, p. 306, no. 181b (with additional bibliography); *RVAp*, Suppl. II, p. 16, no. 4/251 (with additional bibliography); Taplin, *Comic Angels*, pp. 32–34, 41–42, 44, pl. 11.3.

14

strap around his left wrist, stopping the strings with the finger of his left hand as he strikes them with the plektron in his right hand. The strings are brown where they cross the body of the kithara.

The Adolphseck Painter is named for a vase in Schloss Fasanerie, Adolphseck (inv. 179: *RVAp*, I, p. 72, no. 4/51). He was a close associate of the Schiller and Prisoner Painters and like them was a follower of the Tarporley Painter and worked in the Plain style. He painted mainly bell-kraters, most of which have Dionysiac scenes.

PUBLISHED: C. Clairmont, *Yale Classical Studies* 15 (1958), pp. 85ff., pl. 1a; Cambitoglou and Trendall, *Plain Style*, pp. 19–20, no. 3; H. Froning, *Dithyrambos und Vasenmalerei in Athen* (*Beiträge zur Archäologie*, vol. 2, Würzburg, 1971), pp. 39, 41–42, no. 23; C. C. Vermeule, *BurlMag* 115 (1973), p. 118, fig. 77; A. Cambitoglou, *AntK* 18 (1975), p. 59; *RVAp*, I, p. 72, no. 4/52; Rawson, *Marsyas*, pp. 97 (note 14), 200 (no. A37); Maas and Snyder, *Stringed Instruments*, p. 242, notes 44, 59.

15

BELL-KRATER
Attributed to the Hoppin Painter
Ca. 380–370 B.C.
Gift of Alfred Ajami, Esther Anderson, Edith Bundy, Robert S. Czachor, Barbara and Lawrence A. Fleischman, Jonathan H. Kagan, Bruce and Ingrid McAlpine, Josephine L. Murray, Robin Symes, and Catherine C. Vermeule. 1988.532

PROVENANCE: Eisenberg, *Ancient World*, IV, p. 35, no. 105; *Palladion, Antike Kunst, Katalog* 1976 (Basel and Milan, 1976), p. 45, no. 43, illus.

DIMENSIONS AND CONDITION: Height: 36.4 cm; diameter rim: 38.1 cm; diameter body below handles: 26.6 cm; diameter stem: 9.0 cm; diameter foot: 18.1 cm
Recomposed from fragments

SHAPE: Proportionately taller and more slender than cat. nos. 10 and 13, with a taller stem and shorter foot

A: Troilos and Achilles. Achilles, armed with a spear in his right hand and a large round shield in his left, rushes to the left toward the young Troilos, who is on horseback and holding a smaller throwing spear in his raised right hand. Both wear diaphanous short chitons of Italic type, with large white- and yellow-spotted belts and a single strap over one shoulder. Achilles wears boots, and his shield has a star device. Troilos's horse rears in fright as Achilles lunges at it with his spear, the cream-colored butt of which overlaps the tongues of the handle-root at the right. Yellow flowers hang from the upper frame and grow from the lower frame and the sloping ground beneath Achilles, which is composed of red, white, and cream-colored rocks.

14

FRAGMENT OF A BELL-KRATER
Attributed to the Adolphseck Painter
Ca. 380–370 B.C.
Bequest of Miss Grace Nelson. 61.112

PROVENANCE: Christoph Clairmont collection

DIMENSIONS AND CONDITION: Height: 18 cm; width: 15 cm
Recomposed from three fragments; part of the rim is preserved at the top.

The concert of Apollo. Zeus is reclining to the left on a groundline of cream-colored dots, his left arm and side preserved. His himation is wrapped around his waist, and he holds his yellow eagle-topped scepter in the crook of his left arm. Nike or Eros is at the upper right (only wing tip preserved), carrying an embroidered, tasseled fillet. Apollo stands below them at the center, wearing a bordered cape, a broad belt (yellow with black dots), and a richly decorated musician's chiton with long sleeves, embroidered with palmettes, key-pattern, laurel wreaths, and egg-and-dart. Such a rich costume is not inappropriate for a god, but it may also reflect the influence of theatrical costume or the festal gowns worn by mortal citharodes. The god's face is in three-quarter view, and the artist has taken pains with the relief lines of his curly hair and the faint suggestion of budding sideburns. He holds his broad, white kithara erect by the

15

B: Three youths in himatia and white fillets stand in conversation, the middle one holding a staff vertically in his extended right hand.

A laurel wreath circles the vase below the lip. Tongues partly surround the roots of the handles, below which are palmettes and tendrils. The lower frames on either side consist of groups of stopt maeanders to left alternating with saltire-squares.

In Athenian versions of the ambush of Troilos, Achilles is usually shown waiting to leap out and kill Troilos as the latter approaches a spring or pursuing the boy as he flees on horseback. Many South Italian renderings of the subject follow these traditional compositions with only minor variations; see A. Cambitoglou, in *Studies Webster*, II, pp. 1–21, pls. 1.1 - 1.18. In the Hoppin Painter's version, Achilles attacks from the front, and Troilos fights back in a vain effort to escape death. This scene is based on encounters between Greeks and Amazons in Athenian art of the latter part of the fifth century B.C.; see

15

D. von Bothmer, *Amazons in Greek Art* (Oxford, 1957), pl. 78. Even the garments are Amazonian in type; for example, the Lansdowne Amazon (Bothmer, *Amazons*, pl. 89, 3). Compare also the Lucanian bell-krater of about 350 at Yale (1913.323), where a Greek on horseback attacks an Amazon who is on foot: Trendall, *LCS*, p. 121, no. 609, pl. 61, 1– 2; S. M. Burke and J. J. Pollitt, *Greek Vases at Yale* (New Haven, 1975), pp. 84–86, no. 67. Cambitoglou posits a "contrived" South Italian version of the story, with Achilles appearing before Troilos at a turn in the road, but it is more likely that the painter, who perhaps had never depicted the story before, simply borrowed wholesale the more familiar Amazonomachy composition.

The Hoppin Painter is named for a vase formerly in the collection of the classicist Joseph Hoppin and now in the Arthur M. Sackler Museum, Harvard University (inv. 1925.30.48: *CVA* Hoppin-Gallatin 1, pl. 18, 3–4; *RVAp*, I, p. 105, no. 5/17). He was a follower of the Tarporley Painter and, like him, worked in the Plain style. The Hoppin Painter was a skilled draftsman. His human figures have an easy naturalism beyond the capacity of most South Italian vase-painters.

PUBLISHED: *RVAp*, I, p. 108, no. 5/50, pl. 36, 4; A. Cambitoglou, in *Studies Webster*, II, p. 7; *MFA AnnRep* 1988–89, p. 42; *RVAp*, Suppl. II, p. 23 (cited incorrectly as *RVAp*, no. 5/8).

BELL-KRATER
Attributed to the Bendis Painter
Ca. 370–360 B.C.
Gift of Mr. and Mrs. Cornelius C. Vermeule III
in the Name of Cornelius Adrian Comstock
Vermeule. 1983.553

PROVENANCE: Collection of Mr. and Mrs. Cornelius C. Vermeule III (MFA loan 106.64); Münzen und Medaillen A.G., Auktion XVIII, 29 November 1958, no. 147 (entry by H. A. Cahn); A. Ruesch collection, Zürich (Auction Fischer, Lucerne, 1936, p. 5, no. 30)

DIMENSIONS AND CONDITION: Height: 43.1 cm; diameter rim: 43.6 cm; diameter body below handles: 31.8 cm; diameter stem: 10.8 cm; diameter foot: 19.5 cm
Unbroken

SHAPE: Standard Apulian type, like the following two examples (cat. nos. 17–18), which have the same rolled-back handles, tall, disk foot with reserved groove at the top and lower body tapering to a stem. This example has a taller stem than the next two, and the handles are tilted more sharply upward.

A: Bendis stands to the right with a spear held vertically in her right hand. She wears yellow earrings, yellow necklace, embades, a chiton, a yellow belt, a Phrygian cap, embroidered trousers, and a sleeved tunic—appropriate garb for a goddess from barbarian Thrace. Bendis offers a drink from a yellow phiale in her left hand to a hare held by Apollo, who is seated to the left on a folded cloak. Apollo wears a white wreath, and his quiver, decorated with a wave-pattern, hangs at his left side on a baldric. In his left hand he holds a tree that does not really resemble laurel. Hermes stands at the right, wearing a petasos and chlamys, his caduceus in his lowered right hand. The chlamys is pinned at his throat by a yellow brooch. In the field above the hare is a yellow star.

B: Three youths stand clad in himatia. The one at the left holds a strigil in his extended right hand. The middle youth crowns the one on the right with a fillet. The latter holds a staff vertically in his extended right hand.

A laurel wreath circles the vase below the lip. The baseline consists of triple linked maeanders to left alternating with saltire-squares. There are palmettes and scrolling tendrils under the handles, the roots of which are partly surrounded by tongues.

The Bendis Painter was a close associate of the Adolphseck Painter and the Painter of the Long Overfalls. Like them, he was a follower of the Tarporley Painter and worked in the Plain style. This is not his only name-vase, as several other works also represent Artemis-Bendis in oriental costume. The significance of the hare in this example is not clear. For Bendis in South Italian vase-painting, see K.

16

16

Schauenburg, *JdI* 89 (1974), pp. 137–186; see also Z. Gočeva and D. Popov, *LIMC*, III, 1, pp. 95–97; III, 2, pls. 73–74.

PUBLISHED: Cambitoglou and Trendall, *Plain Style*, p. 59, no. 3, pl. 35, figs. 169–170; K. Schauenburg, *JdI* 89 (1974), pp. 182–183; *RVAp*, I, pp. 88 (no. 4/168), 438, fig. 2 h; G. Kokkorou-Alewras, *LIMC*, II, 1, p. 275, no. 739; idem and O. Palagia, p. 320; L. Kahil and N. Icard, ibid., p. 691, no. 915; *MFA AnnRep* 1983–84, p. 42; E. Vermeule, in A. Leonard and B. B. Williams, eds., *Essays in Ancient Civilization Presented to Helene J. Kantor* (Chicago, 1989), pp. 281–282; G. Siebert, *LIMC*, V, 1, p. 345, no. 713a; V, 2, pl. 258; *RVAp*, Suppl. II, p. 483, no. 4/168.

EXHIBITED: Corpus Christi, *Greek Vases*, p. 29, fig. 39; Wellesley College Museum, Jewett Arts Center, October 1 - December 14, 1984.

17

BELL-KRATER
Closely associated with the Judgement Painter
Ca. 370–360 B.C.
Frederick L. Brown Fund. 1976.144

DIMENSIONS AND CONDITION: Height: 36.0 cm; diameter rim: 39.6 cm; diameter just below handles: 28.1 cm; diameter stem: 10.1 cm; diameter foot: 18.3 cm
Reconstructed from fragments; a large fragment is missing at the lower center of the reverse, including the legs of Dionysos. The reverse is somewhat misfired. One piece of the rim above the right handle was broken in antiquity and repaired, as indicated by three pairs of drill holes, two of which are still filled with bronze rods.

SHAPE: See comments on cat. no. 16; in this example, the stem is somewhat shorter and the foot wider and not as tall.

A: Orestes at Delphi. As often in representations of this subject, he clasps the omphalos with one hand and brandishes a sword with the other; one leg is drawn back, and his chlamys swirls behind him to mark his violent agitation. Athena, vertical spear in her right hand, stands at the left, pointing at the young hero with her lowered left hand. She has come to assure Orestes that the Furies will be transformed into beneficent beings, Eumenides. Apollo stands at the right, two yellow arrows in his raised right hand and a laurel branch with white berries in the left. Two Furies sleep in the foreground. A yellow and brown phiale and a bucranium with pendant fillets are in the field above, below a band of dotted egg-pattern and a row of yellow dots that suggest architectural moldings. Athena wears a peplos, a black aegis with white gorgoneion, white scales and yellow snakes, a yellow Attic helmet with two yellow plumes on either side of the crest, white bracelets, and a belt with white spots. Orestes' chlamys is pinned at the throat with a white brooch. His boots are embades, with flaps of skin hanging from the tops. Apollo wears a yellow wreath, shoes, and a cloak over one shoulder. The Furies wear short chitons, belts, and crossed bandoleers with white dots. The Fury at the left holds a spear in her left hand and wears embades, while the one at the right rests her right hand on a spear on the ground and wears different boots; she has yellow snakes entwined in her hair and around her left arm. Groundlines of red and white dots support Athena, Orestes, the omphalos, and the Fury at the left. Three white fillets are draped over the omphalos, which is circled by two wreaths.

B: Dionysos is seated to the right, his cloak folded beneath him; he wears a yellow wreath and holds a stylized plant in his left hand. A maenad with a thyrsos in her left hand stands at the left; she wears a necklace, bracelets, and a radiate stephane, all in yellow, and a belted chiton. Her thyrsos has white dots on the cone and yellow and white chevrons on the staff. A nearly identical figure facing left stands at the right with a palm frond (?) in her left hand.

A wreath of laurel circles the vase below the lip. Tongues partly surround the roots of the handles, below which are palmettes and scrolling tendrils. A band of linked maeanders to right interspersed with a few saltire-squares circles the lower body.

Although not clearly attributable to the Judgement Painter, the leading artist of a large Plain-style workshop, the painting is close in style. For the subject, presumably inspired by the *Eumenides* of Aeschylus, see R. R. Dyer, *JHS* 89 (1969), pp. 38–56; Kossatz-Deissmann, *Dramen*, pp. 102–117, pls. 19–24; and E. T. Vermeule (see reference below). Vermeule noted that the omphalos and altar are combined in one, compared the Athena and Apollo to sculptural types (Athena Medici and Apollo of Metapontum), and wondered if the "virginal and innocent Artemis-quality" (p. 187) of the sleeping Furies might be connected with the appearance of Artemis in several representations of the subject. Vermeule also noted that the subject was appropriate for funerary painting, "with its statement that the implacable powers of evil from the unseen world of the dead can indeed be transformed into beneficent powers of life and fertility, and that man can be forgiven" (p. 185).

PUBLISHED: *MFA AnnRep* 1975–76, pp. 18 (illus.), 22; *RVAp*, I, p. 264, no. 10/33, pl. 87, 5–6; E. T. Vermeule, in *Festschrift von Blanckenhagen*, pp. 186–188, pl. 51, 1–2; Bennett Simon, *Mind and Madness in Ancient Greece: The Classical Roots of Modern Psychiatry* (Ithaca, 1978), p. 107, illus.; Freytag gen. Löringhoff, *Giebelrelief*, pp. 140, 289, no. E 27: dated 370/60–340/30 B.C.; H. Sarian, *LIMC*, III, 1, pp. 832 (no. 49), 840; Schefold and Jung, *Argonauten*, p. 399, note 686; A. Frazer, *The Propylon of Ptolemy II*, in K. Lehmann and P. W. Lehmann, eds., *Samothrace: Excavations Conducted by the Institute of Fine Arts, New York University*, vol. 10 (Princeton, 1990), p. 199, note 134; A. D. Trendall, in *Festschrift Cambitoglou*, p. 213, note 11; *RVAp*, Suppl. II, p. 61, no. 10/33.

17 (Color Plate VI)

17

18

BELL-KRATER
The name-vase of the Painter of Boston 00.348
Ca. 370–360 B.C.
Henry Lillie Pierce Residuary Fund. 00.348

PROVENANCE: E. P. Warren collection; found near Canosa

DIMENSIONS AND CONDITION: Height: 34.0 cm; diameter rim:
38.8 cm; diameter just below handles: 27.4 cm; diameter
stem: 9.1 cm; lower diameter foot: 15.5 cm
Reconstructed from fragments. There are gaps at the upper
border and bottom left on side A, the head of the seated god,
and the head and legs of Silenos at the right. On the reverse
there are gaps in the right background and lower right border.
Two abraded cracks pass through the figure of the youth holding a mirror.

SHAPE: See comments on cat. nos. 16–17. This example is
somewhat broader in profile, with a less abrupt tapering of the
lower body.

A: Athena is seated in the center of the scene, using
her aegis as a cushion. She is playing the auloi next
to a small tree with yellow leaves. The goddess wears
a chiton and bordered himation, which has fallen
around her waist. She has sandals and a necklace. A
youth with a cloak over his left arm and leaning on a
staff holds a white mirror in front of Athena, so that
she can see how her playing distorts her appearance,
a fact emphasized by the lines radiating from her
mouth. Her reflection in the mirror is rendered with
yellow lines. Zeus reclines above and behind her, his
scepter in his left hand; his bordered himation has
fallen around his waist. Below him, the booted Pappasilenos, his hair and beard in orange-yellow slip,
chases a red-orange "Maltese" dog to the right. At
the far left, a maenad in chiton, necklace, and belted
leopard skin approaches with a thyrsos in her left
hand. At the extreme right, the ill-fated Marsyas
approaches the scene on tiptoes, his right hand extended, as though already anticipating the retrieval
of the flutes, which Athena will discard when she
sees how playing them distorts her face.

The arrangement of the figures at various levels,
without groundlines so that they seem to float in a
black void, is characteristic of the painter. The presence of old Pappasilenos suggests the inspiration of a
satyr play. Because of his central location, we might
suppose *he* is Marsyas, but the darker-haired and apparently younger satyr near the handle assumes a
posture not unlike that of the so-called Lateran Marsyas, a Roman statue thought to be based on a fifth-
century work by Myron. Myron's statue showed
Marsyas's surprised reaction to finding the flutes.
His reaction here is thus premature, and his legs are
not in the same position, but the upraised arm and
the backwards lean of the body are clearly similar.

18 (Color Plate VII)

18

The youth with the mirror is not identified by any attribute, but if the tree is a laurel, he may be Apollo. If so, his presence alludes to the outcome of the story, when he defeated the overweening Marsyas in a musical contest and had him flayed alive. For Marsyas, see A. Weis, *LIMC*, VI, 1, pp. 366–378; VI, 2, pls. 183–193. For Myron's sculpture, see G. Daltrop, *Il Gruppo mironiano di Athena e Marsia nei Musei Vaticani* (Vatican City, 1980); and A. Weis, *The Hanging Marsyas Statue* (Ph.D. dissertation, Bryn Mawr College, 1976).

B: A satyr is running to the left, a torch with a cream-colored flame in his left hand. He looks back at a nude youth with a staff in his right hand, a cream-colored fillet on his head, and a draped cloak over his right arm and pulled out by his left hand. To judge by his company, the youth should be Dionysos, but he lacks any identifying attribute. He looks back toward a maenad, with a thyrsos in her left hand, who moves left; she wears a chiton and necklace and has her hair tied in a chignon. At the far right, a satyr with white fillet and a thyrsos in his right hand has turned aside to relieve himself.

A wreath of laurel encircles the vase under the lip. Rays circle the handle-roots, and there are palmettes below each handle. A band consisting of groups of four stopt maeanders to left alternating with cross- and saltire-squares circles the lower body.

The Painter of Boston 00.348 was an associate of the more prolific Judgement Painter and, like him, worked in the Plain-style tradition. A bell-krater in a Virginia private collection with a scene of Iphigenia at Tauris has recently been attributed to the artist by Trendall (*RVAp*, Suppl. II, p. 63, no. 10/48a; L. Kahil and N. Icard, *LIMC*, V, 1, p. 715; V, 2, pl. 469, Iphigeneia 21).

PUBLISHED: G. Jatta, *Annali* 1879, pp. 24ff., pl. D; Jessen, in W. H. Roscher, ed., *Ausführliches Lexikon der griechischen und römischen Mythologie* (Leipzig, 1894–1897), II, 2, cols. 2448–2449; E. Robinson, *MFA AnnRep* 1900, pp. 65–67, no. 24; *AA* 1901, p. 167, no. 24; C. Watzinger, in Furtwängler and Reichhold, III, p. 348, no. 11; Beazley, *EVP*, p. 77; K. Schauenburg, *RM* 65 (1958), pp. 43–44, pl. 30; Cambitoglou and Trendall, *Plain Style*, pp. 18–19, no. 1, pl. 5, fig. 22; MFA, *Gods and Heroes*, pp. 26, 29 (fig. 15); G. Scichilone, *EAA*, V, p. 675; Cambitoglou and Trendall, *Plain Style, Addenda*, p. 425; H. Froning, *Dithyrambos und Vasenmalerei in Athen* (*Beiträge zur Archäologie*, no. 2, Würzburg, 1971), p. 101, note 210; Del Chiaro, *Caere*, pp. 39–40, note 17; K. Schauenburg, *RM* 81 (1974), p. 316, note 30; *RVAp*, I, pp. 23, 258, 264–268, no. 10/48, pl. 89, 2; Schefold and Jung, *Göttersage*, pp. 177, 353, note 351; J. P. Small, *Cacus and Marsyas in Etrusco-Roman Legend* (Princeton, 1982), p. 75, note 26; G. Daltrop and P. C. Bol, *Athena des Myron* (Liebieghaus Monograph 8, Frankfurt, 1983), p. 18, fig. 7; P. Demargne, *LIMC*, II, 1, pp. 1014–1015, no. 620; II, 2, pl. 764;

M. Sguaitamatti, *L'Offrante de Porcelet dans la Coroplathie Géléenne: Étude Typologique* (Mainz, 1984), p. 163, note 8; F. D'Andria, in F. D'Andria and T. Ritti, *Le Sculture del Teatro: I Rilievi con i Cicli di Apollo e Artemide* (Hierapolis: Scavi e Ricerche, II, Rome, 1985), p. 51; *LIMC*, III, 1, p. 927, under no. 925; Rawson, *Marsyas*, pp. 18–19, 23, 192, no. A5, fig. 3; Balensiefen, *Spiegelbildes*, pp. 225–226, no. K 19, pl. 22, 1; *RVAp*, Suppl. II, p. 62, no. 10/48 (with additional bibliography); A. Weis, *LIMC*, VI, 1, pp. 369 (no. 10), 376.

19

SQUAT LEKYTHOS
Attributed to the Lecce Painter
Ca. 370–360 B.C.
Gift of Thomas G. Appleton. 76.59

PROVENANCE: Alessandro Castellani collection; from Ruvo

DIMENSIONS AND CONDITION: Height: 16.5 cm; diameter rim: 3.5 cm; diameter foot: 6.4 cm; diameter body: 9.6 cm Unbroken. The glaze and added colors have flaked away in many places. A missing flake beside the central figure's nose distorts her profile.

SHAPE: Ovoid body, broad grooved foot, vertical handle, short neck, standard lekythos mouth, with flat top

On the body, a woman wearing a clinging chiton, sphendone, yellow necklace, and white earrings and bracelets, is seated to the left on a white rock; she is playing with a bird, a white dove, which has perched on her right knee and looks up at her right hand. Facing her, at the left, stands another woman in similar garb holding a phiale full of offerings in her extended left hand and a wreath in her lowered right hand. To the right of the seated woman, a youth wearing a himation and a wreath leans on his staff to left. He holds a strigil in his raised right hand. Behind him is a blood-splattered altar.

Around the outside of the mouth are two maenads and an ithyphallic satyr, walking to the left and carrying wreaths; the middle maenad also carries a tympanum. Both maenads wear himatia.

Around the middle of the neck is a band of stopt maeanders to left, and below this is a broad band of tongues. A band of wave-pattern circles the shoulder and below this, over the figures, is a row of white dots. The groundline consists of stopt maeanders to left. On the back of the vase is an elaborate palmette complex, from which scrolling tendrils emerge to frame the figures.

The Lecce Painter was one of the many followers of the Tarporley Painter and a close associate of the Hoppin and Truro Painters. Compare the shape and subject of Philadelphia, University Museum, L-64-224, by the same painter (*RVAp*, I, p. 125, no. 5/225; *CVA* 1, pl. 23).

19

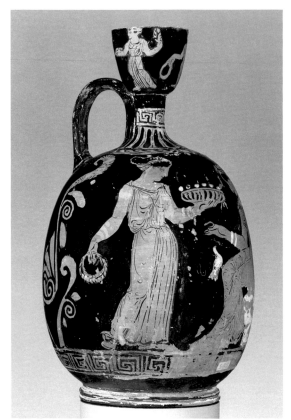

19

19

19

The seated woman with bird, the woman bringing offerings, and the youth standing next to a pillar or stele are all characters familiar from funerary scenes on Athenian white-ground lekythoi. No direct connection is suggested, but a funerary milieu is not unlikely. The strigil and pillar might also suggest the palaestra, but the presence of women should rule this out. For the woman and bird, compare Aphrodite on cat. no. 21.

The addition of decoration on the mouth is very unusual; compare the mouth of an Attic red-figure lekythos in Paris, with Eos and Tithonos: Louvre G.614 (J. de la Genière, in Cambitoglou, *Studies Trendall*, pp. 75–80, pl. 19).

PUBLISHED: Robinson, *Catalogue*, p. 184, no. 503; Cambitoglou and Trendall, *Plain Style*, p. 64, no. 23, pl. 36, fig. 180; idem, *Plain Style, Addenda*, p. 430; *RVAp*, I, pp. 125–126, no. 5/226; J. de la Genière, in Cambitoglou, *Studies Trendall*, p. 78, note 3; K. Schauenburg, in W. Hornbostel et al., *Aus Gräbern und Heiligtümern: Die Antikensammlung Walter Kropatscheck* (Mainz, 1980), pp. 187 (under no. 113), 190, illus.; A. Cambitoglou, *RdA* 5 (1981), p. 6, under no. 7; *RVAp*, Suppl. I, p. 13, no. 5/226.

20

20

OINOCHOE (shape 8)
Ca. 360–350 B.C.
Gift of Edward Perry Warren. 13.93

DIMENSIONS AND CONDITION: Height: 18.0 cm; diameter rim: 9.8 cm; diameter neck: 7.2 cm; diameter body: 13.1 cm; diameter foot: 8.6 cm
Unbroken. The glaze is flaked in places, and the rim encrusted.

SHAPE: A relatively rare type, like a tall mug, with ovoid body and tall, concave neck. Trendall rightly classes it as a shape 8 oinochoe.

A phlyax actor wearing tights and a short, belted tunic is running to the left, fleeing some unseen menace, at which his eye (but not his head) looks back.

The groundline is largely obscured by careless brushwork but may have been running Ss.

The character's haste and his worried, backward glance suggest a larcenous slave on the run from pursuers; compare the Gnathian phlyax on cat. no. 108. For the running slave motif on comic vases, see E. G. Csapo, *AntK* 36 (1993), pp. 41–58. Trendall (*Phlyax*, 1967, p. 66) lists two other oinochoai of this shape with phlyakes; a fourth, with a running phlyax, is in Toronto, ROM 972.182.1 (Csapo, *AntK* 36 [1993], pl. 10, 1). Trendall classes the mask as type B ("Good head of hair, short beard, open mouth").

PUBLISHED: Catteruccia, *Pitture*, p. 70, no. D, *; Bieber, *Theater*, pp. 291, 293, fig. 397; Trendall, *Phlyax*, 1959, p. 48, no. 125; idem, *EAA*, III, p. 708; Bieber, *Theater*, 1961, pp. 142–143, fig. 526; Trendall, *Phlyax*, 1967, pp. 14, 66, no. 129; Webster and Green, *Old and Middle Comedy*, p. 169, no. Ph 129 (dated 350–325 B.C.); E. G. Csapo, *AntK* 36 (1993), pp. 47, 49, 57, no. 1.

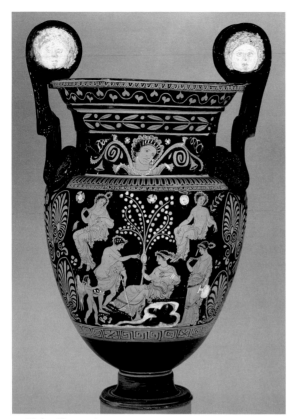

21 (Color Plate VIII)

21

21

VOLUTE-KRATER
Attributed to the Iliupersis Painter
Ca. 365–355 B.C.
Gift of Robert E. Hecht, Jr. 1970.235

DIMENSIONS AND CONDITION: Height with handles: 61.0 cm; height without handles: 52.0 cm; diameter rim: 32.3 cm; diameter neck: 23.1 cm; diameter body: 33.7 cm; diameter stem: 8.8 cm; diameter foot: 15.7 cm
Unbroken. The reverse is slightly misfired.

SHAPE: Standard for the period and not appreciably remote from the late fifth-century Attic prototypes. The same shape, complete with swans' heads, was also produced in bronze in South Italy; for example, Boston 99.943, from Spongano (M. Comstock and C. Vermeule, *Greek, Etruscan & Roman Bronzes in the Museum of Fine Arts, Boston* [Boston, 1971], pp. 315–316, no. 441, illus.).

A: A group of divine or mythological beings is assembled in a garden setting. In the center a woman wearing a chiton, himation, and sphendone is seated to the left by a "reflecting pool" with a white border. She holds up a mirror in her right hand, as a wreathed youth with a cloak about his lower body and left arm leans on the staff in his left hand and offers her a necklace dangling from his right hand. The staff and necklace are white, as are the shoes, bracelets, earrings, and necklace worn by the woman. Be-

low the woman and youth, the terrain is indicated by groundlines of white dots. At the youth's side is the diminutive Eros, wearing a wreath and carrying a phiale full of offerings in his left hand. A second woman holding a white and yellow hydria in her left hand stands at the right; she is dressed and adorned like the seated woman, but her shoes are not white. A tree with round, white leaves grows in the center. In the upper register, seated at left and right, are a woman with a dove on her knee and a youth holding a laurel branch; their position and attributes suggest Aphrodite and Apollo. The goddess wears a chiton and himation, shoes with white detailing, white bracelets and necklace, and a fillet partly covered by her hair. With her right hand she holds the veil behind her head. Apollo wears shoes and a himation; a white wreath is in his hair. A white disk quartered with yellow chevrons floats in the field by Apollo's head, and there are rosettes above the tree and at the upper left.

The necklace recalls the bribing of Eriphyle by Polyneikes, who in Attic and Lucanian representations is normally shown leaning on his staff (see *LIMC*, III, 2, pls. 606–608). Paris and Helen are perhaps less likely possibilities, although the two gods observing the couple were Trojan partisans, and the presence of Eros suggests a love interest. E. Vermeule (cited below) was reminded of the Garden of the Hesperides, but neither Herakles nor the serpent is present.

B: A female stands in the center holding a wreath in her right hand and a cista in her left. On either side of her are two nude youths, the left one seated. Rows of white dots mark the ground below each figure. The woman wears a chiton, white bracelets and earrings, a necklace with white pendants, and a sphendone with radiate white leaves. The youths carry white staffs and wear white fillets. The seated one leans on his cloak, which wraps around to cover his loins. The one at the right has a fillet draped over his extended right hand and his cloak wrapped round his left arm. In the field above are a fillet and other filling ornaments: a "window," a quadrated disk, and a phiale. On the ground by the woman's feet is a cista decorated with maeanders and chevrons and holding three eggs.

On the obverse neck is a female head in three-quarter view, growing from acanthus. She wears a white radiate diadem and earrings. Spiraling yellow tendrils and flowers spring from the white-highlighted acanthus to frame the head. The neck on the reverse is decorated with a complex of palmettes and tendrils. The volutes have mold-made masks representing wide-eyed female heads: white, with features in red-brown dilute glaze. The handles terminate in plastic swan's heads on the shoulders. The palmettes below the handles are particularly rich in conception and execution and are linked by tendrils that enclose the palmettes framing both scenes. There is dotted egg-pattern on the outer rim between the handles.

Below the obverse rim, on the upper register, is a red-figure ivy vine; on the lower register is a laurel wreath with berries. On the reverse, the ivy is black on a reserved ground, and the laurel wreath is of a different and less fine variety (one-directional). A band consisting of groups of linked maeanders to left alternating with saltire-squares circles the lower body. On the shoulders between the handles is a broad band of tongues; on the obverse, these surmount a band of egg-pattern.

The Iliupersis Painter was a prolific and innovative artist, active just before midcentury, whose work set the standard for the large, Ornate-style vases of the second half of the century: volute-kraters with plastic masks on the volutes, increased polychromy, complex floral ornament, multilevel compositions, mourners surrounding funerary naiskoi and stelai. The female head in a floral setting on the neck of this vase is one of the earliest examples of this motif, common on volute-kraters of the second half of the century. See the extensive discussion by Trendall

21

and Cambitoglou; *RVAp*, II, pp. 646–649. In *RVAp*, Suppl. II, p. 46, they compare the drawing of this face to that of a male head, perhaps Orpheus, on a volute-krater in Antibes (ibid., p. 47, no. 8/11a). For the Iliupersis painter, see A. D. Trendall and A. Cambitoglou, in *Études et Travaux* 13 (1983), pp. 405–413. For the masks on the handles, see L. Giuliani, in M. Schmidt, ed., *Kanon: Festschrift Ernst Berger* (*AntK*, Beiheft 15, Basel, 1988), pp. 159–165. Elaborate floral work like that around the head on the neck has been associated with the Sicyonian painter Pausias, who flourished in the second quarter of the fourth century and was said to have developed the art of flower painting (Pliny, *Natural History*, 35.123–125); see *RVAp*, I, pp. 189–190.

PUBLISHED: C. C. Vermeule, *MFA AnnRep* 1969–70, p. 42; E. Vermeule, in *Festschrift Hanfmann*, p. 181, note 18; C. C. Vermeule, *BurlMag* 115 (1973), pp. 117–118, fig. 75; *RVAp*, I, pp. 185, 188–189, 191–192, 194 (no. 8/11), 203, 207, 211, 223, 393, pl. 61, 3–4; Cambitoglou, *Studies Trendall*, p. 52; *RVAp*, II, p. 449, no. 8/11; A. Greifenhagen, *RA* 1982, pp. 156–157; M. Pfrommer, *JdI* 97 (1982), p. 127; D. Salzmann, *Untersuchungen zu den antiken Kieselmosaiken: Von den Anfängen bis zum Beginn der Tesseratechnik* (Berlin, 1982), pp. 15–16, 18, pl. 96, 1; Aellen, Cambitoglou, and Chamay, *Peintre de Darius*, p. 69; Trendall, *Handbook*, pp. 79, 112 (fig. 141), 278; A. D. Trendall, in Descoeudres, *Greek Colonists*, pp. 221–222, pl. 21, 4; *RVAp*, Suppl. II, pp. 44–46, no. 8/11.

22

23

22

SQUAT LEKYTHOS
Ca. 360–350 B.C.
Gift of Barbara Deering Danielson. 1982.658

PROVENANCE: Charles Deering collection

DIMENSIONS AND CONDITION: Height: 10.9 cm; diameter rim: 4.3 cm; diameter neck: 1.4 cm; diameter body: 9.9 cm; diameter foot: 6.0 cm
Unbroken

SHAPE: Trumpet mouth; short, tapering neck; depressed, globular body; grooved, base-ring foot; handle from neck to shoulder

On the body, Eros advances toward an altar at the right, holding a phiale full of white offerings in his left hand. He has bracelets on each arm and a fillet on his head, all in white. A single offering, possibly an egg, sits on the altar. Compare the composition on the reverse of a pelike, cat. no. 24. There is a palmette beneath the handle and one on either side of it. Rays circle the lower neck. The groundline is a simple reserved stripe. The underside of the foot and the fillet between the foot and body are painted with added red.

   The figures and props seem related to the Dijon and Iliupersis Painters (Herrmann). The roundel with seven dots (a patera ?) among the palmettes on the reverse is found on several lesser works of this circle. For the dotted roundel, see *RVAp*, I, pls. 70, 4; 74, 4; 92, 7–8.

For the shape, compare Lecce 957 (*CVA* 2, pl. 51, no. 5); University Museum, University of Pennsylvania L-64-32 (*CVA* 1, pl. 24, 1–2); and Taranto 117509 (J. C. Carter, *The Sculpture of Taras* [*TAPS* 65, pt. 7, 1975], pl. 72e; *RVAp*, I, p. 120, no. 5/163: Truro Painter).

23

SQUAT LEKYTHOS
Ca. 360–350 B.C.
Gift of Barbara Deering Danielson. 1982.659

PROVENANCE: Charles Deering collection

DIMENSIONS AND CONDITION: Height: 11.1 cm; diameter rim: 4.4 cm; diameter neck: 1.5 cm; diameter body: 10.0 cm; diameter foot: 5.9 cm
Unbroken

SHAPE: The same as that of the preceding vase; both may have been decorated by the same hand.

On the body is a youth seated to left on a folded cloak, holding a cista in his right hand, a staff in his left. His wreath and the knots on his staff are in added white.

   There is a palmette beneath the handle and one on either side of it. Rays circle the lower neck. The groundline is a band of dotted egg-pattern. The underside of the foot and the fillet between the foot and body are painted with added red.

24

PELIKE
Associated with the workshop of the Iliupersis
Painter
Ca. 360–350 B.C.
Gift of Edward Perry Warren. 90.160

PROVENANCE: From Capua

DIMENSIONS AND CONDITION: Height: 18.8 cm; width across
handles: 13.1 cm; diameter rim: 11.5 cm; diameter neck:
7.6 cm; diameter body: 14.2 cm; diameter base of body: 9.7
cm; diameter foot: 10.8 cm
Cracked with reattached chips. A chip is missing from the rim.

SHAPE: Typical for minor works in the Plain style and very
much in the Attic tradition, with a short, broad neck, handles
looping down to hug the side of the neck, and a broad disk
foot. Compare the larger, less Atticizing pelike, cat. no. 46.

A: A woman wearing a chiton, earrings, necklace,
and bracelets is rushing to the right, a mirror in her
raised left hand. The jewelry and mirror are white.
She looks back, perhaps at the youth on the reverse.
A floral scroll rises from the ground in front of her.

B: A nude youth, wearing shoes and a white fillet
and holding a large phiale in his outstretched left
hand, strides to the right toward a low, square pillar
or altar.

On both sides, the upper and lower frames consist
of bands of crudely executed dotted egg-pattern.

PUBLISHED: E. Robinson, *MFA AnnRep* 1890, p. 20, no. 8;
idem, *Catalogue*, p. 157, no. 428; Cambitoglou and Trendall,
Plain Style, p. 72, no. 32, pl. 38, fig. 187; *RVAp*, I, p. 309, no.
11/239, pl. 96, 7.

24

24

25

COLUMN-KRATER
The name-vase of the Painter of Boston 76.65
Ca. 360–350 B.C.
Gift of Thomas G. Appleton. 76.65

PROVENANCE: Alessandro Castellani collection; from Ruvo

DIMENSIONS AND CONDITION: Height: 50.6 cm; diameter rim: 36.9 cm; diameter body: 31.7 cm; diameter foot: 16.3 cm
The rim is chipped; otherwise unbroken.

SHAPE: Compare the shape of the earlier column-krater of the Sisyphus Group, cat. no. 9. This later example is typical of its generation in being not taller but more slender and with the neck more flaring. The foot is flared almost to echinus form but retains a reserved groove at the top.

A: A maenad wearing a chiton, kekryphalos, and necklace with yellow pendants stands at the left holding a yellow mirror in her left hand. Before her, at the center, stands a nude youth, probably Dionysos, with a white wreath in his hair and a cloak over one arm. He holds a phiale in his left hand and a thyrsos in the right. At the right is a satyr, a white fillet on his head, carrying a situla in his lowered right hand and a tambourine in his raised left. In the lower right corner is a sprig of laurel, and between the satyr and Dionysos grows a small plant. A rosette floats in the field above.

B: A boy, both arms covered by his himation, faces two youths wearing himatia and holding staffs in their right hands. In the field above are filling ornaments in the form of paired jumping weights.

The panels on either side of the neck repeat the earlier practice, seen on cat. no. 9, of a large ivy vine and clusters of berries, a scheme that continues to be standard on Apulian column-kraters; note the more naturalistic vine in comparison to that on cat. no. 9. The pictures have lateral frames of degenerate ivy and upper frames of tongues. Both groundlines consist of groups of linked maeanders to left alternating with dotted saltire-squares. There is crude ivy on both sides of the rim, wave-pattern on top of the rim, and black palmettes on the handle-plates.

The Painter of Boston 76.65 was a close associate of the Lycurgus Painter. Most of the few works attributed to him are kraters and pelikai. Although this krater is relatively uncluttered in comparison with more elaborate works, the use of added color and the floral filling ornaments place it in the Ornate-style tradition.

PUBLISHED: Robinson, *Catalogue*, pp. 176–177, no. 489; *RVAp*, I, p. 419, no. 16/32, pl. 153, 1–2; M. Bentz, in *CVA* Göttingen 1, p. 23, under pl. 4, 1–3.

25

25

26

26

OINOCHOE (shape 5A)
Attributed to the Monash Group
Ca. 360–350 B.C.
Gift of the Misses Norton. 41.651

PROVENANCE: Lent by the Misses Norton in 1912; Richard Norton collection

DIMENSIONS AND CONDITION: Height: 22.5 cm; diameter upper rim: 10.0 cm; diameter rim: 10.4 cm; diameter neck: 6.1 cm; diameter body: 13.5 cm; diameter base of body: 7.5 cm; diameter foot: 8.0 cm
Unbroken except for small chips on rim and foot; some surface wear

SHAPE: Red-figure oinochoai of shape 5A are relatively uncommon; compare Philadelphia, The University Museum, MS 4801 (CVA 1, pl. 19), and a pair with phlyakes in the Ragusa collection (coll. 4 and 9: Trendall, Phlyax, 1967, pl. 8 c-d).

A youth, nude save for shoes, a himation, and wreath, stands at the left and offers a phiale full of cakes or eggs in his left hand to a female seated on a rock, who holds a stylized branch in her right hand. She wears a necklace, bracelets, and a sakkos, all in white, as well as a chiton and himation. A quadrated disk floats in the upper field.

The head of a bearded silenos on top of the handle is cast from a rather worn mold. The picture has lateral frames of horizontal zigzags and an upper frame

of ivy over a band of dotted egg-pattern. The groundline consists of stopt maeanders and cross-squares. For the ivy, compare that on the shoulder of one of the phlyax vases in the Ragusa collection (Trendall, Phlyax, 1967, pl. 8d).

PUBLISHED: RVAp, Suppl. II, p. 71, no. 11/43a.

27

FRAGMENT OF AN OINOCHOE
Ca. 350–340 B.C.
James Fund and by Special Contribution. 10.204

PROVENANCE: E. P. Warren collection

DIMENSIONS AND CONDITION: Length: 10 cm

Bellerophon, mounted on Pegasus, attacks the Chimaera, who crouches at the lower right. The hero's weapon is a trident, a symbol of his grandfather Poseidon. His cloak is pinned at the throat with a black brooch. He wears laced shoes and a petasos with white dots on the brim and a white cord. Pegasus is a brilliant white, with a flowing mane and brown harness; the muzzle, ears, and hooves are rendered in beige dilute glaze. The Chimaera's lion's head is snarling, with teeth and fiery breath in added white; the goat's head emerging from its side seems lifeless by comparison. A winged figure flies toward Bellerophon, bearing a wreath; one expects Nike, but the white anklet suggests it is Eros, perhaps alluding to Bellerophon's subsequent marriage to Philonoe.

For Bellerophon and Pegasus, see cat. no. 8, with references. Compare the rearing Pegasus on an oinochoe, cat. no. 71. For the Chimaera, see A. Jacquemin, LIMC, III, 1, pp. 249–259; III, 2, pls. 197–209.

PUBLISHED: K. Schauenburg, JdI 71 (1956), p. 64, fig. 8; Brommer, Vasenlisten, 1956, p. 170, no. D 9; ibid., 1960, p. 223, no. D 9; C. Vermeule, BMFA 64 (1966), p. 21, no. 3a, illus.; Brommer, Vasenlisten, 1973, p. 294, no. D 9.

27

ALABASTRON
Related to the V. and A. Group
Ca. 350–340 B.C.
Henry Lillie Pierce Residuary Fund. 00.360

PROVENANCE: E. P. Warren collection

DIMENSIONS AND CONDITION: Height: 28.2 cm; diameter rim:
5.5 cm; diameter neck: 1.8 cm; diameter body: 7.7 cm; diameter foot: 7.6 cm
The mouth is ancient but may not belong. The rim and upper
part of the neck have been reattached.

SHAPE: Footed ceramic alabastra are a South Italian phenome-
non, although the basic shape, without the foot and the tall
neck, is of Attic derivation. For a selection, see K. Schauenburg, JdI 87 (1972), pp. 258–298. Two vertical lugs on the upper body divide the two sides. The wide, black foot has a cyma
recta molding and a reserved groove above the stem.

A: Menelaos and Helen. Eros flies down to crown
the nude Menelaos, who is seated on a diphros at the
center, his white staff propped against the cloak under his left arm. Menelaos wears laced boots, and
Eros has yellow and white shoes and white anklets, a
kekryphalos, and a thigh band of white beads. The
feathers of his wings are white. Below the yellow
stool, on the dotted groundline, are a white bird and
a white quadrated disk, perhaps a ball of wool. Menelaos turns to gesture at Helen, who stands at the
right wearing a chiton, white shoes, diadem, and a
himation that is pulled up over her head like a veil.
The bordered himation is sprinkled with white dots,
and the chiton has a long, central panel decorated
with a white-dotted, crosshatched design. Helen
holds a yellow mirror in her right hand and rests her
left hand on her hip. Her jewelry consists of earrings, bracelets, and a necklace, all in yellow. There
is a rosette in the field above her head. Both Menelaos (ΜΕΝΕΛΑΟΣ) and Helen (ΗΕΛΕΝΑ) are identified by incised inscriptions. To the left of Menelaos, a
woman in a chiton, himation, sakkos, and radiate fillet is playing a harp, elaborately decorated in added
white. Her left foot rests on a low white Ionic column with yellow details. She wears earrings, necklace, and bracelets, all in white.

Judging by the youth of Menelaos, the scene
should be set near the time of his wedding to Helen,
before her elopement with Paris, although in Apulian vase-painting he is sometimes represented as a
beardless youth while at Troy; compare the young
Menelaos on cat. no. 38. The crowning by Eros represents the young prince's fiery desire for his bride.
Eros repeats his action in many scenes of Helen's
reclamation at the Sack of Troy, when Menelaos
is dissuaded from killing his unfaithful wife by the
rekindling of this old flame. If the inspiration for this
scene was Euripides' *Helena*, the setting should be
Egypt.

B: A woman, holding two stacked phialai in her
left hand and a fan (?) in her right, stands to the right
next to a flowering plant. She wears shoes, a chiton,
kekryphalos, white bracelets, and a necklace with
white pendants. Facing her at the right is a youth
seated on a box, decorated with bands of patternwork, and holding a white staff in his right hand.
The youth is nude, save for a cloak around one
shoulder and over his legs, and has what appears to
be a yellow horn on the side of his head, indicating
that he may be a Pan. There is a rosette with yellow
center and yellow-tipped petals in the field above.

Bands of dotted egg-pattern circle the upper and
lower body; the eggs in the lower band have white
cores, and there is a band of yellow pendants below
the upper band on side B.

PUBLISHED: E. Robinson, *MFA AnnRep* 1900, pp. 70–71, no.
27; Caskey and Beazley, II, p. 43, no. 169, pl. 32, 3; Ghali-Kahil, *Hélène*, p. 195, no. 169, pl. 32, 3; Brommer, *Vasenlisten*,
1960, p. 291, no. D 1; K. Schauenburg, *JdI* 87 (1972), pp. 278–
279 (figs. 34–36), 282; Brommer, *Vasenlisten*, 1973, p. 404,
no. D 1; K. Schauenburg in Hornbostel, *Schätze*, p. 359, under no. 308; *RVAp*, I, p. 405, no. 15/48; D. von Bothmer, in
H. De Meulenaere and L. Limme, eds., *Artibus Aegypti: Stu-
dia in Honorem Bernardi v. Bothmer* (Brussels, 1983), p. 16,
note 16; L. Kahil with N. Icard, *LIMC*, IV, 1, pp. 514 (no. 68),
556; IV, 2, pl. 302; Maas and Snyder, *Stringed Instruments*,
pp. 181–183, 195 (fig. 13), 244, note 112; K. D. S. Lapatin,
Hesperia 61 (1992), p. 115, note 31; *RVAp*, Suppl. II, p. 103,
no. 15/48.

28

28 (Color Plate IX)

28   28

29

29

29

EPICHYSIS
Ca. 340–320 B.C.
Bequest of Mrs. Arthur Croft. 01.8373

PROVENANCE: The Gardner Brewer Collection

DIMENSIONS AND CONDITION: Height: 16 cm; diameter neck: 1.5 cm; diameter upper flange of body: 9.4 cm; diameter body: 7.1 cm; diameter base: 9.8 cm
Unbroken. The added white of the wreath is quite worn.

SHAPE: An epichysis is an oil bottle, like a lekythos; although its beaked spout recalls oinochoai of shape 6, it is not a wine jug and is not properly classed as an oinochoe. For the various types of bottles, see the comments under cat. no. 119; compare the shape of cat. no. 122.

On the front shoulder, facing left, is a female head wearing a kekryphalos, earrings, necklace, and radiate stephane, the jewelry all in white. A rosette is in the field at left.

There are rays on the lower neck. A wave-pattern runs around the flange on the shoulder, and a laurel wreath in added white circles the body below. On either side of the juncture of handle and shoulder are large coiling tendrils. Flanking the juncture of handle and spout are two modeled heads of indeterminate sex, apparently cast from a worn mold. On the bottom of the foot is a large X-shaped dipinto in pinkish wash.

30

30

EPICHYSIS

Attributed to the Liverpool Group (Padgett)
Ca. 340–320 B.C.
Gift of E. M. Raymond. 08.165

DIMENSIONS AND CONDITION: Height: 16.6 cm; diameter upper flange of body: 13.3 cm; diameter base: 12.7 cm
The tip of the spout is broken away; otherwise intact. A drop of added white has fallen on the palmette behind the youth.

SHAPE: Wider than the preceding vase, so that the body bears a closer resemblance to a pyxis of type C

On the shoulder, a female with a tympanum in her right hand and a nude youth with a thyrsos in his left hand and a phiale in the right are both seated to the left on low rocks. The woman wears a kekryphalos, necklace, earring, and bracelets, all in white, as well as a chiton. She turns her head to look back at the youth. He has a white fillet around his head and sits upon his cloak. A quadrated disk floats in the field at right.

Large enclosed palmettes are on either side of the handle, filling the rest of the shoulder. There are rays around the base of the neck and dotted egg-pattern around the shoulder flange. A small upright palmette is at the base of the handle, and there are two poorly cast heads of Silenos where the handle joins the spout. A delicate vine of ivy, with incised vine and yellow leaves and berries, runs around the body.

The shape and breadth, the incised ivy vine, the large enclosed palmettes, and the drawing of the woman's drapery indicate an origin within the Liverpool Group; compare Bonn 110 (*CVA* Bonn 3, pl. 30, 3–7); and Turin 4548 (*CVA* Torino 1, pl. 18, 2; *RVAp*, II, p. 638, no. 21/373). The Liverpool Group, associated with the Tarentine workshops of the Darius and Underworld Painters, comprises mostly smaller vessels: cups, jugs, pelikai, lebetes gamikoi, and epichyseis.

PUBLISHED: L. D. Caskey, *MFA AnnRep* 1908, p. 62.

31

31

31

OX-HEAD RHYTON
Ca. 350–325 B.C.
Gift of Henry P. Kidder. 80.590

DIMENSIONS AND CONDITION: Height: 20.0 cm; diameter upper rim: 8.5 cm; diameter outer edge rim: 9.5 cm; smallest diameter body: 5.4 cm; width across ears: 11.2 cm; width across handle and body: 10.3 cm; depth of head (skull to throat): 7.4 cm
Breaks and mends on the forehead and near the mouth are painted to match the original color. The right horn and left ear are rejoined; the right ear and left horn are restored.

SHAPE: The tall cup is wheel-thrown and has a strap handle with lateral ridges. The lip has a flaring ovolo molding below a fillet. There is no hole in the mouth.

The hair between the horns is modeled in relief. There are traces of white slip, but both head and cup are otherwise undecorated.

Undecorated rhyta, probably made specifically for funerary purposes, are at least as numerous as painted rhyta; compare cat. no. 33, and see Hoffmann, *Tarentine*, pls. 54–57. Although Apulian rhyta are in the tradition of Attic ceramic rhyta and both series have their own internal development, both are generally considered to imitate vessels of gold and silver. For a full discussion of Attic and Apulian rhyta, see H. Hoffmann, in *Greek Vases in the J. Paul Getty Museum* 4 (Malibu, 1989), pp. 131–166. For a silver deer's-head rhyton from Apulia, see Hoffmann, p. 156, fig. 23.

PUBLISHED: Robinson, *Catalogue*, p. 170, no. 469; Hoffmann, *Tarentine*, p. 23, no. 100 (C 3).

EXHIBITED: Brockton Art Center, *The Ancient Mediterranean*, p. 50, no. 71; Danforth Museum, Framingham, Mass., "The Mediterranean World," September 1977–March 1978.

32

32

32

DEER'S-HEAD RHYTON
Ca. 350–325 B.C.
Gift of Henry P. Kidder. 80.591

PROVENANCE: From Chiusi

DIMENSIONS AND CONDITION: Height from plane of rim to underside of jaw: 19.8 cm; width of head, ear to ear: 6.5 cm; diameter top of rim: 8.4 cm; diameter base of body above animal head: 2.6 cm; diameter body at central band: 5.5 cm; depth at base of body, including handle: 5.0 cm; length from back of rim to tip of nose: 21.7 cm
The head has been broken and repaired. The left part of the muzzle and part of the right horn are restored.

SHAPE: Grooved moldings articulate the lip and divide the cup into three sections. The tall, tapering lower section of the cup is an unusual feature, as is the way it stands up vertically, away from the small, slightly convex strap handle with lateral ridges, an arrangement recalling much earlier Attic bent rhyta on stands.

The entire vase is glazed black. The head of the deer has short, stubby horns and a narrow muzzle. Hoffmann calls it an antelope's head; this may be correct, for the ears are quite short, but compare cat. no. 64. The shape may be unique; compare the deer's-head rhyton Louvre CA 457 (H. Hoffmann, *Greek Vases in the J. Paul Getty Museum* 4 [1989], p. 162, fig. 28).

PUBLISHED: Robinson, *Catalogue*, p. 111, no. 307; Hoffmann, *Tarentine*, p. 68, no. 416 (A 2), pl. 57, 7.

EXHIBITED: Corning Museum of Glass, Corning, N.Y., September 1 - November 15, 1956.

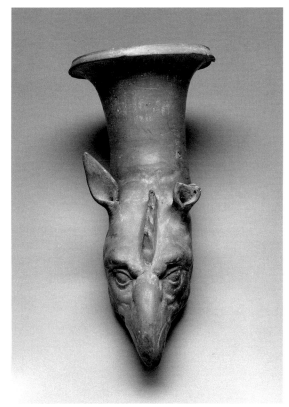

33

33

33

GRIFFIN'S-HEAD RHYTON
Ca. 350–325 B.C.
Henry Lillie Pierce Residuary Fund. 00.361

PROVENANCE: E. P. Warren collection; from Ruvo

DIMENSIONS AND CONDITION: Height: 19.2 cm; upper diameter rim: 8.9 cm; maximum diameter: 9.5 cm; diameter at narrowest point of body: 4.6 cm
Half of the left ear is broken off; otherwise intact.

SHAPE: The wheel-thrown cup is more flaring and trumpet-like than that of the ox-head rhyton, cat. no. 31. The spiky comb, added freehand, is slightly askew.

Unglazed. The lip has an ovolo molding, but no painted patternwork. Like the preceding ox- and deer's-head examples, griffin's-head rhyta were more often decorated in red-figure. For an unglazed example, compare London WT 317: Hoffmann, *Tarentine*, pl. 56, 7.

PUBLISHED: E. Robinson, *MFA AnnRep* 1900, p. 72, no. 29; Hoffmann, *Tarentine*, p. 75, no. 452 (C 7), pl. 56, 5: "Early Group."

34

GUTTUS IN THE SHAPE OF A YOUNG SATYR'S HEAD
2nd half of 4th century B.C.
Gift of Dr. and Mrs. Jerome M. Eisenberg. 1990.350

DIMENSIONS AND CONDITION: Height: 8.9 cm; width: 9.1 cm; diameter mouth: 1.8 cm; diameter rim: 3.0 cm; diameter neck: 1.6 cm
The top of the right ear is restored.

The face is mold-made, with the ears attached separately. The beardless young satyr is grimacing, with knitted brows and deep creases around the mouth and cheeks. The flesh parts are unpainted, but an ocher wash heightens the reddish tone of the clay. Black glaze was used for the hair, eyebrows, irises, and inner mouth; added white for the teeth and the whites of the eyes. The hair is modeled only over the forehead.

Gutti of this type are rare; the closest parallel is Malibu 81.AE.162, in the shape of a young Pan's head: Andre Emmerich Gallery, Inc., *Art of Ancient Italy: Etruscans, Greeks and Romans* (New York, 1970), p. 44, no. 69. A somewhat larger guttus in the Tampa Museum of Art (86.223) is in the shape of a female African's head: Münzen und Medaillen A.G., *Italische Keramik*, Sonderliste U (Basel, Nov. 1984), pp. 60–61, no. 106. Another in the Costantini collection, in the Antiquarium of the Museo Civico in Fiesole, takes the form of a woman's head: *CVA*

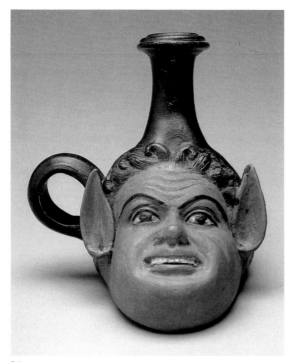

34

34

Fiesole 2, pl. 35, 5–6; V. Saladino in C. Salvianti, ed., *La collezione Costantini* (Milan, 1985), pp. 68 (color illus.), 88 (no. 46), 103–104 (no. 46). The Boston and Malibu gutti, which have been identified as Apulian, have also been considered Etruscan, particularly because of Etruria's rich tradition of sculptural vases; compare for example, the grotesque mask on a miniature jug formerly in the art market: Andre Emmerich Gallery Inc., *Classical Art from a New York Collection* (New York, 1977), no. 46. In fact, however, several points argue in favor of the former ascription. Normal Etruscan gutti (i.e., with rounded body and feet) seem to be late; M.-O. Jentel dates them (with much hesitation) to the third century; *Les Gutti et les askoi à reliefs étrusques et apuliens: Essai de classification et de typologie* (Leiden, 1976), pp. 48–49. This piece and the vividly painted woman in Fiesole, however, seem to belong to the period of red-figure vase-painting in the fourth century. The mouth, moreover, is the stepped Apulian variety rather than the concave collar seen in the Etruscan gutti, and the handle is convex, as in Apulia, rather than strap-like or corded, as in Etruria; see Jentel, *Gutti*, passim. The grimacing satyr and Pan on these unusual figural vases have as much in common with an apotropaic Medusa head (ibid., p. 295, AP III, 7a, fig. 152) as they do with the most hard-faced of the silenoi on conventional Apulian gutti (ibid., p. 273, AP II, 1g, fig. 139). A black-glazed guttus in the form of a bearded satyr's head, said to be from Asia Minor and having a slender vertical spout and a ring handle at the top of the head, was recently in the New York art market (Antiquarium, Ltd.).

PUBLISHED: J. M. Padgett, *MFA AnnRep* 1989–90, pp. 24–25, illus.

35

35

35

Column-krater
Attributed to the Laterza Painter
Ca. 350–340 B.C.
Gift of Thomas G. Appleton. 76.66

DIMENSIONS AND CONDITION: Height: 45.0 cm; diameter rim: 34.5 cm; width across handles: 40.7 cm; diameter neck: 20.0 cm; diameter body: 26.9 cm; diameter stem: 7.6 cm; diameter foot: 14.2 cm
Apparently unbroken. There is considerable repainting on the foot and on the figures and ivy vine on side B, which may mask old breaks or wear.

SHAPE: This krater has a more tapering body than cat. no. 25, and although it is shorter, the neck is proportionately much taller. The echinus foot has a fascia at top.

A: Dionysos and a maenad are walking to the right; each carries a thyrsos, the god's having a long fillet tied to it. Dionysos holds a phiale full of offerings in his left hand; the maenad looks back at him and offers him the wreath in her extended right hand. He wears a yellow fillet and a cloak draped over both arms; she wears a chiton, shoes, a necklace of yellow pendants, yellow bracelets on each arm, and a kekryphalos. The field is filled with rosettes, a fillet, and

ivy leaves. A small plant grows from the rocky groundline.

B: Two youths in himatia and holding staffs in their right hands stand in conversation. Rosettes and a writing tablet with stylus are in the field above them; on either side are tall palmette scrolls.

There are crude tongues on top of the rim and black palmettes on the tops and sides of the handle-plates. The outer rim features a herringbone on the obverse and a zigzag on the reverse. The panels on either side of the neck are painted with large ivy vines and clusters of berries. The pictures have lateral frames of degenerate ivy, upper frames of tongues, and lower frames consisting of groups of stopt maeanders to left alternating with dotted cross-squares.

The Laterza Painter was a close follower of the Snub-Nose Painter and, like him, painted mostly Dionysiac and genre scenes on bell-kraters and a variety of other large shapes, including column-kraters. Both painters worked in the Plain-style tradition of the Dijon Painter.

PUBLISHED: Robinson, *Catalogue*, p. 178, no. 491; *RVAp*, I, p. 330, no. 12/122, pl. 105, 3–4.

36

COLUMN-KRATER
Attributed to the Varrese Painter
Ca. 355–345 B.C.
Gift of Nathan Appleton. 92.2648

PROVENANCE: Thomas G. Appleton collection

DIMENSIONS AND CONDITION: Height: 50.4 cm; diameter rim: 34.5 cm; diameter body: 32.0 cm; diameter foot: 15.6 cm
Most of the rim and large parts of the handle-plates are restored in plaster, with extensive repainting of the wave-pattern and palmettes. On both sides of the neck, the ivy is partially repainted.

SHAPE: Close to the preceding vase, but with a more concave neck

A: At left and right are seated youths, the one at the left holding a tall branch in his left hand, and the other with a yellow kantharos in his right hand. Both are seated on bundles of clothes and are nude except for a yellow fillet and a broad yellow belt, an item of native Italic dress. In the center stands a woman holding a basket of white and yellow loaves in her raised left hand and an oinochoe, half yellow and half white, in her lowered right hand. She wears a chiton, kekryphalos, radiate fillet, earrings, necklace with yellow pendants, and white bracelets on each arm. In the field are two yellow fillets, three rosettes, and a wreath bedecked with a yellow fillet.

B: A boy holding a staff in his right hand faces two youths. All three wear himatia. In the field above are a quadrated disk and two filling ornaments in the form of paired jumping weights.

In the panels on either side of the neck are ivy vines and berries. There are black palmettes on the tops and sides of the handle-plates, a wave-pattern on the outer rim, and a laurel wreath on top of the mouth. The pictures have lateral frames of degenerate ivy and upper frames of tongues and dots. The groundlines consist of groups of stopt maeanders to right alternating with dotted cross-squares.

The Varrese Painter was a prolific and influential painter of midcentury, fond of bright colors and employing a stable of stock figures that reappear time and again on the over 200 vases attributed to him. He influenced a number of younger painters including the Wolfenbüttel and Metope Painters, the Painter of Louvre MNB 1148, and the Painter of Bari 12061.

PUBLISHED: E. Robinson, *MFA AnnRep* 1892, p. 16, no. 23; idem, *Catalogue*, pp. 177–178, no. 490; A. Cambitoglou, *AJA* 61 (1957), p. 112; A. D. Trendall, *Jahrbuch der Berliner Museen* 12 (1970), pp. 176 (no. 14), 178, fig. 13; *RVAp*, I, pp. 319, 345, no. 13/50; K. Schauenburg, *RM* 90 (1983), p. 346, note 56.

EXHIBITED: Corpus Christi, *Greek Vases*, p. 31, fig. 41.

37

SITULA (type 2)
Attributed to the Varrese Painter
Ca. 350–340 B.C.
Gift of Horace L. Mayer and Paul E. Manheim, by
exchange, and the Helen and Alice Colburn Fund.
1992.317

PROVENANCE: Hesperia Arts Auction, Ltd., *Egyptian, Near
Eastern and Classical Greek and Roman Antiquities* (New
York, November 27, 1990), no. 35

DIMENSIONS AND CONDITION: Height to top of ornament: 28.1
cm; height to rim: 26.3 cm; diameter rim: 23.5 cm; diameter
stem: 10.8 cm; diameter foot: 11.7 cm
Unbroken and in good condition; minor scratches; foot
chipped

SHAPE: Deep, with straight sides, a gradually tapering lower
body, and a broad ring foot in two degrees. The turned moldings of the rim consist of a fascia and fillet framing a band of
painted egg-pattern. The "handles" are stamped on the outside with a palmette pattern imitating metal prototypes, but
are not pierced to receive an actual bail handle. For the basic
shape, compare cat. no. 40, also of type 2.

A: Dionysos is seated on a rock or outcropping suggested by a row of white dots; similar dots indicate
the terrain throughout this scene and the one on the
reverse. Two maenads stand on either side of the
god, while at the right a nude satyr has fallen asleep
against a marble louterion. Dionysos is seated to the
right but turns to look at the maenad at the left, who
holds a phiale in her left hand and a pair of yellow
and white fillets in her right. The god's legs are covered by his himation, which has fallen about his
waist to reveal the upper body. His face, drawn in
three-quarter view, is framed by long curly hair and
a thick white fillet, loosely tied at the temples and
decorated with yellow dots. With his left hand he
rests his thyrsos on his lap and with his right holds
out his kantharos, its handles foreshortened, its body
tinted gold over the added white. A drip of glaze has
run down the god's right leg.

The maenad at the left wears a short mantle over a
chiton, the hem and central panel of which are decorated with crosshatching and white dots. Her hair is
tied in back into a tall chignon; the shoes, bracelets,
earrings, necklace, and radiate stephane are rendered
with added white. A dotted fillet hangs behind her at
the left. The maenad at the right leans on the louterion with her left arm, her left foot drawn up; she too
wears white earrings, necklace, and bracelets. The
chiton beneath her himation is plain, without crosshatching. Her hair is pulled back over a white fillet,
which has a small finial in front. In her left hand she
holds a thyrsos; with her right she extends toward

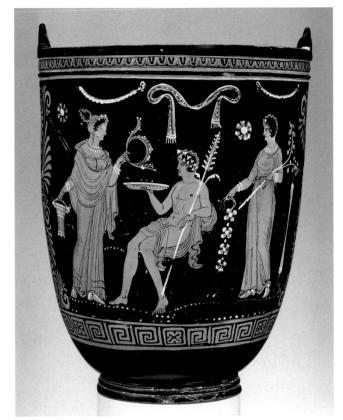

37 B

Dionysos a jug of wine, the fluting of its white body
drawn with dilute glaze. On the ground before her is
a phiale; farther left lies a tympanum.

The sleeping satyr props his head against the louterion with his right arm, his back padded by a himation. Only the context and the thyrsos leaning
against his leg identify him as a satyr, since the ears
and tail are not visible. The face and body are rendered in three-quarter view. A realistic touch is the
coarse black hair covering the chest and belly. He
wears white boots and a fillet identical to that of
Dionysos; the kantharos about to slip from his limp
fingers is also the same. The louterion is drawn with
added white, with the flutes of the stand and other
details in dilute glaze. In the background, arching
over the three right-hand figures like a trellis, is a
grapevine tinted with yellow and white.

B: In this more standardized scene, Dionysos is
seated between two standing maenads; the satyr is
gone and so is the grapevine. The god is seated to the
left, a phiale in his right hand and a thyrsos held
against his left shoulder. He is seated on a himation,
which lies across his lap without covering the genitals. Added white is used for the thyrsos and for the

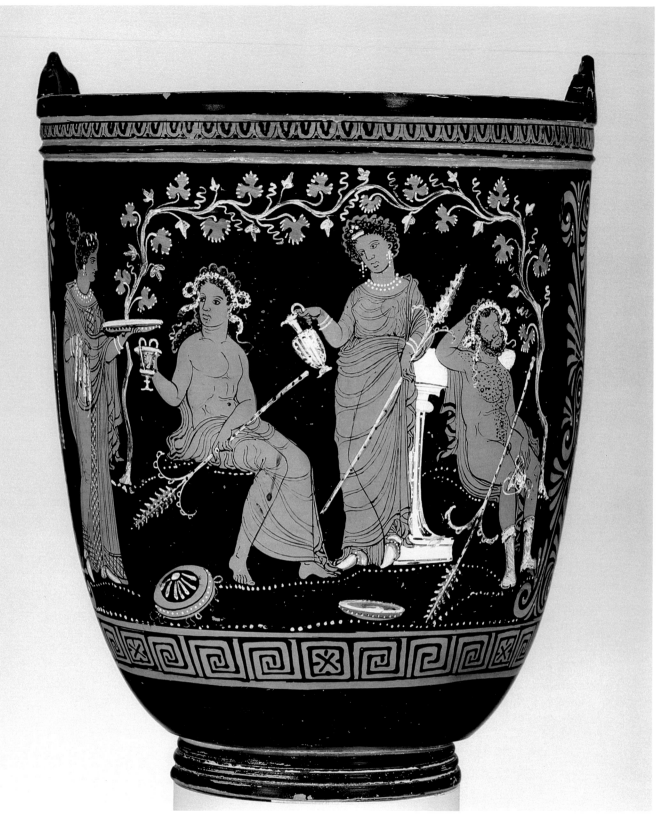

37 A

wreath of ivy on his head. The maenad facing him at the left turns toward him, a wreath in the raised left hand, a situla in the lowered right. She is jeweled and draped like the left-hand maenad on side A, but her chiton is plainer and she wears a kekryphalos. The maenad at the right, with shorter hair, wears a belted chiton without himation; shoes, necklace, earrings, and bracelets are in added white. The white dot on her forehead may indicate a fillet. A garland of white-petaled flowers hangs from her right hand, and in her left arm she cradles a branch with a pendant fillet. Floating in the upper field are a pair of rosettes, a cloth fillet, and two white fillets like those worn by Dionysos and the satyr on side A.

Below the faux handles on either side are two large, enclosed palmettes, their tips touching in the center, flanked by smaller, unenclosed palmettes and tendrils. The band circling the lower body consists of groups of three stopt maeanders to right, alternating with saltire-squares. Around the middle of the rim is a band of dotted egg-pattern. The interior is glazed.

According to Trendall and Cambitoglou (*RVAp*, I, p. 343), "this vase goes very closely in style with no. 34 [a nestoris in a Kiel private collection], and, like it, must be accounted one of the Varrese Painter's better works." Schauenburg compares the shape, ornament, and general style of another situla by the painter, Kiel B 776 (*RVAp*, Suppl. II, p. 89, no. 13/35a), which also has a grapevine over the main scene; see Schauenburg *JdI* 106 (1991), pp. 184–185, pl. 36, 1–3. The chiton of the female flute player on the Kiel situla has crosshatched decoration like that of the Boston maenad, as does the chiton of Helen on cat. no. 28; compare also the peplos of Hippodameia on British Museum F 331 (*RVAp*, I, p. 338, no. 13/5, pl. 109, 2). The situlae of the Group of the Dublin Situlae are not far removed in shape and style. For an example, see Galerie Günter Puhze, *Kunst der Antike*, Katalog 9 (Freiburg im Breisgau, 1991), no. 229; *RVAp*, Suppl. II, p. 105, no. 15/35b.

For South Italian situlae, see K. Schauenburg, *Meded* 43 (1981), pp. 83–89; idem, *RM* 88 (1981), pp. 107–116; idem, *AA* 1981, pp. 462–488; and A. D. Trendall, *NumAntCl* 19 (1990), pp. 117–134, particularly p. 119 and the bibliography on p. 127. For bronze and silver situlae of this type, see B. Barr-Sharrar, in Barr-Sharrar and Borza, *Macedonia and Greece*, pp. 127–130.

PUBLISHED: *RVAp*, I, p. 343, no. 13/35, pl. 111, 2–4; K. Schauenburg, *Meded* 43 (1981), pl. 25, 5–6; idem, *JdI* 106 (1991), p. 185, pl. 36, 4; *MFA AnnRep* 1991–92, p. 52; *RVAp*, Suppl. II, p. 86, no. 13/35.

38

VOLUTE-KRATER
Connected with the work of the Varrese Painter; it is a possible link between the works of the Gioia del Colle Painter and the Painter of Copenhagen 4223 and those of the Darius Painter.
Ca. 340 B.C.
Francis Bartlett Donation of 1900. 03.804

PROVENANCE: E. P. Warren collection; from Ceglie del Campo near Bari

DIMENSIONS AND CONDITION: Height: 124.6 cm; diameter: 56.0 cm
Reassembled from fragments, with only a few small lacunae; the bulge in the right horse of the chariot on the neck is probably due to an air bubble in firing.

SHAPE: Although the size is monumental, the shape is not remarkably different from that of the earlier volute-krater by the Iliupersis Painter, cat. no. 21; the foot and neck, however, are proportionately taller.

A: The death of Thersites. All the principal figures are labeled with incised inscriptions. Rows of white and yellow dots indicating groundlines run throughout the scene on several levels. Achilles (ΑΧΙΛΛΕΥΣ) and the aged Phoenix (ΦΟΙΝΙΞ) are shown at the center within the pavilion of Achilles, an airy structure with a pediment, palmette akroteria, and slender, fluted Aeolic capitals. In the center of the pediment is a slender figure with upraised arms, like the kouros-handle of a patera. The side of the pavilion's floor is decorated with a labyrinthine maeander and saltire-squares. The row of squares above the architrave resembles a Doric frieze but may represent the ends of the ceiling joists. Achilles is seated on a luxurious kline, his cloak beneath him, holding a spear in his right hand and leaning on a pile of cushions, which, like the mattress and coverlets, are elaborately embroidered. Long ringlets frame the hero's face, drawn in three-quarter view. A sword, presumably that just used to decapitate Thersites (ΘΕΡΣΙΤΑΣ), hangs at his side from a white baldric. Phoenix leans on his staff and holds his head in worry. His himation is pulled up over his head; his legs are crossed. The front of the couch is painted white, perhaps to indicate ivory. Its vine decoration is yellow, as is the broad footstool, decorated with egg-pattern. Two chariot wheels, a pair of greaves, a sword, a shield with a gorgoneion device, and a plumed pilos-helmet, all yellow, hang from the ceiling of the pavilion. The decapitated body of Thersites, in shoes and disheveled himation, lies in front of the pavilion. The eyes in the liberated head are shut in death; the

38

ΦΟΙΝΙΞ   ΑΧΙΛΛΕΥΣ

ΘΕΡΣΙΤΑΣ

38

38

grizzled beard shows that Achilles has killed an older man.

Other heroes and divinities are on either side. Agamemnon (ΑΓΑΜΕΜΜΩΝ) approaches from the left, holding a scepter with an eagle finial in his right hand. He wears an embroidered, long-sleeved tunic, embades, and a swirling himation. Agamemnon is followed by the younger Phorbas (ΦΟΡΒΑΣ), who wears embades, a chlamys, and a yellow pilos, and rests a spear on his left shoulder. To the right, Diomedes (ΔΙΟΜΗΔΗΣ), the cousin of Thersites, wearing a chlamys and a white pilos, rushes up to avenge his kinsman. He is accompanied by an Aetolian warrior (ΑΙΤΩΛΟΣ) with a spear, sword baldric, and yellow shield. Diomedes starts to draw his sword, but is restrained by Menelaos (ΜΕΝΕΛΑΟΣ). Menelaos wears a chlamys and has a sword slung at his left side.

In the upper tier are four figures. At the left of the pavilion are Pan (ΠΑΝ) and a seated, winged figure like a Fury, labeled ΠΟΙΝΑ (Vengeance). The Fury wears an embroidered chiton with a white belt, crossed bandoleers, tall boots, and a necklace. White snakes twine in her hair. Her face is in three-quarter view. In her right hand she holds a sword; in her left, a scabbard and spear. Pan is leaning against a tree, a spotted animal skin over his shoulders and a wreath on his horned head. He holds his yellow-brown pedum in his right hand. In the field above is a rosette.

To the right of the building Athena (ΑΘΑΝΑ) sits on a round, yellow shield, wearing chiton, himation, yellow shoes, and white diadem, aegis, bracelets, earrings, and necklace. In front of her, Hermes (ΕΡΜΑΣ) stands with his legs crossed, wearing winged shoes, chlamys, and wreath. He carries his yellow caduceus and petasos in his left hand and a tall branch with a pendant fillet in his right. At the lower left, the helmeted Automedon, wearing a chlamys, kneels with a shield on his left arm and a spear in his right hand, as if guarding the mutilated Thersites. In the foreground and around Automedon (Α[ ]ΤΟΜΕΔΩΝ) and the dead man are objects testifying to the violent action: a broken lustral basin, a tripod, a staff, a footbath, and a variety of metal vases, including two phialai, a kantharos, an oinochoe, and a volute-krater. To the right, a slave or commoner (ΔΜΩΣ), wearing boots and a cloak over his left arm, runs off in horror. Many of the larger yellow objects, like shields, are toned so that more of the white underpainting shows through at either the forward or upper edge to suggest the play of light.

As told in the *Aethiopis*, Thersites was slain in a fit of temper by Achilles, for teasing him about his ill-

38

38

38

38

fated love for the Amazon queen Penthesilea. The Greeks were angry and divided as a result of this brutal act, and Achilles had to sail to Lesbos and sacrifice to Apollo in order to appease his fellow leaders and warriors. The reaction of the character labeled Demos may allude to the revulsion among *hoi polloi*. The emotions aroused are well portrayed by the painter, who represented the anger of Agamemnon, the chagrin of Phoenix, the anguish of Diomedes, and the haughty nonchalance of Achilles. It is interesting that the Fury Poina, a character who turns up in several Apulian mythological scenes where bad business is at hand (cat. no. 42), has her sword drawn; in this context, she must represent the slashing vengeance of Achilles, the personification of his wrath. Trendall and Webster (*Illustrations*, pp. 106–107) suggest the scene may be based on the *Achilles Thersitoktonos* of Chaeremon, a fourth-century dramatist; this may be correct, but if so, the vase-painter has enlarged and elaborated on the stage version, with more protagonists than would be in any single scene.

B: A young man in a chlamys and holding a spear in his left hand stands beside a horse within a white-painted naiskos with a pediment and palmette akroteria. The naiskos has an elaborately decorated plinth (maeanders, lesbian cymatium, key-pattern, scrolling tendrils). There are three figures on either side, in two registers. At left, a seated woman with a phiale is offered a wreath by a wreathed youth leaning on a staff. Below them, a woman runs to the right with a yellow "xylophone" and a basket of offerings. On the right, a wreathed youth seated on his cloak and holding a staff and phiale faces a woman with a wreath in her left hand and a branch in her right. Below them, a wreathed youth with a basket of offerings in his left hand leans on his staff. He holds a flower in his right hand and has shoes and a cloak. All three women wear shoes, chiton, kekryphalos, earrings, bracelets, and necklace. Among the offerings in the baskets are alabastra painted yellow and white. Fillets and rosettes float in the upper field.

The similarity between the pavilion of Achilles on the obverse and the funerary naiskos on the reverse invites comparison between the dead horseman and the greatest of Greek heroes. Achilles was the very embodiment of *arete*, and that is the quality celebrated by the youth's monument. He has joined the heroic dead and, like Odysseus, will see Achilles and the other Homeric heroes in the Underworld. For horsemen as heroes and demigods, see A. Cermanović-Kuzmanović et al., *LIMC*, VI, 1, pp. 1019–1081, especially p. 1025; VI, 2, pls. 673–719.

38

On the obverse neck, in three-quarter view to the left, is the quadriga of Helios, surrounded by a white, yellow, and red nimbus. The god holds a whip in his right hand and is dressed in a long chiton. His presence is an appropriate symbol of renewal and rebirth on a funerary vase; if he is to be associated with the scene below, it may mean that the action there takes place in the morning, with the first rays of the sun revealing the body of the murdered man.

On the reverse neck, Eros is seated on a flower, wearing bracelets, shoes, anklets, necklace, and sakkos; he holds a phiale in his left hand. Elaborate floral ornament and scrolling tendrils, highlighted with added white and yellow, surround both Helios and Eros. The composition with Eros recalls similar scenes on vases of the Alabastra Group and others associated with it; see *RVAp*, II, pls. 232 (5 and 8) and 233 (1–3). For the floral ornament, see the comments on cat. no. 21.

There are two registers of elaborate palmettes under the handles. The latter have plastic female masks on the volutes and black swan's heads on the shoulders. Sprigs of white laurel decorate the obverse handle flanges. A wreath of grape leaves and clusters runs around the foot.

Above both pictures is a double band of egg-pattern. A band consisting of groups of stopt maeanders to left alternating with cross-squares circles the lower body. A band of egg-pattern circles the lip. Below the obverse lip are an ivy vine, a yellow bead-and-reel molding, and a laurel wreath with a central rosette. Below the reverse lip are a laurel wreath, a row of dots, and a band of rosettes.

PUBLISHED: M. Mayer, *NdS* 1900, pp. 509–511; E. Robinson, *MFA AnnRep* 1903, p. 73, no. 70; J. M. Paton, *AJA* 9 (1905), pp. 82–83; idem, *AJA* 12 (1908), pp. 406–416 (figs. 1–2), pl. 19; E. Buschor, *Griechische Vasenmalerei* (Munich, 1914), pp. 216–217, fig. 160; C. Robert, *Archaeologische Hermeneutik: Anleitung zur Deutung Klassischer Bildwerke* (Berlin, 1919), pp. 278–282, figs. 213–214; L. Séchan, *Études sur la tragédie grecque dans ses rapports avec la céramique* (Paris, 1926), pp. 527–530, fig. 156; G. M. A. Richter, *Ancient Furniture: A History of Greek, Etruscan and Roman Furniture* (Oxford, 1926), p. 65, fig. 170; K. Schefold, *Untersuchungen zu den kertscher Vasen* (Berlin and Leipzig, 1934), p. 135; O. Antonsson, *The Praxiteles Marble Group in Olympia* (Stockholm, 1937), pp. 125–126, fig. 16; M. J. Milne, *AJA* 48 (1944), p. 55, no. 29; A. W. Pickard-Cambridge, *The Theatre of Dionysus in Athens* (Oxford, 1946), pp. 87, 89–90, no. 9, fig. 17; J. D. Beazley, *AJA* 54 (1950), p. 322; Chase, *Antiquities*, pp. 98–100, fig. 114; M. Schmidt, *Der Dareiosmaler und sein Umkreis: Untersuchungen zur spätapulischen Vasenmalerei* (Münster Westf., 1960), pp. 41 (note 59), 59; Brommer, *Vasenlisten*, 1960, p. 263, no. D 1; E. Paribeni, *EAA*, IV, pp. 1021–1022; MFA, *Gods and Heroes*, 1962, pp. 89–90, fig. 78; Ginouvès, *Balaneutikè*, pp. 65, 173 (note 3), 316 (note 1); K. Schauenburg, *AntK* 5 (1962), p. 58, note 80, pl. 20; idem, *RM* 69 (1962), p. 32, no. 78 (with ref. to idem, *BJb* 161, 1961, 220); G. Schneider-Herrmann, *BABesch* 37 (1962), pp. 42 (note 8), 48; Chase and Vermeule, *Greek, Etruscan and Roman Art*, pp. 140–141, 151, fig. 130; Ch. Hofkes-Brukker, *BABesch* 38 (1963), p. 67, note 86; Hamdorf, *Kultpersonifikationen*, p. 121, no. 491b; MFA, *Trojan War*, fig. 31; Taranto, *Letteratura*, p. 28, no. 163; G. M. A. Richter, *The Furniture of the Greeks, Etruscans, and Romans* (London, 1966), p. 51, fig. 284; Webster, *Tragedy and Satyr-Play*, p. 74, TV 2; J. Engemann, *Architekturdarstellungen des frühen zweiten Stils* (*RM*, Ergänzungsheft 12, Heidelberg, 1967), pp. 85–86, pl. 61, 5; H. Kyrieleis, *Throne und Klinen* (*JdI*, Ergänzungsheft 24, Berlin, 1969), p. 153, no. 42; M. Bonghi Jovino, in J. Bibauw, ed., *Hommages à Marcel Renard*, III (Collection Latomus 103) (Brussels, 1969), p. 75, note 2; C. Collard, *JHS* 90 (1970), p. 26; C. Letta, *Piccola Coroplastica Metapontina nel Museo Archeologico Provinciale di Potenza* (Naples, 1971), p. 160, note 502; Trendall and Webster, *Illustrations*, pp. 106–107, no. III.4, 2; K. Schauenburg, *JdI* 87 (1972), pp. 281 (note 60), 289 (note 90); A. D. Trendall, *AJA* 76 (1972), p. 338; Brommer, *Vasenlisten*, 1973, p. 356, no. D 1; K. Schauenburg, *RM* 82 (1975), p. 212, note 39; Robertson, *History*, pp. 440, 698, note 211; G. Koch, *Die mythologischen Sarkophage 6: Meleager* (Die antiken Sarkophagreliefs, vol. 12, Berlin, 1975), p. 45, note 43; Schmidt, Trendall, and Cambitoglou, *Grabvasen*, p. 68, note 223; Smith, *Funerary Symbolism*, pp. 85, 259; L. P. B. Stefanelli, *ArchCl* 29 (1977), p. 365; Schneider-Herrmann, *Paterae*, pp. 19 (no. A 2, with additional bibliography), 21; *RVAp*, I, p. liii; J.-M. Moret, *RA* 1979, p. 246, note 180; Lohmann, *Grabmäler*, pp. 60 (note

451), 123 (note 983), 161 (note 1409), 194 (no. A 167), 313, 315; J. Chamay and A. Cambitoglou, *AntK* 23 (1980), p. 43, note 75; A. D. Trendall, *JHS* 100 (1980), p. 275; G. Arrigoni, *ArchCl* 33 (1981), p. 257, note 8; A. Kossatz-Deissmann, *LIMC*, I, 1, pp. 171–172 (no. 794, with additional bibliography), 200; I, 2, pl. 134; O. Touchefeu, ibid., I, 1, p. 267 (no. 61), 273–274; I, 2, pl. 198; U. Höckmann, *Boreas* 5 (1982), p. 85; L. Massei, in *Festschrift Arias*, p. 488, no. 104; *RVAp*, II, pp. 449, 472 (no. 17/75, with added bibliography), 475–476, 478, 492; *RVAp*, Suppl. I, p. 61, no. 17/75; J. Chamay, *AntK* 27 (1984), p. 148, note 12; K. Schauenburg, *JdI* 99 (1984), p. 149, note 57; H. Metzger, in E. Böhr and W. Martini, eds., *Studien zur Mythologie und Vasenmalerei: Konrad Schauenburg zum 65. Geburtstag am 16. April 1986* (Mainz, 1986), p. 161; K. Schauenburg, *RM* 93 (1986), p. 153, note 65; Aellen, Cambitoglou, and Chamay, *Peintre de Darius*, pp. 116–117 (note 6), 224 (note 40); Freytag gen. Löringhoff, *Giebelrelief*, pp. 139–140, 156, 294, no. E 85 (with additional references); A. Kossatz-Deissmann, *LIMC*, III, 1, p. 61, no. 48; H. A. Shapiro, ibid., p. 391; Trendall, *RVP*, p. 247, note 6; L. Giuliani, in M. Schmidt, ed., *Kanon: Festschrift Ernst Berger zum 60. Geburtstag am 26. Februar 1988 gewidmet* (*AntK*, Beiheft 15, Basel, 1988), p. 160, no. 12; K. Schauenburg, *JdI* 104 (1989), p. 41, note 87; Schefold and Jung, *Argonauten*, pp. 246 (fig. 222), 414; M. R. Jentoft-Nilsen and A. D. Trendall, *CVA* The J. Paul Getty Museum, Malibu 3 (Malibu, 1990), p. 10, under no. 77.AE.14; G. Zuntz, *AntK* 33 (1990), p. 106, note 70; K. Schauenburg, *AA* 1990, p. 466, note 90; J. Boardman, in *Festschrift Cambitoglou*, p. 61; N. Yalouris, *LIMC*, V, 1, p. 1010, no. 20; *RVAp*, Suppl. II, pp. 113, no. 17/75 (with additional bibliography), 146.

39

CALYX-KRATER
Close to the Darius Painter (Trendall); Close to the Hippolyte Painter (Padgett and Herrmann)
Ca. 345–335 B.C.
Gift of Edythe K. Shulman. 1985.897

PROVENANCE: Parke-Bernet Sale, *Catalogue*, 5 April 1963, p. 36, no. 99; estate of William Randolph Hearst; collection of H. I. H. Prince Albrecht of Prussia

DIMENSIONS AND CONDITION: Height: 41.0 cm; diameter rim: 41.8 cm; smallest diameter body: 22.2 cm; diameter cul: 24.7 cm; diameter stem: 6.4 cm; diameter foot: 17.9 cm
Unbroken

SHAPE: Standard Late Apulian type, with very wide rim, a slightly concave body, tall handles that curve in to almost touch the sides, a cul tapering to a narrow stem, and a tall spreading foot, separated from the stem by a fillet

A: At the center, Dionysos is seated on his cloak and leaning against some striped cushions. He wears a bracelet and holds a phiale in his right hand. In his left hand he holds a thyrsos with a yellow shaft and a tip in added red and brown. He is crowned by a flying Eros, who holds a smaller phiale. Eros wears a kekry-

39

phalos and yellow bracelets and anklets. A dappled fawn, its pelt tinted with brown dilute glaze, reclines next to Dionysos and looks back toward the god. A maenad, wearing a diaphanous dotted chiton, bracelets, and earrings, and a necklace with white pendants, dances at the right. She carries a thyrsos in her left hand and a torch with a trailing fillet in her right. A feline skin, which is colored with added red on one side and added yellow on the other, dangles from her left arm. At the left, a young Pan is laying a calyx-krater decorated with figures in added yellow at the god's feet. The animal skin pinned at the satyr's throat flies in the wind behind him. A phiale and a white lyre with yellow details lie in the foreground on either side of a small grotto with a rocky border. Ivy hangs from the upper frame, and a rosette floats in the field at the upper left. The terrain throughout is indicated by short groundlines of yellow dots.

B: A young satyr, standing to the right with his left foot on a yellow rock, holds out in his right hand a white kantharos with yellow shading and in his left a wreath and yellow fillet. He offers them to a female seated on a rock, who holds a large phiale in her right hand; in her lowered left hand is a long laurel branch with a pendant fillet. She wears a chiton, shoes, earrings, bracelets, a kekryphalos, and a necklace with white pendants. The satyr wears a yellow fillet and shoes. Two fillets and a "window" fill the field at the top, and a laurel bush grows at the left, behind the satyr. A row of yellow dots represents the groundline.

A wreath of laurel circles the vase below the lip. The lower frame on side A consists of rosettes with yellow centers over a band of egg-pattern; on side B, there are linked maeanders to left, with a dotted cross-square in the center.

The Hippolyte Painter was a forerunner of the Darius Painter. Very few vases have been attributed to him or to his associate the Laodamia Painter. Compare the decorated krater, the diaphanous chiton of Ariadne, the scattered implements, thick white fillets, and subsidiary ornament of the painter's calyx-krater in Basel (BS 468: *RVAp*, II, p. 480, no. 18/13, pl. 170, 3–4).

PUBLISHED: *RVAp*, II, p. 507, no. 18/111 (with ref. to *Verschiedener Deutscher Kunstbesitz* [Sale Catalogue, no. 145, Graupe, Berlin, 27–29 May 1935], no. 926, pl. 85, 2, and also as ex Hearst Estate 3973); *MFA AnnRep* 1985–86, pp. 29 (illus.), 48; *RVAp*, Suppl. II, p. 137, no. 18/111 (as 1985.397).

39

39

40

SITULA (type 2)
Attributed to the Group of Copenhagen 4223
Ca. 340–330 B.C.
Gift of Dr. and Mrs. Jerome M. Eisenberg. 1991.242

PROVENANCE: Sotheby's Sale, London, July 13, 1987, lot 308,
2 color illus.; Galerie Günter Puhze, *Kunst der Antike*, Katalog 6 (Freiburg, 1985), p. 22, no. 226, color plate, and black-
white view of side B

DIMENSIONS AND CONDITION: Height (total): 30.6 cm; height
to rim: 26.4 cm; diameter rim: 24.1 cm; diameter stem: 12.4
cm; diameter foot: 13.2 cm
Unbroken. The added color of the horse's body and the shields
has largely flaked off.

SHAPE: Thick-walled and heavy; the shape is essentially the
same as the earlier situla of type 2, by the Varrese Painter (cat.
no. 37), but the body is more swelling and less straight-sided,
and the handles are taller. The grooved black foot is separated
from the lower body by a flange and a broad reserved band.
The interior is glazed.

A: Amazonomachy. A mounted Amazon is attacking a Greek foot soldier, who advances from the
right. The Amazon wears a short chiton, red trousers, a red, long-sleeved tunic, a belt with black and
white dots, a red Phrygian cap, crossed bandoleers,
and, over the left arm, a short cloak that blows out
behind her. With her left hand she holds the reins of
her rearing steed and with the right hand levels a
long spear. The white body of the horse is tinted yellow in places. The Greek is nude save for embades, a
Corinthian helmet of Italic type (worn on top of the
head), and a chlamys that blows out behind him. He
carries a shield and two short spears in his left hand,
a longer spear in his right. The handle of the sword
hanging at his hip is yellow, the hilt white. The yellow scabbard has a white tip. The helmet and damaged shield are shaded from dark yellow at the edges
to white at their central convexity; the black curls on
the shield are not from the warrior and would have
been covered by the added white. A small plant in
added yellow, white, and brown grows between his
feet. Collapsed on the ground between the two combatants is a dying Amazon, dressed like her mounted
compatriot but without a cap. Her axe and pelta have
fallen beside her. She struggles to her knees, her face
hidden, with red blood pouring from her head and
side. Above, a small Nike flies toward the Greek to
bestow a red and white wreath and red fillet. She
wears white shoes and a kekryphalos, and a long chiton with red hem that distinguishes her from the far
more numerous Erotes in Apulian vase-painting;
compare the Eros crowning Dionysos on the previ-

40

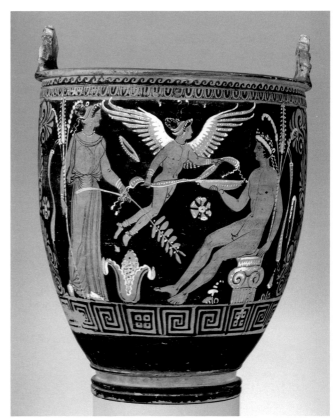

40

ous vase, cat. no. 39. The combatants may be Achilles and Penthesilea, since ordinary Greeks in combat with Amazons do not receive such honors.

B: A woman in a chiton, kekryphalos, and white shoes stands to the right holding a yellow thyrsos with a pendant fillet in her right hand and a laurel branch in her left. She wears bracelets, a necklace, and earrings, all in yellow. At her feet is a large budding acanthus with a yellow center. Before her, an Eros wearing bracelets, earrings, anklets, necklace, kekryphalos, and shoes flies to the right to offer a fillet to a nude youth, who is seated to the left on an Ionic capital. The youth wears a thick yellow fillet with a row of triple dots along its top edge. He holds a phiale in his right hand and a thyrsos with pendant fillet in the left. A rosette and a phiale (?) float in the field. Small plants grow below the youth.

There are elaborate palmettes and tendrils beneath the handles. The broad, circling groundline consists of groups of paired maeanders to right alternating with dotted cross-squares. Below the rim are two bands of ornament: wave-pattern above and dotted egg-pattern below. There is added red in the interstices of the palmettes on the handles.

The Painter of Copenhagen 4223 was a painter of ornate volute-kraters in the generation immediately before the Darius Painter. Compare a situla by the painter, formerly in the New York market, which may also represent Achilles and Penthesilea (*RVAp*, Suppl. I, p. 66, no. 17/54b; D. von Bothmer, *Arts in Virginia* 23:3 [1983], p. 35, fig. 18). The Boston situla may be by the painter himself. For Apulian situlae, see comments on cat. no. 37.

PUBLISHED: *MFA AnnRep* 1990–91, p. 48; *RVAp*, Suppl. II, p. 130, no. 17/54d, pl. 31, 2; ibid., p. 491, no. 17/54b is not in Boston.

41

CALYX-KRATER
Attributed to the Darius Painter
Ca. 340–330 B.C.
Gift of Esther D. Anderson, Edith and Harvey Bundy, Suzanne Dworsky, Leon Levy, Josephine L. Murray, Maurice Tempelsman, Emily T. and Cornelius C. Vermeule, Shelby White, Florence and Leonard Wolsky; and John H. and Ernestine A. Payne Fund. 1987.53

DIMENSIONS AND CONDITION: Height: 63.5 cm; diameter rim: 58.5 cm; minimum diameter body: 33.2 cm; diameter cul: 35.3 cm; diameter stem: 8.4 cm; diameter foot: 24.3 cm
The vase has been reconstructed from large fragments. Some figures have undergone minor restorations to fill gaps. Part of the face of the Fury is missing. Abrasions in the figure of Artemis have been retouched.

SHAPE: Compare cat. no. 39: the body is proportionately taller (the handles reach only halfway up) and is slightly more concave.

A: The exposure of the baby Aigisthos. The figures are arranged in two tiers: divine and semidivine figures above, mortals below. Thyestes (ΘΥΕΣΤΗΣ), dressed in a long-sleeved tunic, a chiton cinched with a broad white belt, a chlamys pinned at the throat, and a pilos with two white dots, hands over his infant son, Aigisthos (ΑΙΓΙΣΘΟΣ), to a hunter to be exposed. His white staff has fallen by his legs. The baby has a red blanket, a bracelet, a string of white charms across his chest, and a fillet tying up his hair. He holds a yellow rectangular object with handle in his left hand. The huntsman wears a bordered chlamys pinned with a white brooch; his two spears stand at the left. Adrastos (ΑΔΡΑΣΤΟΣ), king of Sikyon, stands at the center, gesturing at Thyestes, as though telling him not to hold back. He wears laced shoes and a himation and with his left hand holds a dotted scepter with a white eagle on top. His queen, Amphithea (ΑΜΦΙΘΕΑ), comforts Pelopeia (ΠΕΛΟΠΕΙΑ), daughter of Thyestes and mother of Aigisthos, at the right. Both women wear chitons, bracelets, earrings, and necklaces. The queen has a radiate white diadem and white shoes, while Pelopeia wears a fillet, sandals, and a red belt. As is fitting, the queen's garments are more richly embroidered. Behind Adrastos is an elaborate white (i.e., ivory) throne with a red cushion and a band of red ornament. At the right, between the king and Pelopeia, a necklace hangs from a laurel branch. At the far right, behind Amphithea, is a laurel branch.

From left to right in the register above are five divinities and personifications important to the entire saga. Artemis stands with a bow and arrows in her right hand and an arrow in her left. She wears a short chiton with a broad belt, a tunic with long, spotted sleeves, a white necklace, and a fillet that ties her hair in a chignon. A quiver hangs on her back. Facing Artemis is a little Pan, holding a raised white club in his left hand and a white shell in his right; a bow and quiver hang from the club. He has hairy goat's legs and tall white horns that contrast with the curve of the yellow bow. Apollo is seated to left, his head turned toward the Fury standing at the right. The god holds a large white swan perched on his right thigh and a laurel branch in his left hand. Above him is a yellow sun symbol and below him is a leopard or cheetah. Apollo is wearing a wreath, high boots, and

41 (Color Plate x)

41

41

41

a cloak that cushions his seat and lies across his thighs. The winged Fury leans on the spear in her right hand, her legs crossed, as she looks down on the act of attempted infanticide. She wears a peplos, a broad belt with white circles, a cloak hanging over both shoulders, a tunic with long, spotted sleeves, a necklace, white fillet, embades with yellow liners, a sword and scabbard, and crossed bandoleers with white spots. Yellow snakes twine about her hair. Beyond her at the right, Sikyon (ΣΙΚΥΩΝ), personified by a nude youth, sits on a pair of white Doric columns and holds a scepter with a floral finial in his left hand. In the field above Sikyon and Pan are white bucrania with yellow horns. To the right of Sikyon is a yellow sun symbol. The names of Sikyon and all the figures in the lower register are clearly incised. Some of the larger white objects (the throne, Thyestes' belt, Pan's club) have yellow shading over the added white.

B: Five Dionysiac figures are standing or seated in two registers. Dionysos is seated at the lower center with a thyrsos in his left hand and a phiale on his outstretched right. He wears yellow shoes and a himation that has fallen about his waist. A thick, spotted, yellow fillet is braided in his hair. At the left is a maenad wearing a chiton, shoes, kekryphalos, earrings, bracelets, and necklace, and holding a thyrsos in her right hand and a wreath in her left. Her left foot rests upon a rock, before which grows a laurel bush. Next to this, by Dionysos's legs, is a cylindrical cista with yellow-shaded stripes. At the right is a satyr with a blazing torch in his right hand and a thyrsos in his left. He wears a yellow fillet, and a fawn skin dangles from his left arm. A yellow fillet flutters from his torch. Seated above, at left, is a satyr with a yellow fillet and holding a tympanum in his right hand. He looks across at the maenad at the upper right, who holds a laurel branch in her right hand and a basket of offerings (including a tall cake) in her left. She wears a chiton, necklace, earrings, bracelets, a fillet of white beads, and shoes. Hanging fillets frame the sides of both registers and fill the center of the upper field. A white alabastron with yellow shading lies near the upper satyr. Dotted groundlines define the terrain throughout.

A wreath of laurel circles the vase below the lip. Above each handle is a large palmette. The lower frame on side A consists of alternating lotuses and palmettes above a band of dotted egg-pattern; the reverse consists of groups of maeanders to left alternating with cross-squares with small squares in each quadrant. Below the maeander band is a band of blank eggs.

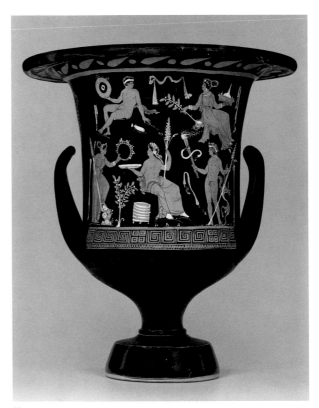

41

The iconography of the primary scene has been explored by Emily Vermeule (*PCPS* 1987; see reference below). The inspiration was probably a play, specifically Sophocles' lost *Thyestes in Sikyon*. No other representation of the subject is currently known. The gods are not mere onlookers here, for Artemis seems to be instructing Pan to find a goat to suckle the baby Aigisthos, who derives his name from his goatish nurse. The Fury, according to Vermeule, "is a pictorial comment on the future of the House of Atreus if Aigisthos should survive to kill Atreus and seduce his cousin Agamemnon's wife." Apollo is present because it was he who told Thyestes that only a child incestuously got from his daughter could be the instrument of his revenge on his brother Atreus. The youth representing Sikyon (where Adrastos would later found the Pythian Games in Apollo's honor) sits on columns that remind Vermeule of Pausanias's statement that tomb monuments in Sikyon take the form of pillars and pediments (Paus. 2.7.2), a possible funerary allusion on a vase that was perhaps made to be a grave offering. A more ominous allusion may be provided by the object held by the infant Aigisthos, which Vermeule interprets as "the hilt of the famous sword Pelopeia took from Thyestes on the night of their reunion. The baby should not have it yet, but the painter signs to us that this is Thyestes' own sword, and that it will be the true instrument of inheritance and revenge, the sword he will wear when sent by Atreus to kill his true father, the sword by which Thyestes will recognize him as his son, the sword Pelopeia will seize . . . to thrust it in her breast, the sword Aigisthos will take, still bloody, to kill Atreus . . . as Atreus sacrificed his brothers" (p. 127). The horrific sequel is represented on cat. no. 42, a Panathenaic amphora by the Darius Painter.

For the childhood of Aigisthos and the death of Atreus, see Apollodoros *Epitome* 2. 13–14; and Hyginus *Fabulae* 87–88. See also L. Séchan, *Études sur la tragédie grecque dans ses rapports avec la céramique* (Paris, 1926), pp. 199–213. For Aigisthos, see R. M. Gais, *LIMC*, I, 1, pp. 371–379; for Adrastos, I. Krauskopf, *LIMC*, I, 1, pp. 231–240; for Amphithea, G. Berger-Doer, *LIMC*, I, 1, p. 723.

Several stylistic and iconographic elements link the vase to other works by the Darius Painter: compare the Artemis and the Apollo-with-swan on a calyx-krater in a Miami private collection (Trendall, *Handbook*, fig. 205; *RVAp*, Suppl. II, p. 150, no. 18/65a, pl. 37, 2); and the Apollo-with-swan on the painter's name-vase in Naples (inv. 3253: *RVAp*, II, p. 495, no. 18/38; Trendall, *Handbook*, fig. 203). The Pan on the Florida vase is in the same position and posture as Sikyon, and the ornament is also similar, as is the scene on the reverse. The little Pan on the Boston krater has a parallel on the painter's calyx-krater in Matera (inv. 12538: *RVAp*, II, p. 501, no. 65), which also has the same subsidiary ornament; see F. G. Lo Porto, *MeditArch* 4 (1991), pl. 2. For the turned legs and ornament of Adrastos's throne, compare a pelike by the Darius Painter in the Macinagrossa collection, Bari (*RVAp*, II, p. 491, no. 18/29, pl. 175, 2).

For the relaxed Fury, compare the garb and posture of the one on Leningrad 4323 (*RVAp*, II, p. 487, no. 18/18, pl. 173, 2); for Furies in South Italian vase-painting, see H. Sarian, in *Iconographie classique et identités régionales* (*BCH*, Suppl. 14, 1986), pp. 25–35. For the grouping of Pelopeia and Amphithea, compare Hecuba and her attendant on London 1900.5–19.1 (*RVAp*, II, p. 489, no. 18/19, pl. 174, 1). For the necklace hanging from a branch, compare the Boston Alkmene krater, cat. no. 43.

The Darius Painter was perhaps the most talented and literate of all Apulian vase-painters. Recent years have seen a host of new vases by the Darius Painter with rare or unique mythological subjects, many of them apparently inspired by lost works of the great Athenian tragedians. This vase and the two following it are among the most splendid of the new mythological works; others include a calyx-krater with the daughters of Anios in a Miami private collection (see ref. above); a volute-krater at Princeton with Medea at Eleusis (inv. y1983–13: *RVAp*, Suppl. I, p. 78, no. 18/41a, pl. 12; A. D. Trendall, *Record of The Art Museum, Princeton University* 43:1 [1984], pp. 4–17); a loutrophoros at Princeton with the mourning Niobe (inv. y1989–29: *Record of The Art Museum, Princeton University* 49:1 [1990], p. 47; *RVAp*, Suppl. II, p. 149, no. 18/56b, pl. 36, 2–3); a loutrophoros in the New York (formerly Basel) Art Market (1992) with Kreousa at Delphi (K. Schauenburg, *AA* [1988], pp. 633–635, figs. 1–3; *RVAp*, Suppl. II, p. 149, no. 18/59c, pl. 37, 1); a volute-krater, also in the New York art market, with Dionysos in the Underworld (*RVAp*, Suppl. II, p. 508, no. 18/41a1); a large pelike in the Getty Museum, with the triumphant return of Andromeda (inv. 87.AE.23: *CVA*, Malibu 4, pls. 198–200; *RVAp*, Suppl. II, p. 151, no. 18/69a, pl. 38, 2); three volute-kraters in Berlin, one with the raid on the camp of Rhesus (1984.39), one with the rape of Persephone (1984.40), the third with Phrixos, Helle, and the ram (1984.41) (L. Giuliani, *Bildervasen aus Apulien* [Berlin, 1988], pp. 6–15; *RVAp*, Suppl. II, pp. 146–147, nos. 18/17a, 18/17b, 18/41b, pls. 35, 1–2, 4); and several major works in Swiss public and private collections (Aellen, Cambitoglou, and Chamay, *Peintre de Darius*, pp. 111–175; *RVAp*, Suppl. II, pp. 145–153, pls. 35–38).

PUBLISHED: A. D. Trendall, in Brijder, *Enthousiasmos*, p. 162; *MFA AnnRep* 1986–87, p. 51; E. Vermeule, *PCPS* 1987, pp. 124–133, 136–137, 146–148, fig. 1; C. C. Vermeule, in Museum of Fine Arts, Boston, *Art for Boston: A Decade of Acquisitions under the Directorship of Jan Fontein* (1987), pp. 72–73, color illus.; M. Conforti, *Museum News* 68, no. 5 (Sept./Oct. 1989), p. 39, illus.; Schefold and Jung, *Argonauten*, pp. 301–303 (fig. 258 bis), 415; K. Schauenburg, *JdI* 105 (1990), p. 91, note 66; *RVAp*, Suppl. II, pp. 8, 145, 151, no. 18/65c, pl. 37, 4; A. D. Trendall, in Rasmussen and Spivey, *Greek Vases*, pp. 174–176, fig. 72; J. M. Hemelrijk, ibid., p. 250.

42

AMPHORA
Attributed to the Darius Painter
Ca. 340–330 B.C.
Collection of Shelby White and Leon Levy and Gift
of the Jerome Levy Foundation. 1991.437

DIMENSIONS AND CONDITION: Height: 88.3 cm; width across
handles: 28.6 cm; diameter rim: 26.5 cm; diameter neck:
7.4 cm; diameter body: 38.8 cm; diameter stem 6.9 cm;
diameter foot: 19.0 cm
Broken and repaired, with some gaps filled with plaster; the
paintings are unrestored. Atreus's lower face is missing, as are
small portions of several other figures, including the head of
Io.

SHAPE: The shape is the standard Apulian Panathenaic type,
though somewhat larger than normal. Amphorae are frequently depicted standing on tombs, and it has been suggested
that their use was primarily funerary (J. R. Green, *Num-
AntCl* 20 [1991], p. 53). This is borne out in the case of this
amphora, which has a hole in the bottom, rendering it useless
as a container.

A, upper register: The death of Atreus. The throne of
Atreus stands frontally in the center; the murdered
king is sprawled upside down upon it, his legs over
one armrest and his head near the floor. His eyes are
closed in death, the bloody wound in his chest
marked by a splotch of red. The throne is largely
painted white, in imitation of ivory; the legs are not
turned, but flat, with cutouts on the sides, like the
legs of a kline. Among the patterns decorating the
throne are chevrons, palmettes, checkerboards, battlements, and a frieze of white figures on a black
ground. The cushion has a wave-pattern, and the
cloth hanging over the back is rendered in added red,
now quite worn. Atreus wears sandals, a himation,
and an elaborately embroidered chiton over a long-
sleeved tunic. His tall scepter leans next to the
throne; the finial is a yellow eagle, and there are
white dots on the shaft. The name of the king
(ΑΤΡΕΥΣ) is incised in the field above the throne.

Two groups of figures stand on dotted groundlines
to either side of the throne. At the left, Thyestes
(ΘΥΕΣΤΗΣ) runs away but looks back at his victim
through hooded eyes. He seems to sneer in disdain,
and a network of lines in diluted glaze give his face a
brutish cast. He wears a pilos, chiton, and chlamys,
the last pinned at the throat with a brooch. With his
right hand he holds up his sword, and with his left
clutches the yellow-tipped scabbard, its white cord
wrapped around his wrist. His son Aigisthos (ΑΓΙΣ-
ΘΟΣ) stands beside him at left, leaning on a tall spear,
whose pointed butt is painted yellow; the blade disappears in the upper frame. The sword in his left
hand is held in the stabbing position, unlike
Thyestes', which is held for thrusting. The yellow

42 (Color Plate XI)

and red scabbard (not striped, like Thyestes') hangs
at his side from a spotted baldric. His face is in three-
quarter view as he gazes at Pelopeia (ΠΕΛΟΠΕΙΑ),
his sister and mother. The unhappy princess stands
at far left, her face turned away from the terrible
sight, both hands raised in horror. She wears sandals, a chiton, and a himation pulled up behind her
head. Her jewelry consists of earrings, bracelets, a
necklace, and a beaded fillet, all in yellow. In the upper field, between Thyestes and Aigisthos, hangs a
white bucranium. The names of all three figures are
incised above their heads.

To the right of the throne stands a winged Fury
([Π]ΟΙΝΗ), Vengeance, who races toward Atreus.
She places her right hand on the back of the throne
and holds a red staff in her left hand. Her wings
spread out behind her on either side, and white
snakes coil in her hair. She wears embades, a short
chiton, a necklace, crossed bandoleers with white
dots, and a yellow belt. The cloak over her left shoulder is tucked under the belt and billows behind her as

42

42

42

she races forward. Her eyes look away from the royal corpse, toward the pair of women at right, identified by inscription as slave women of the palace (ΔΜΩΙΑΙ). They clutch each other in fright, gesturing with their free hands toward their stricken master. Both wear chitons, earrings, necklaces, and yellow shoes; the left one also wears a himation, kekryphalos, and bracelet. A white rosette floats in the field above. Interrupted at their spinning, the servants have dropped a pair of yellow spindles, which lie at their feet. Near these is a knob-handled patera, upended during the struggle.

B, upper register: In the center sit a maenad and the nude Dionysos. The woman, possibly Ariadne, sits to the left and the god to the right, but they turn to face one another. The woman holds a thyrsos in her left arm and a bunch of white grapes in her right hand. She wears yellow shoes, a chiton, himation, kekryphalos, bracelets, necklace, earrings, and beaded fillet. Her feet rest on a dotted groundline. Dionysos holds an open box in his left hand and an empty kantharos in his right; the box is white with yellow shadows, the kantharos yellow with white highlights. He wears a white fillet and sits upon his cloak. On the groundline between him and the maenad are a phiale and a cylindrical cista with yellow rings. Another maenad stands at the right, a torch with a pendant fillet in her right hand and a situla in her left. She wears white shoes, a chiton, fillet, bracelet, necklace, and earrings. A yellow fillet hangs in the field before her. To the left of the seated maenad stand a satyr and another maenad. The satyr holds a bunch of yellow and white grapes in his right hand and a tympanum in his left, which he offers to the seated maenad. The maenad behind him holds a mirror in her left hand and an iynx-wheel in her right. She is dressed like the maenad at right but wears two bracelets and a sphendone. Flowers grow from the dotted groundline at her feet.

Lower register: A continuous frieze of youths, women, and Erotes circles the vase, twelve figures in all. In the center of the group below Atreus, a woman in a chiton, himation, and kekryphalos is seated to the right on a folding stool. With her left hand she touches the strings of the large harp resting on her lap; in her right hand is a ball of wool. She looks back at the nude youth at left, who leans toward her, one foot resting on a rock. He carries a parasol with yellow hatching and a yellow phiale; the cloak over his left arm billows behind him. On the other side of the harpist, another woman leans toward her with one foot resting on a rock. She wears a chiton, himation, and beaded fillet. In her left hand is a phiale, and on her right hand is perched a small white bird. On the ground below the phiale is a thymiaterion. To the right of this woman, a youth with a cloak around his waist is seated on a cista decorated with white patterns. He holds a wreath or crown with an attached fillet in his right hand and a yellow and white box with raised lid in his left. He looks back at the woman behind him at right, who advances with a wreath in her right hand and a diadem and fillet in her left. She wears a chiton, himation, and kekryphalos. A phiale (most of it destroyed) lies at her feet, and there is a rosette in the field before her. Behind her, at right, another woman is seated to the right on a clothes chest, a mirror in one hand and a tympanum in the other. She wears a chiton, himation, and kekryphalos. Before her, an Eros leans toward her with one foot resting on a rock; the rock and most of his face are destroyed. He wears a necklace and bracelets and holds a white wreath in both hands. On the ground behind him at right is a kalathos full of fillets and piled dots. To the right of this, a woman walks to the left but looks back to the right. She wears a kekryphalos, beaded fillet, and an unbelted chiton with a dotted black stripe down the center. In her left hand she holds a cista and in the right a white fan. Following her is a nude youth with a yellow fillet in his hair and a cloak over his left arm. He carries a laurel branch in his left hand and a phiale in the right. To his right, facing in the other direction, a woman in a chiton and kekryphalos is seated on a yellow rock, holding an alabastron and a tympanum. An Eros approaches her from the right, carrying a fillet in both hands. He wears a beaded fillet, necklace, and anklets. The twelfth figure in the frieze, a woman, stands with her back to Eros. She wears a chiton and sphendone and carries a yellow "xylophone" in her right hand and a yellow and white box with raised lid in her left. A cloak hangs from her left arm. Her face and much of her body are destroyed. A yellow fillet hangs in the field between her and the youth with the parasol. The women in the frieze all wear white shoes, as well as bracelets, earrings, and necklaces. Dotted groundlines indicate the terrain.

A vine circles the side of the large, black mouth; the leaves and stem are painted in added red and white. A raised fillet circles the neck at the handle-junctures; above this are tall, upright palmettes alternating with lotuses, with yellow dots above. Below this, on either side, is a band of rosettes and white and yellow dots. The shoulder of the reverse is filled by a broad band of framed tongues, below which is a band of scrolling tendrils in yellow. On the obverse, the rosettes on the neck are set above a band of dotted egg-pattern; below this, on the shoulder, is

42

a large female head, facing frontally. The head emerges from a white acanthus flower and is flanked by spiraling tendrils and flowers. The two yellow horns on the head identify the woman as Io, who appears frequently as a relief mask on volutes but rarely in this position. She wears a yellow necklace, fillet, and earrings; her eyes look off to her right. A small white bird stands at the lower left, an unusual presence in such a stylized bower. There are bands of tongues at the roots of the handles; below these, on either side, is a large complex of palmettes and coiling tendrils, confined to the upper register. Above the upper scene on either side is a band of dotted egg-pattern. A broader band of scrolling tendrils circles the middle of the vase, separating the upper and lower registers. Circling the body below the lower register is a band consisting of linked maeanders to left alternating with cross-squares with small rectangles in each quadrant. There are rays on the tall stem of the foot and a laurel branch with yellow and white

42

Thyestes tells Aigisthos he is his father and convinces him to kill Atreus, as Apollo had once prophesied. In this scene Thyestes also holds a sword, but since there is only one stab wound on Atreus, Thyestes may be offering only moral support. His revenge on Atreus is complete, a fact reinforced by the presence of Poine. The anguished Pelopeia will now seize the fateful sword from Aigisthos and plunge it into her own breast.

Atreus's topsy-turvy posture is unprecedented, which may account for its slight awkwardness; compare the body of the murdered Kreousa, slumped in her throne on a volute-krater by the Underworld Painter (Munich 3296: *RVAp*, II, p. 533, no. 18/283, pl. 195). The Fury's violent movement distinguishes her from the relaxed Poine on the krater with the baby Aigisthos; the absence of a sleeved tunic is a further difference, but compare that worn by the seated Poine on the volute-krater, cat. no. 38, also identified by inscription. The dropped spindles of the two servants and the inscription identifying them as slaves are further unique features. If the scene, like that on the baby-Aigisthos krater, is based on a lost play by Sophocles, the slave women may be from the chorus. Another possible source is Euripides, who also wrote a *Thyestes*; see A. C. Pearson, *The Fragments of Sophocles*, I (Cambridge, 1917), pp. 185 ff.; and A. Nauck, *Tragicorum Graecorum Fragmenta*, 2nd ed. (1889), pp. 480 ff.

For the throne of Atreus, compare the slightly more elaborate seat of Darius on the painter's name-vase, Naples 3253 (*RVAp*, II, pp. 483, 495, no. 18/38, pl. 176, 1); also the throne of Cepheus on Matera 12538 (*RVAp*, II, p. 501, no. 18/65; F. G. Lo Porto, *MeditArch* 4 [1991], pl. 2). For the scepter with eagle finial, compare that of Adrastos on Boston cat. no. 41; and of Xuthus on the Kreousa loutrophoros in the New York art market (see under cat. no. 41); see also Zeus on cat. no. 14 and Agamemnon on cat. no. 38. Although the subject of the Boston amphora is unique, compare a later pair of oinochoai by an artist of the Wind Group, with Orestes and Pylades killing Aigisthos, who is seated on an elaborate, frontal throne: Bari 1014 and Louvre K 320 (*RVAp*, II, p. 933, nos. 28/126 and 28/129, pl. 367, 2). For Atreus, see J. Boardman, *LIMC*, III, 1, pp. 17–18. For the head and the "Pausian" florals on the shoulder, see the comments on cat. no. 21.

PUBLISHED: *MFA AnnRep* 1990–91, p. 48; E. T. Vermeule and F. Z. Wolsky, ibid., p. 27, illus.; G. Nagy, *Greek Mythology and Poetics* (paperback ed., Ithaca, N.Y., 1992), cover illus.; *RVAp*, Suppl. II, pp. 148 (no. 18/47b), 492 (no. 18/47b), pl. 36, 1.

berries on the outer sides of the handles.

The Darius Painter painted several amphorae of this type, some with rare mythological subjects, such as Meleager bringing the boar's skin to Atalanta, or the madness of Lykourgos (*RVAp*, II, p. 497, nos. 18/44–45). This image of the death of Atreus is unique, but it is the natural sequel to the painter's calyx-krater with Thyestes handing over the infant Aigisthos to be exposed (cat. no. 41). Although Thyestes wears a pilos in both scenes and has roughly the same appearance, in the sequel he has a more brutal visage, which suits his role as an abettor of murder. In the scene on the amphora, Aigisthos is now a young man, having returned to his father's side after surviving his exposure with the aid of a friendly nanny goat and being raised by Atreus as his son. Pelopeia also returns as the wife of Atreus. The story is told by Apollodoros (*Epitome* II. 14). Aigisthos, Pelopeia's brother and son, had been sent by Atreus to kill Thyestes, his real father. The sword he carries had been taken from her masked assailant on the night of her rape. Recognizing the weapon,

CALYX-KRATER
Attributed to the Darius Painter
Ca. 340–330 B.C.
Gift of Harry J. Denberg, Jerome M. Eisenberg, and
Benjamin Rowland, Jr., by Exchange; Gift of
Barbara and Lawrence Fleischman; and Classical
Department Curator's Fund. 1989.100

DIMENSIONS AND CONDITION: Height: 56.0 cm; diameter rim:
50.3 cm; minimum diameter body: 20.1 cm; diameter cul:
32.0 cm; diameter stem: 7.7 cm; diameter foot: 21.7 cm
Reconstructed from large fragments, with significant gaps in
the figures of Amphitryon and servant, the scroll held by the
boy beside the altar, the arms of Teiresias, the arms of his boy
helper, and the body and drapery of Hermes. Minor repainting of cracks and gaps (e.g., the left hand of Amphitryon).
Most of the seer's white beard has flaked off.

SHAPE: Similar to cat. no. 41, but somewhat smaller, with
taller handles

A: The rescue of Alkmene, mother of Herakles. Alkmene (ΑΛΚΜΗΝΗ) sits on the altar that her husband
Amphitryon (ΑΜΦΙΤΡΥΩΝ) tried to make into her
pyre. The altar is a rectangular structure of white
stone, with a Doric frieze and black spots on top, perhaps representing ashes. Alkmene is surrounded by
a red, yellow, and white rainbow; she wears sandals,
a white-dotted fillet, chiton, himation, and a third
garment over her shoulders and clutched around her
head like a veil or hood. Her bracelets, necklace, and
earrings are in added white and yellow. Amphitryon,
with lighted torch in his right hand and a long spear
in his left, looks toward his wife. He wears a chlamys
pinned at the throat and a white pilos and has a sword
with a white hilt at his side hanging from a white
baldric. Two young attendants bring wood to the altar; the one at the right has a cloak over one arm, the
one at the left also carries a lighted torch. At the far
right, King Kreon (ΧΡΗΩΝ) of Thebes looks on, his
right hand raised in a questioning gesture, his left
holding a white pilos and a spear. Kreon has a cloak
around his shoulders and a white baldric across his
chest. Zeus is present in the form of a yellow-brown
eagle, which flies to the right above the altar. Above
the eagle, suspended from the upper border, are a pilos in added red and two yellow chariot wheels.

Joining the eagle in the upper register are five figures. To the right of the eagle, Hermes is seated to
the right with his caduceus in his raised right hand
and his petasos in his left; both are white with yellow
shading. He sits upon his chlamys and and is otherwise nude, save for elaborate sandals with yellow
wings. A quiver with a white strap lies at his feet on
the dotted groundline. Facing him, at the upper

43

43

43

43

43

right, is Aphrodite, who sits to the left, holding a branch in her right hand. Eros leans against her right leg and holds a yellow hoop in his right hand; he wears white bracelets, anklets, earrings, and necklace, as well as shoes and a sakkos. Aphrodite wears a chiton, himation, kekryphalos, and white shoes. Her bracelets, earrings, and necklace are white. In her left hand she holds the string of an iynx-wheel. At the upper left is the blind seer Teiresias (ΤΕΙΡΕΣΙΑΣ), apparently present as the foreteller of Herakles' greatness. He is seated to the left, wearing shoes, a himation, a red fillet, a belt with white circles, an embroidered chiton, and a tunic with long, red sleeves. He holds a long staff topped by a figured pinax, perhaps the Kaiberic shrine of Thebes, in his left hand. The shaft of the staff is decorated with white dots and tied with a beaded fillet. A youthful attendant, wearing himation and wreath, is standing in front of him; he gestures toward Teiresias and with his other hand points toward Amphitryon's attempted sacrilege. On the ground around the altar are logs and a bovine skull in yellow: a previous sacrificial victim. A tree grows near Teiresias, apparently laurel, and a branch and beaded fillet or necklace fill the field before Amphitryon. Groundlines of white and yellow dots indicate the terrain throughout the picture. Alkmene, Amphitryon, Teiresias, and Kreon are identified by incised inscriptions.

B: The nude Dionysos is seated on his cloak between two standing maenads, all three holding thyrsoi, the one in the god's left hand also being grasped by the maenad at right, who holds another in her left hand. Both her thyrsos and that of the god have long fillets attached. This maenad looks to the right at a satyr advancing with a torch in his right hand and a situla in the lowered left. The satyr wears a white fillet; a yellow fillet hangs above him. Dionysos holds a phiale full of offerings in his right hand, which he raises toward the maenad at the left, who holds a tambourine in her lowered left hand. Both maenads wear chitons, shoes, kekryphaloi, and white earrings, necklaces, and bracelets. Dionysos wears a yellow wreath. A rosette floats in the upper field, and a bunch of grapes, yellow and white, hangs from the upper border. Flowers grow from the lower border, one large one interrupting the dotted groundline.

A laurel wreath with large berries circles the underside of the rim. Between the handles on side A is a band of rosettes over a narrower band of dotted egg-pattern. The ornament on side B is identical to that on the reverse of cat. no. 41, with groups of stopt maeanders to left alternating with cross-squares, with smaller squares in each quadrant. Below the maeander is a band of blank eggs.

43

43

It is likely that the action and personae are based ultimately on Euripides' lost play, *Alkmene*, a further echo of which may be seen in the elaborate costume of Teiresias. Zeus had sired Herakles by coming to Alkmene in the guise of her husband, Amphitryon. Accused of adultery, Alkmene took refuge on the altar in their house. Zeus heard her supplications and sent Hermes to tell the clouds to bring the rain that put out the fire and formed the rainbow around Alkmene. Shortly thereafter, Alkmene gave birth to her children, Herakles and his half-brother Iphikles (the child of Amphitryon). In the play, Hermes probably spoke the prologue and Zeus the epilogue. Kreon is present because he and Amphitryon have just returned from their campaign against the Teleboans. It is Kreon's daughter Megara who will become Herakles' first wife (see Apollodorus *The Library* 2.4.6–11). Aphrodite and Eros represent the passion of Zeus, who in this version apparently comes in the guise of an eagle to rescue his love.

On Alkmene in ancient art, see A. D. Trendall, in *LIMC*, I, 1, pp. 552–556; I, 2, pls. 413–416; and K. Schauenburg, *AuA* 10 (1961), pp. 87–88. For the necklace hanging from a branch, compare the Boston krater with the baby Aigisthos (cat. no. 41). For Kreon, see K. Birte Poulsen, *LIMC*, VI, 1, pp. 112–117; VI, 2, pls. 49–50. For a close parallel to the figure of Kreon on this vase, compare Menelaos on a krater in the Paul collection, Miami (Trendall, *Handbook*, fig. 205; *RVAp*, Suppl. II, p. 150, no. 18/65a, pl. 37, 2). For the group of Aphrodite and Eros, compare the group from the east frieze of the Parthenon (F. Brommer, *The Sculptures of the Par-*

thenon: Metopes, Frieze, Pediments, Cult-Statue [London, 1979], pl. 105). For the nimbus around Alkmene, compare that surrounding Poseidon and Amphithea on a loutrophoros by the Darius Painter in the Braillard collection, Geneva (Aellen, Cambitoglou, and Chamay, *Peintre de Darius*, pp. 124–136; *RVAp*, Suppl. II, p. 149, no. 18/56a). The motif was handed down by the Darius Painter to his successor, the Underworld Painter, who used it to envelop Eos and Kephalos on a lekythos in Richmond (inv. 81.55: M. E. Mayo, in Mayo, *Magna Graecia*, pp. 133–136, no. 51; *RVAp*, Suppl. I, pp. 83 [no. 18/281b], 219). For the boy with the blind Teiresias, compare a chous by the Darius Painter in Basel (inv. BS 473: *RVAp*, II, p. 503, no. 18/73a; Schefold and Jung, *Argonauten*, p. 66, fig. 46). Compare also a lost vase-painting that M. Schmidt identifies as Teiresias before Oedipus (M. Schmidt, in *Festschrift Hausmann*, p. 241, fig. 1).

PUBLISHED: A. D. Trendall, in Brijder, *Enthousiasmos*, p. 162; idem, *RVP*, p. 140, note 3; idem, *Handbook*, pp. 90, 132 (fig. 206), 262, 279; *MFA AnnRep* 1988–89, p. 42; J. M. Padgett, ibid., p. 24, illus.; idem, *Minerva* 1:6 (June 1990), p. 45, fig. 4; E. H. Spitz, *Image and Insight: Essays in Psychoanalysis and the Arts* (New York, 1991), pp. 250–251, fig. 13.1; *RVAp*, Suppl. II, p. 151, no. 18/65b, pl. 37, 3; K. Schauenburg, *JdI* 106 (1991), p. 194, note 101; K. Birte Poulsen, *LIMC*, VI, 1, p. 115, no. 9; VI, 2, pl. 50.

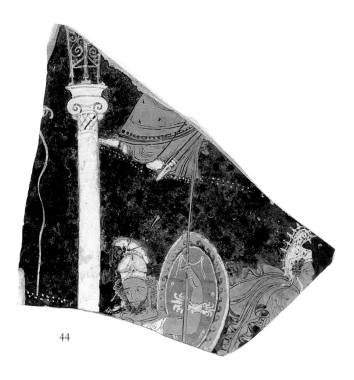

44

44

FRAGMENT OF A VOLUTE-KRATER
Attributed to the Darius Painter
Ca. 330 B.C.
Bequest of Miss Grace Nelson. 61.113

PROVENANCE: Christoph Clairmont collection

DIMENSIONS AND CONDITION: Height: 14 cm; width: 17 cm

The Departure of Amphiaraos. A white Ionic column
topped by a yellow tripod marks the scene's center.
In the upper register, Athena sits to the left with her
spear at her side, her upper body missing. She wears
a himation and peplos; her shoes and the butt of her
spear are white. Amphiaraos stands below with a
spear and a shield; his head, shoulders, and left arm
are preserved; his face is in three-quarter view. He
has a cloak fastened about his shoulders and wears a
white cuirass and a yellow helmet, whose white crest
has a red edge. There is a wave-pattern around the
inner rim of the shield, whose center is red; the
shield's fittings, including its arm band, are yellow.
The helmeted head and cloaked upper body of the
chariot driver (Baton?) are visible at the right. He
wears a chiton, chlamys, and a spiky Phrygian helmet, tinted yellow. The hand and twisted staff visible
at the extreme left may belong to the pedagogue of
the king's sons. The groundlines beneath Athena
and the pedagogue are indicated by double rows of
dots.

Trendall and Cambitoglou (*RVAp*, II, p. 493) note
the close connection with two other volute-kraters,
the closest being Cleveland 88.41 (*RVAp*, II, p. 496,
no. 18/41, pl. 177; Aellen, Cambitoglou, and Chamay, *Peintre de Darius*, pp. 111–114; H. Lohmann,
Boreas 9 [1986], pls. 5–6; E. H. Turner, *BClevMus*
76 [1989], pp. 40–41, 49 [fig. 2], 68, no. 2). On the
Cleveland krater, Artemis is seated above with a
white dog, and the column is absent. Amphiaraos
holds out a phiale in his right hand toward a sorrow-
ing youth, perhaps Alkmaion. The pedagogue is replaced by a youth with a ball and a hoop, possibly
Amphilochos. In the second version by the painter
(Leningrad 1710: *RVAp*, II, p. 490, no. 18/21; H.
Lohmann, *Boreas* 9 [1986], pl. 7, 2), the pedagogue
is in nearly the same position as on the Boston fragment, separated from Amphiaraos only by a Fury,
who on the Cleveland krater steadies the horses of
the quadriga. For the subject, see H. Lohmann,
Boreas 9 (1986), pp. 65–82.

PUBLISHED: C. Clairmont, *AJA* 57 (1953), pp. 90–92, pl. 49,
fig. 8; C. C. Vermeule, *BurlMag* 115 (1973), p. 118, fig. 76; J.
Chamay and A. Cambitoglou, *AntK* 23 (1980), p. 41, no. 22;
I. Krauskopf, *LIMC*, I, 1, pp. 703–704 (no. 74 b), 711; *RVAp*,
II, pp. 484, 486, 493, 503, no. 18/74, pl. 181, 1; Aellen, Cambitoglou, and Chamay, *Peintre de Darius*, p. 113; H. Lohmann, *Boreas* 9 (1986), pp. 68, 81, pl. 8, 3; *RVAp*, Suppl. II,
p. 141, no. 18/74.

EXHIBITED: Fogg Art Museum, *Ancient Art in American Private Collections: A Loan Exhibition at the Fogg Art Museum
of Harvard University*, December 28, 1954 - February 15,
1955 (Cambridge, Mass., 1954), p. 37, no. 300.

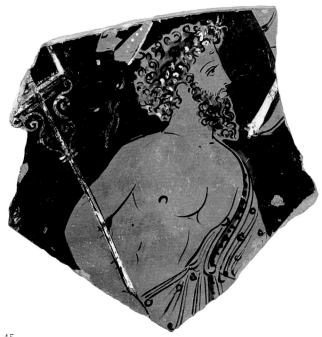

45

45

FRAGMENT OF A VOLUTE-KRATER
Close to the Darius Painter
Ca. 330 B.C.
Lent by Mr. and Mrs. Cornelius C. Vermeule III.
153.64

PROVENANCE: Hesperia Art, Philadelphia; Jacob Hirsch;
Hartwig collection (information from D. von Bothmer)

DIMENSIONS AND CONDITION: Height: 8.0 cm; width: 8.3 cm

Poseidon, holding his white trident against his right
side, is seated to the right; his legs, hands, and lower
body are missing. He wears a bordered and spotted
himation and a yellow and white wreath. In the upper field, behind his head, is a foot and what appears
to be the end of a hanging fillet. At the right, before
the god's face, is a leg (?) and the yellow butt of a
spear or scepter.

A. D. Trendall confirmed the attribution in February 1970 but has not published the piece. Compare
the Poseidon on the Darius Painter's calyx-krater in
Matera (inv. 12538: *RVAp*, II, p. 501, no. 18/65;
F. G. Lo Porto, *MeditArch* 4 [1991], pl. 2).

46

PELIKE
Attributed to the Egnazia Group (Trendall); perhaps
the Painter of Bari 12061 (Herrmann)
Ca. 325 B.C.
Gift of Mrs. S. V. R. Thayer. 10.234

DIMENSIONS AND CONDITION: Height: 43.2 cm; diameter rim:
17.0 cm; diameter neck: 9.0 cm; diameter body: 27.4 cm; diameter stem: 12.5 cm; diameter foot: 16.5 cm
The rim and mouth are broken and repaired, with restorations
in plaster. The handle on side A/B has been broken and reset
with plaster. The seated woman on side B is very rubbed. The
black glaze has a white, cloudy look as the result of misfiring.

SHAPE: Tall, slender neck; nearly spherical body; tall disk foot
with two reserved grooves near the top and bottom; fillet between foot and body; reserved groove below the mouth. Compared with the Plain-style example, cat. no. 24, it has a much
taller neck and handles.

A: At the left, a woman in a peplos, kekryphalos, radiate fillet, and white earrings, stands with one foot
resting on a white rock; she holds a "xylophone" in
her left hand and an alabastron in her right, both
white. She offers the alabastron to a seated woman
holding a mirror in her right hand and a yellow ball
of wool in her left. She too wears a peplos and, like
the first woman, has shoes, bracelets, and a necklace,
all in added white. A white-dotted fillet binds the
tousled hair framing her face, drawn in three-quar-

46 B

ter view. She turns to look at a seated youth holding
a phiale in his right hand and a white staff in the left.
He wears a wreath and sits on a cloak that drapes
over his lap. A large yellow lyre is on the ground beside him at the right, and beyond is a woman standing with a white wreath in her right hand and a fillet
in the left. She wears a chiton, a cloak over both
arms, a sphendone, and white shoes, bracelets, earrings, necklace, and radiate fillet. Above, an Eros is
seated on a cloak, holding a fillet in his right hand
and a phiale and two fillets in his left. He wears a
beaded fillet, necklace, earrings, and anklets, all in
white, as well as shoes. His white wings spread out
on either side. A small bird with a fillet in its feet flies
toward the seated woman. Dotted groundlines of
white indicate the terrain, as does the yellow flower
growing from the lower border. There is a phiale in
the field at the upper right.

The youth might be Dionysos, but the women

46 A

have no maenadic attributes, and there are no vines, kraters, or other articles associated with his cult. The lyre might indicate Apollo, but it is not clearly his; nor are there any certain attributes of the god, not even a laurel branch. Compare the lyre next to Dionysos on cat. no. 53.

B: A woman with a phiale in her right hand and a long branch in the left is seated to the left on a dotted groundline. At left, a nude youth offers her the wreath in his left hand; he wears shoes and uses his cloak to pad the staff he leans on. At right, a woman stands with a tympanum in her right hand and a bunch of grapes in her left. Both women wear shoes, chitons, sphendones, radiate fillets, bracelets, and necklaces. A small laurel grows in the left foreground, in front of the seated woman, and at the right grows a flower. In the field above are a fillet and a narrow "window." Dotted groundlines indicate the terrain.

On the obverse neck are alternating lotus and palmettes above a band of dotted egg-pattern and a row of white dots, like the pendants of a necklace; on the reverse is a laurel wreath with white berries. Beneath the handles are palmettes and scrolls with white dots. A band consisting of groups of stopt maeanders to left alternating with dotted crosssquares circles the lower body.

The vase belongs to a large group of pelikai that are closely interrelated by their similar compositions and decoration and frequently by their amorous themes. Often they display the influence of the Darius Painter, but at times, as in this case, the influence of the Varrese Painter dominates. The drawing of the heads and drapery is especially close to that of followers of the Varrese Painter like the Wolfenbüttel Painter or the Painter of Bari 12061. For the Wolfenbüttel Painter, see *RVAp*, I, pp. 356–358, pls. 114–115; Trendall, *Handbook*, pp. 84, 121, fig. 175. For the Painter of Bari 12061, see Trendall, *Handbook*, pp. 84–85, figs. 179–180; *RVAp*, I, p. 376; Aellen, Cambitoglou, and Chamay, *Peintre de Darius*, pp. 71–83, pl. 17. A calyx-krater in Brussels with the punishment of Marsyas could well be by the same hand as the Boston pelike (Musées Royaux d' Art et d' Histoire R 227: *RVAp*, II, pp. 506–507, no. 18/108: "in the manner of the Darius Painter and possibly by his own hand").

46

PUBLISHED: *RVAp*, II, pp. 512–513, no. 18/146, pl. 183, 4; K. Schauenburg, *Classica et Provincialia: Festschrift Erna Diez* (Graz, 1978), p. 175, note 58; Maas and Snyder, *Stringed Instruments*, pp. 175–176, 242, notes 65–66.

EXHIBITED: Corpus Christi, *Greek Vases*, p. 30, no. 40; Ann Arbor, *Greek Vases*, p. 15, no. 21 (as a wedding on side A); Detroit Institute of Arts, January 5 - March 2, 1977.

47 (Color Plate XII)

47

47

KNOB-HANDLED PATERA
Attributed to the Perrone-Phrixos Group
340–330 B.C.
Gift of Mr. and Mrs. Cornelius C. Vermeule III.
1991.381

PROVENANCE: Lent by Mr. and Mrs. Cornelius C. Vermeule in 1970 (Loan no. 171.1970)

DIMENSIONS AND CONDITION: Height (maximum): 18.5 cm; diameter rim: 47.5 cm; diameter stem (upper molding): 11.2 cm; diameter foot: 16.1 cm
About 40 percent of the rim is missing and restored, along with the adjoining section of vine border. Two knobs are reconstructed. The rest of the vase has been put together from a few large fragments with no significant restoration. Of the exterior, most of side B is missing. The white and yellow vine surrounding the tondo is quite eroded in places.

SHAPE: The bowl is relatively deep for a patera of this type. The flattened rim overhangs both inside and out, the outer descending to take a painted band of dotted egg-pattern. The two handles are grooved along the top and dip slightly in the center where a knob is attached. A pair of knobs on the rim frames each handle, which leans out at an angle. A fillet framed by reserved grooves separates the bowl from the foot, which has a short, broad stem and a narrow beveled disk with two reserved grooves.

Interior: In the tondo, framed by a circle of wave-pattern, are twelve marine creatures: a horn shell (cerith), a wedge clam (donax), a scallop, two dolphins, a cuttlefish, an octopus, a flying squid, a spotted torpedo, a striped perch, an angler-fish, and a

47

dentex. Unlike the sea creatures on fish-plates, the dolphins, squid, angler-fish, and dentex on this patera are arranged in a radial pattern. The backs of the various creatures are tinted with dilute glaze and with white or yellow highlights and markings. Circling the tondo is a white vine.

Exterior: On side A, a nude youth wearing a fillet is seated on folded drapery between a woman at right and an Eros at left. Eros holds a wreath with fillet in his left hand and a laurel branch in his right; the youth holds a phiale on his right hand and branch in his left; the woman carries a situla in her left hand and a dipper in the right. Eros wears a kekryphalos and white bracelets, anklets, earrings, and necklace. The woman wears a chiton, kekryphalos, and white shoes, bracelets, earrings, and necklace. There are fillets, rosettes, and a "window" amid the well-pre-served figures. On side B, only the legs of a draped female seated on a rock at the left and the legs of a male at the right are preserved. The woman wears yellow shoes; the yellow staff by her feet is a thyrsos. She may be a maenad.

Below the handles, between A and B, are elaborate complexes of palmettes and coiling tendrils. The groundline consists of groups of four stopt maeanders to left alternating with cross-squares with circles in each quadrant. There are rosettes on each of the knobs and a dotted egg-pattern around the outer rim. The top of the rim is reserved between the handles.

Compare a similar patera in the Metropolitan Museum of Art, New York (inv. 1989.281.61), formerly in the Schimmel collection (McPhee and Trendall, *Fish-plates*, p. 124, no. IVA/67, pl. 48b; *RVAp*, II, p. 527, no. 18/247), and a second, also from the Phrixos Group, in a Geneva private collection (McPhee and Trendall, *Fish-plates*, p. 124, no. IVA/68a; Trendall, *Handbook*, fig. 207; *RVAp*, Suppl. II, p. 158, no. 18/248a). All three paterae may be by the Phrixos Painter, to judge by the fish on his name-vase, Berlin F 3345, a patera with Phrixos riding over the sea on the ram (*RVAp*, II, p. 526, no. 18/244; McPhee and Trendall, *Fish-plates*, p. 123, no. IVA/65, pl. 48a). McPhee and Trendall, however, have also noted a close similarity to fish on amphorae of the Perrone Group, and, in fact, it is difficult to divide the two groups, just as it is difficult to say how many hands are at work. This Perrone-Phrixos Group was part of the large and diverse Tarentine workshop of the Darius Painter and produced not only these fish-filled paterae but also fish-plates of more customary shape (e.g., cat. no. 49); see McPhee and Trendall, *Fish-plates*, pp. 123–127, pls. 48–50.

PUBLISHED: C. C. Vermeule, *BurlMag* 115 (1973), p. 118, figs. 72, 78; Schneider-Herrmann, *Paterae*, pp. 34 (no. VIII 2), 115 (no. 193), 127, pl. 19, 3; *RVAp*, II, p. 527, no. 18/248; M. E. Mayo, in Mayo, *Magna Graecia*, p. 155, under no. 62; K. Schauenburg, *JdI* 101 (1986), p. 172; McPhee and Trendall, *Fish-plates*, p. 124, no. IVA/68, pl. 48c; N. Kunisch, *Griechische Fischteller: Natur und Bild* (Berlin, 1989), pp. 80–82, fig. 17; *MFA AnnRep* 1990–91, p. 48; J. J. Herrmann, in ibid., p. 27, illus.; *RVAp*, Suppl. II, p. 491, no. 18/248.

EXHIBITED: Fogg Art Museum, *The Discerning Eye: Radcliffe Collectors' Exhibition* (Cambridge, Mass., 1974), no. 4, illus.; St. Paul's School, *The Classical Shape*, no. 32, illus.

48

48

48

KNOB-HANDLED PATERA
Attributed to the Perrone-Phrixos Group
Ca. 340–330 B.C.
Henry Lillie Pierce Residuary Fund. 01.8093

PROVENANCE: E. P. Warren collection

DIMENSIONS AND CONDITION: Height: 10.1 cm; diameter: 43.7 cm; diameter stem: 9.3 cm; diameter foot: 15.0 cm Broken and repaired, with moderate in-painting of cracks. A large fragment is missing from one side, taking with it the head and right hand of the woman on side A and part of the adjacent Eros. There is some of the white vine in the interior and the black glaze under the rim.

SHAPE: Broader and shallower than the previous patera; the handles are more vertical and lack grooves and knobs.

48

Interior: Within a simple circular frame of two reserved stripes, a female head, drawn in three-quarter view, is emerging from a large white flower surrounded by flowers, scrolling stems, and acanthus. The woman or goddess wears a fillet and a yellow necklace. A groundline of dotted egg-pattern creates an exergue with three flowers in it. Surrounding the tondo is a white vine with yellow and white leaves.

A: A nude youth is seated to the right on folded drapery, holding a syrinx in his left hand. Eros flies toward him from the right with a situla (which may have originally been yellow) in his right hand and a wreath in the left. Eros wears shoes, a kekryphalos, necklace, and bracelets. At the far right, a woman is seated to the left, holding a white and yellow fan in her hidden left hand. The object in her right hand is missing, but the traces preserved by her knees suggest it was a fillet. She wears a chiton, himation, shoes, and a yellow bracelet. A large flower grows at the lower center, and rosettes float in the field.

B: A woman is seated to the right, holding a branch in her right hand and a white or yellow "xylophone," now quite eroded, in her left. She wears a chiton, himation, shoes, a kekryphalos, a necklace, and bracelets. In the center stands (or hovers) Eros, wearing shoes, kekryphalos, necklace, bracelets, and anklets. He carries a bunch of grapes in his right hand and a ball (?) in the left. At the right, a nude youth wearing a fillet is seated to the left on his cloak, holding a wreath in his right hand and a tray of offerings in his left. In the field are rosettes and fillets; a laurel grows beside Eros.

Below each handle is a large palmette with smaller sprays in the tendrils on either side. The groundline consists of groups of stopt maeanders to left alternating with dotted saltire-squares.

For the Perrone-Phrixos Group, see comments on cat. no. 47. For floral heads, see comments on cat. no. 21.

PUBLISHED: Schneider-Herrmann, *Paterae*, pp. 81 (no. 103), 127; *RVAp*, II, p. 526, no. 18/246, pl. 192, 2; *LIMC*, III, 1, p. 900, no. 585a.

49

49

49

FISH-PLATE
Attributed to the Perrone-Phrixos Group
340–320 B.C.
Lent by Mr. and Mrs. Cornelius C. Vermeule III.
281.1970

DIMENSIONS AND CONDITION: Height: 4.2 cm; outer diameter rim: 20.4 cm; diameter central depression: 4.0 cm; diameter stem: 4.8 cm; diameter foot: 7.5 cm
Broken and repaired

SHAPE: This and following examples are variations of the standard fish-plate shape, with a shallow, concave upper surface, a central depression offset by a fillet, and a nearly vertical overhanging rim, the height of which, like the profile of the foot, varies from plate to plate. This example has a hollow, spreading foot without moldings.

Interior: Three fish—a striped bream, and two wrasse—with details rendered in added white and with backs darkened with dilute glaze. There are three triangular shells in the field. The shells are highly stylized, but their forms could have been inspired by those of cardites, tellins, or wedge clams, the last of which, though tiny, are particularly abundant in the Mediterranean. The overhanging rim is decorated with a laurel wreath, and the rays in the central depression make of it a rosette. The depression and its surrounding rings are colored with a red wash.

For the Perrone-Phrixos Group, see comments on cat. no. 47. For fish-plates, see McPhee and Trendall, *Fish-plates*, passim; and N. Kunisch, *Griechische Fischteller: Natur und Bild* (Berlin, 1989). For the possible ancient name of these plates (*oxybaphon*) and their manner of use, see McPhee and Trendall, *Fish-plates*, pp. 21–22.

PUBLISHED: McPhee and Trendall, *Fish-plates*, p. 126, no. IVA/85.

EXHIBITED: St. Paul's School, *The Classical Shape*, no. 31, 3, illus.

50

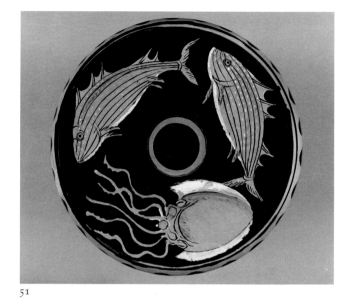

51

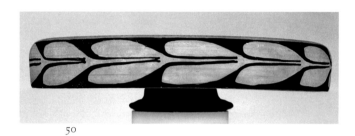

50

51

50

FISH-PLATE
Attributed to the Flatfish Painter
340–330 B.C.
Seth K. Sweetser Fund. 65.564

DIMENSIONS AND CONDITION: Height: 5.0 cm; diameter rim:
22.6 cm; diameter foot: 7.9 cm
A small chip is lost from the rim; otherwise intact. Much of
the added white has been lost.

SHAPE: Spreading foot, faintly ogival, and deep overhanging
rim

Interior: a torpedo, a flatfish, a *coris*, a striped perch,
and two scallops. The added-white details on three of
the fish — gills, spines in the fins and tails — have
nearly worn away; the torpedo never had any added
color but has five large black dots on its back. A band
of dicing circles the upper rim, and around the overhanging rim is a laurel wreath. The central depres-

sion is decorated with wave-pattern around a circular
stripe and central dot. The foot and stem are black.

The Flatfish Painter is named for his propensity to
represent varieties of flatfish, like the one on this
plate: it may be a turbot or a flounder, but one cannot
be certain. The painter is grouped by McPhee and
Trendall among others associated with the workshop
of the Darius Painter and his followers. The dicing
and the wave-pattern around the central depression
are characteristic of the painter; compare a plate in
the Hirschmann collection (G 59: McPhee and Trendall, *Fish-plates*, pl. 42d).

PUBLISHED: C. C. Vermeule, *MFA AnnRep* 1965, p. 67; P.
von Kersburg, *BMFA* 63 (1965), p. 215, illus.; H. Metzger,
Revue des études grecques 81 (1968), p. 121; S. A. Goldblith,
The Red Devil 6 (August 1974), p. 7, illus.; W. R. Biers, *The
Archaeology of Greece: An Introduction* (Ithaca, N.Y., 1980),
pp. 315–316, fig. 10, 49; McPhee and Trendall, *Fish-plates*,
p. 118, no. IVA/5; Söldner, *Bonn* 3, p. 79, under inv. no. 139.

51

FISH-PLATE
The name-vase of the Painter of Boston 282.<u>1970</u>
340–320 B.C.
Lent by Mr. and Mrs. Cornelius C. Vermeule III.
282.<u>1970</u>

DIMENSIONS AND CONDITION: Height: 5.2 cm; outer diameter
rim: 20.0 cm; outer diameter central depression: 4.8 cm; inner diameter central depression: 3.6 cm; diameter stem: 4.4
cm; diameter foot: 7.4 cm
Broken and repaired, with a missing fragment restored near
the ends of the cuttlefish's two middle tentacles

SHAPE: Compared with the previous fish-plate, the overhanging rim is considerably narrower. The reserved, concave stem
flares to a black torus foot.

Interior: A cuttlefish and two striped fish with spiny
dorsal fins, possibly tunny. Parallel rows of yellow-
ish-white dots run down the backs of the fish. Dilute
glaze is used to shadow the cuttlefish and to darken
the upper parts of the fish. A wave-pattern decorates
the overhanging rim. The central depression is black
with a reserved stripe around the edge.

McPhee and Trendall identified the same hand on
three other fish-plates, all of them connected in style
with the Crab Group, which in turn is placed in the
workshop of the Darius Painter; see McPhee and
Trendall, *Fish-plates*, pp. 132–133.

PUBLISHED: McPhee and Trendall, *Fish-plates*, p. 133, no.
IVA/163.

EXHIBITED: St. Paul's School, *The Classical Shape*, no. 31, 4,
illus.

52

SKYPHOS
Attributed to the Alabastra Group
330–320 B.C.
Mary L. Smith Fund. 69.28

DIMENSIONS AND CONDITION: Height: 9.7 cm; diameter body:
9.0 cm; diameter rim: 8.8 cm; diameter foot: 3.8 cm; width
(with handles): 16.0 cm
Unbroken

SHAPE: The so-called Corinthian type of skyphos, with tapering lower body, narrow foot, the widest diameter at midbody,
and delicate, horizontal handles just below the rim

A: A man and woman kiss within the frame of an
open window, the shutters being drawn in clumsy
perspective. Only the heads of the couple are visible.
He wears a white bandeau or padded fillet in his curly
hair; her ringlets fall down from beneath her sakkos,
which is decorated with white dots echoing the beads
of her necklace. On both, the eyes are highlighted
with white, and they look upward as though in ec-

52 (Color Plate XIII)

52

stasy. There are two white phialai under the yellow
frame of the window.

B: Eros, wearing a kekryphalos, shoes, and white
radiate fillet, bracelets, and anklet, flies to the left
carrying a wreath in his right hand.

Under each handle is a laurel plant flanked by rosettes. On the lip, a band of eggs with white and yellow cores extends between the handles on either
side. The rays on the lower body are traditional for
this shape. There are concentric circles on the underside of the foot.

The Alabastra Group was part of the Darius
Painter Workshop and produced mostly vases of that
name. Trendall and Cambitoglou list this cup with
one of similar shape and ornament with Eros on both
sides: Indiana University Art Museum, Bloomington, 77.109 (*RVAp*, II, p. 607, no. 21/27, pl. 233, 3).
For the unusual subject on the obverse of this cup,
see Schauenburg (*RM* 79 [1972]; see reference be-

53

53

low), and compare the female heads in windows on the Etruscan calyx-krater, cat. no. 170.

PUBLISHED: C. C. Vermeule, *MFA AnnRep* 1969–70, p. 40; idem, *BurlMag* 112 (1970), p. 631, figs. 105–106; K. Schauenburg, *RM* 79 (1972), pp. 10, 14, pl. 21, 2; idem, in Hornbostel, *Schätze*, p. 409, under no. 353; *RVAp*, II, p. 607, no. 21/28, pl. 233, 4; *LIMC*, III, 1, p. 893, no. 501g.

53

KANTHAROS
Attributed to the Paidagogos Group
Ca. 335–325 B.C.
Gift of Thomas G. Appleton. 76.60

PROVENANCE: Alessandro Castellani collection; from Canosa

DIMENSIONS AND CONDITION: Height: 13.5 cm; width across handles: 16.2 cm; diameter rim: 10.2 cm; diameter body: 5.3 cm; diameter lower edge of body: 6.6 cm; diameter lower section stem: 1.6 cm; diameter foot: 5.8 cm
Unbroken

SHAPE: Typical for the Paidagogos Group. On either handle, just below the strut to the rim, is a spur pointing outward. A plastic ring circles the center of the tall stem. The foot is a spreading disk with two grooves colored with added white. The body is slender and concave, with a thin, flaring rim. At the juncture of each handle with the rim, facing inward, is a female head in relief, wearing a Phrygian cap.

A: Dionysos is seated on his throne in three-quarter view to the right. The throne has turned legs and no back. The god's himation has fallen about his waist, and he has his feet on a stool, suggesting a cult image. He holds his thyrsos across his lap in his left hand. There is a fillet in his long hair, which falls in ringlets on his shoulder. On the ground are a lyre and a pair of pipes, crossed. A grapevine runs above and on either side of the god. The throne, pipes, grapes, and parts of the thyrsos and stool are in added white, tinted yellow.

B: A maenad in chiton, kekryphalos, earrings, necklace, and bracelets is rushing to the right but looking back to the left. She carries a phiale in her right hand and a thyrsos in the left. On either side of her is a vertical spray of laurel.

The groundlines consist of dotted egg-pattern with yellow cores in the eggs. This ornament and the laurel on side B are standard for the Paidagogos Group, but the grapevine is a special feature in honor of the wine-god. The Paidagogos Group vases are all kantharoi of this type and were produced in the workshop of the Darius Painter.

PUBLISHED: Robinson, *Catalogue*, pp. 186–187, no. 515; *RVAp*, II, p. 610, no. 21/58; *RVAp*, Suppl. II, p. 186, no. 21/58.

EXHIBITED: Cooper - Hewitt Museum, New York, June 4 - October 13, 1985 (D. J. Janson, in H. Johnson, D. J. Janson, and D. R. McFadden, *Wine: Celebration and Ceremony* [New York, 1985], p. 52, illus.).

54

FRAGMENT OF A POT (oinochoe ?)
Attributed to the Ascoli Satriano Painter
330–320 B.C.
Dora S. Pinter Fund. 1986.263

DIMENSIONS AND CONDITION: Width: 14.5 cm; height:
10.8 cm

Pentheus, with a sword in his right hand and a scabbard in his left (both yellow), is attacked by at least
four maenads. He is nude save for a yellow pilos and
the cloak over his left arm. One maenad, perhaps
Agave, reaches for the king's head with her right
hand and holds a thyrsos in her left; the strands of
her black hair are rendered by incision. She wears a
necklace, earrings, and a beaded fillet, all in white.
Her bracelets are yellow. Two white pins secure her
peplos at the shoulders. Her peplos, like those of her
fellow maenads and of Pentheus's cloak, has a black
border, edged with dots. The maenad at the upper
left also carries a thyrsos. At the right are the knee of
a third maenad and the braceleted right hand of a
fourth. In the field at the center is a pendant flower,
perhaps at one end of a beaded chain.

Although Trendall, in *RVP*, listed this as a work of
the Boston Orestes Painter, a Paestan artist, a wealth
of new vases by the Ascoli Satriano Painter has
caused Trendall to reconsider his earlier attribution
and assign this fragment to that northern Apulian
painter, who was deeply influenced by the Paestan
style. This change came too late for the attribution to
be noted in the second supplement to *RVAp*, but in a
recent letter Trendall compares the style, including
dotted borders and pendant flowers, of two oinochoai: Foggia 129328 (*RVAp*, II, p. 720, no. 880),
and a vase in the Swiss art market (*RVAp*, Suppl. I,
p. 127, no. 880a).

The scene on the Boston fragment may have been
inspired by a tragedy of Aeschylus, *Pentheus*, although the *Bacchae* of Euripides is perhaps a more
likely candidate. The subject had a long history in
vase-painting, and no direct theatrical inspiration
need have been involved. For the subject, see Caskey
and Beazley, vol. II, pp. 1–3; Brommer, *Vasenlisten*,
3rd ed., pp. 485–486; A. Greifenhagen, *Berliner
Museen*, N.F. 16 (1966), pp. 2–6; and M. Padgett, in
Antikenmuseum Berlin, *Euphronios der Maler*, ex-
hib. cat. (Milan, 1991), pp. 174–177.

PUBLISHED: *MFA AnnRep* 1985–86, p. 48; Trendall, *RVP*,
p. 255, no. 2/1003a.

54

55

MUG (oinochoe of shape 8M)
Attributed to the A-B-C Group (The Winterthur
Group)
330–320 B.C.
Gift of Michael Filides. 69.55

DIMENSIONS AND CONDITION: Height: 8.2 cm; diameter rim:
6.5 cm; diameter neck: 5.3 cm; diameter body: 7.3 cm; diameter stem: 4.7 cm; diameter foot: 5.3 cm
Pieces of the rim have been reattached.

SHAPE: Oinochoai of shape 8M, with the ring handle confined
to the shoulder, are more common in Gnathian (e.g., cat. nos.
140–142). See A. Cambitoglou, *BSR* 19 (1951), p. 40, note 4.
For some red-figure examples, compare Brunswick AT 687
(*CVA* Braunschweig 1, pl. 40, 3–4); Musée National de Sèvres
180 (*CVA* 1, pl. 42, 11, and 16); and a vase in a private collection (K. Schauenburg, in W. G. Moon, ed., *Ancient Greek Art
and Iconography* [Madison, 1983], p. 263, fig. 17.11). This
example has a broad reserved stem and a turned foot.

A woman's head is in profile to the left, wearing a
kekryphalos, a yellow necklace, and yellow earrings.
The wreath of ivy around the rim has white leaves
and an incised stem. A palmette is under the handle,
and there are scrolling tendrils along the sides. The
floral motifs and parts of the kekryphalos are en-
riched with added yellow.

The A-B-C Group is a subgroup of the Winterthur
Group, which consists primarily of pelikai, kraters,
and choes. Vases of both groups have female heads in
kekryphaloi, with the hair in back doubly secured by
a white fillet with a small loop at the top. These vases
were among the minor pots so copiously produced in
the Darius-Underworld Workshop.

PUBLISHED: C. C. Vermeule, *MFA AnnRep* 1969–70, p. 42;
RVAp, Suppl. II, p. 219, no. 22/635-3, pl. 56, 11.

55

55

LEBES GAMIKOS
Connected with the Woman-Eros Group
Ca. 330–320 B.C.
Gift of Thomas G. Appleton. 76.61 a-b

PROVENANCE: Alessandro Castellani collection; from Ruvo

DIMENSIONS AND CONDITION: Height to rim: 11.7 cm; height to top of handle: 16.8 cm; inner diameter rim: 3.3 cm; diameter body: 9.4 cm; diameter stem: 2.0 cm; diameter foot: 5.0 cm; height lid: 6.7 cm; diameter lid: 5.7 cm; diameter stem of lid: 1.1 cm; maximum diameter finial: 1.7 cm
Unbroken. There is considerable incrustation on side B.

SHAPE: The knob on the lid is barely taller than the two vertical handles. The body is ovoid, with a flattened shoulder. A reserved stem separates the body from the foot, which has a tall, tapering riser (reserved, with a black stripe around the top) and a black base with a cyma recta profile.

A: Eros is seated to the left on a cista or altar decorated with yellow patterns. He holds a phiale in his raised right hand and rests the left on his seat. He wears a kekryphalos, shoes, earrings, necklaces, a bandoleer, bracelets, and a large anklet, all in added color. In the field above the phiale is an ivy leaf, below it a rosette, both touched with added color. Except for some wing feathers and an offering in the phiale consisting of three white dots, all the added color is yellow.

B: A woman in a chiton, kekryphalos, shoes, earrings, bracelets, and necklace is walking rapidly to the right, her head turned back to the left. She carries a mirror in her raised right hand and a wreath in the lowered left hand. A fillet hangs in the field at left, and at upper right is a "window." Many details are in added yellow.

There are tongues on top of the lid and on both shoulders. A band of wave-pattern circles the side of the lid. There are large palmettes on the sides beneath the handles. Tall, coiling tendrils and smaller palmettes flank the figures on both sides. The handles have two broad reserved stripes at their bases; another is at the base of the knob.

Trendall and Cambitoglou listed this vase among those of "coarser style" associated with the Woman-Eros Painter, a painter of skyphoi and lebetes gamikoi in the Darius-Underworld Workshop. In addition to *RVAp*, see A. Cambitoglou, *AJA* 64 (1960), pp. 365–366.

PUBLISHED: Robinson, *Catalogue*, pp. 190–191, no. 526; *RVAp*, II, p. 645, no. 21/453, pl. 240, 9.

EXHIBITED: Corpus Christi, *Greek Vases*, p. 32, no. 43, illus.

56 56

57

KNOB-HANDLED PATERA
Related to the Chur Painter
Ca. 330–320 B.C.
Gift of Thomas G. Appleton. 76.63

DIMENSIONS AND CONDITION: Height: 9.0 cm; diameter rim:
31.3 cm; diameter foot: 9.3 cm
Unbroken

SHAPE: This patera is smaller than the others in the collection;
like cat. no. 47, it has knobs on top of the handles as well as
beside them, but unlike it, the bowl is quite shallow and the
knobs are larger. The foot is in two degrees, with a spreading
riser and a torus base.

Interior: Female head to the left, wearing a necklace
with yellow pendants, yellow earrings, a sakkos decorated with crosses and beads, and a fillet or stephane
with small, yellow oak leaves. In the field at the left
is a yellow fillet. The head is framed by a narrow, circular stripe, around which runs a large white grapevine.

57

57

57

the Oak-Leaf Painter but connected the drawing of the woman's face to the Chur Painter (*RVAp*, II, pp. 671, 693). Compare also the interior of a patera once in the New York market (A. Emmerich Gallery Inc., *Art of Ancient Italy: Etruscans, Greeks and Romans* [New York, 1970], p. 45, no. 72).

PUBLISHED: Robinson, *Catalogue*, pp. 188–189, no. 520; Schneider-Herrmann, *Paterae*, pp. 96 (no. 154), 129; *RVAp*, II, pp. 671 (no. 22/280), 693, pl. 250, 6; Söldner, *Bonn* 3, pp. 52 (under inv. no. 3051), 75 (under inv. no. 134), 78 (under inv. no. 137).

EXHIBITED: Corpus Christi, *Greek Vases*, p. 32, fig. 42; Ann Arbor, *Greek Vases*, p. 15, no. 22; Detroit Institute of Arts, January 5 - March 2, 1977.

58

COLUMN-KRATER
Attributed to the Patera Painter
Ca. 340–325 B.C.
Source unknown. 60.1171
(Found by C. Albert Prior, head of utility, in the furniture storage of the Museum of Fine Arts)

DIMENSIONS AND CONDITION: Height: 42.0 cm; diameter rim: 33.2 cm; diameter across handles: 38.7 cm; diameter neck: 24.0 cm; diameter body: 29.2 cm; diameter stem: 7.6 cm; diameter foot: 14.5 cm
Broken and repaired; two pieces are missing from the wall on side B. Mottling of the black glaze on B and around the legs of the youth on A is due to misfiring.

SHAPE: Compare cat. nos. 35 and 36; the neck of this krater is shorter and less concave than those examples and, in fact, is shorter than most other column-kraters by this painter.

A: A woman in a chiton, shoes, and kekryphalos is seated to the left on a rock. She holds a mirror in her right hand and a wreath in the left. Her jewelry includes bracelets, necklace, and a beaded fillet. A fillet and a large rosette float in the field.

B: Eros is seated to the left on a rock, a cista in his right hand. He wears a necklace, bracelets, shoes, a beaded fillet, and a spiral anklet. In the field are three fillets and three small ivy leaves.

Below the handles, framing the figures, are large palmettes framed by scrolling tendrils. There is much use of added yellow and white throughout both exterior scenes, including stripes and dots on the rocks, fillets and jewelry, shoes, leaves, mirror, parts of Eros's wings, short, dotted groundlines, the cores of the palmettes, and dots in the tendrils. There are white rosettes on the knobs and simple tongues around the outer rim, the top of which is reserved.

Trendall and Cambitoglou compared the "oak-leaf stephane" of the woman in the interior to those of

A: A maenad, with a torch in her right hand and a large basket containing a white cake and sprigs in the left hand, is walking to the left, looking back. She wears a chiton and kekryphalos and has a cloak over her right arm. Her jewelry consists of a bracelet, necklace, and earrings, all in added white and yellow. Her chignon is secured with a white fillet. She is followed by the young Dionysos, carrying a dotted wreath in his right hand and a thyrsos and a cloak in the left. He is nude except for a yellow wreath and fillet. White fillets hang from the torch, the thyrsos, the wreath, and the upper border. There is a rosette in the field at right, a tendril in the lower right corner, and a plant with white berries growing from the dotted groundline. The figures walk on groundlines of white dots.

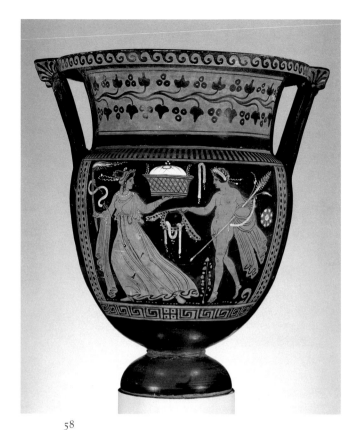

58

58

B: Two youths, wearing shoes and himatia and holding crooked staffs in their right hands, stand facing each other. Filling the field between their heads is a grotesquely enlarged writing tablet. There are stylized jumping weights at the upper left and a quadrated disk with dots at the upper right.

In the panels on either side of the neck are ivy vines with circular berries. A wave-pattern is on the outer rim and small black palmettes on the sides of the handle-plates. There are rays around the top of the rim and black palmettes on top of the handle-plates. The pictures have lateral frames of degenerate ivy and upper frames of tongues. The lower frame on each side consists of groups of four stopt maeanders to left alternating with dotted cross-squares.

The Patera Painter was a contemporary of the Darius Painter. A prolific painter, mostly of large pots with funerary scenes, he seems to have worked at Taranto, Ruvo, and finally Canosa, where he influenced the Baltimore Painter. The ornament and figures on this krater are entirely characteristic. That the rectangle on side B is indeed a writing tablet is made clear on other vases, where the stylus is well defined; compare the stylus and tablet, as well as the youths holding crooked staffs, on London F 295 (*RVAp*, II, p. 742, no. 23/126, pl. 274, 6). Sometimes the rectangle is instead a cista held by one of the youths (e.g., *RVAp*, II, pl. 275, 6, no. 23/145b). For a similar basket with cake and sprigs, compare *RVAp*, II, pl. 274, 2, no. 23/127. For a recent study of the artist, see K. Schauenburg, *AA* 1992, pp. 413–431; see also S. Caranti Martignago, in *Il Carobbio* 5 (1979), pp. 62–70.

PUBLISHED: C. Vermeule, *MFA AnnRep* 1960, p. 36; *RVAp*, II, p. 743, no. 23/141.

59

59

MASTOID SKYPHOS
Connected in style with the Pavia Painter
340–330 B.C.
Gift of Horace L. Mayer. 58.1304

DIMENSIONS AND CONDITION: Height: 9.1 cm; diameter rim: 9.2 cm; diameter body: 8.1 cm; diameter foot: 4.2 cm
Most of each handle is missing. Part of the rim on side B is restored.

SHAPE: Flaring and sharply offset rim, upturned handles, tapering lower body, disk foot with irregular profile. This type of rim, derived ultimately from the native nestoris, is also found on mugs (oinochoai of shape 8N) and kantharoid skyphoi (e.g., *RVAp*, II, pl. 312, 3–4, and pl. 309, 3–4).

A: A woman is seated to the left on two yellow-streaked rocks, holding a yellow box or basket in her right hand. She wears shoes, necklace, earrings, bracelets, and radiate stephane, all yellow, as well as a kekryphalos and chiton.

B: A head of a woman wearing a necklace, earring, radiate stephane, and embroidered sakkos faces to the left. The jewelry is yellow, and the stripes of the sakkos are alternately yellow and white.

There are palmettes under the handles and palmette-scrolls flanking both pictures. The upper frames consist of dotted egg-pattern. A wave-pattern circles the lower body below a pair of stripes. There are crude tongues around the inner and outer rim. The reserved band below the rim is colored with a red wash.

PUBLISHED: *RVAp*, Suppl. II, p. 519, no. 24/254a.

60

SQUAT LEKYTHOS
Attributed to the Menzies Group
Ca. 335–325 B.C.
Gift by Contribution. 89.262

PROVENANCE: R. Lanciani collection; purchased in Rome; from Corato nelle Puglie

DIMENSIONS AND CONDITION: Height: 17.8 cm; diameter mouth: 4.8 cm; diameter body: 7.8 cm; diameter foot: 5.1 cm
The rim is chipped; otherwise unbroken. Incrustation on the foot and the back of the mouth.

SHAPE: The body is slimmer than that of the earlier lekythos by the Lecce Painter (cat. no. 19), and both neck and mouth are taller, the latter flaring to a trumpet shape. A reserved concavity separates the body from the grooved foot.

Eros is seated to the left on a yellow rock, a phiale full of offerings in his right hand and the left hand resting on the rock. He wears shoes, earrings, a necklace, a beaded bandoleer, bracelets, an anklet, a beaded fillet, and a kekryphalos, all rendered with added

60

KANTHAROS
Attributed to the Baltimore Painter
Ca. 330–320 B.C.
Gift of Edward Austin. 76.445

DIMENSIONS AND CONDITION: Height: 14.2 cm; diameter rim: 9.7 cm; maximum width at handles: 16.6 cm; minimum diameter body: 5.5 cm; diameter stem: 1.5 cm; diameter foot: 6.4 cm
The handle without a spur is largely restored. The stem and foot are ancient but alien. The dog's forelegs are badly worn.

SHAPE: Compare the very similar shape of the smaller kantharos of the Paidagogos Group (cat. no. 53); the spurs on this example are lower on the handle, and the struts between handle and rim are crooked. There are modeled female heads, facing inward, where the handles meet the lip. In the middle of the stem is a torus molding. The hollow foot is flaring and grooved at top and bottom.

A: Hermes is seated to the right, his right leg extended. He holds his yellow caduceus in his right hand and in his left a large basket containing a cake. He wears boots and a chlamys; his yellow petasos hangs behind his head. A large white hound stands at his side and faces in the same direction, its head held high as though sniffing the wind. A fillet hangs in the field at left, and there is a vertical branch at right.

white. A white mirror rests precariously on Eros's lap, and there are two rosettes floating in the field. His wings have broad white stripes and rows of white dots. White-dotted groundlines and small flowers mark the landscape.

On the back of the vase is a large palmette, with a scrolling palmette-tendril on either side. There are rays on the lower neck and wave-pattern on the shoulder. A single reserved stripe circles the lower body.

The Menzies Group, including the Menzies Painter, was a large group of minor painters who decorated a great variety of small shapes, perhaps in the workshop of the Ganymede Painter. Eros was a favorite subject.

PUBLISHED: Robinson, *Catalogue*, p. 184, no. 504; *RVAp*, II, p. 838, no. 26/272.

61 B

61 A

B: Athena is seated to the left on a dotted ground-line, holding two stacked phialai in her right hand. She wears a peplos, kekryphalos, shoes, bracelets, earrings, and the aegis, the last with white spots and snakes. Her left hand rests on her shield, and on her lap is her crested Corinthian helmet; both shield and helmet are tinted yellow. Another phiale is on the ground near her seat. A small plant grows at lower right, and a fillet hangs at upper right. At left is a vertical branch.

There is egg-pattern on the lip and on the cul between the handles. The foot, stem, and lower body

62   62

are unglazed.

The Baltimore Painter was a prolific painter of both large and small vases, the large ones with mythological or funerary subjects or both, the smaller ones dedicated to genre. His workshop was at Canosa, where he was influenced by the Patera Painter. He is especially noted for the elaborate decoration of his volute-kraters, on which the figure decoration sometimes extends to the foot. His workshop continued in operation in the last decades of the century under the White Sakkos Painter. For recent studies of the Baltimore Painter, see the bibliography in *RVAp*, Suppl. II, Part 1, pp. xxiii–xxiv. For an Athena by this painter, with similar helmet and aegis, compare Bari, Macinagrossa collection 26 (*RVAp*, II, p. 871, no. 27/57, pl. 333, 2; Trendall, *Handbook*, fig. 253).

PUBLISHED: Robinson, *Catalogue*, p. 187, no. 516; D. B. Hull, *Hounds and Hunting in Ancient Greece* (Chicago, 1964), p. 217, pl. 7; *RVAp*, II, p. 876, no. 27/110c, pl. 336, 5.

62

OINOCHOE (shape 1)
Close to or by the Baltimore Painter
Ca. 330–320 B.C.
Gift of Thomas G. Appleton. 76.54

PROVENANCE: Alessandro Castellani collection; from Canosa

DIMENSIONS AND CONDITION: Height: 25.7 cm; diameter neck: 3.1 cm; diameter body: 11.9 cm; diameter foot: 6.5 cm The handle and a piece of the rim have been reattached; otherwise unbroken.

SHAPE: A small, mold-made head is at either end of the handle, the upper one white with yellow hair, the lower one black. The tapering neck is tall and slender; the body is ovoid, with a flattened shoulder. The trefoil mouth is tightly constricted and flanked by rotellas. The handle is high, with a double ridge. The echinus foot has two grooves around its lower edge and a sharp molding below the juncture with the body.

On the front of the body is a female head in profile to the left, rising from a large white flower. The woman or goddess wears a necklace, earrings, beaded fillet, and striped sakkos; her eye is damaged. On either side of the head is an elaborate floral design with much added white and yellow.

On the front of the mouth is a band of stamped egg-pattern, painted white. There are rosettes on the rotelles by the mouth. Bands of dotted egg-pattern circle the shoulder and the middle of the neck, with white rays on the lower neck between them. The circling groundline consists of triple maeanders to left alternating with dotted cross-squares. On the back of the body is an elaborate palmette complex, highlighted with yellow dots.

For floral heads of this type, see comments on cat. no. 21. For the Baltimore Painter, see comments on cat. no. 61.

PUBLISHED: Robinson, *Catalogue*, pp. 182–183, no. 499; *RVAp*, II, p. 878, no. 27/134; K. Schauenburg, *JdI* 99 (1984), p. 129, note 7.

63

63

ASKOS
Close to the Baltimore Painter
Ca. 330–320 B.C.
Gift of Mrs. Henry P. Kidder. 01.14

DIMENSIONS AND CONDITION: Height: 19.6 cm; length: 16.0 cm; diameter rim: 7.1 cm; diameter foot: 10.4 cm
Unbroken

SHAPE: The so-called "duck askos," with a plump body, concave back, high pointed "tail," single handle, and a spout in place of a head was a type widespread in the fourth century and is found as far away as Athens and Olynthos. Compare B. A. Sparkes and L. Talcott, *The Athenian Agora*, vol. XII: *Black and Plain Pottery of the 6th, 5th and 4th Centuries B.C.* (Princeton, 1970), pl. 80, nos. 1735–1737; D. M. Robinson, *Excavations at Olynthus*, Part XIII: *Vases Found in 1934 and 1938* (Baltimore, 1950), pls. 170–171.

63

On the front, below the mouth, a woman wearing shoes, a chiton, and a kekryphalos is seated to the right on a white-striped rock, looking to the left into the mirror she holds in her right hand. In her left hand is a cista, which, like the mirror, is colored yellow. A large fan, white, with a yellow handle, center, and rim, lies across her shins above her yellow and white shoes. Her jewelry includes yellow bracelets, necklace, and earrings, and a belt of white beads. A yellow fillet secures her chignon. On the ground at left is a kalathos with yellow patterns. A flower grows beside the rock, and there is a dotted groundline below the woman's foot.

There is dotted egg-pattern around the neck and a circling groundline of wave-pattern. At the opposite end, beneath the "tail," is a large palmette; smaller palmettes and scrolls dotted with yellow fill the sides.

Women of the type on this askos are frequently depicted holding offerings and sitting or standing on either side of a grave stele or naiskos, particularly on volute-kraters and amphorae; compare a woman with cista and wreath on a krater by the Baltimore Painter in the Dechter collection, Los Angeles (*RVAp*, II, p. 861, no. 27/3, pl. 319, 3). So common is the scheme that an isolated figure like this is still charged with funerary symbolism.

PUBLISHED: *RVAp*, II, p. 881, no. 27/165.

64

64

DEER'S-HEAD RHYTON
Attributed to the workshop of the Baltimore Painter
Ca. 330–320 B.C.
John Michael Rodocanachi Fund. 63.472

DIMENSIONS AND CONDITION: Length (max.): 25.0 cm; diameter rim: 11.3 cm; diameter body (at base of bowl): 5.5 cm
The tip of the right horn, the tip of the left ear, and most of the left horn have been broken away; otherwise intact.

SHAPE: Compare cat. no. 32.

The deer's eyes are white, with yellow irises outlined and centered with red-orange. The horns are white with red-orange striations. Traces of white remain in the nostrils and ears.

On the front of the neck, Eros flies to the right with a yellow mirror in his extended right hand, a tympanum in his lowered left hand, and a fan, with yellow handle and white feathers, lying across his middle. He wears a kekryphalos, shoes, earrings, bracelets, a beaded thigh band on his right leg, anklets, and a beaded bandoleer across his chest, all in added white. There is a white ivy leaf in the field below. There is a wave-pattern under the rim; large palmettes, linked and enclosed by tendrils, flank the handle at the rear.

For rhyta, see comments on cat. no. 31.

PUBLISHED: C. Vermeule, *MFA AnnRep* 1963, p. 42; Hoffmann, *Tarentine*, p. 61, no. 369 (B 2), pl. 40, 1–2: "Main Group"; *RVAp*, II, p. 885, no. 27/217.

EXHIBITED: Corpus Christi, *Greek Vases*, p. 29, fig. 38.

64

65

65

65

FISH-PLATE

Attributed to the Black and White Stripe Painter
Ca. 340–320 B.C.
Gift of Mr. and Mrs. Cornelius C. Vermeule III in
the name of Cornelius Adrian Comstock Vermeule.
1986.1018

PROVENANCE: Lent by Mr. and Mrs. Cornelius C. Vermeule III (Loan no. 217.65); Hesperia Art, *Bulletin*, XVI, no. 102

DIMENSIONS AND CONDITION: Height: 4.0 cm; upper diameter: 18.0 cm; outer diameter rim: 18.2 cm; inner diameter central depression: 3.5 cm; outer diameter central depression: 4.1 cm; diameter stem: 3.7 cm; diameter foot: 6.9 cm
Unbroken

SHAPE: Hollow, spreading foot; deeply overhanging rim; see McPhee and Trendall, *Fish-plates*, pl. 64, 12, for a comparison with other types.

Interior: Cuttlefish, striped fish (probably a bream), mullet, and a horn shell. Added brown and white have been used for many details, and the bodies of the fish are tinted with brown, dilute wash. The central depression has a rosette; the framed wave-pat-

tern around it is repeated on the overhanging rim, a common feature on fish-plates by this painter.

The Black and White Stripe Painter, named for the vertical stripes like those along the back of the bream on this plate, was associated with the Canosan workshop of the Baltimore Painter. His work exhibits features in common with the Arpi Painter and the Hippocamp Painter, the latter a specialist in fish-plates.

PUBLISHED: C. C. Vermeule, *BurlMag* 115 (1973), pp. 118, 121, figs. 73, 79; McPhee and Trendall, *Fish-plates*, p. 137, no. IVB/31, pls. 58d, 64, 12; *MFA AnnRep* 1986–87, p. 51; I. McPhee and A. D. Trendall, *AntK* 33 (1990), pp. 46, 49.

66

OINOCHOE (shape 1)

Attributed to the Helios Group
Ca. 320–310 B.C.
Gift of H. J. Bigelow. 89.260

PROVENANCE: R. Lanciani collection; purchased in Rome; said to be from Ruvo

DIMENSIONS AND CONDITION: Height: 45.5 cm; height (front at rim): 40.2 cm; diameter neck: 3.5 cm; diameter body: 18.1 cm; diameter stem: 5.5 cm; diameter foot: 11.3 cm
Reconstructed from a few large pieces

SHAPE: The handle has female heads in relief at the mouth and base. Unlike those on the similar oinochoe, cat. no. 62, both modeled heads are glazed black, the lip is undecorated, and the grooved foot has a tall, broad stem. The bottom of the vase is open (diameter of opening: 2.8 cm).

Battle of Greeks and Amazons. In the center, back to back, an Amazon and a Greek are mounted on rearing white horses. The Amazon wears a short chiton, embades, a sleeved tunic (red with white spots), a belt with white dots, and a yellow Phrygian cap. Holding a spear in her right hand, she lunges at a Greek standing at the left who holds a spear in his right hand and a shield on his left arm. The shield is turned with the interior toward the viewer, so that the white porpax and antilabe are visible. He wears a yellow Phrygian helmet with a red crest and two plumes, a chlamys, a yellow cuirass with pteryges, and yellow greaves; on the ground between his feet is an Amazon's cap, with the opening turned toward the viewer. A second Amazon is prostrate on the ground at the right, about to be run through by the mounted Greek, who raises a spear in his right hand, its upper shaft lost in the ornament on the shoulder. The Greek wears a short chiton, a chlamys, a yellow Phrygian helmet without crest or plumes, and a white cuirass. The fallen Amazon wears a short chiton, yellow Phrygian cap, shoes, and red trousers with white spots. She holds a white pelta, like the

66 (Color Plate xiv)   66

66

one lying on the dotted groundline at left, with lacy designs in dilute glaze (a central floral framed by tendrils). Her hatchet has fallen on the ground by her side. Floating in the field at far left and center top are two rosettes; a plant grows at lower left.

A dense complex of palmettes and scrolling tendrils covers the back of the vase. On the neck are white rays beneath a band of white wave-pattern framed by stripes. There is a band of rosettes with white-tipped petals on the shoulder. The groundline consists of linked maeanders to right.

The vases of the Helios Group, all oinochoai, are by late followers of the Baltimore Painter. Compare the Amazonomachy on Leipzig T 956 (*RVAp*, II, p. 932, no. 28/124). The Boston vase is particularly close to the White Sakkos Painter.

PUBLISHED: Robinson, *Catalogue*, pp. 181–182, no. 496; MFA, *Trojan War*, fig. 30A; Oliver, *Reconstruction*, p. 8 (as ex coll. Alessandro Castellani, *Vente à Rome, mars - avril 1884*, lot 123); *RVAp*, II, p. 932, no. 28/123, pl. 366, 2.

67

BOAR'S-HEAD RHYTON
Attributed to the New Milton Group
Ca. 320–310 B.C.
Gift of Mrs. Samuel Dennis Warren. 97.64

DIMENSIONS AND CONDITION: Height: 20.3 cm; outer diameter rim: 10.1 cm; inner diameter rim: 9.3 cm; diameter base of bowl: 5.6 cm
Unbroken. The features of the painted female head are very worn, nearly effaced, and much of the added color is also lost. The black glaze on the boar's head is worn, particularly on the sides.

On the front of the neck is painted a female head in profile to the left; she wears a striped kekryphalos and earrings.

There are palmette-scrolls on either side of the head and crude tongues on the cyma-recta molding of the lip. On the nostrils, mouth, tusks, and forehead crest of the boar are traces of added white and yellow.

The New Milton Group was a small group in the following of the late Baltimore Painter; compare the female head on the deer's-head rhyton Brussels R 446 (*RVAp*, II, p. 944, no. 28/244; *CVA* Brussels 3, pl. 1, 12 [Belgique, pl. 144]).

PUBLISHED: E. Robinson, *MFA AnnRep* 1897, p. 29, no. 16; Hoffmann, *Tarentine*, p. 55, no. 329 (E 14); *RVAp*, II, p. 944, no. 28/245.

67

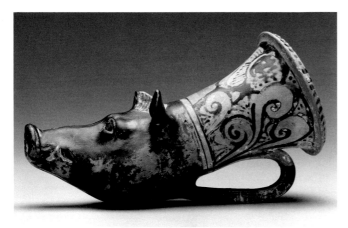

67

68

68

Plate
Connected in style with the Copenhagen Head
Painter
Ca. 320–310 B.C.
Gift of Horace L. Mayer. 58.1279

DIMENSIONS AND CONDITION: Height: 3.7 cm; diameter:
17.7 cm; diameter foot: 4.6 cm
One piece has been reattached, with damage to the woman's
nose and forehead.

SHAPE: Small, with offset rim and small ring foot. A circular
ring in the center of the interior may have been caused during
the turning and trimming of the leather-hard plate.

Interior: A large female head is facing left, wearing a
striped kekryphalos, earrings, a double-strand necklace, and a radiate stephane. Added yellow is used for
the jewelry, the stripes on the kekryphalos, and the
fillet securing the chignon. Floral ornaments are in
the field at left and right.

Circling the tondo is a laurel wreath, half-white
and half-yellow, and around the rim are black
tongues. The outside is black, with a reserved band
around the ring foot.

The Copenhagen Head Painter was a late follower
of the Baltimore Painter, who, like many minor artists of the period, specialized in decorating both large
and small vases with female heads.

PUBLISHED: C. C. Vermeule, *BurlMag* 115 (1973), p. 121, fig.
82; *RVAp*, II, pp. 952–953, no. 28/342.

LOUTROPHOROS
Attributed to the White Sakkos Painter
320–310 B.C.
Mary S. and Edward J. Holmes Fund. 1988.431

PROVENANCE: Eisenberg, *Ancient World*, p. 34, no. 104 b;
Sotheby's Sale, London, December 10, 1984, lot 366

DIMENSIONS AND CONDITION: Height: 80.0 cm; diameter upper rim: 25.0 cm; width upper scrolls: 28.1 cm; width lower
scrolls: 33.2 cm; diameter neck below flanges: 5.2 cm; diameter shoulder: 24.0 cm; diameter center of body: 21.0 cm; diameter bottom of body: 26.3 cm; diameter stem: 7.3 cm;
diameter top of foot: 7.9 cm; diameter foot: 17.0 cm
Broken and repaired, with some restorations in the handles
and considerable repainting in the white areas, most notably
on the horses and the head on the shoulder. The central part of
the octopus has been repainted. Excessive overpainting and
varnish have been removed.

SHAPE: This type of loutrophoros, with a tall, concave, cylindrical body, is exactly like a so-called barrel-amphora except
for the fancy, coiling handles. Sometimes a third type is created by substituting straight handles, like those on an amphora of Panathenaic shape (e.g., Malibu 84.AE.996
[Trendall, *Handbook*, fig. 182; *RVAp*, Suppl. II, p. 144, no.
18/16g]). The Boston loutrophoros has a tall, tapering neck
with a raised fillet around the middle, above which the neck
flares to a broad mouth, consisting of a reserved echinus
topped by an overhanging rim with ovolo cymatium. The
handles are broad and flat. The foot has a tall, tapering stem
and a slender torus base, grooved at the upper edge.

A (upper register): The abduction of Hippodameia. Pelops and Hippodameia stand in a quadriga,
shown in three-quarter view. The chariot, with a red
box and yellow wheels, is drawn to the right by four
galloping white horses, all rearing in unison. A
white hound with its coat streaked with dilute glaze
prances in similar fashion at the right. Hippodameia
wears a chiton, himation, bracelet, earrings, necklace, and one of the white sakkoi that give the artist
his name; all her jewelry is white too. Pelops wears
an embroidered chiton over a red tunic with long
sleeves. His Phrygian cap is yellow, and his belt and
crossed bandoleers have white beads. With his right
hand he holds both the princess and his long scepter,
decorated with white dots and a yellow finial (the latter damaged, but probably an eagle). There are various filling ornaments in the field: stars above,
flowers below, a phiale at the upper right, and a ball
of wool at the upper left.

A (lower register): a woman and a nude youth
with a cloak over his left arm stand on either side of a
white grave monument with a fluted shaft, broad
plinth, and small pediment. The woman holds a
tympanum in her lowered right hand and a casket
with white figures and ornament in her raised left
hand. She wears a chiton, himation, shoes, kekry-

69

phalos, earrings, bracelets, and a necklace. A long
garland of rosettes and white berries trails from her
left hand. The man holds a similar garland in his
raised right hand and a branch with a pendant fillet in
the crook of his left arm. He wears a wreath and a
yellow fillet in his hair. A fillet and a ball of wool
hang in the field.

B: A nude youth and a draped woman with a fillet
in her lowered left hand stand on either side of a tapering grave stele with a black fillet tied around the
shaft. Eggs and other offerings sit on top of the stele.
The woman wears a kekryphalos, shoes, chiton, earrings, necklace, and bracelets. The youth wears a
wreath and has a cloak and branch in his left arm and
a fan with a pendant garland of rosettes in his right
hand. The plinth of the stele, decorated with a white
key-pattern, is so broad that the figures seem to
stand upon it, but the dotted groundline below the
woman shows otherwise. In the field above are a ball
of wool and an ivy leaf. Added white is used for details of the rosettes, fan, ball, leaves, fillet, eggs, berries, jewelry, wreath, and stele.

A female head with a yellow-shadowed Phrygian
cap, perhaps Artemis Bendis, springs from the complex foliage (scrolling tendrils and acanthus) on the
shoulder of side A. Her face is white, with features in
dilute glaze. She looks down to her left, her face
nearly frontal. On the shoulder of side B is a complex
of palmettes and tendrils. Above the chariot scene on
side A, on the broad torus molding, is a frieze of rosettes, and between the two main panels is a band of
marine fauna with extensive use of added white and

69 (Color Plate xv)

69

yellow and shading with dilute glaze: two fish, three shells (horn shell, Venus clam, and scallop), and an octopus. Below, on the bulbous cul of the lower body, are rosettes on side A and a wave-pattern on side B.

The decoration of the neck is complex and differs on A and B. On A is an upper zone of yellow and white diamonds with scalloped edges, then two bands of yellow dots separated by a molded fillet; a

band of rosettes; and a lower zone of white rays. The motif of scalloped diamonds goes back to the Iliupersis Painter; see *RVAp*, I, pl. 64, 5. On B, the rays are black, the rosettes are replaced by chevrons, the molding is framed by black bands, and the upper zone contains a black palmette. There are laurel wreaths down the outer sides of either handle. The obverse edges of the handles have white stripes; the reverse edges have black dots. A band of egg-pattern circles the molding of the rim.

For Pelops and Hippodameia, see L. Lacroix, *BCH* 100 (1976), pp. 327–341; and M. Pipili, *LIMC*, V, 1, pp. 434–440; V, 2, pls. 309–314. For the head and floral ornament on the shoulder, see comments on cat. no. 21. A pair of similar loutrophoroi, one with the Rape of Chrysippos, son of Pelops, has been attributed by Trendall to the White Sakkos Painter (Sotheby's, New York, December 2, 1988, no. 107; *RVAp*, Suppl. II, p. 352, nos. 29/D4 and D6). The Baltimore Painter, colleague and teacher of the White Sakkos Painter, also depicted the abduction of Hippodameia, but as in most Apulian representations of the subject he included the pursuing Oinomaos; once Swiss market (*RVAp*, Suppl. I, p. 151, no. 27/21a).

"The immediate successor and true heir of the Baltimore Painter is the White Sakkos Painter" (Trendall, *Handbook*, p. 99). The influence is indeed obvious, but the White Sakkos Painter has a distinctive style all his own; note especially the moon-faced women with double chins and wisps of hair emerging from their white sakkoi at the temples. A prolific painter of both large and small vases, with a following of minor artists in his Canosan workshop, the White Sakkos Painter was one of the last major Apulian vase-painters of the Ornate style. As his name implies, he favored added color and a rich tapestry of ornament. The prancing, white chariot horses are particularly striking; compare those on the neck of the artist's volute-krater in Matera (A. Bottini, *BdArch* 5–6 [1990], p. 233, fig. 4), and on the neck of a volute-krater in the Getty Museum (Malibu 77.AE.14: *RVAp*, Suppl. I, p. 182, no. 29/C; *CVA* 3, pls. 136, 1 and 138, 1). The horses, too, are a legacy of the Baltimore Painter (e.g., Fiesole, Costantini collection 153 [*RVAp*, II, p. 871, no. 27/55, pl. 332]).

The band of fish on this vase recalls the band dividing the upper and lower registers on the painter's handleless loutrophoros in the Tampa Museum of Art (inv. 87.37: Trendall, *Handbook*, fig. 255; *RVAp*, Suppl. II, p. 353, no. 29/D8, pl. 92, 3–4). The fish on the Tampa vase are by the Sansone Painter, who either collaborated with the White Sakkos Painter or was perhaps the same man. It is not clear that the fish on the Boston loutrophoros are by the Sansone Painter, and there is otherwise no reason to believe they are not by the same artist who decorated the rest of the vase.

PUBLISHED: *MFA AnnRep* 1988–89, p. 42; M. Pipili, *LIMC*, V, 1, pp. 437 (no. 26), 439; V, 2, pl. 312; *RVAp*, Suppl. II, pp. 349–350, 352, no. 29/D5, pl. 91, 3.

HANDLE OF A LOUTROPHOROS

Ca. 330–310 B.C.

Henry Lillie Pierce Residuary Fund. 01.8094

PROVENANCE: E. P. Warren collection; bought in Naples

DIMENSIONS AND CONDITION: Height: 27.9 cm
Broken in four places and repaired. One snailshell-like tendril at the branching of the upper scroll is missing.

SHAPE: The flat handle is S-shaped, with coiled offshoots on both of the larger curves. Since the wave-pattern is normally on the obverse side, this was a left handle (B/A), probably from a barrel-shaped loutrophoros like cat. no. 69.

The flat, outer side is decorated with a laurel branch in red-figure with yellow berries. On the terminal curve at each end is a rosette in white and yellow. A white wave-pattern runs down the narrow edge on one side, terminating in a white stripe on the coils at either end.

70

71

Pegasus, painted in white, with details in yellow, gallops to the left over a flowering plant; a similar plant grows at right. He is not flying, for his left rear hoof touches the dotted groundline. The field is filled with a variety of conventional filling ornaments: rosettes, ivy leaves, fillets, and phialai, all touched with added white or yellow or both.

Two reserved stripes circle the lower body. There are large palmettes on the sides and back and a wave-pattern at the base of the handle. On the shoulder is a band of dotted egg-pattern, and there are white rays on the neck below three horizontal lines.

For the White Sakkos Painter, see comments on cat. no. 69. The vases of the Chariot Group are from his mature phase, when large oinochoai were a favored shape. Trendall and Cambitoglou list eight more examples with this subject: *RVAp*, II, p. 975, nos. 29/180, 29/181, 29/181a, 29/182; *RVAp*, Suppl. I, p. 188, no. 29/182a-b; *RVAp*, Suppl. II, p. 363, nos. 29/182c-d.

PUBLISHED: Robinson, *Catalogue*, p. 182, no. 498; Brommer, *Vasenlisten*, 1960, p. 234, no. D 8; ibid., 1973, p. 308, no. D 8; *RVAp*, II, p. 975, no. 29/179, pl. 382, 2; E. S. Brettman, *Vaults of Memory: Jewish and Christian Imagery in the Catacombs of Rome: An Exhibition* (Boston, 1985), p. 28, no. 133.

71

OINOCHOE (shape 1)
Attributed to the White Sakkos Painter
(The Chariot Group)
Ca. 320–310 B.C.
Gift by Contribution. 89.275

PROVENANCE: R. Lanciani collection; purchased in Rome; said to be from Ruvo

DIMENSIONS AND CONDITION: Height: 40.4 cm; diameter neck: 3.2 cm; diameter body: 15.0 cm; diameter foot: 8.0 cm Broken and repaired. The wave-pattern at the base of the handle is largely repainted.

SHAPE: Unlike the two similar oinochoai described above (cat. nos. 62 and 66), this vase has no modeled heads at the extremities of the handle. The high-swung handle has a double ridge. The foot is "terraced" in four degrees and has a tall reserved stem. A hole passes through the foot of the vase. The mouth has a grooved rim.

71

72

SHAPE: The shape is very close to that of the preceding vase, but it is slightly smaller and has steeper "terracing" on the foot.

In the center, rendered in yellow and white, the head of Nike emerges from a large flower. She looks up to her right, her face in three-quarter view. Her blonde hair escapes in front from beneath her sakkos. A necklace with black pendants circles her fleshy neck, and short wings spread out on either side of the head. Below this is a rich floral pattern of acanthus, flowers, and scrolling tendrils, with many details in white and yellow.

There is a large complex of palmettes and scrolls on the back and a band of dotted egg-pattern on the shoulder. On the neck are white rays below three horizontal lines. Two reserved stripes circle the lower body.

Such heads are usually identified as Nike, although Cambitoglou has suggested some may represent the effeminate Apulian form of Eros; see *RVAp*, II, p. 648, and the comments on cat. no. 21. For the White Sakkos Painter, see comments on cat. no. 69. Compare three jugs in Bari with similar heads of Nike (*RVAp*, II, p. 971, nos. 29/118–120).

PUBLISHED: Robinson, *Catalogue*, p. 182, no. 497; *RVAp*, II, p. 971, no. 29/117.

73

KNOB-HANDLED PATERA
Attributed to the White Sakkos-Stuttgart Group
Ca. 310 B.C.
Gift of Thomas G. Appleton. 76.62

PROVENANCE: Alessandro Castellani collection; from Ruvo

DIMENSIONS AND CONDITION: Height: 11.5 cm; upper diameter rim: 40.5 cm; interior diameter rim: 35.9 cm; maximum diameter rim: 41.4 cm; diameter stem: 8.9 cm; diameter foot: 10.0 cm
One of the knobs is missing; otherwise intact. The profile of the bowl is uneven.

SHAPE: Unlike other paterae of this type in the collection, there are no knobs on top of the handles. The bowl is more conical than cat. nos. 47 and 57. The foot is stepped in two degrees, with a broad reserved stem. The handles are ridged.

Interior: A woman holding a phiale in her left hand and a casket with white figures and ornament in her right is seated to the right on a rock. At the left is a second woman, her left foot resting on a rock and her left arm resting on her knee. She is offering the seated woman the white alabastron she holds in her right hand. Both women wear chitons and white bracelets and shoes; the standing woman wears a white sakkos, the seated woman a kekryphalos and a double necklace with white beads; both have long,

72

OINOCHOE (shape 1)
Attributed to the White Sakkos Painter
Ca. 320–310 B.C.
Gift by Contribution. 89.276

PROVENANCE: R. Lanciani collection; purchased in Rome; said to be from Ruvo

DIMENSIONS AND CONDITION: Height: 39.5 cm; height (front at rim): 31.2 cm; diameter neck: 2.7 cm; diameter body: 14.7 cm; diameter stem: 3.7 cm; diameter foot: 7.9 cm
Unbroken

73

73

white fillets trailing from their head cloths. The seated woman's chiton has slipped off her right shoulder, revealing her breast, an uncommon representation in Apulian red-figure. At the right, a dancing satyr is holding a yellow torch over the women. He wears a nebris rendered in added red and yellow, and a wreath, shoes, and a ring around his right leg, all in added white. In his left hand is a slender yellow pedum. Two flowers fill the field at lower left and right, and there is a pendant white necklace (?) at the top. The two rock outcroppings are banded with added yellow and white, also used to color the flowers. The woman at the left stands on a groundline of white dots.

The baseline consists of a band of dotted egg-pattern, the eggs having white cores. The tondo is framed by concentric bands of wave-pattern and scrolling tendrils, the latter in added white. The knobs by the handles are decorated with white rosettes. On the flattened upper rim, the clay ground is tinted with a red wash. Wave-pattern circles the overhanging rim.

The White Sakkos-Stuttgart Group consists of some late members of the White Sakkos Painter's workshop in Canosa. Their products are often poorly potted and clumsily painted; the exposed breast of the seated woman is a characteristic motif.

PUBLISHED: Robinson, *Catalogue*, p. 188, no. 519; Schneider-Herrmann, *Paterae*, pp. 27 (as 72.62), 33 (no. VII 2, as 72.62), 109–110 (no. 183), 129, pl. 18, 1; *RVAp*, II, p. 980, no. 29/228, pl. 384, 5; Trendall, *Handbook*, pp. 100, 102, 151 (fig. 259), 280; *RVAp*, Suppl. II, p. 347, no. 29/228.

74

KANTHAROS
Attributed to the Kantharos Group
Ca. 320–310 B.C.
Gift of Mrs. Horace L. Mayer. 1978.1346

PROVENANCE: Collection of Horace L. Mayer (Loan no. 4.59)

DIMENSIONS AND CONDITION: Height with handles: 19.1 cm; width across handles: 15.5 cm; diameter rim: 10.9 cm; diameter lower edge of body: 6.4 cm; diameter stem lower section: 2.5 cm; diameter foot: 6.1 cm
Unbroken

SHAPE: Flaring rim; tall, thick stem with reserved fillet in the middle, framed by grooves; foot grooved into three degrees; high, concave handles with struts connecting them to the rim. At the base of each handle is a modeled leaf.

On either side, a female head is facing to the left, wearing a sakkos, earrings, radiate stephane, and necklace, with much use of added yellow. Framing the head are vertical white stripes, which appear to be topped by ivy leaves but in fact are very cursory Ionic columns. There is a flower in the field on side A. The grooves framing the fillet on the stem are painted yellow and red. The side of the foot is tinted red.

That the "ivy-staffs" are in fact Ionic columns is made clear by more carefully executed examples, such as Bonn 118–119 (*RVAp*, Suppl. II, p. 291, no. 27/155a, and p. 188, no. 21/63b; *CVA* 3, pl. 35). They are common framing elements on such kantharoi but are sometimes omitted, as on the following example. The columns may have funerary overtones; compare Malibu 84.AE.996 (*RVAp*, Suppl. II, p. 144, no. 18/16g; *CVA* 4, pls. 179, 2 and 182, 3), where a tomb monument consists of a white Ionic column surmounted by a kantharos.

The Kantharos Group was a large group within the workshop of the White Sakkos Painter. The shape and the decoration with female heads are standard.

PUBLISHED: *RVAp*, II, p. 996, no. 29/396; *RVAp*, Suppl. II, p. 346, no. 29/396 (as 1978.000).

74

74

75

75

75

KANTHAROS
Attributed to the Kantharos Group
Ca. 320–310 B.C.
Gift of Mrs. Horace L. Mayer. 1978.1347

PROVENANCE: Collection of Horace L. Mayer (Loan no. 5.59)

DIMENSIONS AND CONDITION: Height with handles: 19.2 cm; width across handles: 18.4 cm; diameter rim: 12.1 cm; diameter lower edge of body: 6.7 cm; diameter lower section of stem: 2.3 cm; diameter foot: 6.2 cm
Unbroken

SHAPE: Like the preceding example, but with the body broader and the handles wider. The foot is terraced in three degrees and, like the stem and fillet, is all black.

Painting and details are generally as in the previous example but without the white framing elements. On either side, a female head to the left, wearing a sakkos, earrings, radiate stephane, and a necklace. In front of each head is a "window" above and a scrolling floral below.

PUBLISHED: *RVAp*, II, p. 996, no. 29/395.

76

OINOCHOE (shape 1)
Attributed to the Painter of Brunswick 307–8
(Kantharos Group)
Ca. 320–310 B.C.
Bequest of Charles H. Parker. 08.280

PROVENANCE: Alfred Greenough collection

DIMENSIONS AND CONDITION: Height: 22.8 cm; diameter neck: 2.3 cm; diameter body: 10.1 cm; diameter foot 4.6 cm
The neck and handle have been reattached.

SHAPE: Compare cat. nos. 71–72, above; this example has a foot "terraced" in three degrees.

A large female head is facing to the left, wearing a sakkos and yellow jewelry: a necklace, and a radiate stephane. Wave-pattern circles the lower body, and yellow rays decorate the neck, below two yellow horizontal lines. Yellow rosettes and ivy leaves float in the field. The back is painted with a large palmette framed by scrolling tendrils.

The Painter of Brunswick 307–8 is named after two oinochoai in Brunswick (Braunschweig), on which the treatment of the head, as noted by Trendall and Cambitoglou, is almost identical to that on the Boston vase (*RVAp*, II, p. 993). This painter is one of three hands identified within the large Kantharos Group, itself part of the White Sakkos Painter workshop in Canosa.

PUBLISHED: Robinson, *Catalogue*, p. 183, no. 500; L. D. Caskey, *MFA AnnRep* 1908, p. 62; *RVAp*, II, pp. 993–994, no. 29/357, pl. 388, 3.

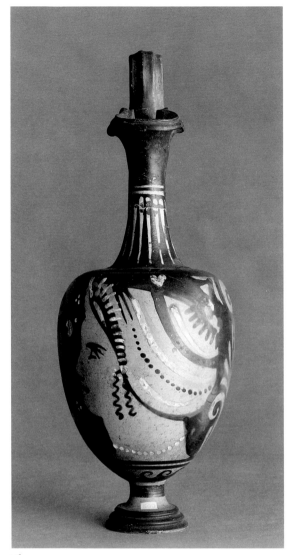

76

77

LEKANIS WITH LID
Ca. 320–310 B.C.
Gift of William Sturgis Bigelow. 98.203a-b

DIMENSIONS AND CONDITION: Height: 10.0 cm; width: 14.7 cm; diameter rim: 8.9 cm; diameter upper body: 9.8 cm; diameter stem: 3.2 cm; diameter foot: 4.7 cm; lower diameter lid: 9.8 cm; maximum diameter lid at carination: 10.0 cm; diameter stem of lid: 1.5 cm; diameter knob: 4.8 cm
A piece is missing from one handle; otherwise intact. There is incrustation on the bowl, and on the lid are dark areas where it was removed.

SHAPE: Standard Apulian lekanis, with horizontal strap handles; offset rim; tapering foot with torus base; low, conical lid with overhanging rim; wide knob with sharp moldings and tall, concave stem.

The lid has two female heads in kekryphaloi to left. Both women are adorned with earrings, necklace, and radiate stephane, all yellow. The sakkoi have detailing in yellow. In front of one head is a yellow ivy leaf; before the other, a flower. In each case, the hair at the back is tied with a yellow fillet. Between the heads are two large, triangular palmettes. On the top of the handle is a black palmette. There are dentil-like tongues around the overhanging rim and between the handles on the bowl.

77

OINOCHOE (shape 3)
Ca. 320 B.C.
Source Unknown. 15.1351

DIMENSIONS AND CONDITION: Height, maximum to top of handle: 12.6 cm; width of neck: 4.3 cm; depth of neck: 4.5 cm; diameter body: 9.4 cm; diameter foot: 7.2 cm
Unbroken. Much of the added white has flaked off.

SHAPE: Standard chous type, with low handle, trefoil mouth, squat, globular body, and wide, flaring foot

Bust of a young Pan facing left. Added white, perhaps originally tinted yellow, is used for the horns, fillet, and the collar of his garment (?). An ivy leaf and scrolling tendril are at right, palm fronds at lower left. The figure panel has lower and lateral frames of simple reserved lines; the upper frame of simple black tongues is unintentionally smeared with black glaze. There is a cross of red wash under the reserved foot.

78

CAMPANIAN
Red-Figure and Plastic Vases

The red-figure vases of Campania differ from those of Apulia and Lucania in several regards. In Campanian, the fired clay is a lighter color, varying from buff to pale brown; it was sometimes coated with a reddish wash to intensify the color. The floral patterns are of a generally different nature from the more exuberant Apulian, with distinctive bellflowers (*Campanulaceae*; e.g., cat. nos. 79, 84) and less use of complex spiraling tendrils. Added white is frequently used for the skin of women (e.g., cat. nos. 84–85, 91–92), and there is generally a greater taste for polychromy. There are fewer mythological subjects and fewer grand display pieces like the kraters and loutrophoroi of the Darius-Underworld workshop. The Samnite warriors who conquered Campania in the late fifth century appear in many scenes, recognized by their plumed helmets and distinctive armor (cat. no. 90); less bellicose Italians may wear loincloths secured with broad belts (cat. no. 84). Some of the larger shapes commonly found in Apulia and Lucania are absent: the volute-krater, the column-krater, the loutrophoros. The hydria is more common than in Apulia, as is the neck-amphora, although never the tall Panathenaic type. Other shapes, like the bail-handled amphora, are unique to the region.

Although it was in Campania that the Greeks first settled in Italy in the second half of the eighth century, in the sixth and fifth centuries the Greeks of Cumae and Neapolis, as well as the predominately Etruscan inhabitants of Capua, continued to import most of their fine wares from Athens, Corinth, and East Greece. Except for the Owl-Pillar group, which produced clumsy imitations of Attic vases in the second half of the fifth century, red-figure workshops did not open in Campania until late in the second quarter of the fourth century. The impetus appears to have been the arrival of immigrant Sicilian potters and painters, perhaps fleeing the political turmoil in their homeland. Three major groups can be distinguished: two at Capua and one at Cumae. Capuan pottery is somewhat more poorly made than Cumaean, with a tendency in larger pieces to develop cracks and fissures. Nonetheless, some of the finest products of the Campanian school originated there.

The first of the Capuan workshops centered around the Cassandra Painter, a precise draftsman fond of elaborate ornament, who was strongly influenced by artists working in the Sicilian style, such as the Chequer Painter (see cat. no. 107). The Cassandra Painter had two schools of followers, one centered around the Parrish Painter, the other around the Laghetto and Caivano Painters. The Parrish Painter was a close follower of the Cassandra Painter but a less talented artist; the amphora in Boston (cat. no. 79), with lounging warriors and a vigorous centauromachy, is one of his better works. The Cassandra-Parrish workshop included several minor artists who decorated mostly small vases, particularly neck- and bail-amphorae, but also oinochoai, such as the one from the Pilos Head Group, with a broad band of tongues filling the shoulder, a common Campanian motif (cat. no. 82). Other followers specialized in kylikes, which show strong Attic influence in both shape and ornament; the Eros on a cup in Boston, however, sits on a typically Campanian landscape element, a volcanic rock speckled with black and white dots (cat. no. 83). Some of the finest Campanian phlyax vases are also from this workshop; the hydria in Boston (cat. no. 80), with its capering actors in padded tights, may date before 350 B.C.

The Ixion Painter represents the final flowering of the Cassandra-Parrish workshop in the last third of the fourth century. He specialized in larger vases, many with mythological subjects. His distinctive style was influenced by contemporary Apulian vase-painting but is characterized by a more liberal use of added color (e.g., cat. no. 90). Among the minor painters associated with the Ixion Painter were those of the Valencia Group; a lekythos from the Group is decorated with a single, large female head (cat. no. 91), which, unlike similar heads on Apulian vases (and those beneath the handles of the Ixion Painter's hydria [cat. no. 90]), is painted with added white. The Ixion Painter also painted a few fish-plates, another product of the Cassandra-Parrish workshop (e.g., cat. nos. 86–87 and 89). Like most Campanian fish-plates, they are distinguishable from Apulian examples by the absence of decoration in the central depression.

The vases of the Laghetto and Caivano Painters, leaders of the other principal school descended from the Cassandra Painter, have a Paestan flavor, and several of their works have been found at Paestum. Both artists were fond of representing the spotted, lava-flow rocks of Campania, whether in mythological scenes or in Dionysiac or genre subjects. The two other major figures in the group were the Painter of B.M. F 63 and the Errera Painter, whose skyphos in Boston is characteristic of his colorful but relatively undistinguished style (cat. no. 84). Several other minor artists were associated with the workshop, and those active at the end of the century can be said to have brought it to a relatively inglorious end.

The second major group of Capuan vase-painters, the AV Group, is named after Avella, although most of their works have been found at Capua. As with the workshop of the Cassandra Painter, the forerunners of the group may have been immigrant Sicilians. The first artist of the group, the Capua Painter, was prolific but of little talent; his influence was small compared with that of the Whiteface-Frignano Painter, who was active about 360–330 B.C. He is named for his predilection for rendering the flesh of women with added white, as on his hydria in Boston (cat. no. 85); his second name comes from the Frignano Painter, whom Trendall has now recognized to be the same artist. The Boston hydria is the painter's most ambitious work, and the serpent guarding the spring is particularly fine, its mottled skin rendered with feathery dilute glaze.

In general, the vases of the AV Group differ markedly from those of the Cassandra Painter's followers. The drawing is sketchier and lacks the precision characteristic of the other school. There are many more scenes of departing warriors in Samnite garb, pouring libations with the assistance of their female relations, also in native costume; and more funerary rites, with the same characters assembled around a tomb monument or grave stele.

Cumaean red-figure began a little later than at Capua, around 350 or so. The large number of vases, many of them found in excavations at Cumae in the nineteenth century, were apparently all produced by the same long-lived workshop. Trendall has divided the development of the fabric into three stages, labeled Cumae A, B, and C. The major figure of the first stage was the CA Painter, whose vases are notable for their bright polychromy, enhanced by the light orange color of the clay and the use of a reddish wash. He painted both large and small vases, rarely with mythological subjects, more often with Samnite warriors and women, symposia, and Dionysiac scenes. The CA Painter had a number of prolific and more modestly talented followers, among whom was the Boston Ready Painter, named by J. D. Beazley after a bell-krater formerly in the Ready collection and now in Boston (cat. no. 92).

Around 330, a strong Apulian influence became apparent in the late work of the CA Painter and his followers. Apulian vase-painters may have emigrated to Cumae in the 330s, when there was a treaty between Taranto and Neapolis, or after the defeat of the Tarentines by the Lucanians and Messapians in 338 B.C. Apulian motifs, such as the "xylophone," were used with increasing frequency, and funerary naiskoi of Apulian type became a frequent motif on hydriai by the CA Painter. The painters of Cumae B represent the second phase of the Cumaean workshop, in which Apulian influence continued but was blended to create a hybrid style still distinctively Campanian, particularly in ornament and the use of added color. Subjects became more limited, with stock figures and repetitious compositions, and there was a general deterioration in the quality of the drawing.

The final phase of the Cumaean fabric, Cumae C, is marked by a further decline in quality. Small shapes, including bottles and lekanides, were decorated with scenes of women or female heads. Drawing became sketchy to the point of impressionism, particularly in the White Bird Group. Among the products of this late phase are the pyxides of the Kemai Group (cat. no. 93) and the eccentric Class of Head-Cruets (cat. no. 94), the latter with plastic heads that foreshadow the molded vessels characteristic of late Hellenistic Campanian, such as the Magenta Ware lamp-filler in the form of a squatting grotesque (cat. no. 96). As elsewhere in Magna Graecia, painted pottery in Campania ended on a poor note, and it was not vase-painters but the muralists of Pompeii who eventually raised Campanian painting to new and unprecedented heights.

NECK-AMPHORA
Attributed to the Parrish Painter
Ca. 350 B.C.
Francis Bartlett Donation of 1900. 03.832

PROVENANCE: E. P. Warren collection; from Campania

DIMENSIONS AND CONDITION: Height: 37.3 cm; diameter rim: 14.2 cm; diameter neck: 7.1 cm; diameter body: 16.0 cm; diameter foot: 10.7 cm
Unbroken. Incrustation on the foot and on the neck, shoulder, and upper right of side A.

SHAPE: The shape differs from most later Campanian neck-amphorae in the relative plumpness of the body, the straightness of the neck, the way the handles touch the underside of the rim, and the absence of a tall stem between body and foot. The shape ultimately derives from early fourth-century Attic neck-amphorae like those painted by the Meleager Painter; e.g., Toronto 388 (Beazley, *ARV²*, p. 1411, no. 40). The foot of this example has a terraced riser and a narrow, straight-sided base. The handles are double-reeded.

A: Three young warriors are lounging in camp. The one holding a staff in his left hand at the upper left is seated on a rock near an Ionic column; the rock is outlined in added white. In the field before him hangs a pilos-helmet. The frowning youth at the lower left leans casually on his staff, his cloak folded over his left arm. He carries an empty pointed amphora on his right shoulder. Like the other youths, he wears an elaborate white fillet or stephane with vertical protrusions in front. He looks back, his face in three-quarter view, toward the youth at the right, who stands with a spear in his raised left hand and rests his lowered right hand on a shield. A chlamys is draped over his left shoulder. There is no clue to the identity of the three youths; they recall the Argonauts relaxing and drawing water on the Etruscan Ficoroni Cista (see comments on cat. no. 167).

B: Eros, maenad, and youth. Eros flies to the left to offer a white fillet to the maenad standing below, her left foot resting on a spotted stone. Eros wears a white radiate crown, bracelets, anklets, and crossed bandoleers. The maenad wears a radiate crown, necklace, and bracelets, all in white, as well as a belted chiton. She holds a thyrsos in her left hand and gestures toward it with her right. A nude youth with a white fillet in his hair and a spear in his right hand is seated on a cloak at the upper left; he turns to look toward Eros, so that his body is in three-quarter view. He supports himself on his left arm, but there is no indication of terrain in the scene except for the stone and the solitary white flower at the lower left.

On either side of the neck, a centaur wielding a tree branch battles a nude young warrior, presum-

79

ably a Lapith, who wears a helmet and carries a shield. On side A, the warrior has a spear in his right hand and a shield in his left; he is being worsted by his opponent, who wields his branch like a spear. The centaur wears a white fillet and has a skin over his left arm. The man is naked save for his Chalcidian helmet; the same is true of the warrior on side B, who is about to stab the centaur with a sword held in his right hand. The centaur has forced aside the warrior's shield, which has a white porpax, and raises the tree branch in both hands behind his head. Instead of a fillet, the centaur wears a white wreath.

The shoulder decoration of alternating lotuses and palmettes, linked by tendrils, looks back to Attic

models. Filling the sides below the handles are large palmettes, flowers, and scrolling tendrils which serve to frame the pictures. The large flowers with dotted stamens and petals are hallmarks of the Parrish Painter. Bands of dotted egg-pattern circle the rim and divide the neck from the shoulder. Above the scenes on the neck are bands of wave-pattern. The groundline circling the lower body consists of groups of four stopt maeanders to right alternating with large saltire-squares, the pattern invariably favored by the artist.

The Parrish Painter was a leading follower of the Cassandra Painter at Capua, active around midcentury. This is one of his finest works, the balanced composition and carefully drawn nudes of the obverse being particularly fine. The figural scenes on the neck are unusual, as is the lotus and palmette ornament on the shoulder.

PUBLISHED: E. Robinson, *MFA AnnRep* 1903, p. 66, no. 18; J. D. Beazley, *JHS* 63 (1943), pp. 72 (no. 1), 73 (fig. 3), pls. 4–5; A. D. Trendall, *Jahrbuch der Berliner Museen* 2 (1960), pp. 28–29; idem, *LCS*, p. 249, no. 144, pl. 99, no. 1; K. Schauenburg, *JOAI* 51 (Hauptblatt) (1976–77), p. 34, note 79; A. Cambitoglou, *Studies Webster*, II, p. 19, note 71.

79

79

80

HYDRIA
Perhaps from the Cassandra-Parrish Workshop
Ca. 360–350 B.C.
Francis Bartlett Donation of 1900. 03.831

PROVENANCE: E. P. Warren collection; Spinelli collection; from Suessula

DIMENSIONS AND CONDITION: Height: 29.8 cm; diameter rim: 11.0 cm; diameter neck: 6.4 cm; diameter body: 18.9 cm; diameter stem upper molding: 5.3 cm; diameter foot: 10.7 cm
Unbroken

SHAPE: Flat shoulder and narrow, concave neck. The profile of the mouth resembles a flattened ovolo. The side handles are set high on the body and tilt sharply upward. The foot has a high, sloping riser with a reserved groove at the top and a reserved flange above the narrow base.

Phlyax scene. Two comic actors face each other in a high-stepping dance. Both wear expressive, bearded masks, trousers, padded tunics, and mock phalli. The tunics and phalli are tinted with dilute glaze. The stage is not represented, and there is no clue to the theme of the play.

The panel has elaborate frames: slanted and addorsed palmettes above, an ivy vine on the left side, a laurel wreath on the right, and a wave-pattern below. The palmettes are of a type not found after midcentury; a relatively early date is also indicated by

80

the careful draftsmanship, the absence of filling ornament, and the geometric composition. Trendall classes the masks as type B; compare the mask worn by the actor on the Apulian oinochoe, cat. no. 20.

PUBLISHED: E. Robinson, *MFA AnnRep* 1903, p. 66, no. 22; Bieber, *Theater*, pp. 283–284, fig. 382; Catteruccia, *Pitture*, p. 59, no. 66 bis, pl. 11; Trendall, *Phlyax*, 1959, p. 49, no. 127; idem, *EAA*, III, p. 709; Bieber, *Theater*, 1961, p. 141, fig. 516; Trendall, *Phlyax*, 1967, pp. 14, 67, no. 132 (with additional bibliography); Webster and Green, *Old and Middle Comedy*, p. 134, no. Ph 132; P. Ghiron-Bistogne, *NumAntCl* 18 (1989), pp. 395 and 401, pl. II, fig. 4.

EXHIBITED: *Theater in Ancient Art*, fig. 31.

81

OINOCHOE (shape 8)
Ca. 350–335 B.C.
Henry Lillie Pierce Residuary Fund. 01.8036

PROVENANCE: E. P. Warren collection; Bourguignon collection; from Capri

DIMENSIONS AND CONDITION: Height: 22.1 cm; diameter rim: 8.2 cm; diameter neck: 4.9 cm; diameter body: 11.7 cm; diameter foot: 8.5 cm
Unbroken; wear on the mouth and handle; incrustation on the foot and parts of the neck and handle.

SHAPE: Round mouth with cyma-reversa molding; tall, concave neck; ovoid body; low strap handle from shoulder to rim; wide, grooved foot in two degrees, with a reserved stem. The shape is uncommon; compare the Apulian juglet, cat. no. 20.

Caricature of Oedipus and the Sphinx. Oedipus is nude except for a pilos, his cloak used only for padding as he leans on his staff to the right. His potbelly recalls the padded costume of comic actors. The sphinx crouches to the left on an irregular pile of mottled rocks. Her body is more human than feline, although somewhat dwarf-like, and she has talons and a large pair of wings. The two protagonists eye one another with insouciant detachment. There is a light wash on the bodies, and on the sphinx are touches of brown shading. Tall plants grow between them and behind Oedipus, and in the field above is what may be a stylized bucranium.

Large palmettes occupy the sides and back. A tall band of unframed black tongues circles the lower neck, and there are two reserved stripes around the lower body and another around the lower edge of the mouth.

Trendall, *Phlyax*, 1967, notes that Oedipus does not seem to be wearing a mask and thus calls this a caricature instead of a stage performance. He is probably correct; however, the painter did give Oedipus the distended phallus of a comic actor and what may

81

81

be the padded costume of one as well. The chest seems naturalistic, but there is a line on the right hip that may be the edge of a garment. The basic composition is traditional for scenes of Oedipus and the Sphinx, going back to the early fifth century (see Moret, *Oedipe*; reference below). Taplin (*Comic Angels*, p. 80, pl. 18.18) discusses the comic treatment of this subject on an Apulian chous (Taranto, Ragusa coll. 74: Trendall, *Handbook*, fig. 137), on which Oedipus and Kreon face a comic sphinx with pendulous breasts, who is perched on a pile of rocks similar to that on the Boston oinochoe; he notes that the faces are more exaggeratedly ugly than mask-like, suggesting macabre visual humor without the reflection of a comedy.

PUBLISHED: E. Robinson, *MFA AnnRep* 1901, p. 34, no. 25; Trendall, *PP*, p. 68 (as Bourguignon collection) (ref. to Hartwig, *Philologus*, 1897, pp. 1–4, pl. 1); Catteruccia, *Pitture*, p. 40, no. 33; Trendall, *Phlyax*, 1959, p. 48, no. 124; idem, *EAA*, III, p. 710; Taranto, *Letteratura*, p. 32, no. 182; Trendall, *Phlyax*, 1967, pp. 15, 17, 87, no. 200 (with additional bibliography); K. Schauenburg, in *Festschrift Hausmann*, pp. 233 (note 42), 235, pl. 52, 2; J.-M. Moret, *Oedipe, la sphinx et les Thébans: Essai de mythologie iconographique* (Rome, 1984), pp. 142–144, 189, pl. 95, cat. no. 194.

82

OINOCHOE (shape 2)
Attributed to the Pilos Head Group
Ca. 340 B.C.
Gift of the Boston Teachers Club in Memory of Mary Ward (September 14, 1884-May 6, 1949). 1970.363

DIMENSIONS AND CONDITION: Height: 24.5 cm; diameter neck: 4.6 cm; diameter body: 13.8 cm; diameter foot: 7.0 cm Reconstructed from a few large fragments. There is a small fragment missing at the top right corner of the picture panel.

SHAPE: A variety of shape 2, with a tall, straight neck, trefoil mouth with grooved rim, low handle, flattened shoulder, and echinus foot.

A centaur wearing a white wreath trots to the left, carrying a sapling with white leaves over his right shoulder and a boulder under his left arm. A hare and two birds hang from the tree. A band of wave-pattern circles the lower neck, and the shoulder is filled by a broad band of tongues. The lateral frames consist of tall, scrolling tendrils enclosed within narrow rectangles. The groundline is a band of dotted egg-pattern. There are large palmettes and floral ornaments on the back.

In Attic vase-painting, the tree branch hung with small game was an attribute of the wise centaur

82

Cheiron. The boulder, however, one would expect to see carried by one of the wild centaurs who broke up the wedding of Perithoos or who attacked Herakles at the well of Pholos. This, then, is an all-purpose centaur, equipped by the artist with all of the traditional attributes but without reference to a specific story or individual. Compare an oinochoe of shape 10, also from the Pilos Head Group, with a very similar centaur carrying a sapling with a dead hare: Vienna 828 (Trendall, *LCS*, p. 271, no. 6/291, pl. 109, 3). For Cheiron, see M. Gisler-Huwiler, *LIMC*, III, 1, pp. 237–248; III, 2, pls. 185–197.

PUBLISHED: C. C. Vermeule, *MFA AnnRep* 1969–70, p. 42; Trendall, *LCS*, Suppl. I, p. 47, no. 291a; C. C. Vermeule, *BurlMag* 115 (1973), p. 121, fig. 80; K. Schauenburg, *JOAI* 51 (Hauptblatt) (1976–77), p. 27, note 36; idem, in *Festschrift Arias*, p. 474, note 15; Trendall, *LCS*, Suppl. III, p. 132, no. 291a.

83

83

83

83

KYLIX (type B)
Compared to the Painter of Zurich 2633
3rd quarter of 4th century B.C.
Henry Lillie Pierce Residuary Fund. 01.8118

PROVENANCE: E. P. Warren collection; from Cumae

DIMENSIONS AND CONDITION: Height: 8.9 cm; diameter rim:
18.5 cm; diameter foot: 7.7 cm; diameter stem: 1.7 cm
Unbroken; minor scratches and incrustation.

SHAPE: Kylix of type B. The handles are tilted upward and
rolled back at the ends, where they flare to nearly twice their
width at the roots. There is an unglazed step between the stem
and the slender foot.

Interior: Eros is seated to the left on a black and
white spotted rock, holding a triangular object with a
vertical handle, possibly a bird trap or a musical instrument. A cloak pads his seat, and he wears a white
bandoleer and (apparently) shoes. His wings are
spotted black and white. His hair is tied in a bun. A
phiale fills the space at lower left. The groundline
consists of a band of dotted egg-pattern above a black
exergue. The circular frame consists of groups of six
or seven stopt maeanders alternating with checkerboards (four in all).

A: A young satyr stands next to a small stele. He
wears shoes and has a cloak over his left shoulder and
arm; he carries a thyrsos in his left hand and a phiale
in his right. He looks back at a youth standing at the
right dressed in a himation and holding a staff in his
right hand. In the field above are a phiale and a quartered circle with dots.

B: A nude youth walks to the left with a phiale in
his left hand and a cloak around both arms; he looks
back at a youth standing at the right with a staff in
his right hand and wearing a richly bordered himation. A circular ornament with a swastika is in the
field at right, possibly a discus.

There are large palmettes under the handles and
smaller ones enclosed by tendrils, which frame the
exterior scenes. There are two concentric circles on
the reserved underside of the foot.

For Eros with what may be a bird trap, compare an
Attic kylix once in Castle Ashby, now at the University of Texas, Austin (CVA Castle Ashby, pl. 40, no.
62). Erotes on some Gnathian vases also hold traps
(e.g., Philadelphia, University Museum, L-64-19
[CVA 1, pl. 36, 2]). In the hands of Eros, they are
probably to be understood as "love-traps." For Eros,
see A. Hermary et al., LIMC, III, 1, pp. 850–942, III,
2, pls. 609–668; and A. Greifenhagen, Griechische
Eroten (Berlin, 1957).

Trendall found the feet and drapery of the youths
to be in the manner of the Painter of Zurich 2633, a

member of the Cassandra-Parrish Workshop, but he thought the faces to be in a different style. The rough checkers and stopt maeanders bordering the tondo recalled to him the Louvre Sacrifice Painter; see Trendall, *LCS*, p. 265.

PUBLISHED: Trendall, *LCS*, p. 265, no. 255, pl. 110, nos. 8–9; G. Schneider-Herrmann, *BABesch* 52–53 (1977–1978), pp. 267, 278, fig. 10a-b; K. Schauenburg, *JdI* 101 (1986), p. 159, note 5; *LIMC*, III, 1, p. 908, no. 666; III, 2, pl. 647.

84

SKYPHOS
Attributed to the Errera Painter
Ca. 340–330 B.C.
Francis Bartlett Donation of 1900. 03.822

PROVENANCE: E. P. Warren collection; from Campania

DIMENSIONS AND CONDITION: Height: 14.2 cm; diameter rim: 14.1 cm; diameter foot: 10.3 cm
Unbroken and in good condition, with some erosion of the woman's features.

SHAPE: The shape descends from Attic skyphoi, with thick walls, a wide disk foot, and handles just below the rim.

A: A youth wearing a white, apicate fillet, a loin-cloth edged with yellow dots, shoes, and a yellow belt stands to the left, his right foot on a rock. With his right hand he holds out a white fillet and with his left a white wreath with yellow ends and central band. The belt and loincloth suggest he is a native Italian; compare the warrior on the painter's neck-amphora in Brussels (A 3550: Trendall, *LCS*, p. 322, no. 704, pl. 126).

B: A white-skinned woman wearing a peplos and yellow bracelets and shoes stands to the left. A belt of yellow beads circles her waist. Her hair is tied up with a white fillet with trailing yellow ends. She holds a white wreath with yellow ends and central band in her extended right hand and rests her left hand on her hip.

A band of egg-pattern circles the rim. Large flowers flank both figures, and there are large palmettes under the handles. The circling groundline consists of two parallel stripes.

The Errera Painter worked in Capua in the third quarter of the century in a workshop that included the Laghetto Painter, the Caivano Painter, and the Painter of B.M. F 63, to whom he is particularly close in style. The beaded belt and plump white wreaths were among his favorite motifs. His women are often painted white.

PUBLISHED: E. Robinson, *MFA AnnRep* 1903, p. 67, no. 24; J. D. Beazley, *JHS* 63 (1943), p. 83, no. 4, pl. 6; Trendall, *LCS*, p. 323, no. 718; idem, *Handbook*, pp. 161, 179 (fig. 285, as the Errera Painter), 280.

84

84

85

HYDRIA
Attributed to the Whiteface-Frignano Painter
Ca. 345–335 B.C.
Helen and Alice Colburn Fund. 69.1142

DIMENSIONS AND CONDITION: Height: 49.0 cm; width with handles: 35.0 cm; upper diameter rim: 16.6 cm; diameter neck: 9.4 cm; diameter body below handles: 27.6 cm; diameter stem: 7.0 cm; lower diameter foot: 15.8 cm
The foot has been restored; otherwise the vase is intact. There are scratches on the figure of Kadmos.

SHAPE: This hydria is taller and more elongated than the earlier example, cat. no. 80, and has more gently sloping shoulders. The neck is tall and concave, the mouth broad and overhanging. The side handles are slender and tilted sharply upward. A thick fillet separates the foot from the lower body.

85 (Color Plate XVI)

85

Kadmos and the serpent. In the upper register is a gabled structure, possibly a heroön or temple, its doors ajar to reveal the foreshortened roof timbers. In the pediment is a female face flanked by tendrils, perhaps an unusually tame gorgoneion. Yellow and black dots represent the nailheads and bosses on the doors. Two white-skinned females are seated on either side of the structure: the one on the left wears a chiton and a red himation and holds a yellow phiale in her left hand; the right one is nude to the waist, where her himation has fallen. Both women wear earrings, necklaces, and bracelets, and the one at the right has a bandoleer of charms. Both wear beaded stephanes of white, and the left one also wears a kekryphalos. The woman at the right looks down at the scene below where Kadmos and a companion battle the coiled serpent, whose white body is tinted with brown dilute glaze. Kadmos is at the left, holding a white spear and a white pointed amphora, both in his left hand. He moves to the left but looks back to the right, his face drawn in three-quarter view. He is naked save for an apicate fillet, a white sword and baldric, and the cloak over his left arm. He leans back with his right hand raised to throw a white stone at the snake, while his companion attacks it with a spear from the right. The companion is nude save for a white pilos and scabbard and the cloak over his left arm. Quadrated phialai float in the field to his right and to the left of Kadmos.

Wave-pattern circles the outer rim, and a laurel wreath circles the lower neck below a band of dotted egg-pattern. The groundline circling the lower body consists of stopt maeanders to right, with two checkerboards at left and right. The reverse is covered with large palmettes and scrolling tendrils, which extend to the areas below the handles. White dots and bars are used to highlight many points within the florals.

The amphora held by Kadmos was to be filled at the spring guarded by the serpent, the offspring of

Ares. Though not visible, the spring is what gives life to the white flowers behind the serpent; their twisting stems are rendered by incising directly into the black glaze. In most such scenes, Kadmos carries a hydria instead of an amphora, but the latter appears in two Paestan versions: a calyx-krater by Python (Louvre N 3157: Trendall, *RVP*, p. 143, no. 2/241, pl. 90), and a bell-krater by Asteas (Naples 82258: *RVP*, p. 85, no. 2/132, pl. 52). In Asteas's version, the woman seated above is identified as Thebe, the personification of the city Kadmos will found. Athena is present to guide the stone flung by Kadmos, and watching from above are the heads of the river god Ismenos and the fountain nymph Krenaia. In her comprehensive publication of the Boston vase, Emily Vermeule (in *Festschrift Hanfmann*; reference below) speculates that the two women might be Thebe and Dirke. M. A. Tiverios (*LIMC*, V, 1, p. 869) suggests Harmonia as another possibility. In the absence of inscriptions, attributes, or closer parallels, it is not possible to assign definite identities to these women, but some combination of the names that have been proposed is likely.

In addition to Vermeule's discussion of the myth of Kadmos and its treatment in art and literature, see Trendall, *PP*, pp. 23–25; idem, *RVP*, pp. 95–96; F. Vian, *Les Origines de Thèbes: Cadmos et les Spartes* (Paris, 1963); and Tiverios, *LIMC*, V, 1, pp. 863–882.

The vase was originally attributed to the White-face Painter alone. Trendall has now recognized that this artist and the Frignano Painter are the same (Trendall, *LCS*, Suppl. III, p. 182). This vase is the artist's most ambitious work, for he normally eschewed mythology for a monotonous series of languid youths, women, and Erotes. Compare the snake and Hesperides on his hydria in the Roš collection, Zurich (Trendall, *LCS*, p. 381, no. 3/139, pl. 147, 1; idem, *Handbook*, fig. 295).

PUBLISHED: C. C. Vermeule, *MFA AnnRep* 1969–70, p. 40; idem, *BurlMag* 112 (1970), p. 631, figs. 107–108; Trendall, *LCS*, Suppl. I, p. 69, no. 139a, pl. 16, 4; E. Vermeule, in *Festschrift Hanfmann*, pp. 177–188, pls. 46–49; K. Schauenburg, *AA* 1971, p. 177, pl. 23; idem, *RM* 79 (1972), p. 7, note 37; Trendall, *LCS*, Suppl. II, p. 214, no. 139a; A. N. Zadoks-Josephus Jitta, *BABesch* 48 (1973), p. 244; Brommer, *Vasenlisten*, 1973, p. 480, no. D 6; *RA* 1974, p. 102; Krauskopf, *Thebanische Sagenkreis*, p. 87, note 320; Trendall, *LCS*, Suppl. III, p. 185, no. 139a; idem, *RVP*, p. 95, note 23; M. Pfrommer, *Studien zu alexandrinischer und grossgriechischer Toreutik frühhellenistischer Zeit* (Berlin, 1987), p. 114, note 709; A. Collinge, *AntK* 31 (1988), p. 11, pl. 3, 3; Schefold and Jung, *Urkönige*, pp. 37 (fig. 26), 364; Trendall, *Handbook*, pp. 164, 182 (fig. 296), 281; G. Berger-Doer, *LIMC*, V, 1, p. 800, no. 7; M. A. Tiverios, ibid., pp. 868–869 (no. 26), 875–879; V, 2, pl. 559.

86

FISH-PLATE
Attributed to the Dotted Stripe Group
350–330 B.C.
Lent by Mr. and Mrs. Cornelius C. Vermeule III.
283.1970

PROVENANCE: Hesperia Art, *Bulletin* XLVII, no. A2, illus. on p. 1.

DIMENSIONS AND CONDITION: Height: 4.2 cm; outer diameter rim: 19.6 cm; inner diameter central depression: 3.7 cm; diameter foot: 8.1 cm
Unbroken; glaze somewhat eroded on the rim.

SHAPE: The shape of this and the following Campanian fish-plates is essentially the same as that of the Apulian examples described above, with a shallow, concave plate, a central depression, a deep, overhanging rim, and a stemmed foot, the last of varying height and profile. This example has a rim of medium breadth and a torus foot with a short stem and a wide, rounded riser.

Interior: Swimming around the black central depression are a torpedo, a striped perch, and a two-banded bream. Various details — fins, gills, eyes, and spots — are in added white. The bodies of all three fish are streaked with brown dilute glaze. A wreath of laurel, tinted with a red wash, circles the overhanging rim. There are glaze stripes around the base of the foot and the underside of the plate.

PUBLISHED: K. Deppert, *CVA* Frankfurt 3, p. 33, under pl. 48, 1–2; McPhee and Trendall, *Fish-plates*, p. 74, no. IIA/62.

EXHIBITED: St. Paul's School, *The Classical Shape*, no. 31, 5 (illus.).

87

FISH-PLATE
Probably by the Heligoland Painter
3rd quarter of 4th century B.C.
Lent by Mr. and Mrs. Cornelius C. Vermeule III.
142.68

PROVENANCE: Sotheby & Co., sale, London, 24 April 1967, no. 160

DIMENSIONS AND CONDITION: Height: 4.9 cm; outer diameter rim: 24.6 cm; inner diameter central depression: 4.7 cm; diameter stem: 5.2 cm; diameter foot: 7.9 cm
Broken and repaired. Many of the added white details have eroded; minor repainting of cracks.

SHAPE: Concave stem; echinus foot.

Interior: Around the central depression are three striped bream, two of them swimming head to head. Added white was used for the gills, fins, tails, bellies, mouths, and other details. The bodies are tinted with streaky dilute glaze. Wave-pattern circles the overhanging rim. A reserved molding surrounds the black central depression.

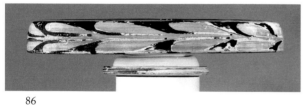

86

88 (Color Plate XVII)

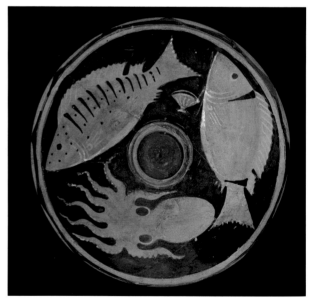

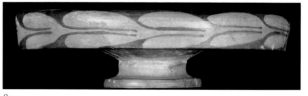

87

89

PUBLISHED: McPhee and Trendall, *Fish-plates*, p. 96, no. IID/40 (as ex Nocera, Fienga), pl. 31 f.

EXHIBITED: Art Museum of South Texas, Corpus Christi, March 1976 - March 1977.

88

FISH-PLATE
Related to the D'Agostino Painter
3rd quarter of 4th century B.C.
Henry Lillie Pierce Residuary Fund. 01.8096

PROVENANCE: E. P. Warren collection; bought in Naples; "said (& truly) to have been found at Santa Maria di Capua"

DIMENSIONS AND CONDITION: Height: 5.6 cm; outer diameter rim: 22.5 cm; diameter top of rim: 21.0 cm; inner diameter central depression: 3.7 cm; diameter stem: 6.3 cm; diameter foot: 7.9 cm
Reassembled from four fragments. The added white vine connecting the reserved ivy leaves is largely effaced.

SHAPE: Narrow rim, wide stem, disk foot.

Circling the central depression are a bream, a striped perch, and an octopus. A band of black dots circles the upper rim; around the overhanging rim is an ivy vine. As usual on Campanian fish-plates, the central depression is black and circled by a broad reserved stripe. The foot is reserved. The fish are carefully drawn, with much attention given to details such as the mouths, gills, mottling of the head and belly, and placement of the stripes. Dilute glaze was used extensively on all three creatures, particularly to define the eight arms of the octopus. The sketchy quality of the dilute glaze may have been achieved by feathering it with a dry brush. McPhee and Trendall draw attention to the unusual use of black for the gills and fins, instead of the more normal white; they note also an affinity with early Paestan fish-plates, particularly in the drawing of the octopus and the use of a dotted outer border.

PUBLISHED: McPhee and Trendall, *Fish-plates*, pp. 97–98, no. II D/62.

89

FISH-PLATE
Attributed to the Bremen Painter
3rd quarter of 4th century B.C.
Lent by Mr. and Mrs. Cornelius C. Vermeule III. 143.<u>68</u>

DIMENSIONS AND CONDITION: Height: 6.0 cm; outer diameter rim: 23.0 cm; inner diameter central depression: 4.4 cm; outer diameter central depression: 5.2 cm; diameter stem: 5.6 cm; diameter foot: 8.1 cm
Broken and repaired. Many of the added white details have eroded.

SHAPE: Relatively deep, overhanging rim; wide, spreading stem; disk foot. The conical lower body and tall stem give this plate added height.

Interior: Circling the central depression are an octopus, a striped bream, a two-banded bream, and a scallop. Added white was used for fins, gills, tails, bellies, the suckers on the tentacles, and other details. The bodies are tinted with dilute glaze. A laurel wreath circles the overhanging rim. A reserved molding surrounds the black central depression.

PUBLISHED: McPhee and Trendall, *Fish-plates*, p. 102, no. IIE/45.

90

HYDRIA
Attributed to the Ixion Painter
330–320 B.C.
Gift of Paul E. Manheim. 1970.238

DIMENSIONS AND CONDITION: Height: 54.0 cm; upper diameter rim: 15.6 cm; diameter neck: 7.5 cm; diameter body just below handles: 27.4 cm; diameter stem (base of body): 7.9 cm; diameter foot: 15.9 cm
Reconstructed from a few large fragments. Some of the added white has been lost, notably on the shield of the soldier at the left. The inpainting of cracks is now discolored.

SHAPE: The neck is taller and more slender than that of the earlier hydria, cat. no. 85, but the mouth and body are similar. The disk foot is grooved and has a tall, tapering stem.

A warrior on the left confronts two like companions, all wearing armor rendered in added white. The pair at the right wear short chitons, cuirasses, belts, and Attic helmets and hold spears in their right hands, which they rest on their shoulders. The one at the left carries a shield on his left arm; the one at the right rests his shield on the ground. Each has one leg drawn back and is listening intently to the helmeted warrior at the far left. This warrior wears a broad white belt over his short tunic and, instead of a full cuirass, wears a smaller, three-disk breastplate. He gestures toward the other two warriors as though addressing them. This action and his distinctive garb may indicate that he is their commander. He has no spear, and his shield has lost nearly all of its white coloring, retaining only the yellow device: a Macedonian star. The damaged device on the middle warrior's shield was perhaps a gorgoneion, while that of the right-hand warrior is a circle of dots. The crests of the two warriors at the right overlap the reserved line that demarcates the shoulder zone. The warrior at the left also wears an Attic helmet, with a long crest and a palmette on the side. A pair of rosettes, edged with white, floats in the upper field at left and right. The curious hook-shaped plant by the warrior

90

90

at the left is a hallmark of the Ixion Painter; compare those on Oxford 1894.5 (Trendall, *LCS*, p. 339, no. 802, pl. 133, 6). Below each side handle is a large female head wearing a spotted sakkos with a bow on top, large white earrings, and a white necklace.

A band of dotted egg-pattern circles the rim, and black tongues nearly encircle the roots of the side handles. The back of the body is filled with an elaborate complex of palmettes, tendrils, and quadrated disks. The groundline circling the lower body consists of a band of wave-pattern. The front of the neck is filled with a large palmette framed by tall flowers. Running around the shoulder is a large ivy vine with attached rosettes; in the center is a large white disk with a yellow cross. The ivy leaves are edged with

white, as are the rosettes. A single reserved stripe circles the stem of the foot.

The Ixion Painter often put large female heads below the handles of his hydriai (e.g., London F 230 [*LCS*, p. 341, no. 813, pl. 133, 2]), which also has similar decoration on the shoulder. For the warriors, compare those on Berlin 4982,45 and Chicago 89.24 (*LCS*, p. 338, no. 784, pl. 131, 1, and p. 339, no. 798, pl. 132, 1–3).

PUBLISHED: C. C. Vermeule, *MFA AnnRep* 1969–70, p. 42; Trendall, *LCS*, Suppl. I, p. 59, no. 813a, pl. 13, 5; C. C. Vermeule, *BurlMag* 115 (1973), p. 121, fig. 81; Trendall, *LCS*, Suppl. III, p. 159, no. 813a.

EXHIBITED: Brockton Art Center, *The Ancient Mediterranean*, p. 27, no. 22; Danforth Museum, Framingham, Mass., "The Mediterranean World," September 1977–March 1978.

91

Sᴏ̨ᴜᴀᴛ ʟᴇᴋʏᴛʜᴏs
Attributed to the Valencia Group
320–310 B.C.
Francis Bartlett Donation of 1900. 03.829

ᴘʀᴏᴠᴇɴᴀɴᴄᴇ: E. P. Warren collection; from Campania

ᴅɪᴍᴇɴsɪᴏɴs ᴀɴᴅ ᴄᴏɴᴅɪᴛɪᴏɴ: Height: 19.3 cm; diameter rim:
5.0 cm; diameter neck: 1.8 cm; diameter body: 9.4 cm; diameter foot: 7.6 cm
Unbroken and in good condition; traces of incrustation.

sʜᴀᴘᴇ: The ovoid body is relatively tall. The broad ring foot is
in two equal degrees, with a groove round the center. The neck
and trumpet mouth are of equal height.

A large female head looks to the left, with the hair in
a sakkos decorated with black stripes and dots and
crowned by a yellow wreath. The woman's face is in
added white. Her features are well drawn, with
downturned mouth, hooked nostrils, and alert,
querying eyes. She wears a chiton but no jewelry.

There are tall, coiling tendrils on the sides and a
large palmette on the reverse. A tall band of tongues
circles the lower neck. A reserved stripe circles the
lower body. The groove on the foot is painted white;
that between foot and body is reserved.

The head vases of the Valencia Group are among
the minor works produced in the workshop of the
Ixion Painter. Trendall compared this head to that on
a chous in St. Petersburg (inv. 2441: Trendall, *LCS*,
p. 345, no. 863).

ᴘᴜʙʟɪsʜᴇᴅ: E. Robinson, *MFA AnnRep* 1903, p. 67, no. 25;
J. D. Beazley, *JHS* 63 (1943), p. 97; Trendall, *LCS*, p. 346, no.
867, pl. 134, no. 5; Söldner, *Bonn* 3, p. 98, under L 86.

Bᴇʟʟ-ᴋʀᴀᴛᴇʀ
The name-vase of the Boston Ready Painter
Ca. 320–310 B.C.
Harriet Otis Cruft Fund. 63.3

ᴘʀᴏᴠᴇɴᴀɴᴄᴇ: Parke-Bernet Sale Catalogue (Kevorkian), 15
December 1962, no. 230; American Art Galleries, Kevorkian
Sale Catalogue, 20 January 1928, no. 322, illus. on p. 163;
Anderson Sale Catalogue (Kevorkian), 19–21 November
1925, p. 53, no. 345, illus.; from the collections of Augustus
Ready and Hagop Kevorkian

ᴅɪᴍᴇɴsɪᴏɴs ᴀɴᴅ ᴄᴏɴᴅɪᴛɪᴏɴ: Height: 39.4 cm; diameter rim:
39.1 cm; diameter body: 30.4 cm; diameter stem: 10.2 cm;
diameter foot: 17.0 cm
A break passes through the stem above the foot; otherwise intact. Many details in added colors have been lost, presumably
when the heavy incrustation, which still survives in places,
was removed. The mottling of the black glaze on side B may
have the same cause.

91

91

92

92

SHAPE: More or less standard for Campanian bell-kraters of this period, with a curvaceous body tapering to a tall stem. The rim is slender and does not extend beyond the handles. The hollow foot has a torus base, a tall, concave riser, and a sloping upper surface.

A: Three women are assembled in a room (to judge by the window-like square at the upper left). The white skin of the women is badly worn and blends confusingly with their hair and kekryphaloi, which are also white. All three wear chitons, and the two at left and right also wear himatia of added white. The woman standing in the center gazes into a yellow mirror held in her right hand; in her lowered left hand is a yellow situla. Her chignon is secured with a long white fillet. She turns toward the woman at the left; between them is a yellow thymiaterion, over which hangs a beaded fillet. The woman at the right, seated on a white stool covered with a yellow feline skin, holds a beribboned thyrsos in her left hand and a cista full of offerings in her right: two white sprigs, two yellow pomegranates, and a cake outlined in white. A yellow bird stands on her lap; it looks more like a goose than a crane, but the latter was a popular women's pet.

The cista, the situla, and the thymiaterion suggest the preparation for a sacrifice, to take place at an altar outdoors; the thyrsos and feline skin suggest the recipient may be Dionysos.

B: Three youths wearing himatia and white fillets stand in conversation, one facing right and two facing left. They are enveloped in their ample cloaks, which they pull taut in front with their right arms. In the upper field at left and right are two "windows"; two cistas decorated with yellow dots hang between the heads of the youths.

A laurel wreath circles the vase below the rim. The groundline circling the lower body consists of a band of wave-pattern. The clay of both bands has been tinted with a red wash that contrasts with the beige of the figure zone. There are large palmettes under the handles, the roots of which are encircled by tongues.

The Boston Ready Painter was among the minor followers of the CA Painter, active during the period when the workshop was under strong Apulian influence. The beefy, draped youths on the reverse are repeated on several bell-kraters, where the women also find parallels (e.g., Michigan 28809 and Naples RC 41: Trendall, *LCS*, p. 516, nos. 609, 614, pl. 201, 3–6).

PUBLISHED: J. D. Beazley, *JHS* 63 (1943), pp. 88–89, fig. 10; C. Vermeule, *MFA AnnRep* 1963, pp. 41–42; idem, *BMFA* 62 (1964), pp. 128–129, illus.; Trendall, *LCS*, pp. 515–516, no. 607, pl. 201, no. 1–2; *FastiA* 18–19 (1968), nos. 381, 383; Smith, *Funerary Symbolism*, pp. 164, 229; see also, p. 146; K. Schauenburg, *RM* 85 (1978), pp. 83–84; Trendall, *Handbook*, pp. 167, 171, 193 (figs. 326–327), 281; Söldner, *Bonn* 3, pp. 93 (under inv. no. 3041), 95 (under L 58); Jentoft-Nilsen, *CVA* Getty 4, p. 40, under inv. no. 71.AE.360.

93

PYXIS
Attributed to the Kemai Group
320–270 B.C.
Purchased. 89.266

PROVENANCE: R. Lanciani collection; bought in Rome; from Canosa

DIMENSIONS AND CONDITION: Height: 11.4 cm; diameter rim: 9.7 cm; diameter neck: 8.8 cm; diameter body: 11.7 cm; diameter foot: 6.4 cm
Unbroken

SHAPE: Globular body; flaring rim; slender echinus foot; conical lid with knob. Two atrophied handles are pressed against the sides of the rim.

Black rays decorate the underside of the rim. On the shoulder is a band of black palmettes separated by single lotus petals; below this is a wreath of white ivy leaves on a black band. On the lid there are two bands of palmettes separated by long tongues or petals. The inner palmettes are painted in black, the outer ones in white on a black ground. The clay is pale brown.

For the Kemai Group, see Trendall, *LCS*, pp. 674–680; and J. D. Beazley, *JHS* 63 (1943), pp. 109–111. The name was coined by Beazley after an inscription on London F 507 (*LCS*, p. 674, no. 4). These pyxides are dated by their association in tombs with very late Campanian red-figure, such as a spouted lebes of the TT Group (Naples 132444: *LCS*, p. 559, no. 916, pl. 220, 5–6). They are minor vessels, and Trendall illustrates only one example (Würzburg 884: *LCS*, p. 674, no. 1, pl. 224, 4).

PUBLISHED: Trendall, *LCS*, p. 675, no. 20.

94

94

HEAD-CRUET
Attributed to the Head-Cruet Class
End of 4th century B.C.
Gift of the Misses Norton. 41.650

PROVENANCE: Lent by the Misses Norton in 1912 (923.12)

DIMENSIONS AND CONDITION: Height: 15.0 cm; diameter base: 13.4 cm; smallest diameter pedestal: 11.7 cm; upper diameter pedestal: 12.2 cm; height at pedestal, red-figure zone: 4.6 cm; height at pedestal: 5.5 cm; just above graffito, clockwise: (1) diameter rim: 4.0 cm; height body and rim: 5.0 cm; diameter body below handles: 5.2 cm; (2) diameter rim: 4.0 cm; height body and rim: 4.7 cm; diameter body below handles: 5.4 cm; (3) diameter rim: 4.1 cm; height body and rim: 5.3 cm; diameter body below handles: 5.4 cm; (4) diameter rim: 4.3 cm; height body and rim: 4.8 cm; diameter body below handles: 5.1 cm
Unbroken; chip on one rim.

Four small, lidded, black-glazed stamnoid pyxides, with rolled-back handles, sit on a cylindrical base decorated with alternating red-figure palmettes in black and white triangular frames. Between each pair of pyxides is a mold-made female head with Phrygian cap, also glazed black. In the center is a black loop handle. The hollow base has concave sides, flaring slightly at the bottom.

Trendall (*LCS*, pp. 570–571; *LCS*, Suppl. III, p. 261) lists several such cruets, including some with the same type of triangular palmettes. To his list may be added two examples recently in the art mar-

93

ket (Christie's, July 11, 1990, no. 182; and Sotheby's, June 20, 1990, no. 198). The jars may have held offerings for the tomb. Like vessels of the Kemai Group, represented by cat. no. 93, they have been found in tombs at Teano in association with late red-figure works of the TT Group.

PUBLISHED: J. D. Beazley, *JHS* 63 (1943), p. 109, no. 11; Trendall, *LCS*, p. 570, no. 1013.

95

PLASTIC MOUSE
Mid-4th century B.C.
Gift of Henry P. Kidder. 80.588

DIMENSIONS AND CONDITION: Height: 7 cm; length: 13.3 cm
The mouth in the middle of the back was broken off at some time; the remaining stump was filed down completely by a modern "restorer." The left ear is missing.

The mouse is painted a lustrous black, with palmettes on each haunch and a grapevine on the back in added white (the leaves and grapes white; the vine itself incised). White is also used for the eyes. The eyebrows, whiskers, and other details are incised.

Compare London G 163, which has a ring handle like a guttus and a pointed spout (Heldring, *Sicilian*, p. 108, no. 5, pl. 36, 6). Heldring places the London mouse among the fourth-century South Italian successors to the plastic mice of fifth-century Sicily (e.g., cat. no. 106). The lack of a narrow, tapering spout on this mouse, or indeed of any secondary aperture for pouring, suggests that it was made for a different function than that of the Sicilian mice. Its classification here as Campanian is no more than tentative.

PUBLISHED: Robinson, *Catalogue*, p. 169, no. 468; M. E. Mayo, in Mayo, *Magna Graecia*, p. 221, under no. 101.

EXHIBITED: San Antonio Museum of Art, San Antonio, 1990-.

95

96   96

96

PLASTIC LAMP-FILLER IN THE FORM OF A SQUATTING GROTESQUE
Magenta Ware
Ca. 120–70 B.C.
Henry Lillie Pierce Residuary Fund. 01.8149

PROVENANCE: E. P. Warren collection

DIMENSIONS AND CONDITION: Height: 9.9 cm; rectangular base: 5.2 cm by 4.0 cm; depth, front to back, including handle: 7.8 cm
The right ear and an ivy leaf beside it are missing; otherwise intact.

This leering, unpainted figure has the chubby build and coarse features of a satyr, although he lacks a tail, and his one surviving ear (left) is not pointed. He wears a wreath of ivy and sits holding a kantharos close to his chest with both hands. His genitals hang on the ground between his feet. The double handle at the back has a thumb-grip in the form of a small square of clay. Above the handle is a cup-shaped filler-hole with strainer. There is a small aperture for pouring in the left upper arm.

Compare a squatting satyr in the National Museum, Belgrade (M. Veličković, *Catalogue des terres cuites grecques et romaines* [Belgrade, 1957], p. 89, pl. 13, no. 29). For Magenta Ware, see R. Higgins, in *The Classical Tradition, The British Museum Yearbook* 1 (London, 1976), pp. 1–32.

PAESTAN
Red-Figure

Excavation of the local cemeteries around Paestum since 1950 has greatly increased our understanding of the red-figure pottery made there. Although Paestum is located in the northwest corner of Lucania, it was firmly in the artistic sphere of Campania. As in Campania, local production of red-figure pottery seems to have been inspired by imports from Sicily as well as by immigrants from the island. Sicilian vases with Dionysiac scenes and theatrical associations, particularly those of the Painter of Louvre K 240 and the Dirce Painter, had a profound influence on the first important Paestan vase-painter, Asteas, whose career began around 360. Asteas set the canons for the subsequent Paestan style, which remained remarkably consistent thereafter. Though sharing many shapes and stylistic traits with Campanian ware, Paestan vases are normally easily distinguishable, not least by their micaceous clay, which fires an orange-brown color, quite different from Campanian.

The favored shapes were the bell-krater (cat. nos. 98–99), calyx-krater, hydria, neck-amphora (cat. nos. 97, 105), and lebes gamikos (cat. no. 102); the chous (cat. no. 100), kylix (cat. nos. 103–104), fish-plate (cat. no. 101), lekanis, and squat lekythos also appear in significant numbers. The bell-kraters have a distinctive shape, with tall, straight sides. The lebetes gamikoi frequently have elaborate lids with a small lekanis supporting a stack of other miniature vessels. The inventiveness of the potters is also expressed in vessels with internal compartments, such as a unique hydria-pyxis painted by Asteas: Tampa 89.109 (Trendall, *RVP*, p. 77, no. 86, pl. 37).

Figures tend to be sleek and smooth-skinned, their thick limbs more suggestive of baby fat than of muscles. They are commonly draped in himatia with distinctive "dot-stripe" borders (e.g., cat. nos. 98–99). Many figures wear white wreaths or beaded fillets, as well as white-beaded bandoleers. As might be expected, the drawing is generally much closer to Campanian than Apulian, with a loose, fleshy quality that eschews the tyranny of the relief line and makes extensive use of impressionistic highlights of added color. Everyone seems to hold some object or another, be it a fillet, phiale, or "skewer of fruit," an obscure but ubiquitous object that may represent a pile of cakes (e.g., cat. no. 102). Most distinctive of all are the tall "framing palmettes," Sicilian in origin, which frame many scenes, particularly on bell-kraters (e.g., cat. nos. 98–99).

Mythological subjects are relatively uncommon; there is only one in Boston's collection (cat. no. 105), with the meeting of Orestes and Elektra at the tomb of Agamemnon. Compared with the mythological works of the Darius Painter and his contemporaries, the Paestan showpieces are somehow less serious in tone, less imbued with the grandeur and cathartic properties of the tragedies that originally inspired them. Dionysiac and genre subjects dominate, and there are many small vases with only a single figure on each side, a large female head, or a bird or animal. Unlike Campanian, few Paestan vases have pictures of departing warriors, Samnite or otherwise. Funerary scenes are rare, and naiskoi do not appear.

In South Italy, only Paestan vase-painters are known to have signed their works; Asteas signed at least eleven, six of them calyx-kraters, all with mythological or phlyax subjects. The mythological works are elaborate, even operatic, with solid, heavyset figures crowding the lower register, and gods, Furies, or satyrs looking down from above, often with their lower bodies concealed.

A younger contemporary and close colleague of Asteas was Python (see cat. nos. 98–99), who signed his name to at least two vases. His style is so close to that of Asteas that they are sometimes difficult to tell apart; the best clues are the two standing figures that normally occupy the reverse, whose himatia are treated with slight but significant differences by the two painters. The Asteas-Python workshop was prolific, and it is not always clear if a particular minor work is from the hand of one of the two principals or by one of their "well-drilled hacks," as Trendall calls them (*Handbook*, p. 203; e.g., cat. no. 102).

A slightly later contemporary of Asteas and Python was the Aphrodite Painter (cat. no. 104), active about 340–330. He seems to have been an Apulian immigrant, to judge by the "xylophones" and floral ornament on some of his early works, and it was he who introduced the tall-necked oinochoe to the Paestan repertory. He soon adopted Paestan motifs and compositional schemes, however, and decorated the local shapes. Both he and the Boston Orestes Painter may be considered late members of the Asteas-Python workshop. The Boston Orestes Painter was a close follower of Python, with a distinctive style and a taste for mythology; the finest Paestan vase in Boston is the neck-amphora that gives the artist his name (cat. no. 105), with Orestes, Elektra, and Pylades at the tomb of Agamemnon. The Boston Orestes Painter is a link with later and less talented Paestan artists, such as the Painter of Naples 1778 and the Painter of Naples 2585. The former was influenced by the Caivano Painter, a Campanian artist who may have worked in Paestum; the latter labored more in the tradition of Asteas.

Contemporary with these painters, and with the late phase of the Asteas-Python workshop, was a large group of Apulianizing vases. These are mostly minor works—lekanides, bottles, and skyphoid pyxides—with some bell-kraters and even a few volute-kraters. They are very Apulian in style, more so than the Apulianizing vases of contemporary Campania, but the vessels are made of good Paestan clay. These were followed in the last decade of the century by works of ever decreasing quality, even barbarization, that brought the fabric to an end by 300 B.C.

NECK-AMPHORA
Attributed to the Black and White Stripe Group
360–350 B.C.
Gift of Joseph H. Clark. 12.423

DIMENSIONS AND CONDITION: Height: 27.8 cm; diameter rim: 11.3 cm; diameter body: 14.5 cm; diameter foot: 7.7 cm Unbroken. Traces of hard incrustation remain in many places, particularly on the mouth, foot, and handles.

SHAPE: The tall neck tapers at the bottom. The tall, double-reeded handles are engaged along the neck, rather than running into it. Both mouth and foot are in two degrees. The ovoid body has a flattened shoulder.

A: A woman, holding a basket and wreath in her right hand and a mirror in the left, is running to the right toward a short stele or altar. She turns to look back, perhaps at the Eros on the reverse. She wears a chiton, shoes, necklace, bracelets, a fillet, and a radiate stephane. Down the center of the chiton are the black and white (or in this case, light yellow) stripes that give the group its name. The basket contains four eggs, which, like the wreath, jewelry, and stephane, are rendered in yellow.

B: Eros, holding a long white fillet in both hands, is moving to the left, away from a short stele or altar. He wears a wreath, shoes, bracelets, and a beaded bandoleer, all in white except the shoes, one of which is red and white. A phiale with black dots is in the field at the lower left.

There are large palmettes on both sides of the neck and under the handles. The shoulder on either side is filled with a broad band of black tongues. A band of wave-pattern circles the lower body.

Compare the nearly identical woman on the pelike Paestum 5639 (Trendall, *RVP*, p. 82, no. 2/116, pl. 43c). The minor vases of the Black and White Stripe Group were produced in the early years of the Asteas workshop.

PUBLISHED: Trendall, *PP*, pp. 50, 124, no. 225, fig. 35; idem, *BSR* 20 (1952), p. 15, no. 312; P. E. Arias, *Dioniso* 36 (1962), p. 9, note 11; Trendall, *RVP*, p. 82, no. 2/115.

97

97

97

98

98

98

BELL-KRATER
Attributed to Python
350–335 B.C.
Gift of Mr. and Mrs. George Washington Wales.
95.834

PROVENANCE: Bought in Naples with cat. no. 99

DIMENSIONS AND CONDITION: Height: 33.0 cm; diameter rim:
33.3 cm; diameter body (below handles): 20.9 cm; diameter
foot: 15.5 cm
A piece has been broken from the rim and reattached.

SHAPE: Characteristic of Python's bell-kraters, with a tall,
slender body with nearly straight sides, a large, spreading
foot, and an overhanging rim that extends beyond the handles. There is a reserved groove around the upper edge of the
hollow foot.

A: Dionysos stands at the left, his thyrsos leaning
against his left arm. He wears shoes, a bracelet, a
beaded bandoleer, a beaded fillet, and a bordered
himation; the thyrsos, jewelry, and beads are all in
yellow. With his right hand, he offers a white egg to
the young satyr at right, who stands with his right
foot on a hummock, bending forward slightly with a
white fillet held in both hands. In the god's left hand
is a yellow wreath or necklace. The satyr has a white
tail and wears shoes, a yellow wreath, and a bandoleer and thigh-chain of yellow beads.

B: A bearded satyr wearing a white and yellow
wreath, shoes, and a beaded bandoleer casually leans
his left elbow on a low pillar, his legs crossed. He

holds a fillet and a tambourine in his left hand,
a fillet and a "skewer of fruit" in his right. At the
lower left, beneath the satyr's extended right hand,
is an altar with offerings on top: three white dots,
possibly eggs.

A wreath of laurel circles the vase below the rim.
A band of wave-pattern circles the lower body. Below each handle is a large palmette. Tall framing palmettes frame both scenes.

The same subjects, in varying compositions, are
very common among the vases of Python, particularly on bell-kraters. Sometimes Dionysos is seated
(e.g., Trendall, *RVP*, no. 2/232, pl. 86a), or it is he
who rests one foot on a rock or hummock (e.g.,
idem, *RVP*, no. 2/237, pl. 87c); sometimes the satyr
facing the god is a bearded adult (e.g., idem, *RVP*,
no. 2/261, pl. 97a). For the posture of the satyr on
the reverse, compare Trendall, *RVP*, no. 2/270, pl.
100a. According to Trendall, *NumAntCl* 19 (1990),
p. 126, the objects in the Paestan "skewer of fruit"
are probably cakes of some kind.

The sizes, subjects, decorative schemes, and common origin suggest that this vase and the following
one (cat. no. 99) were a pair and probably came from
the same tomb.

PUBLISHED: A. D. Trendall, *BSR* 20 (1952), p. 6, no. 70 bis,
pl. 17b; G. Schneider-Herrmann, *BABesch* 51 (1976), p. 69,
no. 30; K. Schauenburg, in *Festschrift Arias*, p. 476, note 55;
Trendall, *RVP*, pp. 161–162, no. 2/301, pl. 106, c, d.

99

99

99

BELL-KRATER
Attributed to Python
350–335 B.C.
Gift of Mr. and Mrs. George Washington Wales.
95.835

PROVENANCE: Bought in Naples, with cat. no. 98

DIMENSIONS AND CONDITION: Height: 32.0 cm; diameter rim:
32.7 cm; diameter body (below handles): 20.9 cm; diameter
stem: 7.0 cm; diameter foot: 16.1 cm
The rim is broken above side A; otherwise intact.

SHAPE: Same as cat. no. 98

A: Dionysos stands to the right facing a maenad or
Ariadne, who offers him a yellow egg (?) held in her
right hand. Both carry yellow thyrsoi and wear
shoes (tinted with dilute glaze), bordered himatia,
and bandoleers with yellow beads. Both wear yellow,
beaded fillets, the maenad's over a sphendone. She is
nude from the waist up and wears a necklace, earring, and bracelet, all yellow. Dionysos lowers a yellow phiale in his extended right hand, apparently
pouring a libation.

B: A satyr runs to the right but looks back to the
left, a white fillet and a dish of white offerings in his
extended right hand and a yellow torch with white
flame in his left. He wears a white wreath, shoes
tinted with dilute glaze, and a bandoleer with white
beads. A leopard skin tinted with dilute glaze hangs
from his left arm. An altar with offerings on top is

beside his left foot, and by his right foot is a short
stele or altar.

The subsidiary ornaments — laurel wreath, wave-
pattern, handle and framing palmettes — are identical to those on the vase's companion piece, cat. no.
98.

PUBLISHED: A. D. Trendall, *BSR* 20 (1952), p. 6, no. 68 bis,
pl. 17a; J. H. C. Kern, *OudMed* 40 (1959), p. 20; K. Schauenburg, in *Festschrift Arias*, p. 476, note 56; Trendall, *RVP*,
pp. 161–162, no. 2/302, pl. 106, e, f.

EXHIBITED: Corpus Christi, *Greek Vases*, p. 33, fig. 44.

100

OINOCHOE (shape 3)
Attributed to Python (or a close associate)
Ca. 340 B.C.
Gift of Mr. and Mrs. William de Forest Thomson.
19.295

PROVENANCE: From Paestum

DIMENSIONS AND CONDITION: Height: 20.7 cm; diameter
body: 13.4 cm; diameter foot: 8.8 cm
Unbroken, save for a chip at the lower front.

SHAPE: Standard chous shape, with trefoil mouth, globular
body, low handle, and wide torus foot. Trendall lists only one
other chous by Python (*RVP*, p. 171, no. 2/371, pl. 117a).

A nude youth, possibly Dionysos, is capering between two altars, the one at the right with offerings on it. He holds a wreath and a "skewer of fruit" in his right hand and a thyrsos with pendant fillet in his left. A bordered cloak hangs from his left arm, and he wears red shoes, a beaded bandoleer, a beaded fillet, and two beaded thigh-chains. The offerings, thyrsos, beads, fillets, wreath, and skewer are all in added white with a distinct orange tint.

The upper frame is a band of dotted egg-pattern; the groundline circling the lower body is a simple reserved line. On the sides are tall framing palmettes, and there is a large palmette below the handle. Flanking the handle are two dotted tympana or phialai.

PUBLISHED: Trendall, *PP*, pp. 73, 122, no. 163, pl. 25 b; Hoorn, *Choes*, p. 114, no. 389; Trendall, *BSR* 20 (1952), p. 12, no. 206; G. Schneider-Herrmann, *BABesch* 51 (1976), p. 67, no. 6; Trendall, *RVP*, pp. 171 (no. 2/372), 214 (under no. 745); Söldner, *Bonn* 3, pp. 100 (under inv. no. 3038), 104 (under L 110).

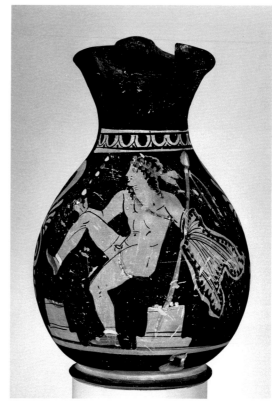

100

100

100

FISH-PLATE
Attributed to the Asteas-Python Workshop
350–330 B.C.
Gift of Dr. and Mrs. Jerome M. Eisenberg.
1988.1120

DIMENSIONS AND CONDITION: Height: 5.7 cm; diameter: 25.8
cm; outer diameter central depression: 5.0 cm; inner diameter
central depression: 3.6 cm; diameter stem: 8.9 cm; diameter
foot: 12.5 cm
Unbroken

SHAPE: Deep, straight-sided overhanging rim; reserved stem
and black torus foot.

Interior: A bream, a striped bream, a red mullet, and
a shrimp swim around the central depression. The
fish are tinted with streaky dilute glaze. Added yellow is used for the shrimp and for stripes and dots in
the fish; added white is used for fins, tails, gills, bellies, mouths, and other details. Wave-pattern circles
the central depression, which is decorated with concentric circles. A band of dots, suggestive of dicing,
runs around the top of the outer rim, and the overhanging rim is circled by a laurel wreath. Compare
the "Paestanizing" dotted band on the Campanian
fish-plate, cat. no. 88.

PUBLISHED: MFA AnnRep 1988–89, p. 42; I. McPhee and A.
D. Trendall, AntK 33 (1990), pp. 41 (no. 27a, as ex J. Haering,
Freiburg), 49, pl. 10, 5.

102

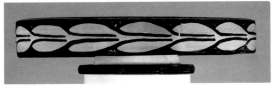

101

LEBES GAMIKOS
Attributed to the Asteas-Python Workshop
350–330 B.C.
Gift of Mr. and Mrs. William de Forest Thomson.
19.299

PROVENANCE: From Paestum

DIMENSIONS AND CONDITION: Height body: 14.1 cm; inner diameter rim: 4.8 cm; outer diameter rim: 5.9 cm; diameter
body: 12.1 cm; diameter stem: 3.3 cm; diameter foot: 7.4 cm;
diameter base of lid: 6.9 cm; height of lid: 6.9 cm
Unbroken

SHAPE: The lid belongs. The tall knob on the lid extends just
slightly beyond the vertical handles. The latter have pointed
protrusions on top and are flanked on the shoulder by plastic
bosses. A low, spreading stem separates the body from the
torus foot, which has a flange around the top.

A: A woman wrapped in a bordered himation is
seated to the right on a stylized plant. She wears a
yellow-orange wreath and earrings and shoes with
yellow soles. She holds a white wreath and a "skewer
of fruit" in her right hand. A white fillet with yellow
ends hangs at the left, and a tympanum and white fillet at the right. The skewered objects are alternately
in added yellow and white.

102

B: A youth is seated to the left on a stylized plant; his bordered himation has fallen around his waist. He wears a wreath and a beaded bandoleer. In his extended right hand are a fillet and a "skewer of fruit." Although he holds a mirror and fillet in his extended left hand, he looks away from his reflection. The skewer, fillets, wreath, and bandoleer are in added yellow and white.

The groundline circling the lower body is a single reserved line. There are tongues on the shoulder and large palmettes under the vertical handles. The lid has large, unframed tongues on the top and wave-pattern around the outer edge. The knob and foot are black; the black handles have reserved stripes around their bases.

Seated figures such as this are a common feature of numerous minor vases from the Asteas-Python workshop. Compare the women on Sydney 49.10 and Paestum 21138 (Trendall, *RVP*, p. 190, no. 2/428, pl. 132c, and p. 205, no. 2/620, pl. 136e).

PUBLISHED: A. D. Trendall, *BSR* 20 (1952), p. 13, no. 255 bis; idem, *RVP*, p. 202, no. 2/593.

103

KYLIX
Attributed to the Asteas-Python Workshop
350–330 B.C.
Gift of Mr. and Mrs. William de Forest Thomson.
19.308

DIMENSIONS AND CONDITION: Height to top of handle: 7.5 cm; height to rim: 5.8 cm; diameter: 21.0 cm; diameter stem: 6.9 cm; diameter foot: 7.7 cm
Unbroken. Most of the added white on the interior has been lost.

SHAPE: The handles are tilted upward and rolled back at the ends, where they are wider than at the roots. The foot has a groove at the base and a low, reserved cylindrical stem.

Interior: A large female head faces left, wearing a dotted hairband and a red necklace with white beads. A white wreath circles the inner rim, and a scrolling tendril, also white, fills the area before the woman's chin; both are nearly effaced. There is a short, reserved scroll at the lower right.

Exterior: A wave-pattern circles the outer rim. The handles are half-black and half-reserved.

In *RVAp*, II, Trendall and Cambitoglou suggested this cup might be placed somewhere near the Apulian Group of Zurich 2660, but in *RVP* Trendall opted for a Paestan origin, "leading on to the work of the Painter of Naples 2585."

PUBLISHED: *RVAp*, II, p. 682, no. 22/426, pl. 252, 12 (Group of Zurich 2660); Trendall, *RVP*, p. 227, no. 2/883, pl. 143, f; *RVAp*, Suppl. II, p. 198.

103

104

PUBLISHED: *RVAp*, II, p. 629, no. 21/261; Trendall, *RVP*, pp. 249–250, no. 2/985, pl. 155, e.

104

KYLIX

Attributed to the Aphrodite Painter
340–330 B.C.
Gift of Mr. and Mrs. William de Forest Thomson.
19.309

DIMENSIONS AND CONDITION: Height: 8.0 cm; diameter: 19.0 cm; diameter stem: 7.9 cm; diameter foot: 8.7 cm
Unbroken

SHAPE: Compare cat. no. 103, with a similar foot and bowl; on this cup, the handles are flared even more.

Interior: A woman is seated to the left on an irregular pile of white rocks with yellow shadow bands. She holds a phiale in her raised right hand and a sprig of ivy in her left, its added color now effaced. She wears a chiton, kekryphalos, shoes, bracelets, earrings, and a necklace; the jewelry is white and the shoes have white spots. The white dots in her lap may be offerings to place in the phiale. There is a rosette above and a scrolling palmette at the left, both with touches of added white. The groundline is a row of white dots. A wreath of laurel with white berries circles the inner rim. In the very center of the interior, concealed by the painting, is a stamped design: a circle surrounded by palmettes.

Exterior: There is a wreath of laurel between the handles on both sides.

This unusual combination of techniques—painting over a stamped design—occurs on a cup of similar shape, also by the Aphrodite Painter (*RVP*, p. 250, no. 2/984, pl. 155d). The Boston cup was originally thought to be Apulian, but a fuller knowledge of the Aphrodite Painter's work has led Trendall to assign it to his hand. The painter was obviously aware of contemporary Apulian vase-painting, whence he may have borrowed the white rock drawn in the Apulian manner; see *RVP*, p. 250.

105

NECK-AMPHORA, WITH TWISTED HANDLES

The name-vase of the Boston Orestes Painter
335–320 B.C.
Henry Lillie Pierce Residuary Fund. 99.540

PROVENANCE: E. P. Warren collection; bought at and said to be from Nola

DIMENSIONS AND CONDITION: Height: 51.3 cm; diameter rim: 20.3 cm; diameter neck: 9.2 cm; diameter body: 23.0 cm; diameter stem: 7.1 cm; diameter foot: 14.5 cm
Unbroken; minor wear on foot and handles.

SHAPE: Paestan neck-amphorae frequently have twisted handles, and these often come up to touch the mouth, as on this example. The mouth is wide and in two degrees. The foot is tall, with a rather bulbous stem and torus base. The body is slender and tapering; the neck is concave.

A: The meeting of Elektra, Orestes, and Pylades at the Tomb of Agamemnon. The tomb is represented by a white Ionic column topped by three eggs; two more eggs sit at the base of the column. At the right is Elektra, standing on the beige platform supporting the column and wearing a spotted himation and a black chiton with incised pleats. Incision is also used for the strands of her black hair, which makes a bold contrast against the white of her skin. Her cheek has a touch of yellow, and her hair is cut short in mourning. She carries a yellow hydria of water in her left hand and a red fillet in her right. The water is for cleaning and purifying the tomb, and the fillet will be tied around the column shaft. Standing at the left, beside the platform, are Pylades and Orestes. Both youths wear chlamides and shoes (Orestes' are intricately cut and laced). Each carries his spear in one hand and his pilos and sword in the other, the latter in a red scabbard. The chlamys and pilos of Orestes are yellowish beige, while those of Pylades are white. Orestes and Elektra have not yet recognized each other, for he is looking back at Pylades, and she is busy decking the column. In the upper corners, marked off by rows of yellow dots, two Furies observe the scene below, their lower bodies concealed. Both wear yellow snakes in their hair, and the one at the right is winged and brandishes snakes in both hands.

In a panel on the obverse neck is a Siren standing on a dotted terrain. She holds a white fillet and a tray of offerings in her left hand and gazes into the yellow mirror held in her right. She wears a kekryphalos and a beaded fillet. Her nude torso is complete to the waist, where the bird's body begins; the latter is spotted, with a striped tail and black and white

105 (Color Plate XVIII)

105

wings. Before her, at the lower left, is an altar with a pile of white eggs on it.

B: A youth wearing a yellow wreath, shoes, a bordered himation, and a bandoleer of white beads stands facing a woman in shoes, bordered peplos, kekryphalos, and beaded fillet. The youth holds a yellow staff in his right hand and a yellow fillet and egg in his left; the woman has a mirror in her right hand, and a fillet and a "skewer of fruit" in her left (all yellow). A white rosette floats in the field be-

tween their feet. In the upper corners are the heads bound with white fillets of a woman and a youth, who peer from behind a continuous groundline, like the outline of a hill. The contrast with the snake-haired Furies on the obverse is hard to miss, but these more benign observers can hardly be the Eumenides.

On the neck of side B, a youth in a bordered himation stands to the left between two framing palmette-scrolls.

A band of wave-pattern circles the lower neck. Above the Siren on the obverse neck is a band of egg-pattern. On the obverse shoulder is a wreath with a flower in the center; a broad band of tongues fills the reverse shoulder. In framed panels under each handle are palmettes, flowers, and spiraling tendrils. The groundline circling the lower body consists of wave-pattern.

Episodes from the *Oresteia* of Aeschylus inspired many South Italian vase-paintings. This and similar scenes obviously are based on the recognition scene in the *Choephoroi*; see Trendall and Webster, *Illustrations*, pp. 41–44; Kossatz-Deissmann, *Dramen*, pp. 92–102, pls. 13.2–18; and I. McPhee, *LIMC*, III, 1, pp. 709–719. Many elements — Ionic column, eggs, hydria, and winged Furies — appear in other versions. Kossatz-Deissmann notes that the short hair and black dress of Elektra are repeated on a Campanian hydria with this subject: Würzburg L 874 (Trendall, *LCS*, p. 408, no. 318; Kossatz-Deissmann, *Dramen*, p. 94, pl. 14, 2). The version on a contemporary Campanian neck-amphora by the Danaid Painter shows the eggs on top of the column and has remarkably similar ornament on the shoulder: Hamburg, Termer collection (Trendall, *Handbook*, fig. 307; idem, *LCS*, Suppl. III, p. 208, no. 3/495a; Kossatz-Deissmann, *Dramen*, frontispiece). On a calyx-krater by the Aphrodite Painter, where the scene has shifted to Delphi, the Furies peer from windows and are identified by inscriptions as Poina and Teisiphone: Tampa, Zewadski collection (Trendall, *RVP*, p. 245, no. 2/971, pl. 150). The Siren on the neck is included on another Paestan version, a neck-amphora by the Painter of the Geneva Orestes: Geneva HR 29 (*RVP*, p. 57, no. 2/1, pl. 15). Asteas put a Siren on the neck above a scene of Orestes at Delphi (San Antonio, Denman collection: *RVP*, pp. 96–98, no. 2/133, pls. 53 and 54a), and one wonders whether in these instances these death-daemons may be more than ornamental.

PUBLISHED: E. Robinson, *MFA AnnRep* 1899, pp. 84–86, no. 38; *AA* 1900, p. 220, no. 38; Weicker, in W. H. Roscher, ed., *Ausführliches Lexikon der griechischen und römischen Mythologie*, IV (Leipzig, 1909–1915), col. 637, fig. 30; P. Jacobsthal, *Die Melischen Reliefs* (Berlin, 1931), pp. 169–170, fig. 50; D. M. Robinson, *AJA* 36 (1932), p. 402; Chase, *Antiquities*, pp. 97–98, fig. 113; Trendall, *BSR* 20 (1952), p. 16, no. 351; Brommer, *Vasenlisten*, 1960, p. 322, no. D 1; Ginouvès, *Balaneutikè*, p. 262; Chase and Vermeule, *Greek, Etruscan and Roman Art*, pp. 140, 150, fig. 129; see S. Stucchi, *EAA*, V, p. 743, on the painter; MFA, *Illustrated Handbook*, 1964, pp. 76–77, illus.; E. Diehl, *Die Hydria: Formgeschichte und Verwendung im Kult des Altertums* (Mainz, 1964), p. 141; MFA, *Trojan War*, fig. 43; Taranto, *Letteratura*, pp. 18–19,

105

no. 100; Trendall, *LCS*, p. 427, note 1; idem, *PP*, pp. 79, 125, no. 258, pl. 29; Webster, *Tragedy and Satyr-Play*, p. 138, PV; Trendall and Webster, *Illustrations*, pp. 42–44, pl. III, I, 6; Brommer, *Vasenlisten*, 1973, p. 450, no. D 1; Del Chiaro, *Caere*, p. 116, note 43; F. D'Andria, *NSc* 29 (1975), Supplemento, pp. 387, 389; G. Schneider-Herrmann, *BABesch* 51 (1976), p. 69, no. 33; MFA, *Illustrated Handbook*, 1976, pp. 108–109, illus.; K. Schauenburg, in Hornbostel, *Schätze*, p. 380, under no. 328; H. Hoffmann, ibid., p. 396, under no. 341; Kossatz-Deissmann, *Dramen*, pp. 94–95, pl. 14, 1; Lohmann, *Grabmäler*, pp. 304–305, P 2; J. A. Barlow and J. E. Coleman, *AJA* 83 (1979), p. 224; P. E. Arias, *Gnomon* 52 (1980), p. 537; S. Gogos, *JOAI* 55 (Hauptblatt) (1984), pp. 50–51, fig. 19; Prag, *Oresteia*, p. 119, note 88; Aellen, Cambitoglou, and Chamay, *Peintre de Darius*, p. 268; G. Schneider-Herrmann, in Brijder, *Enthousiasmos*, p. 176, note 6; Freytag gen. Löringhoff, *Giebelrelief*, p. 290, no. E 42 (with reference to P. C. Sestieri, *Dioniso* 22, 1959, 45) (date 350/340–300 B.C.); I. McPhee, *LIMC*, III, 1, pp. 714 (no. 41), 718; III, 2, pl. 547; H. Sarian, ibid., III, 1, pp. 831 (no. 37), 840; Trendall, *RVP*, pp. 58–59, 174, 252, 254–256 (no. 2/1004), 259–260 (under no. 1024), pl. 158; A. J. N. W. Prag, *JHS* 108 (1988), p. 293; R. Hurschmann, *JdI* 103 (1988), p. 62, notes 93, 95; Trendall, *Handbook*, pp. 205–206, 282, figs. 389–390; K. Schauenburg, *JdI* 104 (1989), p. 39, note 78; Carpenter, *Art and Myth*, p. 244, fig. 352; Jentoft-Nilsen, *CVA* Getty 4, p. 48, under inv. no. 80.AE.153.

EXHIBITED: Virginia Museum of Fine Arts, Richmond, May 12–August 8, 1982; Philbrook Art Center, Tulsa, November 20, 1982–January 9, 1983; Detroit Institute of Arts, February 7–April 10, 1983 (A. D. Trendall, in Mayo, *Magna Graecia*, pp. 18, 22 [color illus.]; M. E. Mayo, ibid., pp. 237–239, no. 112, 2 illus. [dated 330 to 310 B.C.]).

SICILIAN
Red-Figure and Plastic Vases

The Museum of Fine Arts does not possess a representative sampling of Sicilian wares — it owns only one fine skyphos and a charming little mouse — but a basic understanding of the development of Sicilian vase-painting in the fourth century is essential for understanding the Campanian and Paestan schools.

Red-figure pottery in Sicily developed in two distinct phases. The earliest began around 410 B.C. and lasted until about 370, when production dropped dramatically. The main centers of production seem to have been Himera and Syracuse. Attic influence in this early period was so strong that it is difficult to say whether some vases were made in Sicily or Athens; this is particularly evident in the works of the Chequer Painter (cat. no. 107), which reflect the influence of such Attic artists as the Meidias Painter and the Jena Painter.

In the second quarter of the fourth century, some Sicilian potters and painters apparently emigrated to Campania, possibly to escape the political upheavals in Sicily. Their arrival marks the beginning of red-figure production in Campania and Paestum, and once again it is sometimes difficult to distinguish what is Sicilian and what is an early product of these first workshops in the Bay of Naples. The skyphos by the Chequer Painter (cat. no. 107) was found in Campania, but it is an early work and was probably imported from Sicily. Of greater influence was the Dirce Painter, whose style, transmitted by his immigrant pupils, strongly affected both Campanian and Paestan artists.

In Sicily, red-figure production continued on a limited scale in the area of Syracuse, but it was not until Timoleon reestablished political stability around 340 B.C. that the second major phase began; thereafter, Sicilian red-figure was remarkably uniform in its shapes, subjects, and ornaments. Two main groups are discernible: the Lentini-Manfria Group and the Etna Group, the former centered around Syracuse and Gela, the latter found at sites near Mt. Etna, particularly Centuripe. Vases of the Lentini-Manfria Group show the strong influence of the Campanian CA Painter, and it is likely that one or more of his pupils came — or returned — to Sicily from Cumae at this time.

In both groups, larger vessels appear, particularly calyx-kraters, but the favorite shapes are smaller: skyphoid and spherical pyxides, bottles, lekythoi, and lekanides. Women figure prominently as subjects: sitting with their maids or with Eros, conversing, preparing for weddings, lounging in the women's quarters. In many cases, the subject is reduced to a large female head.

The third major late Sicilian group is the Lipari Group, produced on the island of Lipari. The vases are characterized by the extensive use of added colors, a style akin to that of the later polychrome vases of Centuripe. The chief artist was the Lipari Painter, who worked in both the polychrome and the red-figure style. The favorite subjects were once again women. Lipari was sacked in 304 B.C., and production of painted pottery came to an end; red-figure production in Sicily itself had apparently ceased about a decade earlier.

106

106

Plastic mice of this type have been convincingly identified as Sicilian by Heldring (see references below); this example she assigns to her Randazzo Group. A close parallel, not included in her lists, was recently in the Paris market (A la Reine Margot, *Mémoire de la Beauté: La Toilette et la Parure de l'Égypte Prédynastique aux Mérovingiens* [Paris, 1987], p. 23, no. 38.4, illus.). In 1990, another example was seen in a gallery in Rome (Simotti-Rocchi). Heldring suggests that such vessels may have been used for cult purposes (*Sicilian*, p. 13). The tapering spout, however, suggests a feeding cup; one can easily picture the mouse hanging from cords over a cradle.

PUBLISHED: C. C. Vermeule, *MFA AnnRep* 1968, p. 33; idem, *CJ* 66 (1970), p. 21, figs. 21A-B; B. Heldring, *Meded* 39 (1977) pp. 15, 17, pl. 15, 1 ("market"); Heldring, *Sicilian*, p. 59, no. 8 ("Rome, art market") (ref. to *Arch Tr* 13, 1979, pl. 22, 2); I. McPhee, *AJA* 87 (1983), p. 567; H. Menzel, *Die römischen Bronzen aus Deutschland*, III: *Bonn* (Mainz, 1986), p. 65, under no. 134.

EXHIBITED: Tampa Museum of Art, Tampa, 1991 - .

106

PLASTIC VASE IN THE FORM OF A MOUSE
Attributed to the Randazzo Group
Ca. 450–410 B.C.
Gift of Mathias Komor. 68.581

DIMENSIONS AND CONDITION: Length: 15.5 cm; height: 8.0 cm

The mouse crouches with its front paws under its chin and its tail curled up beneath itself. The mouth of the vessel, in the center of the back, is flanked in front and back by a pair of stringholes. A narrow, tapering spout emerges at a 45-degree angle between the rear stringhole and the tail. A black ivy vine is painted on the back as though it were running through the holes. The ears, eyes, eyebrows, and neck fringe are also painted black, as are the tops of the mouth, spout, and stringholes.

107

SKYPHOS
Attributed to the Chequer Painter
Ca. 400 B.C., or slightly earlier
Francis Bartlett Donation of 1900. 03.824

PROVENANCE: E. P. Warren collection; Marcello Spinelli collection; from Campania

DIMENSIONS AND CONDITION: Height: 21.2 cm; diameter rim: 23.9 cm; diameter base of body: 50.7 cm; diameter foot: 16.6 cm
Unbroken. The added white coloring of the thyrsos on side A and the kid on side B has largely flaked off.

SHAPE: Very much in the Attic tradition, with stout walls, wide torus foot, and horizontal handles just below the rim.

A: Death of Pentheus. A maenad, probably Agave, carries the head of her son Pentheus in her left hand and a yellow and white sword in her right. She advances to the right, preceded by a maenad holding in her right hand a straight vine branch resembling a thyrsos, rendered in white. Both women wear belted peploi with black borders, their breasts indicated by circular swirls. Agave's hair is tied in a bun with a white fillet. The hair of the maenad and of the decapitated and beardless Pentheus is wild and windblown.

  B: Two maenads, dressed like those on side A, move to the left and the right, their heads raised and their drapery swirling about them. Each wears a white wreath and holds a thyrsos in one hand, while

107

107

with the other they support a kid, which they are about to tear apart.

There is a band of dotted egg-pattern around the rim. The groundline circling the lower body consists of groups of three linked maeanders to left alternating with saltire-squares. Below the handles are large palmettes with buds and coiling tendrils. Like the shape, the ornament is strongly Atticizing; the checker pattern that gives the artist his name is not employed.

The Chequer Painter was active in Sicily at the end of the fifth century and in the early years of the fourth. Like this vase, several of his works have been found in Campania, where he may have emigrated later in his career; this early work may be an import from Sicily. For recent comments on the painter, see A. D. Trendall, in *Kotinos: Festschrift für Erika Simon* (Mainz, 1992), pp. 301–305; among the new works listed by Trendall, compare the maenads on a calyx-krater formerly in the Freiburg market (p. 301, no. I, pl. 66, 1).

PUBLISHED: P. Hartwig, *JdI* 7 (1892), p. 163; E. Robinson, *MFA AnnRep* 1903, pp. 66–67, no. 23; L. Curtius, *BWPr* 88 (1929), p. 15, note 1; H. Philippart, *Iconographie des Bacchantes d'Euripide* (Paris, 1930), p. 67, no. 155 (with additional bibliography); Caskey and Beazley, II, p. 2; Brommer, *Vasenlisten*, 1960, p. 343, no. D 4; A. D. Trendall, in L. Bernabò-Brea and M. Cavalier, *Meligunìs Lipára*, II (Palermo, 1965), pp. 272, 275; Trendall, *LCS*, p. 199, no. 14, pl. 79, no. 4; Brommer, *Vasenlisten*, 1973, p. 486, no. D 4; M. Schmidt, in Mayo, *Magna Graecia*, p. 29; Trendall, *LCS*, Suppl. III, p. 93, no. 20.

GNATHIAN WARE

Gnathian ware is named for the site of Egnazia (ancient Gnathia), on the Adriatic coast of Apulia, where many vases of this type were excavated in the mid-nineteenth century (e.g., cat. nos. 117, 119, 129, 132). Although there is no evidence that such pots were actually made at Gnathia, most examples are indeed of Apulian origin. Production began sometime around 360 B.C. at several centers in Apulia and continued well into the third century, at least as late as the Roman conquest of Taranto in 273 B.C.

Gnathian pottery is distinguished from most other wares by the technique of decoration, which consisted of covering most or all of the surface with black slip, usually by dipping, and then applying the decoration in added colors — slips of white and red — directly onto the black surface. This method differs from the Six's technique of some fifth-century Attic and Etruscan pots in that most details are not incised into the added colors but painted with a brush; if incision exists, it is directly on the black ground (e.g., the altar on cat. no. 111, the woman on cat. no. 108, and the wavy vines on several examples). By coating the white slip with a thin wash of diluted black slip, a yellowish tint was produced, useful for representing metalwork or blonde hair (e.g., cat. no. 132). The same diluted glaze could be used for shading and a variety of color tones, thus modeling the figures and imparting a sense of three-dimensionality.

The same added colors also appear on red-figure vases, particularly in the subsidiary ornament of larger vessels, such as the necks of volute-kraters. Indeed, Gnathian ware probably owes its origin to such red-figure artists as the Varrese Painter, who not only reveled in polychrome ornament but was also one of the first to use extensive added colors on figures in naiskoi. In the second half of the fourth century, many Gnathian and red-figure vases may have been produced in the same workshops, and one suspects that Gnathian artists may have painted the white heads decorating the shoulders and necks of some red-figure vases; for example, the shoulder of the loutrophoros by the White Sakkos Painter (cat. no. 69).

The first artist to paint figures entirely in added colors and isolate them against the black of the vase was the Konnakis Painter, named after an inscription on a fragment in Taranto. The phlyax actor on cat. no. 108, a favorite subject, is brilliantly conceived, the vivid colors perfectly complementing the lurid expression of the mask and the earthy emotions in the breast of the character. The absence of superfluous ornament increases the impact of such isolated figures, and this is all the more effective when the vessel is a large one, such as a calyx- or bell-krater. When the drawing is superlative, however, as on the lekythos, cat. no. 111, a smaller vase may also serve.

These early works are relatively few, although important new examples have come to light, including some that extend the activity of the Konnakis Workshop as late as the 330s; for example, a calyx-krater in the German art market with a pedagogue close in style to those of the Darius Painter. It was not until early in the third quarter of the fourth century that production of Gnathian pottery boomed in the form of a variety of smaller shapes, particularly skyphoi, cup-skyphoi, and squat lekythoi. One shape that found particular favor with both Gnathian and red-figure painters was the epichysis, an oinochoe that may combine its narrow, beaked spout with a flattened, flanged, or teardrop body (see cat. nos. 119, 121–122). Gnathian potters seem to have delighted in experimenting with a variety of small shapes, including bottles, juglets, kantharoi, and kotylai. Calyx-kraters disappear after the early period, volute-kraters are small and rare, and column-kraters and Panathenaic amphorae never show up at all.

One important scheme of decoration developed on pelikai, with a single figure, frequently Eros, isolated on the body, and one or more bands of ornament on the neck (e.g., cat. no. 117). A more common decorative scheme also developed soon after midcentury, with a vine — usually grape, but sometimes ivy — framing a single object, such as a pendant mask (cat. no. 118). On smaller vessels, there is often a single, horizontal grapevine, without lateral pendants, set below narrower bands of patternwork. The vine may have a single row of pendant leaves and grapes (cat. no. 127) or two rows back-to-back (cat. no. 115).

Another common scheme is a female head between scrolling tendrils and flowers (see cat. nos. 116, 132), similar to those on the necks of red-figure volute-kraters. Like the latter, the Gnathian heads usually wear a sakkos or kekryphalos, so that it is sometimes difficult to determine if it is a woman or

Eros. A Phrygian cap may indicate Orpheus; a pair of wings, Nike.

Because the majority of Gnathian vases are decorated with purely ornamental motifs, either florals or patternwork or both, attribution to specific hands is difficult. For example, the florals on the situla, cat. no. 110, place it within the Konnakis workshop, but in the absence of figure decoration, we cannot say whether it is by the Konnakis Painter. Webster identified a number of early groups, such as the Naples Harp Group (cat. no. 114) and the Boston Group (cat. no. 116). Among the followers of the Rose Painter, active about 340–330 B.C., were the Painter of the Louvre Bottle and the artists of the Dunedin Group, the latter including such subgroups as the Dotted-spray Group (cat. no. 118). The Laurel Spray Group, also descended from the workshop of the Rose Painter, gave rise to the Knudsen Group (cat. nos. 140–142), which lasted well into the third century. To judge by their clay, the vases of the Knudsen Group may have been made at Canosa, while those of the Rose Painter and the Dunedin Group were produced at Taranto.

A major development at the end of the fourth century was the introduction of ribbed vases. This was not a totally new idea, as ribbing appears on Attic vases of the late fifth century and on a few Apulian red-figure examples of the mid-fourth century. In Gnathian ware, the practice was first introduced in the workshop of the Painter of the Louvre Bottle but quickly became widespread. On some pieces, mostly early, the ribs may be broad and carefully executed, with rounded tips, but on many later works, the "ribs" are merely shallow scratches. Metalware may have been the initial inspiration, but the practice was soon adapted for all manner of vessels.

The vogue for ribbing seems to have inspired experiments in shapes and decorative schemes. Vines have smaller leaves and slender, winding stems. Many bottles and lekythoi are decorated with a white net-pattern that covers the body in lieu of ribbing (cat. nos. 123–125). Kantharoi are a favorite ribbed shape, either with knotted handles and a molded lip (cat. nos. 128–129), or with ring handles and a straight lip (cat. no. 136). There was a renewed interest in large shapes, now covered with elaborate ribbing; for example, the skyphoid-krater (cat. no. 131) and the bell-krater with lion's-head handles and friezes of frolicking Erotes (cat. no. 130), a favorite subject on ribbed vessels of the period.

Other regions of South Italy also produced pottery of Gnathian type, particularly Sicily, Paestum, and Campania. The favorite Campanian type was a stemless kylix having an ivy vine with an incised stem around the interior (cat. no. 144). In Campania, painted decoration was frequently combined with stamped ornament (cat. no. 143). The technique was also employed in Etruria, inspiring such imitations as cat. nos. 162 and 163.

Gnathian Ware, Apulian

108

CALYX-KRATER
Attributed to the Konnakis Painter (Webster)
Ca. 350 B.C.
Henry Lillie Pierce Residuary Fund. 00.363

PROVENANCE: E. P. Warren collection; Forman collection at
Pippbrook House, Dorking, Surrey (Forman Sale Catalogue,
no. 370)

DIMENSIONS AND CONDITION: Height: 29.9 cm; diameter rim:
31.9 cm; diameter at base of wall: 18.1 cm; diameter stem
above foot molding: 5.8 cm; diameter foot: 14.5 cm
Broken and mended in antiquity with five pairs of rivet holes
and one single hole from the ancient repair. Broken and repaired again in modern times; minimal restoration except for
infill for two missing rim fragments.

SHAPE: The same as that of many contemporary red-figure
and Gnathian calyx-kraters, with a relatively short, broad
body and the handles extending more than halfway up toward
the rim, curving inward at the top. A fillet separates the lower
body from the tall, sloping foot.

A: A phlyax actor in the guise of an old man is running to the left on a groundline of white dots. He
wears a white cloak, a red, padded tunic with yellow
sleeves, yellow trousers, and a red fillet. His feet,
mask, and hands are red-brown; his pendant phallus
is red; the hair and beard are white. He helps himself
along with the slender yellow staff in his extended
right hand. A shower of sweetmeats, probably stolen, spills from his cloak as he runs. Perhaps he is an
old slave who has raided the larder and whose crime
is revealed by his own greedy haste; compare the larcenous slave Xanthias on a bell-krater in the Moretti
collection, Milan, who stuffs a stolen cake into his
tunic (Trendall, *Phlyax*, 1967, p. 38, no. 45, pl. 2).
Trendall identifies the mask of the Boston phlyax as
type G: "scanty white hair, considerable beard,
hooked nose" (ibid., pp. 12, 79).

B: A woman is standing with her body nearly
frontal and her head in profile to the right. The flesh
of her feet and face are painted white, and her flowing hair, pulled back and tied, is yellow. The rest of
her draped body is rendered entirely by incision directly on the black ground. She is wrapped in a himation, which reveals her body while falling down
the left side in ample folds. Her arms are concealed:
the left resting on the hip, the right one pulling the

108 (Color Plate XIX)

108

drapery taut. Her body is pierced by three drill holes from the ancient repair.

There are a few other calyx-kraters that combine poychrome figures in the Gnathian technique on the obverse with incised figures on the reverse; for example, New York 10.210.17 a-d (M. E. Mayo, in Mayo, *Magna Graecia*, pp. 261–262, no. 119), and St. Petersburg (no number: Forti, *Gnathia*, pl. 11, a). The polychrome subject is often a phlyax (e.g., London F 543: Trendall, *Phlyax*, 1967, p. 79, no. 178; Forti, *Gnathia*, pl. 17, b), but sometimes a tragic actor may be intended, as on the famous fragment in Würzburg, with an actor holding the mask of a bearded king (Forti, *Gnathia*, pl. 10, a); compare the pedagogue, a standard dramatic role, on a calyx-krater recently in the German art market, almost certainly by the Konnakis Painter (Galerie Gunter Pühze, *Kunst der Antike*, cat. 10 [1993], no. 220).

The Konnakis Painter is named for an inscription on a krater fragment in Taranto with a drunken hetaira in added white (Forti, *Gnathia*, pl. 10, b). Such inscriptions are rare on Gnathian phlyax vases, but the coy phlyax on an unpublished calyx-krater in the Zewadski collection, Tampa, is identified as "Derkylos." The Konnakis Painter decorated other shapes as well, such as a bell-krater with a comic Prometheus in Malibu (Getty 82.AE.15: F. C. Frel, in *Studies Mildenberg*, pp. 51–55, pl. 7), and an unpublished situla of type 1 in the Fleischman collection, New York, with a dark-skinned phlyax.

PUBLISHED: E. Robinson, *MFA AnnRep* 1900, p. 82, no. 38; H. Bulle, *Festschrift für James Loeb* (Munich, 1930), pp. 30–31, figs. 19a-b; R. Zahn, in Furtwängler and Reichhold, III, p. 180, note 5 (i); Bieber, *Theater*, pp. 279 (figs. 376–377), 281; T. B. L. Webster, *JHS* 71 (1951), pp. 223 (no. 40), 224–225, 230–231; Catteruccia, *Pitture*, pp. 64–65, no. 77, pl. 12; Trendall, *Phlyax*, 1959, p. 54, no. 149; T. B. L. Webster, *AntK* 3 (1960), p. 32; A. D. Trendall, *EAA*, III, p. 709; Bieber, *Theater*, 1961, p. 138, fig. 502, a-b; Forti, *Gnathia*, pp. 44, 55 (note 25), 59, 61–62, 99–100, 106 (note 10), 107 (note 13), pl. 12a-c; Taranto, *Letteratura*, p. 31, no. 175; S. Winkelmann, *JOAI* 50 (Hauptblatt) (1972–73), p. 164, note 19; Trendall, *Phlyax*, 1967, pp. 12, 14, 79, no. 177 (with additional bibliography); Webster, *Gnathia*, p. 5, no. 2; *NSc* 28 (1974), Suppl., p. 460, under no. 39; Webster and Green, *Old and Middle Comedy*, p. 109, no. Ph 177; M. E. Mayo, in Mayo, *Magna Graecia*, pp. 261–262, under no. 119; F. C. Frel, in *Studies Mildenberg*, pp. 53–54; J. R. Green, in *Greek Vases in The J. Paul Getty Museum* 3 (Malibu, 1986), pp. 115, 117, figs. 3 a-b, 123, note 33; E. Borgna, *ArchCl* 42 (1990), pp. 391–392, fig. 4.

EXHIBITED: *Theater in Ancient Art*, fig. 33.

108

108

109

FRAGMENT OF A KRATER
Attributed to the Konnakis Group
Ca. 350–340 B.C.
Cornelia Prime Lowell Fund. 22.679

PROVENANCE: E. P. Warren collection

DIMENSIONS AND CONDITION: Height: 11.0 cm

The lower half of a draped, standing figure is incised directly on the black ground. To judge by the previous vase (cat. no. 108), the absence of added white should indicate a male. His right leg is bent, as though he were leaning or walking to the right. The two rounded areas at the front of the waist are the concealed hands, from which the himation hangs in folds terminating in small weights.

For similar incised figures, see the comments on cat. no. 108; this vase too may have been a calyx-krater.

109

110

SITULA
Attributed to the Konnakis Group (Webster)
Ca. 340–330 B.C.
Henry Lillie Pierce Residuary Fund. 01.8098

PROVENANCE: E. P. Warren collection; bought in Rome

DIMENSIONS AND CONDITION: Height to top of handle: 27.0 cm; inner diameter rim: 14.7 cm; outer diameter rim: 17.0 cm; diameter body: 19.8 cm; diameter stem: 10.4 cm; diameter foot: 11.2 cm
Unbroken. The added color is worn, particularly the white tripod.

SHAPE: There is a strainer behind the spout, which is in the form of a comic mask of an old man. The bail-handle consists of two thick, rolled cylinders. The body is widest at the shoulder, constricting to a wide mouth with a flattened rim. The lower body tapers to a simple disk foot, convex in profile.

The comic mask of the old man has white hair and beard, a red face, a red fillet, and a larger padded fillet in white. The spout itself is painted yellow. Beneath the spout is a white tripod with three laurel branches draped with lobed fillets. The stems of the laurel are red-brown. On the opposite side of the rim, at the root of the handle, is a rather benign-looking mask of Herakles modeled in relief, with a yellow beard, red face, and yellow lionskin.

Below the rim on each side is a grapevine with a red central stripe, the grapes alternately red and orange, the leaves yellow, and the tendrils white. From the ends of both grapevines hang incised vines of ivy, with yellow leaves. A broad, reserved band with a black stripe near the top circles the lower body above the disk foot. There is a large X-shaped dipinto on the bottom of the foot rendered in pinkish wash.

Webster (*Gnathia*, p. 6) recognized the same hand on a chous, London 67.5–8, and a lekythos, Oxford 1881.100.

For situlae of this type, see K. Schauenburg, *AA* 1981, pp. 462–488; J. R. Green, *Museum News* (Toledo Museum of Art) 22, no. 2 (1980), pp. 28–33; K. T. Luckner, in Mayo, *Magna Graecia*, pp. 271–272, no. 130; and A. Kossatz-Deissmann, *AA* 1990, pp. 505–520. For the mask of Herakles, compare a situla in the Bill and Linda Houston collection, on loan to the Tampa Museum of Art (inv. 7.2.89). For the spout in the form of a comic mask, compare Lecce 1631 (Bernardini, *Vasi*, p. 26, pl. 58, 10). A similar spout, but with a satyr-mask, is found on a situla in Toledo (inv. 73.7: Green, *Museum News*, p. 29, fig. 6; Luckner, *Magna Graecia*, p. 271, detail a.) These situlae clearly imitate metal vessels; for example, compare two bronze situlae from Bolsena, also with masks of Herakles (Vatican 12806 and 12808: P. J.

110

110

110

Riis, *ActaA* 30 [1959], p. 15, fig. 12). Most ceramic examples come from Apulia, but metal examples are found also in Etruria, Macedonia, and Northern Greece; see B. Barr-Sharrar, in Barr-Sharrer and Borza, *Macedonia and Greece*, pp. 127–131. For the debate over whether the metal vessels are primarily Greek, Etruscan, or Macedonian in origin, see A. Oliver, Jr., in *Antiquities from the Collection of Christos G. Bastis* (New York, 1987), p. 223, no. 129.

PUBLISHED: T. B. L. Webster, *AntK* 3 (1960), pp. 31–32, 35, no. 54, pl. 8, figs. 4–5; idem, *Tragedy and Satyr-Play*, p. 80, no. GV 5; idem, *Gnathia*, p. 6, no. 14; idem, *Old and Middle Comedy*, p. 53, no. GV 6 b; Webster and Green, *Old and Middle Comedy*, p. 162, no. TV 3c; J. R. Green, *Museum News* (Toledo Museum of Art) 22, no. 2 (1980), p. 33, figs. 13–14; *Het verhaal bij het materiaal* (Utrecht, 1980), p. 115, note 7; K. Schauenburg, *AA* 1981, p. 462, note 3; M. Pfrommer, *JdI* 98 (1983), p. 262, note 143; M. Candela, *BABesch* 60 (1985), pp. 32 (no. C 3), 33–35, 46–47, 52, 69, figs. 46–47.

111

SQUAT LEKYTHOS
Ca. 350 B.C.
Henry Lillie Pierce Residuary Fund. 01.8106

PROVENANCE: E. P. Warren collection; Somzée collection (A. Furtwängler, *Sammlung Somzée: Antike Kunstdenkmäler* [Munich, 1897], p. 68, no. 98, pl. XXXIX); van Branteghem collection (Hôtel Drouot, Paris, *Collection van Branteghem: Catalogue des monuments antiques, vases peints, terres cuites*, May 30-June 1, 1892, no. 231).

DIMENSIONS AND CONDITION: Height: 21.2 cm; diameter rim: 5.0 cm; diameter neck: 1.6 cm; diameter body: 11.0 cm; diameter foot: 8.0 cm
Unbroken and in excellent condition

SHAPE: Mirrors that of many contemporary red-figure Apulian lekythoi, with a tall body, grooved disk foot, concave neck, and tall, flaring mouth.

111 (Color Plate xx)

Eros is seated to the right on a cube-shaped block or altar, his legs crossed and his left hand resting on his knee. He is nude except for his yellow shoes. With his right hand he holds out a yellow wreath, which he regards with a rather disgusted look. The altar is incised directly on the black ground in three-quarter view (the base in profile). Eros is painted with brown skin delicately shaded with strokes of lighter hue. His hair, pulled up in a tall chignon, is blonde and his wings yellow and white. The groundline is a wavy white line. Compare a pelike in Taranto with a seated Eros holding a wreath (Forti, *Gnathia*, pl. 6). For the combination of incised block and polychrome figure, compare a krater fragment in Taranto (Forti, *Gnathia*, pl. 33, c).

112

SKYPHOS
Attributed to the Konnakis Group (Webster)
Ca. 340–330 B.C.
Gift of the Estate of Alfred Greenough. 86.151

DIMENSIONS AND CONDITION: Height: 11.1 cm; diameter rim: 8.3 cm; diameter body: 8.9 cm; diameter stem: 3.3 cm; diameter foot: 4.2 cm
Broken and roughly repaired. Much of the added white has been lost.

SHAPE: Descends from the skyphos of Corinthian type. The lower body is narrow and tapering. The widest diameter is at midbody below the handles. The foot is in two degrees. The handles angle upward slightly.

On one side, the rim is decorated with two bands of white herringbone framed by incised lines, from which hang white fillets and festoons, now almost entirely effaced. On the opposite side is a single band of herringbone, below which is a large white ivy vine, whose leaves and berries are now for the most part effaced, leaving the incised vine as the most visible element. A black stripe circles the reserved lower body.

PUBLISHED: Robinson, *Catalogue*, p. 185, no. 510; Webster, *Gnathia*, p. 7, no. 10.

112

113

SKYPHOS

Ca. 340–330 B.C.

Gift of Horace L. Mayer. 58.1305

DIMENSIONS AND CONDITION: Height: 9.6 cm; width across
handles: 14.0 cm; diameter rim: 7.5 cm; diameter body: 8.1
cm; diameter stem: 2.8 cm; diameter foot: 3.6 cm
Broken and repaired. Much of the added paint has been lost.

SHAPE: Resembles that of cat. no. 112, but the body is less
plump, tapering more at the bottom, and the foot is a simple
disk.

Of the painted decoration, only faint traces and incised lines remain. The rim on both sides is decorated
with egg-pattern. On one side, there is a red and yellow fillet below the rim, framed by incised lines. Below this are a row of dots and a large grapevine with a
red central stripe and grapes and leaves. Vertical red
stripes seem to support the ends of the vine. On the
other side, three pendant ivy vines with incised
stems hang from the egg-pattern on the rim; a rosette filled one of the intervals. The lower body is reserved, with a single black stripe. Compare *CVA*
Naples 3, pl. 73, 3.

114

CUP-SKYPHOS

Attributed to the Naples Harp Group (Webster)

Ca. 340–330 B.C.

Anonymous Gift. 15.256

DIMENSIONS AND CONDITION: Height: 8.7 cm; width across
handles: 18.2 cm; diameter rim: 11.5 cm; diameter body:
12.0 cm; diameter stem: 5.4 cm; diameter foot: 6.2 cm
Unbroken

SHAPE: A common Gnathian shape, with a roughly hemispherical body, a ridge separating the gently spreading foot
from a short, wide stem, and sharply angled handles that roll
back on themselves like the metal prototypes they mimic.

The rim on one side is decorated with a band of
white, dotted egg-pattern, the eggs outlined with incision. Below this are a red and yellow fillet framed
by incised lines, a row of yellow dots, and a yellow
and white grapevine with a red central stripe (a so-
called Oxford vine). On the other side, in the handle-
zone, is a single white wreath with an incised stem.

PUBLISHED: Webster, *Gnathia*, p. 17, no. 31 (as 15.526).

113

114

115

115

CUP-SKYPHOS
Ca. 340–330 B.C.
Gift of Mrs. Henry P. Kidder. Res. 23.214

DIMENSIONS AND CONDITION: Height: 6.4 cm; diameter rim:
9.7 cm; diameter body: 10.0 cm; diameter stem: 5.0 cm; diameter foot: 6.0 cm
Unbroken

SHAPE: Very close to cat. no. 114, but smaller, with a shallower bowl and wider foot.

On one side, the rim is decorated with a band of
white, dotted egg-pattern, the eggs outlined by incision. Below this are a band of yellow dots and a yellow grapevine with a red central stripe. The rim on
the other side is decorated with a white wreath with
an incised stem. The concavity between body and
foot is colored with a rose wash.

   This combination of shape and decoration is relatively common (e.g., Lecce 1401: Bernardini, *Vasi*,
p. 11, pl. 19, 16).

116

BOTTLE
The name-vase of the Boston Group (Webster)
Ca. 340–330 B.C.
Purchased 1880. 80.623

PROVENANCE: Bought by C. C. Perkins

DIMENSIONS AND CONDITION: Height: 14.3 cm; upper diameter rim: 4.4 cm; diameter body: 8.0 cm; diameter foot: 5.3 cm
The lip is partially restored.

SHAPE: Sometimes called an alabastron, but with little resemblance to the traditional form (e.g., cat. no. 28); the generic
term "bottle" is perhaps preferable. Compared with examples
of the next quarter century, the neck is wider, the body more
sack-shaped, and the mouth smaller; compare cat. no. 124.
The grooved foot is in two degrees.

On one side is a female head in profile to the left,
flanked by spiraling tendrils in yellow and white.
The woman's skin is white and her hair blonde; her
red kekryphalos is decorated with white esses, and a
white fillet trails behind her neck. She wears a necklace of tiny black dots. Above and below are bands of
white, dotted egg-pattern framed by incised lines,
and there are white rays on the lower neck.

PUBLISHED: Robinson, *Catalogue*, p. 190, no. 525; Webster,
Gnathia, p. 22, no. 6.

116

117

PELIKE
Ca. 330–320 B.C.
Gift of Thomas G. Appleton. 76.56

PROVENANCE: Alessandro Castellani collection; from Gnathia

DIMENSIONS AND CONDITION: Height: 23.7 cm; diameter rim:
11.8 cm; diameter neck: 5.3 cm; diameter body: 13.5 cm; diameter stem: 6.0 cm; diameter foot: 8.3 cm
Intact except for a chip in one handle

SHAPE: Pelike of type 2, with a reserved molding at the top of
the neck, and with the foot separated from the lower body by a
reserved stem. The cyma recta foot has a flange around the
top.

117

OINOCHOE (shape 3)
Related to the Dotted-spray Group (Webster and Green)
Ca. 340–330 B.C.
Gift of Miss B. H. Lyman. 31.143

DIMENSIONS AND CONDITION: Height: 10.4 cm; diameter neck: 2.4 cm; diameter body: 8.5 cm; diameter foot: 4.2 cm
Unbroken

SHAPE: A variety of the standard Apulian chous, with trefoil mouth, tall, tapering neck, nearly spherical body, and a foot in two degrees. There is a red lion's head modeled at the end of the handle where it touches the rim.

All of the decoration in white appears to be modern, but the artist may have been following an original design. On the neck are a white wreath with pendant sprays and a female mask hanging from a cord. On the body below is a large white disk, badly eroded. Compare the plastic lion's head and painted mask on Lecce 3572: Bernardini, *Vasi*, pl. 37, 6. For masks on Gnathian vases, see T. B. L. Webster, *JHS* 71 (1951), pp. 222–232; idem, *AntK* 3 (1960), pp. 30–36.

PUBLISHED: T. B. L. Webster, *AntK* 3 (1960), p. 35, no. 34h; idem, *Gnathia*, pp. 20–21, no. 9; idem, *Old and Middle Comedy*, p. 55, no. GV 16m; Webster and Green, *Old and Middle Comedy*, p. 197, no. TV 26h.

118

Eros, wearing a kekryphalos and necklace, is seated to the left on a seat covered with a red cloak, his feet resting on groundlines of white dots. He holds a yellow phiale in his raised right hand. His skin is white, and his wings are white and red. In the field at left are a yellow fillet and ivy leaf.

On the obverse neck are three bands of ornament: dotted egg-pattern, battlements, and a row of pendants resembling a necklace. The battlements are yellow, the eggs and necklace white. The entire reverse is undecorated. The stem of the foot and the broad groove below the overhanging rim are tinted with reddish wash.

PUBLISHED: Robinson, *Catalogue*, p. 178, no. 492; MFA, *Art in Bloom*, 1985, p. 135, illus.

119

EPICHYSIS
Ca. 340–320 B.C.
Gift of Thomas G. Appleton. 76.58

PROVENANCE: Alessandro Castellani collection; from Gnathia

DIMENSIONS AND CONDITION: Height: 19.6 cm; height to handle attachment at mouth: 14.0 cm; diameter neck: 1.6 cm; diameter body: 7.4 cm; diameter stem: 3.8 cm; diameter foot: 5.7 cm
Unbroken

SHAPE: This variety of epichysis has the usual narrow, beaked spout and high-swung handle, but with a pear-shaped body and cyma recta foot; compare cat. no. 120. The same shape is frequently decorated in red-figure (e.g., Toronto C.680: Robinson, Harcum, and Iliffe, *Greek Vases*, pl. 71, no. 386). The modeled female faces on either side of the juncture of handle and rim are standard on both this type and the more conventional epichysis (e.g., cat. no. 122).

None of the ornamental bands framed by incised lines completely circles the neck or body. In the middle of the body is a white and yellow grapevine with a red central stripe, the so-called Oxford vine. Below this is a band of white, dotted egg-pattern. On the neck and shoulder are five superimposed bands of ornament: white egg-pattern at top and bottom framing zigzags, key-pattern, and running esses, all in yellow.

Webster (*Gnathia*, p. 6) thought the vine wreath on this epichysis and the one on the chous London 67.5–8 (*CVA* 1, pl. 5, 5) were by the same hand. With these he compared the vine on a squat lekythos of the Konnakis Group (Oxford 1881.100).

PUBLISHED: Robinson, *Catalogue*, p. 183, no. 501; Chase, *Antiquities*, p. 117, fig. 142; Chase and Vermeule, *Greek, Etruscan and Roman Art*, pp. 141, 152, fig. 131; Webster, *Gnathia*, pp. 6, 18.

120

EPICHYSIS
Ca. 330 B.C.
Henry Lillie Pierce Residuary Fund. 01.8112

PROVENANCE: E. P. Warren collection; bought in Bari

DIMENSIONS AND CONDITION: Height to the top of handle: 18.2 cm; height to handle attachment at mouth: 14.0 cm; diameter neck: 1.7 cm; diameter body: 8.9 cm; diameter stem: 5.7 cm; diameter foot: 6.5 cm
Unbroken

SHAPE: See the comments on cat. no. 119; this example has a more spherical body and a wider foot. On either side of the juncture of handle and rim are modeled female faces.

The bands of ornament framed by incised lines do not fully circle the body. At midbody is a broad

119

120

wreath with leaves alternately beige, yellow, and
white. Below this is a band of crudely executed, incised and white-painted egg-pattern. Below the
white rays on the neck are three superimposed bands
of ornament: incised and white-painted egg-pattern,
a red and yellow fillet, and white scrolling tendrils. A
rosy wash colors the concavity between body and
foot.

Compare a jug in the Dechter collection, Los An-
geles: K. Hamma, ed., *The Dechter Collection of
Greek Vases* (San Bernardino, 1989), p. 66, no. 39.
Compare also two jugs once in the Swiss market:
Italische Keramik, Münzen und Medaillen AG,
Sonderliste U (Basel, 1984), nos. 86–87.

121

121

EPICHYSIS
Ca. 330 B.C.
Henry Lillie Pierce Residuary Fund. 01.8113

PROVENANCE: E. P. Warren collection; bought in Bari but
marked "Lecce"

DIMENSIONS AND CONDITION: Height: 14.6 cm; diameter
neck: 1.7 cm; diameter body: 9.9 cm; diameter foot: 9.3 cm
Unbroken

SHAPE: In this type of epichysis, the body is neither flanged
nor teardrop-shaped but flattened, like that of the squat lekythos, cat. no. 123. The modeled faces flanking the juncture of
handle and rim are from molds so worn that they have lost all
definition. The foot is a simple torus.

The neck is offset and decorated with white rays. On
the body is a broad wreath with alternating red and
white leaves and an axial yellow roundel. Above this,
on the shoulder, is a band of yellow and white scrolling tendrils. Below the wreath and above the tendrils
are bands of dotted egg-pattern, with the eggs outlined by incision. The upper eggs are alternately yellow and white; the lower are all white.

Compare the ornament (and provenance) of the
preceding vase (cat. no. 120).

122

EPICHYSIS
Ca. 330 B.C.
Gift of Edward Austin. 76.450

DIMENSIONS AND CONDITION: Height: 16.3 cm; height to handle attachment at mouth: 11.8 cm; diameter neck: 1.5 cm;
diameter upper flange: 8.8 cm; diameter body: 5.4 cm; diameter foot: 8.2 cm
Unbroken

SHAPE: This is the more standard form of Apulian epichysis,
with a spreading foot, concave body, and a domed shoulder set

122

off by a broad, flat flange. On either side of the juncture of handle and rim are two modeled female faces.

A band of white, dotted egg-pattern circles the shoulder on top of the flange, the eggs outlined by incision. The key-pattern on the front of the body is white and yellow; the rays on the neck are white. The broad wreath on the shoulder has a yellow knot in front, with leaves alternately red and white and separated by strands of white dots. Rows of yellow dots frame the wreath above and below.

Compare the decoration of an epichysis in Naples (*CVA* 3, pl. 71, 2).

PUBLISHED: Robinson, *Catalogue*, p. 183, no. 502.

123

123

SQUAT LEKYTHOS
Ca. 320–300 B.C.
Gift of Miss Helen Griggs. 12.1179

PROVENANCE: Said to be from Cumae

DIMENSIONS AND CONDITION: Height: 9.6 cm; diameter rim: 4.8 cm; diameter neck: 1.7 cm; diameter body: 10.6 cm; diameter foot: 9.3 cm
The mouth is reattached, and there is plaster fill and repainting on the neck.

SHAPE: Depressed, lentoid body, more flat than squat; wide ring foot, flaring mouth, vertical strap handle. Compare the "flat" epichysis, cat. no. 121.

There are yellow rays on the neck; a yellow stripe framed by white stripes nearly circles the shoulder, stopping at the handle. Circling the body is a broad band of white, crosshatched lines forming a net-pattern. A red stripe framed by white stripes circles the lower body above the foot.

This type of decoration is more commonly found on taller lckythoi or bottles, such as cat. nos. 124 and 125. Compare *CVA* University Museum, University of Pennsylvania, pl. 37, 5; Hayes, *Black-Gloss*, pp. 150–152, no. 250; *CVA* Copenhagen 7, pl. 277, 8; *CVA* Fogg Museum, pl. 36, 11; *CVA* Gotha 2, pl. 85, 1; *CVA* Stuttgart 1, pl. 60, 11–13, and *CVA* Taranto, pl. 1, 5.

PUBLISHED: Robinson, *Catalogue*, p. 185, no. 506.

124

124

BOTTLE
Ca. 320–300 B.C.
Purchased 1880. 80.624

PROVENANCE: Bought by C. C. Perkins

DIMENSIONS AND CONDITION: Height: 12.8 cm; diameter upper rim: 4.2 cm; maximum diameter rim: 4.9 cm; diameter

neck: 1.6 cm; diameter body: 7.4 cm; diameter stem: 4.1 cm;
diameter foot: 5.0 cm
Unbroken

SHAPE: A standard shape of the end of the fourth century;
compare the earlier bottle, cat. no. 116. The beveled mouth is
broad and overhanging, with a flat molding at the top; the reserved stem is short and wide.

White rays circle the neck. The body is covered by a
network of white, crosshatched lines. Around the
shoulder is a yellow stripe framed by two white
stripes. Two yellow stripes circle the lower body.

Both the shape and the decoration are common;
see, for example, Capua 8079 (*CVA* 4, pl. 2, 5) and
Lecce 1297 (Bernardini, *Vasi*, p. 22, pl. 46, 6). J. R.
Green has dated the vogue for such "reticulate" decoration, also applied to lekythoi, to the period 320–
300 B.C. (*CVA* University Museum, University of
Pennsylvania 1, p. 33).

PUBLISHED: Robinson, *Catalogue*, p. 190, no. 524.

125

125

BOTTLE
Ca. 320–300 B.C.
Gift of Horace L. Mayer. 58.1307

DIMENSIONS AND CONDITION: Height: 13.7 cm; diameter upper rim: 4.1 cm; maximum diameter rim: 4.6 cm; diameter
neck: 1.7 cm; diameter body: 7.3 cm; diameter stem: 3.3 cm;
diameter foot: 4.3 cm
Unbroken. The surface is encrusted in many places.

SHAPE: Compare cat. no. 124; in this example, the mouth is
less ponderous and the stem is tall and flaring.

The crude white rays on the neck are framed above
and below by red stripes framed by white stripes.
The body is covered with a network of white, crosshatched lines, below which is a red stripe.

126

LEKYTHOS
End of 4th century B.C.
Gift of William Sturgis Bigelow. 98.202

DIMENSIONS AND CONDITION: Height: 19.2 cm; diameter rim:
4.7 cm; diameter neck: 1.8 cm; diameter body: 8.0 cm; diameter stem: 3.5 cm; diameter foot: 5.4 cm
Unbroken

SHAPE: Ovoid body; pedestaled foot with narrow base; tall
neck and trumpet mouth

The body is decorated with a net-pattern of black
crosshatching on a reserved ground. There are white
dots at the intersections of the lines and at the core of
each wave in the band of wave-pattern around the
shoulder; a second band of wave-pattern, without

126

dots, circles the lower body. There are rays on the upper neck.

Lekythoi of this type are relatively common; see, for example, Lecce 892 (*CVA* Lecce 2, pl. 50, 18). They are not properly classified as Gnathian at all, for there is no use of superimposed colors. Nonetheless, they so much resemble Gnathian bottles and lekythoi with net-patterns in added white, like cat. nos. 123 and 124, that it seems permissible to include this example here, especially as no other category claims priority.

The decoration is clearly inspired by vases of the Attic Bulas group of the end of the fifth and the first half of the fourth centuries. Bodies decorated with black net-patterns highlighted with white dots are extremely common, and even an occasional wave-pattern turns up. The tall, ovoid body and pedestaled foot of the Boston lekythos, however, are unknown in Greek fabrics and identify it firmly as Italiote; compare J. D. Beazley, *BSA* 41 (1941–1945), pp. 10–21, pls. 3–4; see also R. Hirschmann, *Jahrbuch des Museums für Kunst und Gewerbe Hamburg* 9/10 (1990–1991), pp. 39–42.

127

127

SKYPHOS
Attributed to the Dotted-spray Group (Webster); attributed to the Knudsen Group (Green)
Ca. 300 B.C.
Gift of Miss Helen Griggs. 12.1180

PROVENANCE: Said to be from Capua

DIMENSIONS AND CONDITION: Height: 8.6 cm; diameter rim: 7.6 cm; diameter body: 7.9 cm; diameter stem: 3.3 cm; diameter foot: 4.2 cm
One handle has been restored with the handle of another ancient but slightly smaller skyphos.

SHAPE: Compare cat. no. 113; the handles are more horizontal, the body shorter and less sharply tapering.

On one side there is a band of white egg-pattern on the rim, and below this are a red and yellow fillet framed by incised lines, a row of yellow dots, and a white and yellow grapevine hanging from a red stripe. On the other side, in the handle-zone, is a single white wreath with an incised stem.

The shape and decorative scheme recall earlier skyphoi, such as cat. no. 113, but the drawing of the vine and egg-pattern links it with the Knudsen Group of the early years of the third century (e.g., cat. no. 141).

PUBLISHED: Robinson, *Catalogue*, p. 186, no. 511; Webster, *Gnathia*, p. 21, no. 16 (as 22.1180).

128

KANTHAROS
Attributed to the Painter of the Louvre Bottle (Green)
End of 4th to early 3rd century B.C.
Gift of Dr. Henry J. Bigelow. 88.320

DIMENSIONS AND CONDITION: Height: 14.8 cm; width across handles: 16.9 cm; diameter rim: 11.4 cm; diameter neck: 8.2 cm; diameter body: 9.9 cm; diameter stem: 2.4 cm; diameter foot: 6.2 cm
Unbroken

SHAPE: Occasionally referred to as a krateriskos (e.g., by Webster; see reference below). The "Knot of Herakles" on either handle functions as a thumb-grip. An angular groove sharply bifurcates the rim. The neck is concave, the body rounded and tapering. The foot is in three degrees of rounded, torus-like moldings; the sloping stem is of moderate height. The shape is sometimes greatly enlarged for use as a krater (e.g., Forti, *Gnathia*, pl. 26, e).

128

There is vertical ribbing on the body, topped on either side by a white stripe. On either side of the neck is a branched spray in yellow. There are white rays on the roots of the handles and white spots on the foot. The stem of the foot is painted a dull red.

For a list of parallels, see Webster, *Gnathia*, p. 27.

PUBLISHED: Robinson, *Catalogue*, p. 186, no. 514; Webster, *Gnathia*, p. 27, no. 12; J. R. Green, *BICS* 18 (1971), p. 36.

129

KANTHAROS
Beginning of 3rd century B.C.
Gift of Thomas G. Appleton. 76.57

PROVENANCE: Alessandro Castellani collection; from Gnathia

DIMENSIONS AND CONDITION: Height: 16.0 cm; width across handles: 19.3 cm; diameter rim: 13.2 cm; diameter neck: 9.0 cm; diameter body: 11.5 cm; diameter stem: 2.6 cm; diameter foot: 6.4 cm

SHAPE: Close in shape to cat. no. 128; the stem of the foot is taller.

The body has vertical ribbing, topped on either side by a white stripe. On either side of the neck is a yellow ivy wreath with berries. There are yellow rays on the roots of the knotted handles and a row of yellow strokes on the foot. The stem of the foot is painted a dull red.

To the comparable examples listed by Webster may be added a pair in the Royal Ontario Museum, Toronto: inv. 923.13.114 and (with a taller neck) 923.13.123 (Hayes, *Black-Gloss*, pp. 155–157, nos. 255–256); also Stockholm NM 2132 (E. Rystedt, *Grekisk Keramik* [Stockholm, 1985], p. 23, fig. 20).

PUBLISHED: Robinson, *Catalogue*, p. 186, no. 513; Webster, *Gnathia*, p. 28, no. 5.

EXHIBITED: Tampa Museum of Art, Tampa, 1991–

129

130 (Color Plate XXI)

130

BELL-KRATER
End of 4th century B.C.
Henry Lillie Pierce Residuary Fund. 01.8126

PROVENANCE: E. P. Warren collection (According to the Museum's records, "the provenance can be ascertained," but apparently this was never done.)

DIMENSIONS AND CONDITION: Height: 45.5 cm; width at handles: 43.5 cm; diameter rim: 45.7 cm; diameter body at belt: 31.4 cm; diameter stem: 9.0 cm; diameter foot: 18.5 cm Unbroken. The figures on side B are quite worn. A red stripe may have flaked off the wing of the first Eros on side A.

SHAPE: The two mold-made handles are in the shape of lions' heads. As on the later skyphos, cat. no. 133, there are two zones of ribbing on the body, that of the lower body being less carefully executed, without the rounded tips of the upper tier. The foot is in two degrees, with a tall stem and a flange above the spreading base. The mouth consists of a broad echinus with a flaring, overhanging rim, grooved at the top.

Yellow and white dotted egg-pattern circles the overhanging rim, forming a cymation. Between the two zones of ribbing is a smooth, unribbed band of alternating yellow rosettes and palmettes. White stripes frame the upper band of ribbing and the smooth central band. Figure decoration is confined to the handle-zones, below the rim.

130

130

A: A pudgy young Eros dressed as a charioteer is driving a yellow biga with red spots drawn by white hounds. The hounds have spotted red girths and incised reins looped as martingales. The wreathed driver wears a yellow gown and a red long-sleeved tunic with yellow dots. At the left, preceding the biga, another nude, white-skinned Eros runs along with a torch in his right hand and one of the reins in his left; he wears a wreath, necklace, bracelets, anklets, and yellow shoes. His wings are red, white, and yellow. Two white birds fly above the biga, which is followed by a third Eros with shoes and jewelry like the one in front; he prances along in a kind of goose step while playing the double flutes. From the groundline by the handles, flanking the scene, grow stout yellow vines, heavy with grapes.

B: Two boys and two girls are playing together. The boy at right, wearing a red tunic, white hat, and yellow boots, holds a stick above a little white dog. A girl stands behind him, and behind her is a nude boy with a red cloak, who has fallen to one knee. A second girl tries to help him up, or is it she who has knocked him down? The boys have yellow skin, the girls white skin and yellow and white chitons. At the upper left, a small white Eros carrying a sword flies off to the left. Yellow, scrolling tendrils flank the scene.

For the general decorative scheme, compare London F 545 (*CVA* 1, pl. 1, 7). For Eros driving a chariot (drawn by leopards, not hounds), compare the kantharos Naples 81007 (*CVA* 3, pls. 54–55). For the fluting Eros, compare the boy on a ribbed oinochoe in Cleveland: inv. 52.16 (K. Hamma, in Mayo, *Magna Graecia*, pp. 274–275, no. 135). Compare also the polychrome child dressed as a hunter on a fragment from a similar krater in Taranto (*CVA* 3, pl. 22.3). The handles in the form of lions' heads are common; see Bernardini, *Vasi*, pls. 57–58.

PUBLISHED: L. Viola, *NSc* 1886, p. 101, no. 1: Manduria; K. Schauenburg, *Bonner Jahrbuch* 155/156 (1955/56), p. 84, note 180, pl. 13; Forti, *Gnathia*, pp. 34 (note 29), 60, 77, 101, 103, 107 (note 21), 126 (note 33), 165 (note 9), pl. 20, a; Webster, *Gnathia*, pp. 4, 24 (no. 6), 25–26, 31–33, pl. 3 a; S. Winkelmann, *JOAI* 50 (Hauptblatt) (1972–73), p. 164 (as Forti, pl. 20 c); G. Siebert, *Recherches sur les Ateliers de Bols à reliefs du Péloponnèse à l'époque Hellénistique* (Paris, 1978), p. 269; K. Schauenburg, *RM* 87 (1980), p. 55, note 197; R. Bianchi Bandinelli, *La Pittura Antica* (Rome, 1980), p. 73; *LIMC*, III, 1, p. 912, under no. 720; F. Rumscheid, in *CVA* Göttingen 1, p. 55, no. 4.

131

131

SKYPHOS-KRATER
End of 4th or early 3rd century B.C.
Gift of Nathan Appleton. 99.123

DIMENSIONS AND CONDITION: Height: 35.0 cm; diameter rim: 28.7 cm; diameter body: 28.3 cm; diameter stem: 13.0 cm; diameter foot: 16.8 cm
Unbroken save for chips in the rim

SHAPE: This large, heavy vessel is more suitable for mixing than for drinking wine, in spite of its skyphos shape. The straight-sided body abruptly tapers to a simple disk foot. The handles are tilted upward slightly.

The vertical ribbing on the body is carefully executed and topped by a red stripe. On either side of the rim is a white and yellow swan flanked by yellow grapevines. The top of the foot is painted a dull red.

Compare a ribbed bell-krater once in the German market, with similar decoration on the rim; Galerie Günter Puhze, *Kunst der Antike*, Katalog 5 (Freiburg, 1984), no. 225.

PUBLISHED: E. Robinson, *MFA AnnRep* 1899, p. 86, no. 39.

132

BOTTLE
End of 4th or beginning of 3rd century B.C.
Gift of Thomas G. Appleton. 76.55

PROVENANCE: Alessandro Castellani collection; from Gnathia

DIMENSIONS AND CONDITION: Height: 21.0 cm; diameter upper rim: 5.8 cm; maximum diameter rim: 7.0 cm; diameter neck: 2.4 cm; diameter body: 12.2 cm; diameter stem: 6.5 cm; diameter foot: 8.1 cm

SHAPE: The spreading foot is unusually wide for a bottle. The grooves between the ribs are broad and deep and are not perfectly vertical. The mouth resembles that of cat. no. 124.

132

On the shoulder, flanked by yellow scrolling tendrils, is a female head facing left, with white skin, blonde hair, necklace, earring, and a small hairnet confined to the back of the head, where the emerging hair is tied with a fillet. The body of the vase is circled by two bands of ribbing divided by a band of yellow and white scrolling tendrils, framed by yellow stripes. A band of yellow rays framed by stripes circles the neck. A white fillet separates the body from the foot. Finger-marks at the bottom show that the slip was applied by dipping.

The division of the ribbing into two sections is an uncommon feature on a bottle. Webster (*Gnathia*, p. 31) lists three late examples whose shape and floral ornament differ from the Boston vase; compare also *CVA* Naples 3, pl. 68, 13–14. Another bottle in Naples, with undivided ribbing, has a woman's head on the shoulder (*CVA* Naples 3, pl. 68, 12). The florals on the bellyband may be compared with the band of tendrils dividing the ribbing on a bell-krater, London F 545 (*CVA* 1, pl. 1, 7); compare also the shallow krater Toronto 923.13.113 (Hayes, *Black-Gloss*, pp. 158–159, no. 260), which also has a woman's head flanked by scrolling tendrils below the rim. The carelessly executed ribbing points to a date at the beginning of the third century, but the head and tendrils recall earlier compositions (e.g., cat. no. 116). Compare the head on the shoulder of a ribbed Gnathian lebes gamikos in Schloss Fasanerie, Adolphseck 224 (*CVA* 2, pl. 91, 6 and 10).

PUBLISHED: Robinson, *Catalogue*, pp. 189–190, no. 523.

EXHIBITED: Tampa Museum of Art, Tampa, 1991 -.

133

SKYPHOS
Possibly connects with the Group of Lecce 1047D (Webster)
Early 3rd century B.C.
Henry Lillie Pierce Residuary Fund. 01.8121

PROVENANCE: E. P. Warren collection; bought in Brindisi

DIMENSIONS AND CONDITION: Height: 17.5 cm; diameter rim: 13.2 cm; diameter body: 14.0 cm; diameter stem: 3.3 cm; diameter foot: 7.1 cm
The glaze is greenish and iridescent, perhaps an intentional effect created by increasing the firing temperature.

SHAPE: A large cup, deep, thin-walled, and well-potted, with a gradually tapering body and horizontal handles; compare the feet of the two kantharoi, cat. nos. 128 and 129.

There is ribbing on the lower body and in a second band around the upper body, the two areas separated by a smooth, unribbed band decorated with yellow wave-pattern. The ribbing is carefully executed, with rounded tips. The upper section is framed by white stripes, and another stripe runs above the lower section. On either side of the rim is a yellow ivy vine with berries. There are yellow rays on the handles and a row of yellow strokes on the foot. The stem of the foot is painted red.

The band dividing the ribbing into two areas is an unusual feature on a skyphos. Webster (*Gnathia*, p. 28) lists four related examples, none with the bellyband, of which the closest in shape may be Karlsruhe B 912 (*CVA* 2, pl. 82, 14); compare also Toronto 923.13.117 (Hayes, *Black-Gloss*, pp. 156–157, no. 258).

PUBLISHED: Webster, *Gnathia*, p. 28, no. 19.

EXHIBITED: Tampa Museum of Art, Tampa, 1991 - .

133

134

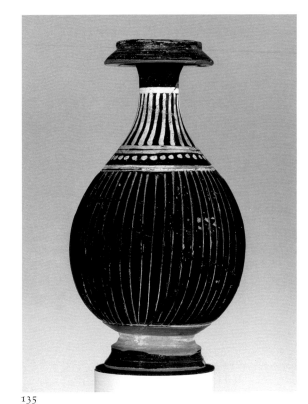

135

134

BOTTLE
Probably early 3rd century B.C.
Gift of Edward Jackson Holmes. 41.914

DIMENSIONS AND CONDITION: Height: 16.2 cm; diameter upper rim: 4.5 cm; outer diameter rim: 5.2 cm; diameter neck: 1.9 cm; diameter body: 9.1 cm; diameter stem: 4.2 cm; diameter foot: 5.3 cm
Unbroken

SHAPE: Compare cat. nos. 124 and 132.

There is vertical ribbing on the body. Yellow rays circle the neck, and a yellow "necklace" runs round the shoulder. The stem above the foot is tinted a dull red.

135

BOTTLE
Probably early 3rd century B.C.
Gift of Horace L. Mayer. 58.1308

DIMENSIONS AND CONDITION: Height: 11.6 cm; diameter upper rim: 3.2 cm; maximum diameter rim: 4.0 cm; diameter neck: 1.4 cm; diameter body: 6.5 cm; diameter stem: 2.7 cm; diameter foot: 3.7 cm
Broken and repaired

SHAPE: Compare cat. no. 134; the mouth is narrower and more flaring; the foot consists of a tall, sloping riser above a slender disk.

The body has vertical ribbing. There are yellow rays on the neck. Around the shoulder is a band of yellow dots framed by white stripes.

136

RING-HANDLED KANTHAROS
Early 3rd century B.C.
Purchased, 1880. 80.622

PROVENANCE: Bought by C. C. Perkins

DIMENSIONS AND CONDITION: Height: 8.0 cm; width across handles: 15.3 cm; diameter rim: 8.8 cm; diameter body: 9.6 cm; diameter stem: 3.4 cm; diameter foot: 4.3 cm
Unbroken

SHAPE: In this simple form of kantharos, there is no neck, no overhanging mouth, no tall, stemmed foot, and no knotted handles. Body and rim resemble those of a skyphos. The foot is a cyma recta, with a reserved, concave stem.

The ribs on the body are topped on either side by a red stripe. The rim is decorated with wave-pattern framed by stripes; on one side the waves are yellow below and black above, and on the other side the opposite.

For the shape, see Green, *Gnathia*, pp. 12–13, pl. 21b; J. R. Green, *AA* 1977, pp. 556–557.

PUBLISHED: Robinson, *Catalogue*, p. 187, no. 517.

136

137

SKYPHOS
Early 3rd century B.C.
Gift of Dr. Henry J. Bigelow. 88.321

DIMENSIONS AND CONDITION: Height: 10.5 cm; diameter rim: 7.8 cm; diameter body: 8.0 cm; diameter stem: 2.0 cm; diameter foot: 4.2 cm
One handle is repaired with an alien piece, apparently ancient.

SHAPE: The reserved stem of the foot is offset from the body, which seems to nestle inside it. The foot is steeply terraced in three degrees. For the general shape, compare the more elegant skyphos, cat. no. 133.

There is vertical ribbing on the body. On either side of the rim is a band of yellow wave-pattern framed by multiple white stripes. Much of the wave-pattern on one side has been repainted in white. The reserved stem of the foot is decorated with two black stripes.

Compare Lecce 3882 (Bernardini, *Vasi*, p. 11, pl. 19, 6).

PUBLISHED: Robinson, *Catalogue*, p. 185, no. 509.

137

138

SKYPHOS
Early 3rd century B.C.
Gift of Dr. Henry J. Bigelow. 88.322

DIMENSIONS AND CONDITION: Height: 10.5 cm; width across handles: 14.1 cm; diameter rim: 7.5 cm; diameter body: 7.7 cm; diameter stem: 1.6 cm; diameter foot: 4.1 cm
Unbroken

SHAPE: Similar in shape to the preceding cup, cat. no. 137, but with a foot in two degrees, closer to that of cat. no. 133. The stem of the foot is divided from the body by a deep incision that cuts off the tips of the ribs.

There is vertical ribbing on the body, topped on either side by a row of yellow dots above a white stripe. On either side of the rim is a band of yellow wave-pattern framed by yellow stripes. There is a row of yellow spots on the foot. A single black band circles the reserved stem.

PUBLISHED: Robinson, *Catalogue*, p. 185, no. 508.

138

139

140

139

CUP-SKYPHOS
Early 3rd century B.C.
Gift of Misses Sara and Elizabeth Gaskell Norton.
12.795

PROVENANCE: Charles Eliot Norton collection

DIMENSIONS AND CONDITION: Height: 7.3 cm; height with
handles: 9.0 cm; diameter rim: 7.5 cm; diameter body:
8.0 cm; diameter stem: 1.9 cm; diameter foot: 4.0 cm
Each of the sharply angled handles is only partly preserved;
otherwise intact. One side is heavily encrusted.

SHAPE: The body is essentially the same as that of the ring-
handled kantharos, cat. no. 136, while the foot is similar to
that of the preceding cup, cat. no. 138. The handles are tilted
sharply upward.

The body has vertical ribbing, topped on both sides
by a white stripe, which extends beneath the handles. Around the rim is a yellow wave-pattern
framed by yellow stripes. There is a row of yellow
dots on the grooved, echinus foot. The concave stem
is reserved.

140

MUG (oinochoe of shape 8M)
Attributed to the Knudsen Group (Green)
Early 3rd century B.C.
Purchased 1880. 80.625

PROVENANCE: Bought by C. C. Perkins

DIMENSIONS AND CONDITION: Height: 11.6 cm; width across
handle: 8.0 cm; diameter rim: 7.1 cm; diameter neck: 6.0 cm;
diameter body: 7.6 cm; diameter stem: 3.5 cm; diameter foot:
4.4 cm
The rim and handle are chipped; otherwise intact.

141

SHAPE: Compare the red-figure example, cat. no. 55. This Gnathian example has a reserved stem topped by a fillet; the foot is in two degrees.

The incised ribs on the body are rough and shallow. Below the handle, beneath the black glaze, is an incised star. On the rim is a band of yellow egg-pattern above a chain of yellow circles with dotted pendants, the whole resembling a necklace. The lower body is reserved.

Compare cat. nos. 141–142. K. Schauenburg, in W. G. Moon, ed., *Ancient Greek Art and Iconography* (Madison, 1983), p. 278, note 23, lists several other Gnathian examples; see also *CVA* Locarno, Rossi Collection (Switzerland 5), pl. 53, 9–19. In a few cases the decoration transcends pure ornament; for example, the kantharos and kylikes on Athens 2306 (Forti, *Gnathia*, pl. 3, c). For the incised design beneath the black glaze, compare Bonn 161 (Green, *Gnathia*, pl. 21a).

PUBLISHED: Robinson, *Catalogue*, p. 185, no. 507.

142

141

MUG (oinochoe of shape 8M)
Attributed to the Knudsen Group (Green)
Early 3rd century B.C.
Gift of Mr. and Mrs. George Washington Wales. 95.837

PROVENANCE: According to an old paper label on the bottom of the mug, it was found in Egypt; bought in Athens for $5.00.

DIMENSIONS AND CONDITION: Height: 11.5 cm; width across handle: 9.0 cm; diameter rim: 6.7 cm; diameter neck: 5.5 cm; diameter body: 7.6 cm; diameter stem: 4.4 cm; diameter foot: 5.8 cm
Rim broken and reattached

SHAPE: See the comments on cat. no. 140; the foot of this example is broader.

The shallow, vertical incisions on the upper body imitate ribbing but do not extend all the way down. There are three superimposed bands of ornament on the neck below the white egg-pattern on the rim: a red and yellow fillet, white key-pattern, and white dots. None of these circles the neck completely. Incised lines separate the bands of ornament. A black stripe circles the reserved lower body.

Bands of alternating red and yellow rectangles, often with wavy outlines, as on this mug, have been convincingly identified as fillets by J. R. Green; see H.-U. Cain, H. Gabelmann, and D. Salzmann, eds., *Festschrift für Nikolaus Himmelmann* (Mainz, 1989), p. 223.

142

MUG (oinochoe of shape 8M)
Attributed to the Knudsen Group (Green)
Early 3rd century B.C.
Gift of Mr. and Mrs. Isaac O. Rankin. 22.632

PROVENANCE: Lent by Dr. I. O. Rankin in 1912 (as 134.12)

DIMENSIONS AND CONDITION: Height: 10.2 cm; width across handle: 8.5 cm; diameter rim: 7.1 cm; diameter neck: 5.1 cm; diameter body: 7.4 cm; diameter stem: 3.6 cm; diameter foot: 4.7 cm
Unbroken

SHAPE: Compare the shape of cat. nos. 140 and 141. In this example, the mouth is flared, the body rounder, and the foot less flared.

The ribbing on the body is shallow and irregular and does not extend all the way down; a white stripe marks the terminus. The black glaze is otherwise undecorated. The stem above the foot is reserved.

PUBLISHED: *MFA AnnRep* 1912, p. 157.

Gnathian Ware, Campanian

143

PLATE
4th century B.C., perhaps the 2nd quarter
Gift of Horace L. Mayer. 58.1268

DIMENSIONS AND CONDITION: Height: 3.8 cm; outer diameter
rim: 24.2 cm; diameter foot: 10.6 cm

SHAPE: Broad and shallow, with a thick, grooved rim and ring
foot.

The interior and the upper part of the exterior wall
are glazed black. In the center of the interior is a
stamped design consisting of a central rosette surrounded by linked palmettes. Around this is a band
of linear incisions imitating rouletting, made by
stuttering a stick on the surface as it spun on the
wheel. This in turn is circled by an ivy vine painted
in added white.

For the imitation rouletting, compare the Teano
Ware plate, cat. no. 148.

143

144

STEMLESS KYLIX
Late 4th century B.C.
Francis Bartlett Donation of 1900. 03.823

PROVENANCE: E. P. Warren collection; from Campania

DIMENSIONS AND CONDITION: Height: 6.0 cm; height with
handles: 7.5 cm; diameter rim: 10.2 cm; diameter stem:
4.4 cm; diameter foot: 4.6 cm
Unbroken

SHAPE: Hemispherical body; long handles, tilted upward and
turned back at the ends; high disk foot with a groove around
it.

Around the inner rim is an ivy wreath or, more
accurately, a row of ivy leaves, in white.

For the shape, without wreath, compare *CVA*
Capua 3, pl. 16, 8. Another example, with wreath,
was recently in the New York market; Ariadne Galleries Inc., *Ancient Art 1987* (New York, 1986),
no. 94.

PUBLISHED: E. Robinson, *MFA AnnRep* 1903, p. 67, no. 26.

144

Gnathian Ware, Paestan

144a

STEMLESS KYLIX
320–300 B.C.
Gift of C. Granville Way. 72.1488

PROVENANCE: Hay collection

DIMENSIONS AND CONDITION: Height: 4.4 cm; width with
handles: 17.5 cm; diameter rim: 11.8 cm; diameter stem:
4.6 cm; diameter foot: 4.8 cm
One handle is broken and reattached. The glaze is dull and
brownish and has flaked from the center of the interior. The
exterior is encrusted.

SHAPE: Flaring ring foot with a deep groove around the lower
part. The handles have flaring "shoulders" and roll back
slightly at the ends.

144a

A wreath with berries circles the inside of the rim.
The leaves are modulated from white at their base to
orange at their tips. The berries vary from orange to
white, and the stem is incised.

The decorative scheme resembles that of the Apulian Red Swan Group, but the tondo is vacant, and the
gracefully drawn leaves have blunt tips that curl outward (unlike the conventional laurel seen in the Red
Swan Group). The glaze is poorer than the glossy
black of the Apulian fabric.

The same wreath appears in added color on the exterior of two bolsals in the Naples Museum; *CVA*
Naples, Museo Nazionale 3, pl. 63, nos. 10, 13.
Leaves that curl outward as these do alternate with
conventional laurel leaves on the shoulders of Campanian and Paestan red-figure vases, such as a Paestan amphora in Boston, cat. no. 105; Trendall, *LCS*,
pp. 322–323 (no. 711, pl. 126, 6), 397 (no. 262, pl.
154, 3–4), 430 (no. 495, pl. 171, 2); Trendall, *RVP*,
nos. 2/135 (pl. 57a), 2/1004 (pl. 158), 2/1028 (pl.
164a), 2/1025 (pl. 164b), 2/1036 (pl. 165a), 3/40 (pl.
173d). These composite wreaths seem to have been
executed regularly in superposed color, as here. The
closest parallels, however, seem to be the wreaths
around the tondos of late Paestan kylikes by the
Painters of Naples 1778 and Naples 2585. In these
wreaths, curling leaves again alternate with straight

144a

leaves, and, in addition, the stems are incised; Trendall, *RVP*, nos. 3/58 (pl. 175a), 3/441 (pl. 203a), 3/
465 (pl. 209f), 3/487 (pl. 212a), 3/488 (pl. 212b). It
seems likely that this kylix and the bolsals in Naples
were executed in an allied workshop. The yellowish
clay of this cup, however, suggests that the kiln lay
outside of Paestum itself; Trendall characterizes the
clay of Paestum as orange-brown and micaceous
(Trendall, *RVP*, p. 266).

XENON GROUP

Xenon ware is a distinctive Apulian fabric named after a vase in Frankfurt with the inscription +ENON (ξενών) (Beazley, *EVP*, p. 219, 1). Like Gnathian vases, Xenon vases are decorated with added color over black glaze, but the shapes are different from those of Gnathian ware, and the only color used is a matte red. Xenon vases tend to be small, and many are miniature: toys or tomb offerings for children. The most common shapes are mugs, oinochoai, skyphoi, sessile kantharoi (cat. no. 145), lekanides, and nestorides (cat. no. 146). The decorative motifs include ivy vines, laurel wreaths, key-pattern, running esses, chevrons, maeanders, wave-pattern, and the occasional bird, animal, or human figure. Some examples have Greek inscriptions, yet it is possible, considering the nestorides, that the entire group is the product of native, semi-Hellenized Italians. It is not known where pottery of this type was produced, but the inland sites of Ruvo and Canosa are likely candidates. Most seem to date from the second and third quarters of the fourth century.

Stemless kylikes of the Red Swan Group are so close to Xenon ware in technique and ornament that there is good reason to believe they were made by the same artisans. On most examples, the tondo of the kylix is decorated with the bird that gives the group its name, but other motifs appear, including horses, vessels, and human heads. The central figure is usually surrounded by a laurel wreath similar to those on Xenon vessels.

145

145

145

SESSILE KANTHAROS
First half of 4th century B.C.
Gift of Edward Austin. 76.451

DIMENSIONS AND CONDITION: Height: 10.1 cm; diameter rim: 11.3 cm; diameter body: 8.3 cm; diameter foot: 5.9 cm
Unbroken. The glaze is a lustrous black but has flaked off severely in several areas to reveal the dull brown clay.

SHAPE: Deep, straight-sided body, flaring rim, two vertical strap handles, disk foot. An irregular groove circles the foot for half its circumference.

In the upper zone of each side, a laurel wreath runs from right to left. On one side only, blossoms branch off from the stem. In the lower zone, a wave-pattern, executed differently on each side, runs from left to right. Each band of ornament is bordered by stripes drawn freehand. The stripes are interrupted in the handle-zone. The underside of the foot is without black glaze but washed with red. Decoration in added color is orange washed with red.

The vase is an Apulian imitation of Attic kantharoi of the fifth- and early fourth-century Saint-Valentin class; S. Howard and F. P. Johnson, *AJA* 58 (1954), pp. 191–207, pls. 32–34. For a recent discussion of Xenon group kantharoi, see Hayes, *Black-Gloss*, p. 115, nos. 195–196.

PUBLISHED: Robinson, *Catalogue*, no. 408.

146

NESTORIS
Ca. 360–330 B.C.
Gift of Horace L. Mayer. 58.1303

DIMENSIONS AND CONDITION: Height with handles: 15.2 cm; diameter rim: 8.8 cm; diameter neck: 6.6 cm; diameter body: 10.6 cm; diameter stem at top of foot: 2.4 cm; diameter foot: 4.8 cm
Unbroken. The painted decoration is so worn as to be barely discernible.

The added red decoration is set within panels on either side of the upper body: on one side a swan standing between upright palmettes, on the other, a central palmette flanked by disconnected lotus buds and half-palmettes. There are rays on the outside of the everted rim.

This nestoris is small enough to be called miniature, but many nestorides are even smaller; for example, a pair once in the J. V. Noble collection and now in the Tampa Museum of Art (inv. 86.117–118), each only 5 cm tall (M. E. Mayo, in Mayo, *Magna Graecia*, p. 304, no. 159). Beazley called the shape a "kantharoid" (*EVP*, pp. 218–219), which it is, but it is clearly also a variant of the Lucanian and Apulian nestoris (e.g., cat. no. 4), descended from the native trozella. The palmette decoration is somewhat unusual, as is the swan; compare a nestoris in the Japanese market (N. Horiuchi, *Catalogue*, no. 4 [1990], no. 29).

146

TEANO WARE

Teano ware is a type of pottery named for the northern Campanian town of Teano, where it is found in the local cemeteries and where it was probably made. Rare examples with Oscan inscriptions suggest it was produced in a native workshop. It is related to Gnathian ware, since the painted decoration is applied over the black glaze coating the vessel. Open shapes were favored, particularly plates (cat. no. 148), skyphoi, and stemmed bowls (cat. no. 147); other popular types were oinochoai, kernoi, and plastic vessels in the shape of birds. The decoration combines a profusion of stamped ornament—usually combinations of dotted circles and egg-pattern—with florals and patternwork in added white and yellow. On the plates and bowls, stamped and painted ornament may alternate in concentric bands. The stamped ornament occasionally seems to have been filled with added white, although this may be difficult to distinguish from remnant incrustation. Ivy vines have small leaves with incised stems. Sometimes there is only stamped ornament, other times only painted. Teano was produced in the last quarter of the fourth century and the early years of the third, disappearing shortly after the end of Campanian red-figure.

147

147

STEMMED BOWL
Ca. 310–280 B.C.
Francis Bartlett Donation of 1900. 03.825

PROVENANCE: E. P. Warren collection; from Campania

DIMENSIONS AND CONDITION: Height: 9.2 cm; diameter rim: 13.5 cm; diameter foot: 7.3 cm
Chipped rim and foot but otherwise intact

SHAPE: The bowl is shallow and carinated, the lip broad and flat. The foot is a wide cylinder, with a deep groove around the middle set off by simple moldings.

The egg-pattern around the upper and lower sections of the foot is incised, and the eggs have white-painted centers; the same technique is used for the egg-pattern around the outer edge of the lip, where

147

white dots separate the eggs. The egg-pattern around the inner edge is stamped. Between the inner and outer edges is a row of dotted circles, also stamped. Around the lower body on the outside is a band of stamped egg-pattern with a row of dotted circles above. Inside the bowl there is a central radiating design composed of stamped U-shapes and circles. Red-tinted ovals are incised between the radiate arms. A necklace of circles and U-shapes rings the inner walls of the bowl. A vine with incised stem and white leaves and berries is painted on top of the foot. The incised grooves on the sides of the foot are tinted red.

For the shape, compare *CVA* Capua 3, pl. 1, 12 (Italia, pl. 1304).

148

148

PLATE
Ca. 310–280 B.C.
Francis Bartlett Donation of 1900. 03.826

PROVENANCE: E. P. Warren collection; from Campania

DIMENSIONS AND CONDITION: Height: 6.6 cm; diameter: 25.2 cm; diameter foot: 10.5 cm
Unbroken

SHAPE: The rim is broad and flat, the bowl shallow, the foot low and cylindrical.

On the foot, a row of white dot-clusters separates two opposing bands of egg-pattern, with each egg incised around a core of added white. The same design, stamped instead of incised and painted, appears in circular bands on the rim and in the interior. The inner band of egg-pattern, defined by incised grooves, is framed by rows of stamped circles and bands of rouletting. At the center, four palmettes surround a stamped human face of crude design. Between the palmettes are clusters of stamped U-shapes, stamped circles, and incised ovals. Just inside the rim, on the upper wall, a band of stamped circles and U-shapes imitates a necklace.

148

CANOSAN WARE

Canosa, the ancient Canusium, was a town in the central Apulian region of Daunia. In the fourth century, Canosa was a major producer of red-figure vases in the Greek style — the Baltimore and White Sakkos Painters had their workshop there — and also of vessels in traditional Daunian shapes and styles. In the early third century, red-figure vases faded from popularity, and a new style emerged with roots in the native tradition. The old geometric decoration on Daunian askoi was replaced with a variety of floral motifs executed in polychrome tempera on a ground of white slip. Plastic decoration sprang exuberantly from rims and bodies: flowers, female heads, Medusas, dogs, tritons, horses, and full-length female figurines. These inventive, sometimes bizarre vessels, with their pastel colors, are the hallmark of the Canosan style.

A favorite type was the Skylla-askos, such as cat. no. 149, with the fearsome female monster rising up behind the mouth of the vessel, dogs springing from her waist, and the handle replaced by her undulating, serpentine body — all this painted in brilliant colors. Another type of askos featured a large mask of Medusa in high relief below the spout, sometimes with a row of horse-protomes above and a file of draped women or Nikai standing around the neck. Similar treatment is accorded another traditional Daunian shape, the cuspidor-shaped sphageion.

Other common Canosan shapes descended from the red-figure repertory, particularly volute-kraters and tall-necked oinochoai. The kraters may have several draped women and Erotes seated on the rim and even standing on top of the handles. Many oinochoai have mold-made bodies in the form of a female head, sometimes with radiate floral crowns. Often the spout has been dispensed with altogether and replaced with one to three draped female figures; the vase is thus useless as a vessel, confirming speculation that Canosan vessels were made exclusively for the tomb. Other shapes include pyxides with relief scenes on the lid or with feet in the shape of birds. The plastic decoration and the rich polychromy of the painted designs combine to make Canosan ware one of the most exuberant of ancient fabrics.

149

ASKOS
Attributed to the Group of the Skylla Askoi
Ca. 300 B.C.
Henry Lillie Pierce Residuary Fund. 99.541

PROVENANCE: E. P. Warren collection; from Canosa

DIMENSIONS AND CONDITION: Height: 38.0 cm; length: 30.3 cm
Unbroken. The vase has no bottom and can have had only a funerary function. The painted decoration is quite worn, particularly on the dolphins and griffins on the sides.

A modeled figure of Skylla stretches along the top, her long, undulating body painted with black and red spots on a blue-streaked white ground. Two spotted dogs spring from her waist on either side of the vessel's mouth, which she holds in her hands. Skylla has red hair and a tunic with pink stripes and yellow rosettes. On the rim of the mouth, by Skylla's left hand, is a modeled fish, painted blue; by her right hand is a blue phiale with a small cake inside. The mouth is red on the inside and pink and white on the outside. On the front of the vase is a large frontal face, female, with big eyes and thick red lips. The face is outlined in red but is left reserved in the white ground that underlies all the added colors on the vase. Small flowers grow from the top of the face, and there is a round disk at the apex. On either side of the body is painted a large griffin rearing over a leaping dolphin. Though badly damaged, both griffins were apparently outlined in black, with peach-colored bodies and blue wings. Traces of the same peach color are preserved on the dolphins, now white. Between the griffins and the face on the front are large white palmettes topped with rosettes; a brown palmette covers the rear of the vase. The background between the face, the griffins, and the palmettes is lavender. The dolphins are surrounded by black. The shoulder and lower body of the vase are painted red.

For askoi of this type, see K. Schauenburg, *RM* 87 (1980), pp. 29–56; F. van der Wielen, *Genava* 26 (1978), pp. 143–149; Oliver, *Reconstruction*, pp. 11–12; and H. Lohmann, *AA* 1979, pp. 204–209. The face on the front is borrowed from red-figure Apu-

149 (Color Plate XXII)

149

lian askoi (e.g., an askos by the White Sakkos Painter in the New York market; *RVAp*, Suppl. II, p. 353, no. 29/I). There are, in fact, a few Skylla askoi decorated in red-figure, which Trendall and Cambitoglou date to ca. 300 B.C. (*RVAp*, II, pp. 1025–1026, nos. 45–47, pls. 396, 6, and 397). On at least one occasion, the askos is dispensed with and a plastic Skylla forms the base of a rhyton (e.g., a red-figure example of about 330 B.C. in Matera; A. Bottini, *BdArch* 5–6 [1990], p. 234, fig. 5). Polychrome askoi were made throughout the first quarter of the third century, but the Boston vase may date from no later than 300 B.C.

The shape of the Boston askos as well as the figure of Skylla and the face painted on the front are closely paralleled by a polychrome askos in Bari (inv. 6003: Schauenburg, *RM* 87, pls. 9–10). Trendall and Cambitoglou (*RVAp*, II, p. 1026) follow Lohmann and Schauenburg in wondering if the molded handle

might sometimes be a tritoness, but on this vase the dogs leaping from the waist should identify the woman as Skylla. In some examples, both Skylla and the vessel itself are winged (e.g., Antiquarium, Ltd., Fine Ancient Arts Gallery, *Myth and Majesty* [New York, 1992], no. 26).

PUBLISHED: E. Robinson, *MFA AnnRep* 1899, pp. 86–87, no. 40; Shepard, *Monster*, p. 65, pl. 13, fig. 83; P. Jacobsthal, *Early Celtic Art* (Oxford, 1944), p. 149; A. Greifenhagen, *CVA* Mannheim I, p. 56, under pl. 45; D. von Bothmer, *AJA* 64 (1960), p. 100; MFA, *Gods and Heroes*, 1962, pp. 40–41, fig. 27; MFA, *Trojan War*, fig. 50 A; J. L. Keith, in *The Pomerance Collection of Ancient Art* (Brooklyn, 1966), p. 100, under no. 117; Oliver, *Reconstruction*, pp. 6, 11–12, pl. 7, fig. 4; Brommer, *Vasenlisten*, 1973, p. 444, no. 3; idem, *Denkmälerlisten*, III, p. 304, no. 9; H. Lohmann, *AA* 1979, pp. 204–205, no. 6; K. Schauenburg, *RM* 87 (1980), pp. 30 (no. 3), 42, 46, pl. 12, 1–2; *RVAp*, II, p. 1025; H. Lohmann, *JdI* 97 (1982), p. 230, note 133; F. van der Wielen-van Ommeren, in *Canosa* II (Bari, 1983), p. 126, note 130.

CENTURIPE WARE

Most examples of this ware have been found in the area around Centuripe, a small town in eastern Sicily, where they were apparently made. The vases are usually found in tombs, sometimes in contexts suggesting production in the third century B.C., a dating consistent with internal stylistic evidence. The technique of manufacture is further proof of their exclusively funerary use, for the decoration is one-sided, the applied reliefs fragile and often lightly attached, and the tempera paint — applied after firing — too fugitive to tolerate persistent, everyday use.

Many of the vases are composed of separate, unjoined elements; for example, cat. no. 152, with a foot, bowl, lid, knob, and finial. This shape is variously described as a bell-krater, pyxis, or lebes and may be handleless or, like cat. no. 151, equipped with large, tilted handles, seemingly borrowed from the other major shape, the lekanis. A typical lekanis is cat. no. 150, with a conical bowl, tall foot, and high, conical lid; the florals and head of Medusa in relief on the rim are also standard on this shape.

On kraters, elements of the rim, lid, knob, and finial are frequently articulated by relief moldings of architectural derivation, such as egg-and-dart and bead-and-reel. The join of foot and base may be concealed by a calyx of acanthus. Rosettes and animal heads along the rim and lower edge of the lid imitate gutter-spouts and the carvings on metopes, and may be separated by triglyphs.

Both lid and bowl are usually painted on one side, although the design on the lid may be purely ornamental (e.g., cat. no. 151). The tempera paint is applied over a chalky white slip, but this, itself, may be tinted, and backgrounds range in color from pink to dark blue. The quality of the drawing is often quite high, with skillful use of shading and highlights, and faces routinely drawn in three-quarter view. The vast majority of figures are women, who sit or stand in groups of three, four, or five, swathed in heavy drapery of blue, white, yellow, and pink. There is no indication of either landscape or an interior setting, save for a few props and pieces of furniture. The exact meaning is often unclear, but many examples are painted with Dionysiac or nuptial ceremonies, rites of passage and transformation appropriate for their use as grave offerings. Others continue the old funerary motif of a seated woman attended by her maids. In style, the vase-paintings probably reflect contemporary murals and panel-paintings and are thus important evidence for the palette and style of these lost works.

150

LEKANIS
Early 3rd century B.C.
Arthur Tracy Cabot Fund. 1970.478

DIMENSIONS AND CONDITION: Height body: 31.0 cm; diameter rim: 31.7 cm; diameter body below handles: 27.9 cm; diameter foot: 16.9 cm; height lid: 45 cm; diameter rim: 31.8 cm; diameter knob: 8.4 cm
Broken and repaired, with considerable erosion of the painted surfaces. The foot was made separately but has been glued to the lower body by a modern restorer. The lid was created in four parts, which have now been glued together.

SHAPE: Conical bowl with carinated rim; tall, conical lid with carinated rim; tilted strap handles with side flanges; tall foot with an echinus above a slender disk base; complex knob and finial (see description below).

The handle-zone is decorated with applied relief consisting of a central head of Medusa flanked by a floral scroll populated with tiny Erotes. A bead-and-reel molding defines the lower border. The background is pink, and the vines and upper and lower borders are gilded. Medusa has an idealized face, a pair of wings on her head, and pendant earrings. Her face is beige, her eyes white with black irises. Her hair and earrings are gilded, and her wings pink and blue. The strap handles, with their angular flanges, are pink with a gold stripe. The lower body is painted with large petals, turning the body into a kind of lotus. The front row of petals is blue below and pink above. A second row of petals behind and between them is red below and beige above. The black background above the tips of the petals continues on the reverse of the lower body, which is entirely black. The foot is white, and the fillet above it is gilded.

The rim of the lid is painted with broad pink leaves outlined in black on a white ground; above this, in front, is a plastic bead-and-reel molding. The complex knob has a pink, egg-shaped finial, with five yellow, upright, plastic leaves (one missing) above a yellow, plastic bead-and-reel molding. The shaft below is painted with pink, white, and yellow stripes, and below this is a large flange with an egg-and-dart molding painted pink and beige.

The painting on the conical, main zone of the lid is so badly damaged that only the basic composition can be reconstructed. The scene comprises two female servants who hold a pink object with vertical

150

projections, perhaps a radiate stephane or a large and elaborate hat, over the head of a seated, veiled woman. The background is painted black. The female figures were painted entirely over a white ground. The servants have white skin, and their hair and features are drawn in red. They wear wreaths with large white leaves, white chitons, and striped himatia. Framing the scene on either side is a large ovoid form, which is flanked by a tendril that curls toward the figures.

PUBLISHED: C. C. Vermeule, *MFA AnnRep* 1969–70, p. 42; P. Deussen, *OpRom* 9, no. 14 (1973), pp. 126, 130 (fig. 5), 132; C. C. Vermeule, *BurlMag* 115 (1973), p. 122, fig. 86; U. Wintermeyer, *JdI* 90 (1975), pp. 141, 144, 146–148, 150, 155, 157, 161, 163, 170–171, 175, 180 (fig. 2), 210 (no. K 4), 213, 219, 233; H. B. Siedentopf, *CVA* Nordrhein-Westfalen 1, p. 40, under pl. 31; I. Krauskopf, *LIMC*, IV, 1, pp. 298 (no. 130), 328; IV, 2, pl. 173.

151

151

BELL-KRATER
Early 3rd century B.C.
Arthur Tracy Cabot Fund. 1970.479

DIMENSIONS AND CONDITION: Height body: 39.5 cm; diameter rim flange: 37.6 cm; diameter body above rim: 34.0 cm; diameter foot: 18.3 cm; height lid: 18.6 cm; diameter rim: 37.2 cm; diameter finial (lower flange): 15.6 cm; diameter finial (upper flange): 9.3 cm
Broken and repaired, with a few missing pieces and considerable erosion of the painted surfaces.

SHAPE: Deep, bell-shaped body; triple-reeded handles, tilted sharply upward from below the rim; flattened rim; tall foot with an echinus above a slender disk base; domed lid with a flattened rim and a knob with a cyma reversa profile. Wintermeyer calls this shape a pyxis, perhaps because of the lid (see reference below); he may be technically correct, but it is perhaps less misleading to follow A. D. Trendall (*BMMA* 13 [1954–1955], p. 161) and refer to these large, deep pots as bell-kraters, even if they never tasted wine.

The decoration is confined to one side. Above the white, high-stemmed foot, the body nestles in a bed of modeled acanthus leaves and berries on a pink ground. The berries are gilded, and the leaves are blue with gilded stems. Circular impressions make it clear that plastic rosettes or phialai were attached

above the berries. The rim between the handles is decorated with a gilded leaf-and-tongue molding in applied relief, above which is a band of painted rectangles in red, pink, and blue outlined in black on a white ground. The handles are in pink and gold, with gilded, plastic leaves at the roots (much damaged).

The scene painted on the body comprises a seated female flanked by two maids. The women have white skin and wear wreaths of light blue leaves with a central yellow oval. Their features and hair are red, and their chitons are white. The servant at the left, who wears a skimpy red himation with yellow stripes, proffers a phiale with a tall pile of circular offerings to her mistress. The servant on the right holds a parasol outlined in yellow above the seated woman's head. A pink bow hangs from the upper edge of the scene behind this servant. Tall scrolls frame the scene, and under each handle is what appears to be a large white leaf. The domed lid is painted with three rows of white leaves, in shape more like acorns than ivy, interspersed with four tall, vertical leaves in pink. On both the body and lid the background is black. The gilded knob is hollow and painted red on top.

For the decoration of the rim, compare Syracuse 35946; U. Wintermeyer, *JdI* 90 (1975), p. 205. For the iconography of this and similar scenes, see J. R. Green, *North Carolina Museum of Art Bulletin* 14, no. 4 (1990), pp. 49–59.

PUBLISHED: C. C. Vermeule, *MFA AnnRep* 1969–70, p. 42; idem, *BurlMag* 115 (1973), p. 122, fig. 84; U. Wintermeyer, *JdI* 90 (1975), pp. 142, 145–147, 150–151, 159, 161, 163, 165, 170–171, 175, 184 (fig. 10), 210, 218–219, no. K 34; idem, in P. Gercke et al., *Funde aus der Antike: Sammlung Paul Dierichs Kassel* (Kassel, 1981), p. 133, under no. 61.

152

BELL-KRATER
Early 3rd century B.C.
Gift of Mohammad Yeganeh. 1983.558

DIMENSIONS AND CONDITION: Total height: 79 cm; height finial: 12.9 cm; height lid: 15.5 cm; height body: 32.1 cm; height foot: 17.2 cm; diameter finial (flange): 9.4 cm; diameter finial (neck): 5.0 cm; diameter lid (upper molding): 10.0 cm; diameter lid (at carination behind astragal): 26.7 cm; diameter lid (lower): 31.1 cm; diameter urn (rim behind astragal): 33.3 cm; diameter urn (at top of figure zone): 27.6 cm; diameter urn (lower molding body): 14.5 cm; diameter urn (stem): 8.2 cm; diameter urn (foot): 20.3 cm
Broken and repaired, with considerable erosion of the painted surfaces. On the lid, parts of the attached dolphins are missing, and some appear to have been reattached. The neck and limbs of the hippocamp on the lid at the far right are missing.

152

SHAPE: The vase is made in four separate parts: foot, body, lid, and finial. Unlike the preceding vase, this krater apparently never had handles. The stemmed foot is taller and tapering, while the nearly conical lid is closer to that of the lekanis, cat. no. 150.

The tall foot is painted pinkish white, and its lower step is painted rose. On the finial of the knob, which is covered with a white wash, are five gilded, upright, plastic leaves. On the lid below the concave stem is a plastic egg-and-dart molding. On the lower edge of the lid, below an applied bead-and-reel molding, is a band of fish, dolphins, and hippocamps in applied relief. Around the upper rim of the body, framed by applied bead-and-reel and leaf-and-tongue moldings, is a band of alternating rosettes and lions' heads in applied relief. On the lower body, between bead-and-reel and egg-and-tongue moldings, is a band of relief foliage, including rosettes, water leaves, and acanthus leaves. Small applied ovoid projections suggest olives or tightly closed buds. The applied reliefs are all on a black ground; all the plastic moldings and reliefs are gilded, save for the leaves on the lower body, which are pink with gilded stems and borders.

The scene on the body, painted on a pink ground, focuses on a woman seated on a white throne-like chair with turned yellow legs outlined in brown. She is surrounded by three maids; the one at her left shades her with a parasol. The seated woman holds a vertical scepter in her left hand, suggesting that she is a goddess, perhaps Persephone. The maid with the parasol has rather dark skin. Her face is rendered nearly frontally, like that of her mistress and the maid at the left. The maid at the far right stands in profile to the left holding a dark red rectangular object framed on two or three sides with white; it may be a casket rendered in confused perspective, but its flat effect, abetted by two rows of faint white signs in the red field, suggests that it might be a tablet with writing. All four women wear chitons, himatia, and jewelry. Their drapery is outlined with black. The himatia of the maid at the left and the maid holding the parasol are white with pink overfolds, and their chitons are light pink. The parasol is white. The seated woman and the maid at the far right have yellow-brown himatia with pink overfolds. The seated woman has a pink chiton, and the maid at the far right has a pink and white chiton. The women's faces are painted pink and red with white highlighting. Their hair is reddish black. White fillets tied in bows hang from the upper edge of the dark pink background.

On the lid is painted the bust of a winged woman on a dark pink ground. Her flesh is orange-pink, and her hair and eyebrows are reddish black. Her lips are pink, and her nose is highlighted with white. The pupils of her eyes are black, and her hand, wings, and chiton are outlined in black.

In both pictures, the women's features are well drawn, with subtle shading and use of highlights, but the techniques and characterizations are different enough to be the products of two different hands.

Compare the seated woman and the maid with a parasol on a bell-krater at the University of Catania; P. E. Arias and M. Hirmer, *A History of 1000 Years of Greek Vase Painting* (New York [1962]), color pl. LII.

PUBLISHED: J. J. Herrmann, *MFA AnnRep* 1983–84, p. 22, illus.; ibid., p. 42.

152

152

CATALOGUE OF THE COLLECTION

Etruscan and Faliscan

ETRUSCAN AND FALISCAN

Red-figure vase-painting had a long and somewhat tormented period of gestation in the lands between the Tiber and the Arno. Since many of the greatest examples of Archaic red-figure from Attica went into the rich tombs of the area, the technique was undoubtedly well known there. Throughout most of the fifth century, however, the best that local producers could muster was a strange imitation of the red-figure technique. Etruria was in a sense a refuge for an Athenian failure. Vases with the appearance of red-figure were created by applying red clay over the uniformly black-glazed surface of the vessel. Interior detail was provided by cutting through the added red to the underlying black. This procedure — variously called Six's technique, added color, or superposed color — had been invented and used in early fifth-century Athens, where its career was short-lived and cheerfully undistinguished. It was surely a Greek who brought the technique to Etruria, where it established itself for over a century and a half. One of the earliest of these vases was signed by a certain Praxias, making use of the Chalcidian Greek alphabet, which was employed in Reggio in South Italy, whence this Praxias probably came. An Etruscan name in the Etruscan alphabet was also painted on the same vase. The style of the figures in the Praxias Group is often quite close to that of Athenian work of the end of the Archaic period, perhaps imitated from the fine red-figure vases available in Etruria. The main center of production for the Praxias Group was at Vulci, but a branch of this activity seems to have been set up at Chiusi (C. Laviosa, *BdA* 4, 43 [1958], p. 305).

On the two examples of the Praxias Group in Boston (cat. nos. 153–154), the figures recall the creations of the Attic "Mannerists," whether the Pan Painter, Myson, or others of that circle. The actions and settings, however, seem slightly more mannered and bizarre than anything that might be expected from Athens; the satyrs who turn handsprings over their winecups or chase roosters represent a particularly rustic kind of physical comedy; the gesture of surprise of the spear-carrying youth seems strangely unmotivated. There is nonetheless a vigorous independence to these compositions.

The fate of vase-painting in superposed color during the second half of the fifth century is currently rather unclear. Pianu has suggested that this period was a virtual void until vase-painting was reintroduced to Etruria from Athens around 400 B.C. (Pianu, *Figure rosse*, p. 3; idem, *Sovradipinte*, pp. 1–2; idem, *MEFRA* 90 [1978], pp. 171–173). Although Athens may have had a direct influence on Etruscan red-figure at that time, Pianu's reconstruction is hard to accept for vases with superposed color. It seems more probable that the late Archaic or early Classical style of the Praxias Group continued in stereotyped form to the end of the century. This kind of continuity is suggested by an Etruscan column-krater with superposed color in the von Matsch collection, Vienna (*CVA* Deutschland 5, Wien 1, pp. 30–31, pl. 22 [Deutschland, pl. 248]); at first glance, the vase looks much like the Praxias Group column-krater in Boston (cat. no. 153), but, as Hedwig Kenner pointed out (ibid., p. 31), details of figure drawing and ornament are based on Attic models of the end of the fifth century. The tradition of the Praxias Group may have survived in Campania as well as Etruria, since trivialized versions of "sub-Archaic" vases with added color are preserved in the Naples Museum, and the Campanian series seems to merge into typical fourth-century production (*CVA* Naples, Museo Nazionale 3, pl. 53, nos. 1–6). In any case, at the beginning of the fourth century, painting in superposed color exhibited an entirely new range of types and styles emanating from a number of regions on the west coast of Italy: Campania and Paestum as well as Etruria (A. G. Pontrandolfo, *MEFRA* 89 [1977], pp. 42–44; Hayes, *Black-Gloss*, pp. 120–121, no. 206). A group of oinochoai of type II, Beazley's Demoness Group (*EVP*, p. 218), shows a particular vitality in breaking with sub-Archaic traditions in the late fifth and early fourth century B.C. Hayes is uncertain whether the group is Campanian or Etruscan (*Black-Gloss*, p. 123, no. 207), but the ornament of this group unmistakably foreshadows that of the Etruscan Sokra Group. Many new impulses certainly came directly from Athens (cf. an Etruscan oinochoe in superposed color of the late fifth century in Toronto [Hayes, *Black-Gloss*, pp. 123–124, no. 208]), but it is unlikely that the technique of superposed color itself would have spread to all these Italian sites from Attica, where it apparently had long been extinct.

The fourth-century Etruscan production of vases in added color has been divided into an earlier and a later phase by Pianu on the basis of a technical detail: on the earlier vases details are incised into the added red (as in the fifth century), while the later ones are without this articulation. With a few exceptions like the owl-skyphoi (glaukes) (e.g., cat. no. 161), the unincised vases belong to the second half of the century (Pianu, *MEFRA* 90 [1978], p. 169). The main production of the first half of the fourth century, the Sokra Group, takes its name from the inscription Sokra(tes) on the foot of a kylix found at Falerii. The inscription, apparently that of the potter, makes it clear that Greeks were involved in this workshop, yet the vases were standardized and repetitious to a degree seen neither in Attica nor in South Italy. The palmette and tendril ornament anachronistically remains thin and wiry like the ornament of fifth-century Attic vases (or the Demoness Group), while the victorious athletes, who alternate with stocky, draped youths, become as slender and willowy as those on contemporary Attic cups of the second quarter of the century (the fragment, cat. no. 158, is one of the better pieces).

The city of Falerii (modern Città Castellana) in the Tiber valley was apparently a center of production of Sokra Group vases. The Faliscans who inhabited the city and region were not pure Etruscan stock, since they spoke a language akin to Latin, but their vase production during the fourth century is intertwined with that of Etruria proper; artistic influences were exchanged, and there was an active trade in pottery between Etruria and Falerii, all of which often makes it difficult to determine where the works were produced. The six vases of the Sokra Group in Boston, for example, seem to have come from Chiusi or its neighborhood, and it is possible that a branch of the workshop existed there, since, as noted previously, a branch of the Praxias Group had been established earlier at Etruscan Chiusi. This kind of intimate relationship between the two linguistically distinct cultures makes it necessary to treat their fourth-century vase-painting together. For the sake of convenience and by tradition, the two are often summed up under the single heading of "Etruscan."

Throughout the first half of the fourth century, craftsmen in the Etruscan-Faliscan area working in added red imitated minor but charmingly decorative types of fifth-century Attic pottery; the owl-skyphos (cat. no. 161) is an example of this survival of an earlier Greek tradition in central Italy. Many of the later Etruscan vases in superposed color, like the condiment server (cat. no. 162) and the kantharos (cat. no. 163), follow contemporary fashion in imitating the Gnathian pottery of Apulia.

True red-figure seems to have sprung up more or less autonomously in several places in west-central Italy during the late fifth and earlier fourth centuries, and production had a somewhat disconnected quality; a multitude of groups can be identified whose points of origin often remain uncertain or controversial. There is difference of opinion also about the chronology of Etruscan and Faliscan red-figure. Italian scholars tend to push its beginnings ever later into the fourth century. Beazley, who was aware of this impulse, offered well-reasoned grounds for maintaining that true red-figure began in the late fifth century (*EVP*, pp. 31–32), and his arguments still appear to be valid. Disagreement continues about the dating of the later phases.

The subject matter and technique of red-figure vase-painting can be as Greek in tone in Etruria as in South Italy, but at times the artists of Etruria or Falerii lapsed into local and even primitive aberrations. In the sporadic red-figure production of the late fifth century, vases were painted purely with the brush; the Attic technique of relief line seems not to have been in use. Thereafter, however, the more important figural compositions tended to be executed with the use of relief line, while decorative elements and lesser figural compositions were outlined and detailed with broader brushwork. Such technical observations, made first by John Beazley (*EVP*, p. 25), have suggested a division of fourth-century Etruscan red-figure production into an earlier and a later phase; relief line is characteristic of the earlier phase and disappears again in the later phase, roughly the second half of the fourth century. This convenient method of distinguishing early from late fourth-century production (which is quite analogous to Pianu's way of dating vases in superposed color) does not seem to work, however, with complete consistency; the kylikes of the northern Etruscan Tondo Group, for example, make use of relief lines but have been dated by Harari and others to the second half of the fourth century (*Gruppo Clusium*, pp. 100, 107–110).

The craftsmen of Vulci began their production of red-figure vases at a relatively early date, probably by the end of the fifth century. Their approach has an old-fashioned quality that makes it especially difficult to date. The painters of Vulci copied details, figures, or even entire passages from substantially older fifth-century Attic vases. An element of this approach can be observed in the palmette ornament on a stamnos (cat. no. 164) by a follower of the Painter of London F 484, one of the earlier red-figure artists of Vulci. In a way typical of this workshop, the ornament does not display the compact massing customary in the fourth century but clings to a freer and more open kind of composition current in the late fifth. There is also some of this spideriness of the ornament on vases of the Sokra Group, seen particularly in the tightly wound S-curve spirals. The figures on the stamnos display a spontaneity that falls somewhere between barbarism and the rustic charm of folk art.

The most coherent and polished tradition emerged in Falerii — according to current views, around 380 B.C. Many of the earliest Faliscan vases have an extremely close relationship to those of early fourth-century Athens. The kylix with Hades seated by an altar to Persephone (cat. no. 165) is a good example of the solid, rather rough but workman-like approach characteristic of Attic followers of the Meleager or Jena Painters and their Faliscan imitators. The draperies bordered with wave-patterns, the floating effect of a figure seated in the landscape, and the sharply geometricized contour lines of the anatomy are all features of the style. The kylix seems to be related to the work of the Diespater Painter, who is thought by Pianu to have been an Athenian working at Falerii (*MEFRA* 1978, p. 171; on the painter, see Beazley, *EVP*, pp. 73–76). The Nazzano Painter was an especially robust and energetic practitioner of this emphatic style of figure composition. It seems quite possible that he too was an Athenian; if a craftsman of such modest talents as the Sokrates who gave his name to the Sokra Group was a Greek, then the Nazzano Painter's far more respectably Attic style at least raises the question of a foreign training.

On less ambitious Faliscan vases or on subordinate parts of vases, such as the exteriors of kylikes, figures are executed with less care and in a more stereotyped manner, but this too is typical of and probably drawn from Attic work of around 400 B.C. On the exterior of the kylix with Hades, the carelessly rendered athlete and girl and the tapestry-like effect of the solidly packed palmettes are typical of Attic kylikes of the time. Unlike Attic vase-painters, however, the Faliscan artist made use of broadly brushed lines, rather than wiry relief line, to define forms on the exterior of his cup. The exuberant fleshiness of the ornament on Faliscan vases like the kylix, moreover, quickly went beyond anything seen in Athens.

Other painters who seem to have been connected with the Faliscan school had different points of contact with Greek art. The stamnos with the binding of Amykos (cat. no. 167) must have been inspired by a famous Greek masterpiece, presumably a panel-painting, that made its way to central Italy; the composition was also copied on the famous Ficoroni Cista from Palestrina near Rome. On the stamnos, which could have been produced at Falerii, the style of drawing is much looser and more spontaneous than in the work of the Nazzano Painter and his circle. The oblique poses represent a more sophisticated naturalism than the frieze-like compositions of the previous Faliscan vase-painters. In a fragmentary kylix (cat. no. 168), this looser, more naturalistic style has an exceptional fineness. The iconography and composition are highly unusual, and the anatomy is beautifully articulated. This fluent style of drawing, with its undulating rhythms, has more in common with Early Apulian work such as the krater by the Tarporley Painter (cat. no. 10) or the fragment with the death of Aktaion (cat. no. 11) than with most early fourth-century Attic drawing, and this may be one of the probably numerous cases where a Greek migrant from South Italy had an important influence on early Etruscan or Faliscan practice.

The subject matter of these earlier Etruscan red-figure vases is clearly derived from the Attic repertoire. Bacchic imagery and athletic scenes dominate, but Etruscan and Faliscan iconography is not without its surprises and its own particular emphases. As pointed out earlier, the depiction of the punishment of Amykos (cat. no. 167) may be related to the presence of a major Greek painting on Italian soil. The comic scene with Polydeukes and the egg of Helen on the reverse of the same vase reflects the influence of Greek comedy, which is not known to have been performed in Etruria in the fourth century. The Nazzano Painter had a taste for Greek myths with particularly emotion-fraught scenes of violence. In the case of his krater with Telephos taking the infant Orestes hostage on the altar (cat. no. 166), the subject may also have had a relevance for an Italic setting since Telephos was regarded as the ancestor of the Etruscans. Funerary overtones may be present in some early Faliscan subject matter. The kylix with Hades (cat. no. 165) could well have been designed with burial in mind. The violent events depicted on the Nazzano Painter's kraters could also be regarded as scenes of deliverance, perhaps alluding to hopes for a better fate in the afterlife.

It should be noted that even the most Athenian of these artists, the Diespater Painter, labeled the characters on his name-vase in the Villa Giulia in Faliscan rather than in Greek (Beazley, *EVP*, p. 73; Martelli, *Ceramica*, pp. 193, 315, no. 143.1). In this catalogue, however, the figures are identified with their Greek names unless it appears essential to introduce the local Italic terminology. For instance, the local terms seem appropriate for various death-daemons seen in later red-figure, such as the winged woman, perhaps Vanth, on kraters of the Etruscan Funnel Group (cat. nos. 171–172) and the Charun on the Faliscan skyphos-krater (cat. no. 173).

Around the middle of the fourth century, another workshop was founded, this time in northern Etruria. It may have started its production in Chiusi and perhaps later moved to Volterra; its products included those of the Clusium Group. Its earlier cups show a close relation to those of the Faliscan school, but at the same time they have a special energy and exuberance. There is also a fondness for oblique and frontal views in the better works, like the cup in Boston (cat. no. 169). Convoluted poses and gestures, which had long been endemic in Etruscan art, are particularly characteristic of the early phase of this production around the middle of the fourth century. The decorative compositions are highly emphatic and stylized, as are lesser supporting figures, like

those on the exteriors of cups; these figures frequently have absurdly elongated beards and hairstyles.

This northern Etruscan workshop was also responsible for a great number of fine plastic (i.e., sculptural) vases, which take up forms produced in Athens in earlier times: duck-askoi and head-kantharoi. The careful finishing and the occasional use of gilding on these vases make it clear that they held a position of prestige among the ceramic products of the Etruscan-Faliscan area. The northern Clusium Group production was imitated elsewhere with varying degrees of success. Some southern imitations of northern duck-askoi, like those currently ascribed to Tarquinia (cat. no. 180), have the lively quality of folk art. Other products of as yet unidentified Etruscan or Faliscan centers can be excellent variations on established themes. The head-kantharoi of the Negro-Boy Group (cat. nos. 178–179) are fine pieces displaying a broad and charming stylization of a common Attic and Clusium Group type.

Two other plastic vases in Boston are ambitious and unusual examples of ceramic "engineering." Both are true rhyta: vases in the tradition of the Persian Empire that are a kind of drinking horn without a proper foot and with a mouth to be filled at one end and a spout for pouring at the other. In one (cat. no. 177), the design problem was made more challenging by coupling two heads back to back; one is a beautifully modeled, expressive image of a classical warrior, while the other is a caricature of a barbarian. The comical intent of the vase is clear; it must have been satirizing the drinking customs of the Greeks and Eastern barbarians, who used rhyta as showpieces at heroic or Bacchic banquets and at ceremonies of fraternization or treaty-making. The juxtaposition of a Greek-looking and a Semitic-looking head on the vase might also allude to the military conflict between the Sicilian Greeks and the Semitic Carthaginians that had been going on for more than a century. The trick amphora with plastic reliefs (cat. no. 176) is an even more ingenious example of the potter's craft. Its painted decoration of animal friezes is also unusual in a fourth-century setting and is probably a consciously barbaric touch to reinforce the associations of the rhyton form. Such vessels were clearly made for performances before cosmopolitan audiences in the context of a banquet rather than for purely funerary display.

In spite of the controversy surrounding the location of the various schools of Etruscan vase-painting, it seems clear that Vulci continued to be an important producer of red-figure vases in the second half of the century. A fragmentary krater in a robust and cheerful style (cat. no. 170) represents the more conservative side of Vulci's production: that of the Alcestis Painter and his workshop and followers. In its ornament and in the floral setting of its figures, the krater has links with Faliscan and Apulian vases of the first half of the century. Its cheerful figures and heavy draperies with dentilled borders reflect the influence of Paestum on ceramists at Vulci in the middle of the fourth century. At the same time, the vase is characteristic of later Etruscan vase-painting in mixing black silhouette ornament with the usual red-figure. Foliate ornament rendered in black became more common throughout the second half of the century, as in kraters of the Funnel Group, probably also from Vulci (cat. nos. 171–172), and in the duck-askos ascribed to Tarquinia (cat. no. 180). Black ornament became the sole decoration of numerous smaller vases (pitchers and plates) produced at Tarquinia and other Etruscan and Faliscan sites during the later fourth and earlier third centuries B.C.

The more innovative aspect of vase design in the second half of the century at Vulci is provided by the Funnel Group, a workshop or group of workshops of which the principal seat of production is usually placed at Vulci but which also seems to have had an offshoot at Tarquinia. In the Funnel Group, vases are covered with a grid of large-scale, highly stylized triangular or diamond-shaped patterns. The central element of tongue patterns frequently becomes a funnel-like, elongated triangle that gives the group its name (see cat. nos. 171–172). The shapes as well as the decorative vocabulary of Funnel Group vases are simplified, and they tend to be very elongated and soft in contour.

Among the most notable developments seen in later Etruscan vases is the emergence of subject matter connected with the funerary function that many of them fulfilled. Simultaneously, the subject matter often takes on a more distinctly Etruscan character.

Two Funnel Group calyx-kraters in Boston (cat. nos. 171–172) are entirely typical in showing a winged woman, who is probably the Etruscan daemon Vanth, often associated with Charon as a spirit of the Underworld. On the other side of one of these vases (cat. no. 172) is a satyr, who may allude to the original function of the calyx-krater as a container for wine in a festive, Dionysiac context. Maurizio Harari has conjectured that such satyrs represent the protective, preservative role of Dionysiac initiation. The tympanum is mystically offered to the deceased whose ashes rest in the vase or the tomb, and by means of the sound of the tympanum, the death-daemon is held at bay (*OudMed* 70 [1990], p. 34). A fragmentary krater (cat. no. 170) probably showed Vanth and a satyr-like daemon flanking a woman to be conducted to the Underworld. A monumental skyphos (cat. no. 173) is a major example of these new, later fourth-century interests; not only is the subject of one side — Alcestis taking the place of her husband Admetos in the Underworld — highly appropriate for a funerary function, but, in addition, Charon has become Charun, an Etruscan death-daemon with wings, hooked nose, jutting chin, and snakes in his bristling hair.

One of the important formal developments in late Etruscan vase-painting was the introduction of hatching to create softer, more illusionistic modeling within the limitations of a linear technique. This hatching, which often takes the form of dotted lines, can be seen in the Alcestis skyphos and in the phiale with the procession of geese (cat. no. 174), where it suggests the soft undulations of human anatomy or rows of feathers.

The gentle, spreading shapes, rendered with a broadly brushed line, seen in the phiale and (to a lesser extent) in the skyphos, are characteristic of the late production of Falerii. This late Faliscan Fluid Group already has its precedents in earlier Faliscan productions like the kylikes with broadly brushed exteriors (see cat. no. 165). In many small Fluid Group vases, like the skyphos with a woman's head and a bird (cat. no. 175), the forms become puffy, even bloated, and highly simplified. A workshop stemming from this late Faliscan tradition established itself at (Etruscan) Caere and turned out large numbers of stylized, simplified red-figure vases in almost industrial fashion.

A softness of touch and a breadth of form had been endemic in Faliscan vase-painting from its beginnings, initially being reserved for the exteriors of cups. The introduction of the dotted or hatched "illusionistic" technique suited this predilection admirably and was linked to truly progressive developments. Soft, spreading forms, however, could easily be debased in careless, simplified editions. Just this kind of decline affected Etruscan red-figure generally. Original formulations by more ambitious, committed artists tended to be multiplied in watered-down mass-production, although fine work appeared sporadically (usually executed in the Gnathian technique of several superposed colors). It may be that the Roman conquest of most of the Etruscan cities by around 280 B.C. played an important role in the termination of their tradition of figure-decorated vases.

VASES WITH SUPERPOSED COLOR

153

COLUMN-KRATER
Etruscan
Attributed to the Praxias Group
Ca. 480–450 B.C.
Gift of Henry P. Kidder. 80.595

DIMENSIONS AND CONDITION: Height: 28.3 cm; width across handles: 28.0 cm; diameter rim: 23.5 cm; diameter neck: 16.6 cm; diameter at shoulder: 22.8 cm; diameter top step of foot: 8.4 cm; diameter stem: 7.4 cm; diameter foot: 10.3 cm
Unbroken. Most of the decoration, which is somewhat worn on side A, is in added red, with incised details in the figures.

SHAPE: Very Attic in style, with only a few details, such as the foot in three degrees and the flatness of the rim, to betray its native origin.

A: A satyr is about to turn a handspring over a sky-phos. Although he is moving to the left, his torso is depicted frontally.

B: A wreathed satyr chasing a cock bends over to the right as he reaches for the bird. Unlike the satyr on side A, he is represented in profile.

Around the top of the rim is a wreath, composed of thick masses of leaves, and on top of each handle-plate is an octopus. The ivy vine on the outer face of the rim is drawn in black glaze on the reserved clay, but the vines framing the sides of both pictures are in added red, like the rest of the ornament. The upper frames are crude, unframed bands of egg-and-dart (or tongue-and-dart). The groundline is a simple stripe that circles the lower body.

Both the style of the figures and the shape of the vessel betray a strong Attic influence, but other features are non-Attic: the differences in the foot and rim already mentioned, the form of the wreath on the rim, the egg-and-dart ornament, and the use of superposed color with incised details on a krater. Within the Praxias Group, the satyrs are perhaps best compared to those on a hydria in the Thorvald-sen Museum, Copenhagen (T. Melander, *Thorvald-sens graeske Vaser* [Copenhagen, 1984], p. 45, fig. 23).

Vases of the Praxias Group are thought with virtual unanimity to have been produced at Vulci.

PUBLISHED: Robinson, *Catalogue*, pp. 173–174, no. 484; Beazley, *EVP*, p. 197, no. 45 bis.

153

153

154

STAMNOS
Etruscan
Attributed to the Praxias Group (the same painter as cat. no. 153)
Ca. 480–450 B.C.
Gift of Henry P. Kidder. 80.596

DIMENSIONS AND CONDITION: Height: 25.0 cm; diameter rim: 15.2 cm; diameter neck: 13.2 cm; diameter body: 21.6 cm; diameter top step of foot: 8.9 cm; diameter lower step of foot: 10.2 cm
Unbroken. The decoration is in added red, now somewhat worn, especially on side A, with incised details in the figures.

SHAPE: The shape copies Attic models of the second quarter of the fifth century, but this type of foot in two degrees is not found on Attic stamnoi.

A: A youth with a chlamys over his left shoulder and arm walks to the left. His head is turned back, perhaps to look at the ram he is leading to the altar at left. He holds a knife in his raised right hand and one of the ram's horns in the left. A plant with leaves like thyrsos heads grows in the background at the right.

B: A youth is striding to the left with a spear in his lowered left hand and his right arm outstretched. He wears a fillet, and his cloak hangs around both shoulders. It may be at him that the youth on side A is looking, although it is not clear why an armed man would be hastening to intrude on a sacrifice.

A band of crude, unframed egg-and-dart circles the upper shoulder; compare those on the column-krater, cat. no. 153.

The painter, who also decorated the preceding column-krater (cat. no. 153), was imitating Attic models; his style recalls that of the Pan Painter. For the subject of side A, compare an Attic kylix fragment by the Kleomelos Painter (Malibu 83.AE.323: *Getty-MusJ* 12 [1984], p. 246, no. 72). Within the Praxias Group, a stamnos from Chiusi is close in style (Florence, inv. Vagnonville 14: Martelli, *Ceramica*, p. 189, pl. 140). For the curious plant on side A, compare the one on another stamnos of this type, now lost (Beazley, *EVP*, p. 197, no. 39; A. Greifenhagen, *RM* 85 [1978], pl. 23).

Like other vases of the Praxias Group, this piece was probably produced at Vulci.

PUBLISHED: Robinson, *Catalogue*, p. 174, no. 485; Beazley, *EVP*, p. 197, no. 37 bis.

154

154

155

156

155

156

155

Skyphos
Probably Faliscan
Attributed to the Sokra Group
375–350 B.C.
Gift of J. J. Dixwell. 76.233

PROVENANCE: From Chiusi

DIMENSIONS AND CONDITION: Height: 16.1 cm; diameter rim:
15.4 cm; diameter body: 15.6 cm; diameter stem: 8.5 cm; diameter foot: 9.1 cm
Reconstructed from three fragments with no lacunae. Most of
the red slip has worn off, leaving only the incision and the
shadows of the figures and ornament.

SHAPE: Deep skyphos of Attic type, with horizontal handles
tilted slightly upward and disk foot

156

The decoration is in added red, with incised details in
the figures. On both sides, a draped youth stands to
the left, a stylized flower in his outstretched right
hand. There are large palmettes and scrolls beneath

the handles and a wreath running above both figures. The groundline consists of two red stripes.

Compare Pianu, *Sovradipinte*, pl. 15, no. 19.

PUBLISHED: Robinson, *Catalogue*, p. 173, no. 482; Beazley, *EVP*, p. 203, no. 31; G. Pianu, *MEFRA* 1978, p. 167, no. 108.

156

SKYPHOS
Probably Faliscan
Attributed to the Sokra Group
375–350 B.C.
Gift of J. J. Dixwell. 76.236

PROVENANCE: From Chiusi

DIMENSIONS AND CONDITION: Height: 15.3 cm; diameter rim: 16.1 cm; diameter stem: 8.2 cm; diameter foot: 8.6 cm
Broken and repaired, with no lacunae.

SHAPE: Same as cat. no. 155

The decoration is in added red, with incised details in the figures. On both sides, a draped youth stands to the left. There are large palmettes and scrolls beneath the handles. The continuous groundline consists of two red stripes.

PUBLISHED: Robinson, *Catalogue*, p. 173, no. 483; Beazley, *EVP*, p. 203, no. 30; G. Pianu, *MEFRA* 1978, p. 167, no. 107.

157

KYLIX
Probably Faliscan
Attributed to the Sokra Group
375–350 B.C.
Gift of J. J. Dixwell. 76.239

PROVENANCE: From Chiusi

DIMENSIONS AND CONDITION: Height: 8.8 cm; diameter rim: 21.4 cm; diameter stem: 1.9 cm; diameter foot: 9.4 cm
A large piece of the rim is restored, and part of the interior frame, below the youth's feet, is crudely repainted. A large section on the opposite side has been reattached. The added color on the exterior is badly worn.

SHAPE: Kylix of type B; handles squared off and turned back slightly.

The decoration is in added red, with incised details in the figures.

Interior: A nude youth stands frontally, his head turned to look at the phiale in his outstretched right hand. The circular frame consists of groups of four linked maeanders to right alternating with cross-squares.

157

157

A and B: On either side are two nude youths; on side B only their lower legs remain. There are palmettes and scrolling tendrils around the handles. On the reserved bottom of the foot there are two small concentric circles in the center and another circular stripe near the edge.

Compare Pianu, *Sovradipinte*, pl. 3, no. 3.

PUBLISHED: Robinson, *Catalogue*, p. 174, no. 486; Beazley, *EVP*, p. 202, no. 12 bis; G. Pianu, *MEFRA* 1978, p. 164, no. 29.

158

158

158

KYLIX FRAGMENT
Probably Faliscan
Attributed to the Sokra Group (Pianu)
375–350 B.C.
Gift of John James Dixwell. 76.828

PROVENANCE: Probably from Chiusi (said to have been
deaccessioned from a "public collection in Chiusi" in 1875)

DIMENSIONS AND CONDITION: Height: 3.3 cm; diameter:
14.5 cm

The decoration is in added red, with incised details in
the figure.

    Interior: A nude youth stands frontally, looking
to his right. He holds a fillet in his right hand and a
mantle in his left. He wears a headband. A stylized
wreath composed of chevrons and dots and framed
by double stripes surrounds the tondo.

    A and B: On either side are the lower parts of two
draped youths facing one another. There are palmettes and scrolling tendrils on the handle sides, between the pairs of figures. The groundline is a double
stripe.

PUBLISHED: G. Pianu, *MEFRA* 1978, p. 165, no. 45; see Robinson, *Catalogue*, p. 94, for provenance.

159

SQUAT LEKYTHOS
Probably Faliscan
Attributed to the Sokra Group (Pianu)
375–350 B.C.
Gift of William Sturgis Bigelow. 13.78

PROVENANCE: Lent by William Sturgis Bigelow, 1877

DIMENSIONS AND CONDITION: Height: 9.6 cm; diameter rim:
2.6 cm; diameter neck: 1.3 cm; diameter body: 6.8 cm; diameter foot: 4.9 cm.
Unbroken. The decoration is in added red, but most of the
color has flaked off, leaving only traces of incision.

SHAPE: The mouth is convex as in Attic lekythoi of the fifth
century. The quasi-spherical body suggests an Attic model of
430–400 B.C. Compare B. A. Sparkes and L. Talcott, *The
Athenian Agora* 12, *Black and Plain Pottery of the 6th, 5th
and 4th Centuries B.C.* (Princeton, 1970), nos. 1124, 1129.

On the front, a draped figure of indeterminate sex is
standing to the left. There is a palmette on the back,
scrolling tendrils on the sides, and rays around the
shoulder; all but the rays and parts of the figure's
cloak are now effaced.

Beazley associated this lekythos with the Phantom Group, but Pianu restricts the group to the unincised oinochoai of shape 7, which, he argues, belong to the second half of the fourth century.

Compare Pianu, *Sovradipinte*, pl. 17, no. 22.

PUBLISHED: Robinson, *Catalogue*, p. 174, no. 487; L. D. Caskey, *MFA AnnRep* 1913, p. 89; Beazley, *EVP*, p. 206; G. Pianu, *MEFRA* 1978, p. 183, no. 314.

159

160

PELIKE
Probably Faliscan
Attributed to the Sokra Group (Pianu)
375–350 B.C.
Gift of William Sturgis Bigelow. 13.86

PROVENANCE: Lent by William Sturgis Bigelow, 1877; from Chiusi

DIMENSIONS AND CONDITION: Height: 10.0 cm; diameter rim: 5.4 cm; diameter neck: 3.3 cm; diameter body: 7.1 cm; diameter foot: 5.1 cm
Unbroken. The added color is badly flaked, and there is extensive incrustation on the surface.

SHAPE: The vase has an overhanging torus rim and is solidly planted on a torus foot. It is a short-bodied version of minor Attic pelikai of around 420 B.C. Compare J. Boardman, *Athenian Red Figure Vases: The Classical Period* (London, 1989), pp. 97, 109, fig. 213.

The decoration is in added red, and details of the figure are rendered with incision.

On either side is a draped woman standing to the left, her hair pulled back and tied. On each side, the upper frame is a band of crude, linear tongues set within a rectangular panel. The circling groundline consists of two red stripes. Scrolling tendrils flank each handle.

Beazley associated this pelike with the Phantom Group, but, as mentioned in the entry for cat. no. 159, Pianu restricts the group to the unincised oinochoai of shape 7.

Compare Pianu, *Sovradipinte*, pl. 16, no. 21.

PUBLISHED: Robinson, *Catalogue*, p. 175, no. 488; L. D. Caskey, *MFA AnnRep* 1913, p. 89; Beazley, *EVP*, p. 206; G. Pianu, *MEFRA* 1978, p. 183, no. 308.

160

161

SKYPHOS (glaux)
Probably mid-4th century B.C.
Gift of Horace L. Mayer. 58.1296

DIMENSIONS AND CONDITION: Height at rim: 8.8 cm; width
across handles: 14.4 cm; diameter rim: 7.8 cm; diameter
stem: 5.1 cm; diameter top of foot: 5.5 cm
Unbroken

SHAPE: One handle is vertical and the other horizontal, as is
typical of skyphoi decorated with owls (hence the name given
the shape: glaux [i.e., owl]). Typical of glaukes with added
color is the incurving rim.

The decoration is in creamy added white, without incision.

A and B: An owl flanked by vertical twigs of olive
stares out with large, round eyes. The beak and the
dot and circle of the eyes are reserved in black. The
circling groundline is a double stripe.

For Etruscan owl-glaukes and the Attic vases that
inspired them, see Beazley, *EVP*, pp. 200–201; F. P.
Johnson, *AJA* 59 (1955), pp. 119–124, pls. 35–38;
M. T. Falconi Amorelli, *ArchCl* 24 (1972), p. 105, pl.
44, 1; and Pianu, *Sovradipinte*, pp. 55–62, pls. 50–
56 (compare especially pl. 51, no. 93). M. Del Chiaro
emphasizes the role that Apulian glaukes could have
had in disseminating the form (*ArchCl* 24 [1972],
pp. 107–108).

Etruscan glaukes with applied red owls have double groundlines, which are not found in true red-
figure glaukes. This common feature suggests that
the glaukes with applied color belong to a common
workshop tradition. The owls with incision, on the
other hand, do not have reserved beaks and eyes, and
they stand solidly on straight legs. Most of the unincised owls prance on bent legs, as in this example.
The typological differences suggest that the workshop tradition had branched out or subdivided itself.
The owls with incision, in any case, are probably earlier. In spite of the absence of incision in most Etruscan glaukes, Pianu is unwilling to date them to the
second half of the fourth century; he feels they are
too closely tied to fifth-century Attic models to per-
mit so great a chronological displacement (Pianu, *Sovradipinte*, p. 55). Pianu believes these cups were
produced at Falerii, although many have been found
at Tarquinia.

161

162

FOUR-PART FOOD OR CONDIMENT SERVER
2nd half of 4th century B.C.
Gift of William Sturgis Bigelow. 13.87

PROVENANCE: Lent by William Sturgis Bigelow in 1877

DIMENSIONS AND CONDITION: Clockwise from the (misfired)
jar at the top of the photograph: (1) Height: 9.7 cm; diameter
rim: 7.6 x 8.0 cm; diameter body (on diagonal): 10.3 cm; diameter foot: 5.1 x 5.0 cm; (2) height: 8.8 cm; diameter rim:
8.2 x 7.6 cm; diameter body (on diagonal): 10.2 cm; diameter
foot: 5.0 x 4.8 cm; (3) height: 9.0 cm; diameter rim: 7.6 x 8.0
cm; diameter body (on diagonal): 10.0 cm; diameter foot: 5.0
x 4.9 cm; (4) height: 9.0 cm; diameter rim: 7.6 x 7.6 cm; diameter body (on diagonal): 10.0 cm; diameter foot: 5.0 x 5.1
cm
Unbroken

SHAPE: Formed of four small jars, joined together, with a basket handle. The jars have flaring collars, carinated shoulders,
tapering lower bodies, and disk feet.

Around the outer body of each jar is a yellow and
white grapevine framed by stripes. The shoulder of
each jar is decorated with white rays, carelessly executed.

A virtually identical multibodied vase is in the
Tarquinia Museum (Pianu, *Sovradipinte*, pl. 103,
no. 244).

The use of added color in these vases is perhaps
less a holdover from earlier Etruscan vases in this
technique than a conscious imitation of contemporary Apulian Gnathian ware.

In a modern setting, very similar four-part metal
containers are used to serve chutney and other
sauces in Indian restaurants. The Etruscan ceramic
products may have played a similar role at ancient
banquets. Franz Messerschmidt has collected several
second-century Etruscan vessels made up of a cluster
of four jars and concluded that they were for serving
food; they were placed in tombs to provide furnish-

ings for eternity (*RM* 46 [1931], pp. 48–53, pls. 3–6). One example found in a tomb in Vulci (now in the British Museum) contained four swan's eggs, while another had lids on each of the jars, which therefore must have been intended for some different sort of nourishment. A Teano Ware cluster vase from Teano itself in the Metropolitan Museum of Art, New York (09.221.46f) also has lids on its four jars (*RM* 46 [1931], p. 52, pl. 5c; called Gnathian. The attribution to Teano and information on its provenance are due to Dietrich von Bothmer; private communication, Elizabeth Milleker.). Other Italic cluster vases, perhaps of the earlier third century, have been found in Ruvo and in Constanza on the Black Sea (J.-P. Morel, *Céramique campanienne: Les formes* [Bibliothèque des Écoles Françaises d'Athènes et de Rome 244, 1981], p. 436, nos. 9311–9312, pl. 217). Another Teano Ware cluster vase is in the Museum of Art and Archaeology, University of Missouri, Columbia (92.74).

PUBLISHED: Robinson, *Catalogue*, p. 189, no. 522; L. D. Caskey, *MFA AnnRep* 1913, p. 89.

162

163

KANTHAROS
Etruscan
2nd half of 4th century B.C.
Gift of Mr. and Mrs. William de Forest Thomson.
19.300

DIMENSIONS AND CONDITION: Height: 11.0 cm; maximum width across handles: 11.7 cm; diameter rim: 6.9 cm; diameter neck: 5.9 cm; diameter body: 8.1 cm; diameter stem: 2.3 cm; diameter foot: 4.3 cm
On one side, the thumbpiece and half of the handle are missing; otherwise intact.

SHAPE: Tall, straight-sided neck, shallow shoulder, tapering body, stemmed foot in two degrees. There are small, square thumbpieces on both of the slender double handles.

On either side of the neck is an ivy vine with reddish leaves and berries and incised stems. A groove, gouged freehand through the dull black glaze before firing, circles the body.

Highly similar kantharoi have been excavated at Tarquinia. Only the profiles of the rims differ significantly; compare Pianu, *Sovradipinte*, pl. 104, nos. 248–249. Compare also the decoration and shape (except the handles) of a vase in the Museum of Fine Arts, Houston (H. Hoffmann, *Ten Centuries that Shaped the West: Greek and Roman Art in Texas Collections* [Houston, 1971], p. 437, no. 198).

These kantharoi are evident imitations of contemporary Apulian Gnathian ware.

163

RED-FIGURE AND PLASTIC VASES

164

STAMNOS
Etruscan
Attributed to the Workshop of the Painter of London
F 484 (Herrmann)
Ca. 390–370 B.C.
Gift of William Sturgis Bigelow. 13.73

PROVENANCE: Lent by William Sturgis Bigelow, 1877

DIMENSIONS AND CONDITION: Height: 29.2 cm; diameter upper rim: 17.7 cm; diameter neck: 12.0 cm; diameter body: 23.7 cm; diameter stem: 7.3 cm; diameter foot: 11.1 cm
Unbroken. The vase was heavily repainted in modern times. Much of the applied coating was removed in a recent cleaning. Blackened shellac (?) still clings tenaciously and darkens or obscures much of the reserved areas, while zones of black glaze have been abraded away (probably providing the reason for the overpainting). Within the figures, much of the detail survives only in preparatory sketch lines.

SHAPE: Tall, tapering body; foot in two degrees. The neck is rather tall for a stamnos. The handles, rather than rolling back slightly, begin their pronounced backward curve from the point of attachment.

A: Two draped female figures touch one another affectionately. At the left is a woman in a chiton. The object in her right hand may be a small pail. Traces of added white survive on her face and arms. At the right is a figure in a chiton and himation. Faint traces of added white on the face indicate that this figure too is female. She is crowned with a wreath of laurel or olive in added color.

B: Two nude androgynous youths encounter one another. Faint traces of male genitals survive in the youth at the left. He wears a bandoleer in added yellow and carries a pail or situla that was covered with added white. Both have long, undulating locks of hair in slightly diluted glaze that descend just in front of and behind their ears. The youth at the right places one hand on the shoulder of the youth with the bandoleer and reaches out with the other hand, which his companion seems to fend off. The scene may be one of rejected courtship.

There are pairs of large, addorsed palmettes oriented vertically below and on either side of the handles. The tongues circling the upper shoulder are alternately black and reserved, the latter with black tips. The circling groundline consists of groups of stopt maeanders to right alternating with checker-

164

164

boards. Inverted tongues seem to have decorated the rim.

Beazley did not associate this vase, whose deplorable modern retouching discouraged attention, with any well-defined group. The character of the palmette decoration, however, seems unmistakably linked to the Painter of London F 484, an early ceramist of Vulci active in the last decade of the fifth century; the closest comparison seems to be that painter's name-vase in London (Beazley, *EVP*, pp. 43–45, pls. 7, 2; 8, 1, 2; for the date of the Painter of London F 484, see Jolivet, *Recherches*, p. 10). In both stamnoi, the palmettes spread their fronds and float freely on the surface with large circles flanking the tip of the central frond. In the work of the Painter of London F 484, the palmettes are even more spacious, and there are foliate embellishments, which are missing in this impoverished imitation. The lively, though primitive figure style of the painter of this stamnos is not alien to that of the Painter of London F484, who was characterized by Beazley as having "the rude charm of popular art." It is probable that this vase was made at Vulci.

PUBLISHED: Robinson, *Catalogue*, p. 193, no. 530; L. D. Caskey, *MFA AnnRep* 1913, p. 89; Beazley, *EVP*, p. 301.

164

165

165

KYLIX
Faliscan
Ca. 380–360 B.C.
Henry Lillie Pierce Residuary Fund. 01.8114

PROVENANCE: E. P. Warren collection; bought in Rome

DIMENSIONS AND CONDITION: Height: 8.1 cm; width across handles: 26.5 cm; diameter rim: 19.8 cm; diameter foot: 8.5 cm; diameter stem: 1.5 cm
Reconstructed from fragments with some pieces missing along the rim. On both A and B, the faces of the figures are missing.

SHAPE: Kylix of type B; the handles squared and rolled back slightly.

Interior: A wreathed and bearded man wearing a himation with a wave-pattern border is seated to the right. His scepter, with lotus finial, held vertically in his left hand, identifies him as a king, perhaps Zeus himself. He looks toward an altar with Ionic volutes and moldings of eggs and wave-pattern, on which stands a cock. Also on the altar is an egg or, more probably, a pomegranate in added color. In the field before the altar is an elaborate rosette or phiale.

A and B: On either side, a nude young athlete stands in conversation with a woman clad in a belted chiton, both gesturing with their hands.

There is a large palmette under each handle. Flanking the handles and framing the figures are large palmettes enclosed by tendrils linked to the palmettes beneath the handles. The exterior groundline consists of two stripes.

The circular frame of the tondo consists of groups of stopt maeanders to right alternating with saltire-squares. The bottom of the foot is reserved except for

165

165

broad stripes around the center and the outer edge (the resting surface) and a slender stripe just within the outer edge.

If it is Zeus who is represented in the cup's interior, the association with a cock is unusual, though not unprecedented. The cock is the sacred bird of the youthful Zeus Felchanos of Phaistos (A. B. Cook, *Zeus: A Study in Ancient Religion*, II, 2 [Cambridge, 1925], pp. 946–947, figs. 838–841; III, 2 [Cambridge, 1940] p. 1042, note 9). Beazley interpreted the figure as Zeus with the cock of Ganymede. It seems more likely, however, that Hades rather than Zeus is intended. On Locrian pinakes, Hades and Persephone are frequently shown together with roosters and pomegranates. Although Hades occasionally holds the pomegranate, the rooster is usually held by Persephone (R. Lindner in *LIMC*, IV, 1, pp. 375–379 [nos. 49–61], 391–392; IV, 2, pl. 213). The objects on the altar would thus allude to Persephone. The association between the cock, the pomegranate, and the altar seems more appropriate for a major divinity like Persephone than a minor demigod like Ganymede. How influence passed from the rather geographically limited and specific cult at

Locri to Etruria, however, is not immediately apparent. Stylistically, the painter of this kylix looked to Athens rather than to South Italy.

PUBLISHED: Beazley, *EVP*, p. 111, no. K, pl. 26; A. D. Trendall, *Vasi italioti ed etruschi a figure rosse e di età ellenistica* (*Vasi antichi dipinti del Vaticano: La Collezione Astarita nel Museo Gregoriano etrusco*), III (Vatican City, 1976), p. 35, under pl. XIX, 1–2.

166

CALYX-KRATER
Faliscan
Attributed to the Nazzano Painter (Cahn)
Ca. 380–360 B.C.
John H. and Ernestine A. Payne Fund. 1970.487

PROVENANCE: Andre Emmerich Gallery Inc., *Art of Ancient Italy* (New York, April 4–29, 1970), pp. 32–33, no. 45, 2 illus. (entry by H. A. Cahn).

DIMENSIONS AND CONDITION: Height: 49.1 cm; width including handles: 40.9 cm; outer diameter rim: 53.7 cm; inner diameter rim: 52.1 cm; diameter at base of wall: 27.0 cm; diameter cul: 29.4 cm; diameter stem molding: 10.2 cm; diameter body above stem molding: 9.9 cm; diameter foot: 22.0 cm
A horizontal break runs around the middle of the vase. The upper zone is reconstructed from fragments with a few pieces missing in the lip. There is a crack through the palmette band on the reverse. The artist neglected to fill in the background above the heads of Iris and Artemis.

SHAPE: Standard for the Nazzano group and, like contemporary South Italian calyx-kraters, descended from Attic prototypes: flaring body with overhanging rim; tall handles; fillet between lower body and tall, spreading foot.

A: Telephos and the infant Orestes. Telephos, the wounded Mysian king, is seated on the altar in the palace at Mycenae with a dagger in his left hand and the infant Orestes in the other. The child is represented with white skin and wearing a wreath. He stretches out his arms imploringly toward his father, Agamemnon, and another man, perhaps Menelaos or Odysseus or the seer Kalchas. Agamemnon rushes toward the altar, his long scepter in his right hand, but is restrained by the second man. The king wears a sleeved tunic, a long chiton, and a himation that trails from his left arm. His garments are richly embroidered with stars, wave-pattern, palmettes, and egg-pattern. The same is true of the chitons of Telephos and "Kalchas," both of whom also carry himatia and wear embades. At the right, the nurse, raising her arms in panic, has dropped a basket, possibly the baby's cradle. At her right stands the mantled Clytemnestra, pouring a libation with a phiale in her lowered right hand. Like the nurse, she wears bracelets and a richly embroidered chiton and himat-

166 (Color Plate xxiii)

166

166

166

ion but has the latter pulled over her head. Both women have white skin, as do all the females in the scene except Athena.

In the upper tier, the gods look down on these earthly events; from left to right are Athena, Iris, Apollo, Artemis, Zeus, and Hermes. At either end of the row of gods, above each handle, is a nude, white-skinned Eros. The one at the left places his left hand on Athena's white, foreshortened shield, and with his right offers the goddess a phiale full of offerings, including two pomegranates. The other Eros stands with his body partly turned to the left, his wings spread out on either side behind him. In his left hand he holds a metal jug, and with his right he reaches toward the tympanum next to Hermes' left leg. He wears nothing but shoes and a bracelet; his counterpart on the other side wears shoes, anklets, a bandoleer, and a wreath. Athena is seated with her legs to the right but looks back at the fruit offered by the Eros. Her right hand touches her shield, and the left holds her short spear in a vertical position. Her helmet has a long white crest, and her scaly aegis has a white-faced gorgoneion in the center. She wears bracelets, shoes, a necklace of white beads, and a richly embroidered peplos. To the right of Athena, Iris runs to the right toward the central group of Apollo and Artemis. Iris wears a short, embroidered chiton, embades, and bracelets. Her hair is tied in back with a white fillet, and there is a fillet of white beads round her head. She holds her caduceus in her outstretched left hand. Although Apollo is seated with his legs toward Iris, he does not see her approaching, having turned his head to the right to converse with Artemis. The god is seated on his cloak and holds a garlanded laurel branch in his left arm. He wears a wreath of laurel and two crossed bandoleers of white beads. Artemis stands facing Apollo, her bow in her upraised left hand and her right arm across her chest. She wears the same boots, chiton, bracelets, and fillets as Iris and also has a cloak over her left arm. Behind her, at the right, Zeus is seated with his legs to the right but looks back toward Artemis. His right hand is raised in front of his chest, and with his left arm he cradles his striped scepter. There is a wreath in his hair, and his cloak has fallen around his waist. To the right of Zeus, the nude Hermes stands with his right foot resting on an unseen support. He wears boots, a petasos, and a cloak pinned at the throat and holds his caduceus in his right hand. The garments of all the figures are richly embroidered, like those worn by actors.

B: Dionysos and Ariadne stand between two capering satyrs. The god moves to the left atop a low, viny hummock while looking back at his white-skinned consort, who rests one foot upon a low altar. He is nude except for a wreath and the bordered cloak around his shoulders. Ariadne wears an embroidered chiton with a wave-pattern border as well as bracelets, earrings, a necklace, and a white fillet. Both carry thyrsoi in their left hands, and Dionysos also holds his kantharos in his right hand. A fillet trails from his thyrsos. The satyr at the left wears crossed bandoleers of white beads, and the one at the right holds a metal jug in his right hand. Both wear white wreaths. A variety of disks, rosettes, ivy leaves, and phialai float through the field as filling ornaments.

Bands of dotted egg-pattern circle the rim and also frame the enclosed, upright palmettes in the handle-zone of the cul. A wreath of laurel and berries circles the vase below the overhanging rim.

The Nazzano Painter is one of the most clearly defined artistic personalities in Faliscan vase-painting. His robust and somewhat rough, angular style is closely related to that of Athenian artists of the beginning of the fourth century like the Meleager Painter or the Oinomaos Painter. He frequently made use of their two-tiered compositions and ornate draperies, and the elaboration and richness of his work compare favorably with that of many of his Athenian predecessors and contemporaries. His mythological narratives often have an amusing quality because of their energy and vividly concrete detail. Some of his compositions, like this one, are relatively well ordered, while others, which may be later, are almost chaotic. Given that the only two Etruscan vase-painters known have Greek names — Praxias and Sokra(tes), both working in added red — it is possible that the Nazzano Painter too was a Greek, presumably an Athenian.

Cahn (in *Art of Ancient Italy*, cited above), followed by Trendall and Webster (*Illustrations*, p. 104), connected the scene on this vase with the *Telephos* of Euripides. Keuls (in *Festschrift Cambitoglou*; see reference below, pp. 87–94) has developed the Euripidean connections of this and other representations of the Telephos story even further; she points out that Clytemnestra is introduced into the story only by Euripides, who evidently felt the need for dramatic male-female interaction. Neither Clytemnestra nor other females participate in earlier representations of the story. Nonetheless, there is no need to assume a direct theatrical influence. Although Euripides was popular among South Italian Greeks, there is little evidence that he or his fellow playwrights were much performed in Etruria, let alone Falerii. The elaborate costumes are like those worn by actors, but this detail, like the basic conception of the subject and the composition, could have been transmitted from Attica via the channel of vase-painting. A good parallel for both subject and composition is provided by Berlin 3974, a roughly contemporary Attic calyx-krater (Bauchhenss-Thüriedl, *Der Mythos von Telephos* . . . , see reference below, pp. 26–28, pl. 2; De Puma, *RM* 87, see reference below, pp. 17–18, pl. 5, 2; J. Boardman, *Athenian Red Figure Vases: The Classical Period: A Handbook* [London, 1989], fig. 357).

As Richard De Puma has pointed out, the inhabitants of west-central Italy had a special reason to be interested in Telephos; he was regarded as the ancestor of the Etruscans, at least by the Greeks. The connection emerges in the obscure poem *Alexandra*, written by Lycophron in the third century B.C. Telephos was the father of Tarchon (of Tarquinia) and Tyrsenos (who provided the Greek name for the Etruscans, *Tyrsenoi*). The literary tradition can probably be traced back to the early third century. Lycophron's verses in the *Alexandra* touching on this subject are thought to be derived from a lost history by Timaeus of Tauromenium (*Alexandra* 1245–1249; in *Callimachus . . . Lycophron . . . Aratus . . .* [Loeb edition], p. 422; J. W. Salomonson, *OudMed* 38 [1957], pp. 29–30; R. D. De Puma, *RM* 87 [1980], p. 15). In Roman Imperial times, the tradition was modified slightly, and Telephos became the ancestor of the Latins. Telephos nursed by the hind was often paired with representations of Romulus and Remus and the wolf (Salomonson, *OudMed* 38 [1957], pp. 20–44; L. de Lachenal in A. Giuliano, ed., *Museo Nazionale Romano: Le Sculture*, I, 5 [Rome, 1983], pp. 1–2, no. 1). This and the other Etruscan vases with Telephos collected by De Puma may provide the earliest evidence for this legend's taking root in central Italy itself.

PUBLISHED: C. C. Vermeule, *MFA AnnRep* 1970–71, p. 36; C. Bauchhenss-Thüriedl, *Der Mythos von Telephos in der Antiken Bildkunst* (*Beiträge zur Archäologie*, no. 3, Würzburg, 1971), pp. 28–32, pl. 3; Trendall and Webster, *Illustrations*, p. 104, pl. III.3, 49; Brommer, *Vasenlisten*, 1973, p. 472, no. D8; C. C. Vermeule, *BurlMag* 115 (1973), pp. 121–122, figs. 83, 85; J. Schelp, *Das Kanoun der Griechische Opferkorb* (*Beiträge zur Archäologie*, no. 8, Würzburg, 1975), p. 83, note 411; E. Zwierlein-Diehl, *Gnomon* 47 (1975), p. 70; MFA, *Illustrated Handbook*, 1976, p. 111, illus.; C. Vermeule, *Roman Art: Early Republic to Late Empire* (Boston, 1978), pp. 17–18, 187, 236–237, fig. 21; R. D. De Puma, *RM* 87 (1980), pp. 17–18, pl. 5, 1; I. Krauskopf, *LIMC*, I, 1, pp. 261 (no. 18), 274–276; I, 2, pl. 193; J.-M. Moret, *RA* 1982, p. 133, note 102; H. Bloesch, in *Greek Vases from the Hirschmann Collection* (Zurich, 1982), p. 105, under no. 42; K. Schauenburg, *RM* 90 (1983), p. 348, notes 70, 78; I. Krauskopf, *LIMC*, II, 1, pp. 344 (no. 50), 356, 359, 785 (no. 75); II, 2, pl. 587; A. Kossatz-Deissmann, *LIMC*, V, 1, pp. 755–756 (no. 154), 758–760; E. C. Keuls, in *Festschrift Cambitoglou*, pp. 92, 94, pl. 20:3.

167

STAMNOS
Possibly Faliscan
Attributed to the Painter of the Oxford Ganymede
1st half of 4th century B.C.
Gift of W. A. Gardner. 07.862

PROVENANCE: E. P. Warren collection

DIMENSIONS AND CONDITION: Height: 36.8 cm; width with handles: 37.1 cm; upper diameter rim: 21.1 cm; outer diameter rim: 23.5 cm; diameter body at level of handles: 31.5 cm; diameter top of foot: 9.7 cm; diameter stem: 6.7 cm; lower diameter foot: 15.4 cm
Broken and repaired, with a few small fragments missing; reconstructed from large fragments. Three of the ketos protomes terminating the handles are partly or entirely missing. The face of Amykos is destroyed.

SHAPE: The neck is short and concave. The unpainted handles are modeled in the shape of a pair of sea monsters (ketoi); their sinuous bodies intertwine to form the handles proper, with a head and a tail emerging at either end. The stem is offset from the lower body, and its echinus base rests on the recessed upper surface of the disk foot, which has a groove around its outer edge.

A: Polydeukes is binding Amykos to a tree trunk in front of a fountain, which consists of a stream flowing from the center of a flower into a tub. A plant, a folded cloak, and an alabastron are represented on the ground below. Polydeukes braces himself with one knee against the tree to draw tight the bindings, which themselves consist of young saplings. Like Amykos, he is infibulated and wears leather boxing thongs.

B: Hermes, Polydeukes, and a satyr old and fat enough to be called Silenos are shown in a scene possibly inspired by a satyr play. Hermes stands at the left, his right leg propped on the tendril of an adjacent palmette. He wears high-laced sandals and a winged helmet and carries his caduceus in his left hand. He looks back to the right at Polydeukes, who stands looking at the egg in his left hand that contains his sister Helen. In his other hand is a mattock, with which he will crack open the egg. Approaching from the right is Silenos, wearing shoes and carrying a situla in his right hand and a phiale in his left.

There are elaborate complexes of palmettes, tendrils, and flowers under the handles. The rim is circled by a band of egg-and-dart, and a band of large tongues runs around the shoulder. The groundline is a continuous reserved stripe with a stripe of diluted glaze through its center. Quadrated disks fill spaces within the floral complexes. On the reverse, the areas below Silenos and between the heads of Hermes and Polydeukes are filled with, respectively, a dotted disk and two pendant chevrons.

Amykos, king of the savage Bebrykes of Bithynia,

167

167 (Color Plate XXIV)

167

his presence. Silenos comes up with a bucket of water to wash the egg (or perhaps hoping to boil it!). The presence of Silenos suggests the influence of satyric drama; compare the phlyax actor on an Apulian bell-krater, who cracks open Helen's egg with an axe (Bari 3899: *RVAp*, I, p. 148, no. 96; *LIMC*, IV, pl. 291, Helene 5). According to Horace, Polydeukes and his brother Kastor were also born from an egg (*Sat.*2.1.26). Evidence that this story was known early enough to be parodied by an Apulian vase-painter of the mid-fourth century may be provided by an unpublished Gnathian bell-krater recently in the New York art market, with an actor in female guise watching an egg on an altar give birth to an erect phallus.

PUBLISHED: S. N. Deane, *MFA AnnRep* 1907, p. 52, no. 3; Shepard, *Monster*, p. 64, pl. 13, fig. 82; P. L. Williams (Lehmann), *AJA* 49 (1945), p. 340, note 44; Beazley, *EVP*, pp. 4–5, 57–61, 298, pl. XIV; G. A. Mansuelli, *EAA*, I, p. 334; F. Brommer, *Satyrspiele: Bilder griechischer Vasen* (2nd ed., Berlin, 1959), p. 85, no. 227; P. Bocci, *EAA*, III, p. 791; Brommer, *Vasenlisten*, 1960, pp. 346 (no. D 2), 361 (no. D 1), 363 (under no. D 6); Caskey and Beazley, III, p. 72 (under no. 163); Herbig and Simon, *Götter*, p. 41, under pl. 21; P. Zazoff, *Etruskische Skarabäen* (Mainz, 1968), p. 117, note 43; Brommer, *Vasenlisten*, 1973, pp. 490 (no. D 2), 512 (no. D 1), 515 (under no. D 9); Krauskopf, *Thebanische Sagenkreis*, p. 87, note 312; G. Foerst, *Die Gravierungen der Pränestinischen Cisten* (Rome, 1978), p. 48; F. Roncalli, *JdI* 95 (1980), p. 264; Sommella, *Enea nel Lazio*, p. 239, under D 224; G. Beckel, *LIMC*, I, 1, p. 739, no. 4; I, 2, pl. 594; A. Weis, *AJA* 86 (1982), pp. 24, 28, 30, 33 (no. 2), pl. I, fig. 2; V. Jolivet, *RA* 1983, p. 17 (as 07.802); R. Blatter, *LIMC*, II, 1, p. 594, under no. 10; J.-P. Thuillier, *Les jeux athlétiques dans la civilisation étrusque* (Rome, 1985), pp. 152 (no. 2.2), 218–219, 220 (note 111), 375, 580; R. D. De Puma, *LIMC*, III, pp. 604 (no. 73), 608.

compelled all strangers to box with him, otherwise denying them drink from the spring. Polydeukes, a skilled boxer, overcame him and punished his hubris by binding him. Except for the fountain, the composition of side A is very close to that on the bronze Ficoroni Cista in the Villa Giulia; the postures of the figures are nearly identical, and the cloak and alabastron are present at the base of the tree.

For the subject in Etruscan art, see G. Beckel, *LIMC*, I, 1, pp. 738–742; I, 2, pls. 594–597 (the Ficoroni Cista is p. 739, no. 5, pl. 595); and Beazley, *EVP*, pp. 58–60. For the cista, see T. Dohrn, *Die Ficoronische Cista in der Villa Giulia in Rom* (Berlin, 1972).

The subject of side B may be unique. Beazley listed two vases and eight mirrors representing either Hermes or Polydeukes delivering the egg of Helen to Leda or Tyndareos or both (*EVP*, pp. 115–116). Both the god and the hero are present on this vase, but Silenos is a poor substitute for either of the two recipients. Beazley suggested that Polydeukes has just discovered the egg while loosening the soil in the palaestra with his mattock, a preparation for exercising on the hard ground (*EVP*, p. 60). The egg had been hidden there by Hermes, which explains

168

FRAGMENT OF A KYLIX
380–350 B.C.
Gift of Dr. William N. Bullard. 90.69

DIMENSIONS AND CONDITION: Preserved diameter: 9.9 cm. The heads of all three figures on the interior are missing. The foot and much of the tondo of the cup are preserved and are now set within a restored kylix made of blackened plaster. No traces of exterior scenes are preserved.

Interior: A nude male holds the struggling Eros in a tight embrace, as though crushing him. Athena, identified by her aegis and wearing a bordered peplos and shoes, stands at the right, one foot resting on a

168

low support. Her right hand rests on her knee. If the object leaning against Athena's footrest is a club, the man is Herakles, but the identification is not certain.

Beazley (*EVP*, p. 298) noted the "fine style" and "unique subject." In the richness and freedom of its composition and in its rendering of anatomy, the cup outdoes practically all other Etruscan kylikes, but the surprisingly mannered arrangement of the undulating hemline looks forward to the kylikes of the Clusium Group (cat. no. 169). No ancient author mentions any animosity between Herakles and Eros, but an allegorical meaning may be intended: the hero conquers love, just as he overcomes old age when he attacks Geras. Some Attic vases show Aphrodite punishing the mischievousness of Eros; perhaps the god of love has been caught trying to steal Herakles' weapons, as the satyrs occasionally are shown doing.

PUBLISHED: Beazley, *EVP*, p. 298; G. Colonna, *LIMC*, II, 1, p. 1062, no. 154; II, 2, pl. 780; E. Mavleev, *LIMC*, III, 1, pp. 811–812, no. 6 (as 90.96); S. J. Schwarz, *LIMC*, V, 1, p. 217, no. 158.

169

KYLIX
Northern Etruscan
Attributed to the Clusium Group (Beazley);
attributed to the Tondo Group, Painter B (Harari)
350–325 B.C.
Henry Lillie Pierce Residuary Fund. 01.8123

PROVENANCE: E. P. Warren collection; bought in Rome

DIMENSIONS AND CONDITION: Diameter: 22.3 cm
Reconstructed from fragments; many pieces lost, particularly in the area of the missing handles. On both A and B, the head of the larger woman is missing. In the interior, the maenad's face is damaged, as is much of the satyr at the right.

SHAPE: Kylix of type B

Interior: Three figures are dancing on a bead-and-reel groundline. In the center, an ecstatic maenad in a bordered chiton whirls about to the tune of the double-pipes, played by the frontal satyr-boy at the left. She wears earrings, and a pin fastens her chiton at the shoulder. Dilute glaze is used to tint the folds of her garment. Her fingers are long and curved, like claws. At the right, a satyr in a leopard skin stands on tiptoes and washes (?) his hands in a pedestaled louterion; he, too, has curious hands, which are bent far back as they touch at the wrists. A thyrsos stands behind the louterion, and an object, almost entirely missing now, hangs from a peg at the far left. Beazley (*EVP*, p. 114) thought that the peg might be a goat's horn tipped with a ball and that the object is an alabastron; it could also be a flute case. The circular frame of the tondo consists of groups of stopt maeanders to right alternating with checkerboards.

A and B: On either side, a nude woman stands in a relaxed posture, her left hand on her hip and a drinking horn in her raised right hand. She wears a necklace, shoes, and earrings, and her wavy hair streams out behind her as though blown in the wind. Facing her at the left is a large, fat woman dressed in a curious gown, with a broad vertical stripe. Her left breast is exposed, and her left arm is massive and heavy.

Below each handle and framing the figures are large, enclosed palmettes with tendrils and flowers. The groundline is a single reserved stripe.

It is possible that the figures on the exterior were meant to be humorous, but there is a disquieting solemnity about them as well, shared also by the grotesque maenad of the interior. The exterior figures are closely paralleled by those on the kylix Geneva 23471 (M. Cristofani, in Martelli, *Ceramica*, pp. 237

169

169

169

hands of the maenad and satyr as the "Etruscan-dancer hand"; compare the hands of the girl on Villa Giulia 43608 (*CVA* 2, pls. 12, 1–3, and 17, 5). The pattern of the groundline in the interior he compared to one on the Bucciosanti mirror (E. Gerhard, ed., *Etruskische Spiegel*, V [Berlin, 1884–1897], pp. 44–46, pl. 35).

The early and finer productions of the Clusium Group, like those of the Tondo Group, are usually ascribed to Chiusi, but recent scholarship has tended either to shift this production to Volterra or, like Cristofani (in Martelli, *Ceramica*, pp. 49, 329), to consider it simply a northern Etruscan workshop.

PUBLISHED: Beazley, *EVP*, pp. 6, 68, 114, no. 9, pl. 27, 1–3; G. Maetzke, in *Studi in onore di Aristide Calderini e Roberto Paribeni*, III (Milan-Varese, 1956), pp. 259–260; Ginouvès, *Balaneutikè*, p. 116, note 12; D. W. Rupp, *ArchCl* 24 (1972), p. 20; F.-H. Pairault-Massa, *RA* 1980, p. 82; Harari, *Gruppo Clusium*, pp. 31 (no. 12, with additional bibliography), 113–114, 125, pl. 7, 2–3; A. D. Trendall, *JHS* 101 (1981), p. 216.

170

CALYX-KRATER

Etruscan
In the Neighborhood of the Funnel Group (Beazley); related to the Alcsti Group (Herrmann)
3rd quarter of 4th century B.C.
Gift of E. M. Raymond. 08.201

DIMENSIONS AND CONDITION: Height: 45.9 cm; maximum height base of body to rim: 32.0 cm; diameter rim: 33.8 cm; diameter body above handles: 19.7 cm; diameter cul: 22.8 cm Broken and repaired. The foot and half of handle A/B are modern. Large pieces of the body are missing. The vase has recently undergone conservation work in which the old repainting was removed.

SHAPE: The body is proportionally shorter and broader than in the Funnel Group examples (cat. nos. 171–172). It is, on the other hand, more slender than that of the earlier krater by the Nazzano Painter (cat. no. 166). The rim flares but little, barely extending beyond the handles.

A: At the left, a nude youth, wearing shoes and a white stephane and bandoleer, stands facing right with his left foot resting on a rock. He gestures toward the central figure or figures, who are almost entirely missing. At the far right are the remains of a draped female (?) figure who also has a foot propped up, presumably on a rock. The reserved area behind the hair and the wing-tips (?) appearing close to the handle suggest that the figure was winged. Thus it is probably Nike or an Etruscan death-daemon like Vanth. If it is Vanth, then the satyr-like youth at the left is probably a death-daemon as well. White plants rise from the groundline and hang from the upper border.

[fig. 180], 331). Cristofani attributes the Geneva cup to the "Montediano Painter," and this kylix (or at least its exterior) must be from the same hand, as is a cup in the Vatican (inv. Z 89: Trendall, *Vasi antichi*, II, pl. 60 b-c). Compare also the figures on the exterior of Florence 92093/a (*San Martino ai Colli* [Rome, 1984], pp. 57, 61–62, no. 42).

Harari (*Gruppo Clusium*, p. 31) attributes the interiors of some of these cups to two different painters: Painter B for this piece and Painter C for that in the Vatican. Trendall (*JHS* 101 [1981], p. 216) objects to the distinction between the interiors as "perhaps too finely drawn." Like others before him, however, Harari points out that the stylized exteriors and the more naturalistic interiors could well have been executed by different hands (*Gruppo Clusium*, pp. 120–121). That one hack could work for two different expert craftsmen within a workshop does not seem improbable, and the distinction between Painters B and C still seems valid.

Beazley (*EVP*, p. 114) referred to the curious

170

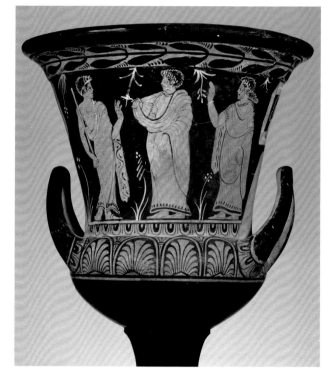

170

170

170

B: A youth wearing a himation and holding a staff stands to the right in conversation with a woman wearing a cloak and a tunic or chiton bordered with black strokes. Another draped woman stands at the far right. The women wear white wreaths, and the youth wears a white stephane and a long, white necklace. White plants grow from the groundline and hang from the upper frame. Above each handle is a female head with white radiate stephane facing right in a window.

A wreath of black laurel circles the vase below the rim. On either side of the cul, in the handle-zones, are broad bands of enclosed upright palmettes, with narrower palmettes in between. Bands of egg-pattern circle the handle-roots. The groundlines on both sides consist of egg-and-dart pattern. Between the roots of each handle is a black palmette.

Beazley noted that the heads in the windows over the handles recall those on some South Italian vases (e.g., cat. no. 52). The vegetation springing up and hanging down onto the field may also reflect South Italian influence (cf. the krater by the Hoppin Painter, cat. no. 15). The relatively elaborate and classical treatment of the ornament provides a link with calyx-kraters of the first half of the fourth century, like those by the Nazzano Painter of Falerii (cat. no. 166); by the Painter of London F 484, a craftsman of Vulci, in the Villa Giulia (inv. 55638: Martelli, *Ceramica*, pl. 165, 1); and by the workshop of the Alcestis Painter in Malibu (inv. L 74.AE48: Martelli, *Ceramica*, pl. 169). Both of the last have been ascribed to Vulci. At the same time the black laurel wreath links this krater, as Beazley pointed out, to the Funnel Groups, which are generally considered to come from Vulci. Jolivet's confidence that it can "sans doute" be joined to the Berlin Funnel Group, however, seems excessive. In both shape and style it differs from the standardized Funnel Group production.

The Boston krater seems more at home in another workshop of Vulci: that of the Alcestis Painter. Solidly classical kraters with this relatively rich decoration at the base of the handles and body and in the cul appear frequently in this tradition. The large spreading palmettes with small triple palmettes or lotus buds between them appear (executed in black-figure) on the krater in Malibu (Martelli, *Ceramica*, pl. 169) and in red-figure on a krater in Trieste from Tuscania (G. Q. Giglioli, *L'arte etrusca* [Milan, 1935], pl. 277, 1). On a modest krater of the Alcestis workshop in the Vatican, the large palmettes are executed in red-figure and the small lotus in black, just as on the Boston piece (Trendall, *Vasi antichi*, II, pp. 238–239, pl. 62, a, b; Z 110). Kinky hair, outlined by a reserved

area, is common in this group, and in this respect the Boston krater is particularly close to that in the Vatican. The landscape props, such as a little hill with a cave below it, turn up on most of these vases, as do the heavy draperies with black borders trimmed with dots. The effect is also rather Paestan, an influence that has been noted in the midcentury work of Vulci (M. Cristofani in Martelli, *Ceramica*, pp. 46–47). Beazley compared the Boston krater to a stamnos in the Walters Art Gallery, Baltimore (48.63), that was found just south of Cerveteri. It too could be a product of the Alcestis workshop.

PUBLISHED: L. D. Caskey, *MFA AnnRep* 1908, p. 62; Beazley, *EVP*, pp. 145, 301; K. Schauenburg, *RM* 79 (1972), p. 9, pls. 20, 21, 1; A. Greifenhagen, *AA* 1981, p. 277; J. G. Szilágyi, *CVA* Budapest 1, p. 86, under pl. 34; Jolivet, *Recherches*, p. 73.

171

CALYX-KRATER
Etruscan
Attributed to the Frontal Funnel Group Workshop (Del Chiaro)
Ca. 330–300 B.C.
Gift of Horace L. Mayer. 58.1278

DIMENSIONS AND CONDITION: Height: 38.5 cm; diameter rim: 31.0 cm; diameter body: 15.8 cm; diameter cul: 19.0 cm; diameter stem: 7.2 cm; diameter foot: 15.9 cm
Broken and repaired from a few large fragments, with no lacunae. Many of the added white details on side A, chiefly highlighting of the wings and drapery, have flaked off, giving the figure a somewhat ghostly appearance.

SHAPE: Compared with the earlier calyx-krater by the Nazzano Painter (cat. no. 166), the body is taller and more slender, the cul more bulbous, the handles more vertical, the rim less flaring, and the foot taller.

A: A winged woman, probably Vanth, an Etruscan Fury, faces the front but looks back to her left. She wears a peplos with a white belt and carries a white torch in her left hand. Her face has an anxious expression. Added white highlights the drapery folds and feathers and is used to contour the upper part of the wing.

B: Winged woman. The costume and pose are nearly identical to those on side A, but reversed, with Vanth moving to her right. Unlike her counterpart on side A, she carries no torch.

The figures are set within simple panels framed by reserved lines. Above each handle is a large palmette pointing downward, and between these and the figure-panels are tympana (?) hanging from white fillets; the left one on side B lacks a fillet. A wreath of

171

171

black laurel circles the vase below the rim. In the handle-zones of the cul are broad bands of vertical stripes and funnel-shaped tongues. The rim is decorated with vertical stripes, alternately short and long.

The shape and decorative scheme are entirely characteristic of the Funnel Group; compare Vatican Z 96, Z 97, and Z 98 (Trendall, *Vasi antichi*, II, pl. 64 a–f). Trendall calls the winged women on Z 96 (pl. 64, a and d) Nikes, and so they may be. The torch seen here on side A, however, is an unusual attribute for the Greek Nike and may identify the female as a Fury, as Del Chiaro proposed. The Etruscan Lasa is normally nude. Cristofani prefers to identify such figures as Vanth, an Etruscan adaptation of the Greek Fury. Compare the Vanth identified by inscription in a fresco in the François Tomb, at Vulci, who also wears a peplos (M.-F. Briguet, in L. Bonfante, ed., *Etruscan Life and Afterlife* [Detroit, 1986], p. 162, fig. IV-96). For Vanth, see E. Paschinger, *JOAI* 61 (1991/92), pp. 33–48.

Del Chiaro felt that the Funnel Groups worked at Tarquinia rather than Vulci, where they had previously been located. Jolivet (*Recherches*, pp. 72–76), followed by Cristofani (in Martelli, *Ceramica*, no. 171), returns the majority of the Funnel Group workshops, including the one responsible for this vase, to Vulci.

PUBLISHED: Del Chiaro, *Funnel Group*, pp. 36–38 (no. 1), 47, pl. 35; Jolivet, *Recherches*, pp. 74, 76 (as 59.1278).

EXHIBITED: Corpus Christi, *Greek Vases*, p. 36, fig. 49; Ann Arbor, *Greek Vases*, p. 16, no. 23; Detroit Institute of Arts, Detroit, January 5–March 2, 1977.

172

CALYX-KRATER
Etruscan
Attributed to the Vatican Funnel Group Workshop (Del Chiaro)
Ca. 330–300 B.C.
Gift of Horace L. Mayer. 59.1066

DIMENSIONS AND CONDITION: Height: 39.5 cm; height without restored foot: 30.2 cm; diameter rim: 31.9 cm; diameter body: 15.3 cm; diameter cul: 17.9 cm
Broken and repaired. The foot and most of handle A/B are modern. Parts of the cushion and of the satyr's face, hair, and tail are restored. Most of the added white details are eroded.

SHAPE: Like cat. no. 171, but with the body less concave.

A: A beardless young satyr in high boots is walking to the left, carrying a large striped cushion. He has rounded human ears and a black tail. Three rings surrounded by dots in added white are placed on the

172

background. A loop in added white hangs from the cushion.

B: Vanth or Nike stands frontally but looks to her right. She wears a long-sleeved tunic and a belted chiton with a flouncy overfold and large pins (dotted circles) at the shoulders. If the semicircular objects on or in front of her feet are shoes, they are very crudely foreshortened. Her empty right hand is raised with the thumb extended in an emphatic but inscrutable gesture. Her left hand rests on her hip but is hidden by the sleeve.

Cushions like that on side A are carried by figures on other vases in the Vatican Funnel Group. On Vatican Z 100, a stamnos by the same painter who decorated this krater, a youth holds a pillow in a manner nearly identical to that of the Boston satyr. The woman on the reverse of the stamnos, also carrying a pillow, wears the same chiton with flowing overfold and curious shoes as the Boston Vanth (Trendall, *Vasi antichi,* II, pl. 63, i and k).

The subsidiary ornament is similar to that on cat. no. 171, but without the tympana.

For the location of the workshop of this vase at Vulci, see comments under cat. no. 171.

PUBLISHED: Del Chiaro, *Funnel Group,* pp. 29–30 (no. 3), 41.

172

173

SKYPHOS-KRATER
Faliscan
Affinities with the Fluid Group (Beazley); related to the Berlin Funnel Group Painter (Del Chiaro)
2nd half of 4th century B.C.
Catharine Page Perkins Fund. 97.372

PROVENANCE: E. P. Warren collection; probably from Falerii

DIMENSIONS AND CONDITION: Height: 38.5 cm; width across handles: 52.4 cm; diameter rim: 36.5 cm; diameter body: 36.7 cm; diameter stem: 16.3 cm; diameter foot: 20.6 cm
Reassembled from a few large fragments with no lacunae

SHAPE: This "skyphos" is too large for a drinking-cup and may have been used as a krater; compare the Gnathian skyphos-krater, cat. no. 131. For the shape, compare the skyphoi, cat. nos. 155 and 156.

A: A bearded man is taking leave of his wife. If Beazley was correct in identifying them as Admetos and Alcestis, the winged death-daemon with a hooked nose and snaky hair who flies in behind them has come to take Alcestis to the Underworld in place of her husband. Though lacking a hammer, his usual attribute, the daemon must be Charun, the monstrous Etruscan version of Charon, ferryman of Hades; see E. Mavleev and I. Krauskopf, *LIMC,* III, 1, pp. 225–236; III, 2, pls. 174–185. Admetos wears

173

173

a tebenna, the rounded Etruscan cloak, and boots; the daemon a belted tunic; Alcestis a peplos, himation, shoes, a tall headdress, earrings, and a necklace. As on side B, many details of musculature are rendered with dotted lines. At the left is a funerary monument in the form of a column topped by a cone-shaped finial. Beside it at left, a tympanum or patera floats in the field. The altar at the right has pedimental parapets decorated with crude black palmettes.

B: A young man killing an older man. The murder takes place before a closed door of a palace, the rooftiles of which are visible above. Both figures wear cloaks. The victim has been knocked to the ground and looks up at his murderer, who is about to swing down the sword in his right hand. A large horn painted with stripes and zigzags floats in the field at right.

Below each handle is a large complex of palmettes and flowering tendrils. The continuous groundline consists of groups of stopt maeanders to right alternating with saltire-squares with chevrons in the interstices.

Beazley identified the scene on side B as Orestes taking revenge on Aigisthos. Del Chiaro, arguing that the out-of-doors setting and unheroic mood did not suit the Greek saga, opted for a local Italic interpretation such as the assassination of Servius Tullius, sixth king of Rome. Servius was slain *near* his house by servants of Arruns Tarquinius (Livy 1.48). For the scene on side A, compare a vase from Vulci with Alcestis and Admetos embracing between Charun and a snake-wielding death-angel (Paris, Cabinet des Médailles 918: Beazley, *EVP*, pl. 30, 1–2; Martelli, *Ceramica*, p. 222, pl. 170).

This is an extraordinary and beautiful vase, one of the great works of Etruscan vase-painting. There are no relief lines or sketch lines. The drawing is unusually fine and precise. The dotted lines of the musculature on side B are very unusual, perhaps experimental. Although the vase does not fit perfectly into the Funnel Group, it displays analogous subject matter (similar murder scenes) and several similar subsidiary ornaments, as Del Chiaro has pointed out. Cristofani does not accept Del Chiaro's effort to place the Funnel Group workshop at Tarquinia and instead prefers Vulci. If the (distant) association with the Funnel Group is to be accepted, this vase should probably also be referred to Vulci. Warren's report of a probable provenance from Falerii, on the other hand, seems to favor Beazley's association of the vase with the Faliscan Fluid Group.

PUBLISHED: E. Robinson, *MFA AnnRep* 1897, pp. 28–29, no. 15; Beazley, *EVP*, pp. 166–167, 303, pl. 37, 1–2; Chase,

173

Antiquities, pp. 137–138, fig. 178; M. A. Del Chiaro, *The Genucilia Group: A Class of Etruscan Red-Figured Plates* (University of California Publications in Classical Archaeology 3, no. 4, Berkeley, 1957), pp. 302–303, pl. 27b; Brommer, *Vasenlisten*, 1960, pp. 321 (no. D 2) (as 97.3.72), 352 (no. D 2); L. Guerrini, *EAA*, III, pp. 248–249; Chase and Vermeule, *Greek, Etruscan and Roman Art*, pp. 196, 214, fig. 207; E. Richardson, *The Etruscans: Their Art and Civilization* (Chicago, 1964), pp. 67, 109, 151–152, 177, 242–243, 284, pl. 42; J. Boardman, *Greek Art* (New York, 1964), p. 256, ill. 240; Herbig and Simon, *Götter*, pp. 3, 20, 45, pl. 32, 2; G. Hafner, *RM* 72 (1965), p. 48, note 45; J. M. C. Toynbee, *Death and Burial in the Roman World* (Ithaca, 1971), pp. 14, 283, note 21; K. Schauenburg, *RM* 79 (1972), pp. 6–7; E. Macnamara, *Everyday Life of the Etruscans* (London, 1973), pp. 107–108, fig. 59; Brommer, *Vasenlisten*, 1973, pp. 449 (no. D 2, as 97.3.72), 498, no. D 2; A. Rallo, *Lasa: Iconografia e Esegesi* (Florence, 1974), pp. 36, 41, pl. 22, 2; Del Chiaro, *Funnel Group*, pp. 13, 22–24 (no. 1), 53, pl. 14 (the attribution given above); O. Alvarez, *The Celestial Brides: A Study in Mythology and Archaeology* (Stockbridge, Mass., 1978), pp. 38–39, 159, illus. 13; L. B. van der Meer, *BABesch* 52–53 (1977–1978), pp. 65, 108 (fig. 29); O. J. Brendel, *Etruscan Art* (New York, 1978), pp. 348–349, fig. 271; Harari, *Gruppo Clusium*, p. 206, note 87; Sommella, *Enea nel Lazio*, p. 242, under D 226; P. J. Riis, *Etruscan Types of Heads: A Revised Chronology of the Archaic and Classical Terracottas of Etruscan Campania and Central Italy* (Det Kongelige Danske Videnskabernes Selskab Historisk-filosofiske Skrifter 9: 5, Copenhagen, 1981), p. 31; R. M. Gais, *LIMC*, I, 1, p. 376, no. 29 (with additional bibliography); I, 2, pl. 290; M. Schmidt, ibid., p. 541, no. 55; G. Pianu, *DialArch*, N. S. 3: 1 (1981), pp. 141–142; C. Peyre, in P. -M. Duval and V. Kruta, *L'Art celtique de la période d'expansion: IVe et IIIe siècles avant nôtre ère* (Geneva, 1982), p. 59, pl. III, fig. 4; V. Jolivet, *CVA*

174 (Color Plate xxv)

Louvre 22, pp. 24–25, under pl. 4, 8–13; idem, *Recherches*, pp. 23, 72–73, 95; Prag, *Oresteia*, pp. 101, 127, note 45, pl. 45b; A. H. Armstrong, ed., *Classical Mediterranean Spirituality: Egyptian, Greek, Roman* (New York, 1986), p. 173, fig. 12; Freytag gen. Löringhoff, *Giebelrelief*, p. 122; E. Mavleev and I. Krauskopf, *LIMC*, III, 1, pp. 230 (no. 53), 235; III, 2, pl. 179; H. Blanck, in H. Blanck and G. Proietti, *La Tomba dei Rilievi di Cerveteri* (Rome, 1986), pp. 46–47, fig. 35; F. Gilotta, *ArchCl* 38–40 (1986–88), p. 239; Cavagnaro Vanoni and Serra Ridgway, *Vasi etruschi*, p. 112; M. Harari, *OudMed* 70 (1990), p. 37, note 43; Y. Morizot, *LIMC*, VI, 1, p. 79, no. 48.

174

PHIALE MESOMPHALOS
Faliscan
Attributed to the Fluid Group
330–310 B.C.
Gift of Henry P. Kidder. 80.539

DIMENSIONS AND CONDITION: Diameter: 22.5 cm; exterior diameter omphalos: 4.7 cm; interior diameter omphalos: 3.0 cm
Reassembled from two fragments

The striking design of this phiale is unique. The outside is glazed black. The interior has a row of white dots and a band of egg-and-dart pattern around the black omphalos. Around this, a broader band is painted with six geese, alternately reserved and in added white, with feathers, eyes, and other details in black and dilute glaze. The geese are walking with wings partly spread, and there are large, stylized flowers or tympana below each of the leading or right wings. The outer frame of the tondo, a simple reserved line, functions as a groundline for the birds and for five small palmettes in added white.

PUBLISHED: Robinson, *Catalogue*, p. 189, no. 521; Beazley, *EVP*, p. 158, pl. 36, 6.

175

SKYPHOS
Faliscan
Possibly the Fluid Group (Beazley); attributed to the Barbarano Group (Cavagnaro Vanoni and Serra Ridgway); attributed to the Circle of the Full Sakkos Painter (Padgett and Herrmann)
Late 4th century B.C.
Gift of Miss Helen Griggs. 12.1181

PROVENANCE: Said to be from Cumae

DIMENSIONS AND CONDITION: Height: 8.4 cm; diameter rim: 8.6 cm; diameter body below handles: 8.5 cm; diameter stem: 4.1 cm; diameter foot: 4.6 cm
Unbroken. The added white of the woman's skin on side A is almost entirely worn away, destroying many of her features, including the eyes.

SHAPE: Compared with the earlier skyphoi of the Sokra Group (cat. nos. 155–156) and the skyphos-krater with Alcestis and Admetos (cat. no. 173), the handles are larger and the lower body more abruptly tapering.

A: A large female head wearing a sakkos is in profile to the left. There are traces of yellow on the spotted sakkos.

175

175

B: A bird, possibly a dove, stands in profile to the left, its feathers drawn in black, yellow, and white.

There are palmettes and scrolling tendrils under the handles and framing the figures.

Similar skyphoi from Tarquinia (e.g., Tarquinia 69708 and 69710) have been assigned to the Barbarano Group by Cavagnaro Vanoni and Serra Ridgway (*Vasi etruschi*, p. 85, no. 69). Within this group, very similar skyphoi, again from Tarquinia, have been attributed to the Full Sakkos Group by Pianu (*Figure rosse*, nos. 60, 62, 70, 73–75). The inspiration may have been Campanian skyphoi such as Budapest T.777 (*CVA* 1, pl. 48, 4–7).

PUBLISHED: Robinson, *Catalogue*, p. 186, no. 512; Beazley, *EVP*, p. 302: he thought the skyphos might belong to the Fluid Group, but his notes on the vase did not give this specific attribution.

"TRICK" AMPHORA-RHYTON
Related to the Clusium Group
370–350 B.C.
Henry Lillie Pierce Residuary Fund. 00.362

PROVENANCE: E. P. Warren collection; Forman collection, Pippbrook House, near Dorking, Surrey (Forman Sale Catalogue, no. 347, citing de Bammeville collection, Sale Catalogue, no. 35).

DIMENSIONS AND CONDITION: Height: 15.1 cm
A fragment from the lip has been reattached; otherwise unbroken. The red wash is worn, particularly on the handle reliefs.

SHAPE: The form is that of a transport amphora, with a knob in place of a flat foot. Functionally, it is a true rhyton, with a wide mouth at one end and a spout at the other. Extra refinements or complications are present, however. The ingenious workings of this "trick" vase and of a very similar vase by the same artist in the Allard Pierson Museum, Amsterdam, were analyzed by J. V. Noble (*PAPS* 112; see reference below). The double-walled construction allows wine to enter through both the mouth and the bottom knob. A hole in the bottom of the innermost chamber communicates with the reservoir in the outer chamber. By stopping the hole in the foot with one finger and with another finger closing the hole in one of the hollow handles, one can empty the inner chamber via the mouth and then "magically" refill it by removing the finger from the handle-hole. The illusion is thus given of a seemingly empty vessel refilling itself. It could also be conjectured that two portions might be served from the vessel: one from the mouth and one from the base. In the Achaemenid empire and on its fringes among the Thracians and Scythians, the amphora-rhyton was apparently used for ritual fraternization, and such vessels were equipped with multiple serving spouts to fill several drinking cups simultaneously (Venedikov and Gerassimov, *Thracian*, pp. 72–73, figs. 123–124; A. Mincev, *Pulpudeva* 3 [Sofia, 1980], pp. 184–185; Piotrovsky, Galanina, and Grach, *Scythian*, figs. 265–267).

On either side of the neck, an owl stands frontally between stacks of dotted chevrons. There are two tiers of animals on either side of the body, those on the shoulder lacking a groundline.

A: On the shoulder, a dog chases two hares to the right; the hare in the middle has shorter ears than the one in front, and were it not for its short tail, it might also be taken for a dog. In the lower tier, two boars square off for combat, oblivious to the lion (?) approaching from the right.

B: On the shoulder, two spotted rams are butting heads. In the lower tier, a bull falls to the left between a lion and a lioness with pendulous teats.

On both handles are applied reliefs of a frontal female head above a larger profile head of a goose, both

176

176

of which were coated with a red wash. A band of stopt maeanders to the right circles the shoulder below the neck. On either side of the rim is a band of egg-pattern, and below this is a molding painted with bead-and-reel. Red wash was applied to the handle reliefs, the bead-and-reel, and the reserved band above the bottom knob. The other reserved areas were given a brown wash, with the exception of the rim, which remains in the original pale tan clay.

The fine quality of the applied reliefs recalls the plastic vases of the Clusium Group in general, but the strongest analogies are with a duck-askos in the Villa Giulia where the head of the genius riding on each wing is shown frontally and in a similar scale (50581: Harari, *Gruppo Clusium*, pp. 61 [no. 36], 154–155, pl. 40, 1–2). Harari does not think that the askos was made in Chiusi. The trick amphora can hardly be from the northern Etruscan workshop, either, since its painted decoration has loose, sketchy forms quite unlike the emphatically patterned figure painting characteristic of the Clusium Group. The animals are modeled with harsh, curved lines, which recall the modeling lines on the stamnos by the Painter of the Oxford Ganymede (cat. no. 167). The vase's ornament is limited but unusual. The simple, disconnected maeanders on the shoulder are seen on the Phuipa cup from Vulci, where the large eyes and rough modeling of figures are also comparable (Vatican G 112: Beazley, *EVP*, pp. 55–56, pl. 12; Martelli, *Ceramica*, no. 167). The black bead-and-reel on the neck is a rare form that appears on the bell-krater of the Argonaut Group in Florence (4026: Beazley, *EVP*, pp. 33–35, pl. 9, 1). An astragal with incomplete reels appears on the groundline of a kylix of the Clusium Group (cat. no. 169). The stacks of diamonds flanking the owls on the neck are also highly unusual. They recall the checkerboards of elongated diamonds on Athenian cups of the Saint-Valentin class (S. Howard and F. P. Johnson, *AJA* 58 [1954], pp. 191–207, pls. 32–33).

In spite of the Boston rhyton's connections with the Clusium Group, which is usually dated in the second half of the century, several points argue in favor of a date for it in the first half of the century. First, it makes use of relief line, a relatively early technique, and, second, the owls on the neck make it clear that it was influenced by fifth-century Athenian glaukes (see the discussion of cat. no. 161); both considerations make it desirable to place the rhyton as early as possible. This argument is also supported by the stacks of elongated diamonds flanking the

176

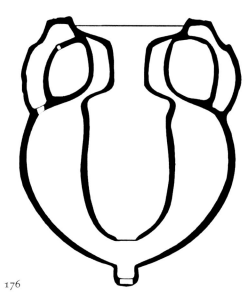

176

owls since they could well have been inspired by the
ornament of the fifth-century Saint-Valentin vases.

The rows of animals on this rhyton are somewhat
unusual in fourth-century Italic vase-painting. On
the other hand, animals are a principal theme in contemporary Scythian metalwork, including the great
Chertomlyk amphora-rhyton (Piotrovsky, Galanina, and Grach, *Scythian*, figs. 188–195, 265–268).
They may have been used on the Boston vase to
reinforce the barbaric associations of the rhyton
structure.

PUBLISHED: E. Robinson, *MFA AnnRep* 1900, pp. 71–72, no.
28; R. Lullies, *RM* EH 7 (1962), p. 40, note 31; J. V. Noble,
PAPS 112 (1968), pp. 373–374, figs. 8, 11.

177

PLASTIC RHYTON
Etruscan
Attributed to the Bruschi Group
Late 4th century B.C.
Francis Bartlett Donation of 1900. 03.795

PROVENANCE: E. P. Warren collection; Bruschi collection;
found at Tarquinia

DIMENSIONS AND CONDITION: Length: 18.5 cm; width across
handles: 13.1 cm; width across ears of warrior: 8.9 cm; depth
from crest of helmet to grotesque nose: 12.5 cm
The mouth of the vase is broken in several places; fragments
are missing in the area below the left side of the helmeted warrior. There is one break in the head zone.

SHAPE: There are no close parallels outside its group. With a
wide mouth at one end and a spout at the other, it is a true rhyton, a kind of ritual serving vase normally used together with
a phiale.

This unusual vessel is composed of two mold-made
faces set back to back: the upper one a bearded Greek
warrior with curly hair and wearing a Corinthian
helmet pushed up on top of his head; the lower one a
caricature of a bearded man, perhaps a Syrian or
Phoenician, with a broad nose, almond eyes, and
thick, smiling lips. The warrior's mouth is open and
pierced. Below his chin is a scallop-shaped opening,
partly restored, with angled incisions on the yellow-
brown painted rim. In the top of his helmet, which is
coated with a wash of dilute glaze, is a small spout,
the tip broken off. The warrior's hair is black and his

177

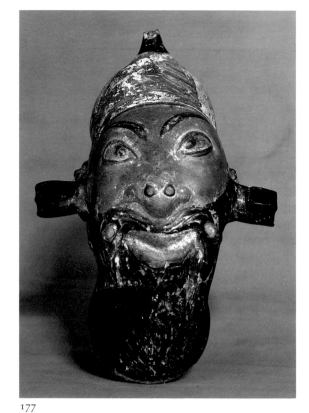

177

177

skin a light brown. The whites of the eyes are properly colored. A double-channeled handle is set on either side, below the ears.

Four "warts" on the "Syrian's" nose and by his mouth provide a resting surface for the vessel. He has brown skin and large white eyes with black pupils; unlike the warrior's, the eyes are outlined in black. The "Syrian's" long beard forms the underside of the rhyton's mouth.

The vase is loosely connected with the double-headed kantharoi of the Clusium Group (Harari, *Gruppo Clusium*, pp. 65–68, 70–72, pls. 41–43, 49–55). Both the kantharoi and the rare examples of rhyta with a single head (double-headed rhyta are otherwise unknown) have the mouth above the head and the spout below, the reverse of what is seen here; compare the gold head-rhyta in the Panagyurishte Treasure (Venedikov and Gerassimov, *Thracian*, figs. 125–127; A. Mincev, *Pulpudeva* 3 [Sofia, 1980], pp. 177–188).

Beazley (*EVP*, p. 190) pointed out two vases, a complete vessel in the Vatican (Z 129) and a fragment in the Todi Museum (487; Trendall, *Vasi antichi*, II, pp. 254–255, pl. 66j; *CVA* Musei Comunali

Umbri, Todi, pl. 9, 5) that not only are the closest parallels for this rhyton in style and composition but also help to explain the inversion of the relationship of spout and mouth. The complete example in the Vatican again has two heads back to back; one is a bald Oriental similar to the "Syrian" here, and the other is a balding grotesque, whose aquiline nose gives him an Eastern flavor as well. The latter has a gaping mouth and asymmetries that strongly recall masks of both Atellan farce and New Comedy (cf. Bieber, *Theater*, 1961, pp. 100–101, 248, figs. 377, 381, 820). Since the gaping comic mouth could conveniently be used as the mouth of the vase, there is a certain logic (missing in the Boston rhyton) in putting the spout in the tops of the heads. Turning the heads upside down to pour from the spout, moreover, increases the comic effect.

The Vatican piece is unmistakably humorous in intent, while the Boston rhyton is more ambivalent, since the warrior's head is not a caricature. Nonetheless, it seems likely that both vases were intended as parodies of foreigners, including Greeks as well as Semites, and their drinking habits. It is not improbable that the Etruscans knew that rhyta were used in the drinking rituals of the lands surrounding the Aegean and the Black Sea. (On these rituals, see Venedikov and Gerassimov, *Thracian*, pp. 72–77; H. Hoffmann, *Greek Vases in the J. Paul Getty Museum* 4 [1989], pp. 157–160.) Rhyta of fourth-century type have even been found as far south as the Golan Heights (M. Hartal, *Israel Exploration Journal* 37 [1987], p. 271, fig. 2). In the Thracian realm, at least, these rituals had a Bacchic character, in which comedy would be entirely appropriate. The designers of the Etruscan rhyta seem to have played on a considerable knowledge of the geographic and cultural associations of this exotic type of vessel.

A relationship to the rhyta of the Bruschi Group has been observed in a miniature Etruscan jug with a grotesque face applied like a mask to its front (Andre Emmerich Gallery Inc., *Classical Art from a New York Collection* [New York, 1977], no. 46).

PUBLISHED: *MonAnt* 36 (1937), col. 485; Beazley, *EVP*, pp. 189–190, pl. 40, figs. 7–8; Trendall, *Vasi antichi*, II, p. 254; G. Hafner, *RM* 77 (1970), p. 57, pl. 27, 3; Harari, *Gruppo Clusium*, p. 175, note 106; Pianu, *Figure rosse*, p. 145; U. Mandel, *Kleinasiatische Reliefkeramik der mittleren Kaiserzeit: Die 'Oinophorengruppe' und Verwandtes* (*Pergamenische Forschungen* 5, Berlin, 1988), p. 206, note 1497.

178

178

PLASTIC MUG IN THE FORM OF AN
AFRICAN BOY'S HEAD
Attributed to the Negro-Boy Group
2nd half of 4th century B.C.
Gift of W. A. Gardner. 07.863

PROVENANCE: E. P. Warren collection

DIMENSIONS AND CONDITION: Height: 16.6 cm; diameter rim: 11.0 cm; smallest diameter rim above head: 8.6 cm; depth, eyebrow to handle: 15.1 cm; neck, side to side: 6.5 cm; neck, front to back: 6.9 cm; diameter foot: 8.8 cm
Reconstructed from fragments. Part of the left rim and the left cheek are restored.

SHAPE: The vase is generally like mugs of the Clusium Group, but the lip is much lower. Concave neck; broad, flaring mouth; vertical handle with concave profile.

Circling the bottom of the neck is a band of dotted egg-pattern framed by stripes. The boy's snail-shell curls were applied separately, as was the rosette on the forehead. The eyes, set deeply beneath sharp brows, are large and heavily lidded; the whites and a ring around the pupil are reserved. Added red is used for the lips, the philtrum, the petals of the rosette, and a stripe around the side of the foot. On the reserved underside of the foot are two concentric black circles. Beazley saw a connection between the careful

178

179

finishing of the underside of this and the following
vase (cat. no. 179) and that of other head-vases and
duck-askoi from Clusium (*EVP*, p. 305). The connection between the Negro-Boy Group and the Clusium
Group is fully accepted by Pianu (*Figure rosse*, no.
141). Harari, however, denies that Beazley offered a
sufficient basis to make the link and excludes the
Negro-Boy Group from the Clusium Group
(*Gruppo Clusium*, p. 174).

This and the following vase (cat. no. 179) are two
of the most striking members of Beazley's Negro-
Boy Group; the closest parallel, as Beazley noted, is
Villa Giulia 16338 (Beazley, *EVP*, p. 187, pl. 40, 6).
One may add to Beazley's list a mug formerly in the
Zurich art market (Fortuna, *Antikenkatalog* 13
[1989], no. 1). Vessels of this type first appeared in
Athens in the late sixth century (e.g., Boston
00.332: J. D. Beazley, *Attic Black-Figure Vase-
Painters* [Oxford, 1956], p. 614); Beazley considered
the later Attic examples inferior to these Etruscan
variations on the theme.

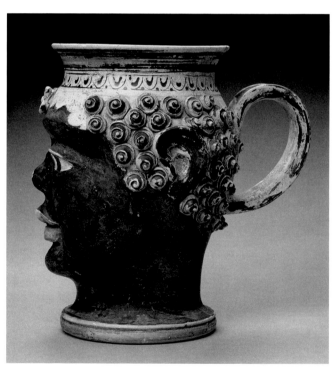

179

PUBLISHED: Beazley, *EVP*, p. 187, no. 2, pl. 40, 5; F. M. Snow-
den, Jr., in J. Vercoutter et al., *The Image of the Black in
Western Art*, I: *From the Pharaohs to the Fall of the Roman
Empire* (New York, 1976), pp. 173–174, fig. 210.

179

PLASTIC MUG IN THE FORM OF AN
AFRICAN BOY'S HEAD
Attributed to the Negro-Boy Group
2nd half of 4th century B.C.
Gift of W. A. Gardner. 07.864

PROVENANCE: E. P. Warren collection

DIMENSIONS AND CONDITION: Height: 16.0 cm; diameter rim:
10.2 cm; smallest diameter rim above head: 8.3 cm; depth,
eyebrow to handle: 15.3 cm; neck, side to side: 6.4 cm; neck,
front to back: 7.0 cm; diameter foot: 8.8 cm
The curls on the left side of the forehead are broken away and
lost. The vase is otherwise intact, except for abrasions of the
black glaze, as on the tip of the nose and on the handle.

Nearly identical to cat. no. 178.

PUBLISHED: Beazley, *EVP*, p. 187, no. 3.

180

180

DUCK-ASKOS
Etruscan
Last 3rd of 4th century B.C.
Gift of Henry P. Kidder. 80.575

DIMENSIONS AND CONDITION: Length: 16.0 cm; height: 11.4
cm; diameter rim: 3.7 cm; diameter foot: 4.9 cm
Unbroken

SHAPE: A well-known type, this askos is rather crudely modeled in the form of a duck. The spout is in the duck's beak, and
above the tail is a circular mouth with a short neck. A flanged
handle extends from the tail to the neck.

There are stripes on top of the mouth and head and
on the covert feathers; the primary feathers are represented more or less naturalistically. On both necks
(i.e., below the head and the mouth) are horizontal
stripes with pendant vertical stripes. The eyes are
mere dotted circles. There are two broad bands of
maeanders on the back beneath the handle, and on
the breast and below the tail are black palmettes: the
one on the breast curled inward, that to the rear out-
spread.

Beazley (*EVP*, pp. 191–192) compiled a list of such
askoi and remarked on their inferiority to those of
the earlier Clusium Group. Del Chiaro (*RA* 1978;
see reference below) has studied these later duck-
askoi and assigns the Boston example to his type
A.2, which he believes was produced in Tarquinia
(see reference below). Pianu (*Figure rosse*, pp. 150–
151) admits that the majority of such askoi have
been found at Tarquinia but sees no specific connection with the other wares ascribed to that city. The
use of black-figure palmette ornament connects

180

them strongly with Vulci, as in vases like the fragmentary krater with black-figure palmettes under
the handle (cat. no. 170).

PUBLISHED: Robinson, *Catalogue*, p. 170, no. 470; Beazley,
EVP, p. 191, no. 3; M. Del Chiaro, *RA* 1978, p. 31, no. 7;
Harari, *Gruppo Clusium*, p. 135, note 17.

GLOSSARY

Alabastron. A small, elongated vessel for perfumed oils; normally handleless.

Amphora. A vase with two vertical handles from neck to shoulder, with variations in shape of neck and body. Fine, decorated examples were used for storage and serving of wine or oil.

Antilabe. The hand-grip of a shield.

Aryballos. A small oil vessel, usually globular.

Askos. A spouted flask with handle across the top.

Aulos. A reed instrument similar to the oboe but popularly called a flute or pipe; always played in pairs.

Bucranium. An ox skull.

Chiton. A long, loose gown worn next to the skin, of wool or linen, secured by a belt and sometimes sleeved.

Chitoniskos. A short chiton, worn usually by men but also by active females, such as Artemis or the Furies.

Chlaina. A shawl-like mantle.

Chlamys. A short cloak for riding or traveling, fastened on one shoulder with a pin.

Chous. A broad-bodied pitcher with trefoil mouth (oinochoe of shape 3).

Cista. A storage box; in ritual use it held sacred utensils.

Diphros. A type of four-legged stool.

Embades. High boots of animal skin with flaps at the top.

Epichysis. An oil bottle with a slender neck, constricted spout, and single vertical handle.

Exaleiptron. A vase for scented water or oil, with a deep inner rim to prevent spillage; sometimes called a plemochoe.

Flabellum. Fan.

Glaux. A skyphos with one vertical and one horizontal handle; named for the owl (*glaux*), which is frequently the principal decoration.

Gorgoneion. The disembodied head of the gorgon Medusa.

Guttus. A small oil flask with an angled spout and single ring handle, probably for filling lamps.

Himation. A rectangular woolen cloth worn wrapped around the body as a cloak.

Hydria. A water jar with two horizontal side handles and one vertical handle at the back.

Iynx-wheel. A wheel holding wryneck birds (or symbolic equivalent); used as a love charm.

Kalathos. A tall, tapering basket used in wool-working.

Kalpis. A hydria with neck and body forming a continuous curving profile; vertical handle from shoulder to neck.

Kantharos. A wine cup with two high-swung handles.

Kekryphalos. A head-scarf from which hair emerges at the back.

Ketos. A sea monster.

Krater. A deep, two-handled, wide-mouthed vase for mixing wine and water.

Krateriskos. A drinking cup in the shape of a calyx-krater.

Kylix. A shallow, two-handled wine cup, usually with a stemmed foot.

Lebes. A mixing bowl with rounded body designed for placement on a stand; also called a dinos.

Lekanis. A shallow, two-handled bowl with knobbed lid.

Lekythos. An oil flask with single vertical handle; may be tall, with offset shoulder and slender neck, or squat, with plump body and rounded shoulder.

Louterion. A washbasin, often supported by a pedestal.

Loutrophoros. A tall, slender amphora with long, vertical handles, to carry water for nuptial and funerary ritual use.

Naiskos. A small shrine or tomb monument, with a pediment supported by columns or antae.

Nebris. A fawn skin, as worn by Dionysos and his retinue.

Nestoris. A jar with flaring mouth and high-swung, angular handles from rim to shoulder, derived from a native Messapian shape, the trozella.

Oinochoe. A wine pitcher.

Omphalos. Literally "navel"; the low, rounded stone, associated with Apollo, that marked the center of the earth at Delphi.

Palaestra. An area or building for teaching and practicing wrestling and other sports.

Panoptes. "All-seeing" or "multi-eyed": applied to Argos, who, according to myth, had many eyes.

Patera. A saucer-like dish with a single handle.

Pedum. A shepherd's staff, frequently carried by Pan.

Pelike. A storage jar with wide mouth, large low belly, and two vertical handles.

Pelta. A small, light leather shield, frequently crescent-shaped.

Petasos. A broad-brimmed hat worn by Hermes, horsemen, hunters, and travelers.

Phiale. A saucer-like offering dish with a hollow boss at the center to facilitate the pouring of libations; in South Italian vase-paintings, it frequently is shown holding food offerings instead of wine.

Phlyax. A type of farce or comedy performed in South Italy.

Pilos. A brimless felt cap or a metal helmet of similar shape.

Pinax. A wooden or clay tablet, with painted decoration.

Porpax. The arm band of a shield.

Pteryges. Small flaps of leather or metal attached to the lower edge of a breastplate.

Pyxis. A round, lidded container for holding cosmetics or jewelry.

Rhyton. A vessel made with a spout opposite the mouth so that liquid flows through it. Rhyta often have the form of an animal's head or a drinking horn. The horn-shaped vessels from Apulia are called rhyta even though they lack the spout of a true rhyton.

Rotella. A disk; on some oinochoai and hydriai, rotellas flank the juncture of handle and rim.

Sakkos. A snood; a bag-like hair covering, secured by a drawstring.

Situla. A deep, bucket-shaped vase.

Sphageion. A bowl with a broad, flaring rim, like a cuspidor. Its form originated with the Daunians, a native people of Apulia.

Sphendone. Literally "sling"; a leather or cloth headband, wider in the center.

Stamnos. A wine jar, usually lidded, with a wide mouth, bulbous body, and two small horizontal handles.

Stephane. A tiara-like crown.

Streptos. A twisted bread roll.

Strigil. A curved metal instrument used for scraping oil from the skin, especially after athletic exercises or bathing.

Thymiaterion. An incense burner, normally with a tall stand.

Thyrsos. A Dionysiac staff, decked with ivy and vine leaves, sometimes surmounted by a pine cone.

Trozella. A jar with flaring mouth and high-swung angular handles from rim to shoulder; related to the nestoris shape. It originated with the Messapians, a native people of Apulia.

Tympanum. Tambourine.

CONCORDANCE

Catalogue number	Accession number
1	00.366
2	76.50
3	Res. 41.56
4	1971.49
5	172.1970
6	76.455
7	97.605
8	00.349a
9	1970.236
10	1970.237
11	03.839a-b
12	13.206
13	69.951
14	61.112
15	1988.532
16	1983.553
17	1976.144
18	00.348
19	76.59
20	13.93
21	1970.235
22	1982.658
23	1982.659
24	90.160
25	76.65
26	41.651
27	10.204
28	00.360
29	01.8373
30	08.165
31	80.590
32	80.591
33	00.361
34	1990.350
35	76.66
36	92.2648
37	1992.317
38	03.804
39	1985.897
40	1991.242
41	1987.53
42	1991.437
43	1989.100
44	61.113
45	153.64
46	10.234
47	1991.381
48	01.8093
49	281.1970
50	65.564
51	282.1970
52	69.28
53	76.60
54	1986.263
55	69.55
56	76.61a-b
57	76.63
58	60.1171
59	58.1304
60	89.262
61	76.445
62	76.54
63	01.14
64	63.472
65	1986.1018
66	89.260
67	97.64
68	58.1279
69	1988.431
70	01.8094
71	89.275
72	89.276
73	76.62
74	1978.1346
75	1978.1347
76	08.280
77	15.1351
78	98.203a-b
79	03.832
80	03.831
81	01.8036
82	1970.363
83	01.8118
84	03.822
85	69.1142
86	283.1970
87	142.68
88	01.8096
89	143.68
90	1970.238
91	03.829
92	63.3
93	89.266
94	41.650
95	80.588
96	01.8149
97	12.423
98	95.834
99	95.835
100	19.295
101	1988.1120
102	19.299
103	19.308
104	19.309
105	99.540
106	68.581
107	03.824
108	00.363
109	22.679
110	01.8098
111	01.8106
112	86.151
113	58.1305
114	15.256
115	Res. 23.214
116	80.623
117	76.56
118	31.143
119	76.58
120	01.8112
121	01.8113
122	76.450
123	12.1179
124	80.624
125	58.1307
126	98.202
127	12.1180
128	88.320
129	76.57
130	01.8126
131	99.123
132	76.55
133	01.8121
134	41.914
135	58.1308
136	80.622
137	88.321
138	88.322
139	12.795
140	80.625
141	95.837
142	22.632
143	58.1268
144	03.823
144a	72.1488
145	76.451
146	58.1303
147	03.825
148	03.826
149	99.541
150	1970.478
151	1970.479
152	1983.558
153	80.595
154	80.596
155	76.233
156	76.236
157	76.239
158	76.828
159	13.78
160	13.86
161	58.1296
162	13.87
163	19.300
164	13.73
165	01.8114
166	1970.487
167	07.862
168	90.69
169	01.8123
170	08.201
171	58.1278
172	59.1066
173	97.372
174	80.539
175	12.1181
176	00.362
177	03.795
178	07.863
179	07.864
180	80.575

CONCORDANCE

Accession number	Catalogue number
72.1488	144a
76.50	2
76.54	62
76.55	132
76.56	117
76.57	129
76.58	119
76.59	19
76.60	53
76.61a-b	56
76.62	73
76.63	57
76.65	25
76.66	35
76.233	155
76.236	156
76.239	157
76.445	61
76.450	122
76.451	145
76.455	6
76.828	158
80.539	174
80.575	180
80.588	95
80.590	31
80.591	32
80.595	153
80.596	154
80.622	136
80.623	116
80.624	124
80.625	140
86.151	112
88.320	128
88.321	137
88.322	138
89.260	66
89.262	60
89.266	93
89.275	71
89.276	72
90.69	168

90.160	24
92.2648	36
95.834	98
95.835	99
95.837	141
97.64	67
97.372	173
97.605	7
98.202	126
98.203a-b	78
99.123	131
99.540	105
99.541	149
00.348	18
00.349a	8
00.360	28
00.361	33
00.362	176
00.363	108
00.366	1
01.14	63
01.8036	81
01.8093	48
01.8094	70
01.8096	88
01.8098	110
01.8106	111
01.8112	120
01.8113	121
01.8114	165
01.8118	83
01.8121	133
01.8123	169
01.8126	130
01.8149	96
01.8373	29
03.795	177
03.804	38
03.822	84
03.823	144
03.824	107
03.825	147
03.826	148
03.829	91
03.831	80
03.832	79
03.839a-b	11

07.862	167
07.863	178
07.864	179
08.165	30
08.201	170
08.280	76
10.204	27
10.234	46
12.423	97
12.795	139
12.1179	123
12.1180	127
12.1181	175
13.73	164
13.78	159
13.86	160
13.87	162
13.93	20
13.206	12
15.256	114
15.1351	77
19.295	100
19.299	102
19.300	163
19.308	103
19.309	104
22.632	142
22.679	109
Res. 23.214	115
31.143	118
41.650	94
41.651	26
41.914	134
Res. 41.56	3
58.1268	143
58.1278	171
58.1279	68
58.1296	161
58.1303	146
58.1304	59
58.1305	113
58.1307	125
58.1308	135
59.1066	172
4.59	= 1978.1346
5.59	= 1978.1347
60.1171	58

61.112	14
61.113	44
63.3	92
63.472	64
153.64	45
65.564	50
68.581	106
142.68	87
143.68	89
69.28	52
69.55	55
69.951	13
69.1142	85
1970.235	21
1970.236	9
1970.237	10
1970.238	90
1970.363	82
1970.478	150
1970.479	151
1970.487	166
171.1970	= 1991.381
172.1970	5
281.1970	49
282.1970	51
283.1970	86
1971.49	4
1976.144	17
1978.1346	74
1978.1347	75
1982.658	22
1982.659	23
1983.553	16
1983.558	152
1985.897	39
1986.263	54
1986.1018	65
1987.53	41
1988.431	69
1988.532	15
1988.1120	101
1989.100	43
1990.350	34
1991.242	40
1991.381	47
1991.437	42
1992.317	37

INDEXES

Index of Artists

Index of Mythological Subjects

Numbers refer to the catalogue entries.

Selected General Index

Numbers refer to the catalogue entries.